REA

Frommer's®

Poland

1st Edition

by Mark Baker and Kit F. Chung

Here's what the critics say about Frommer's:

"Amazingly easy to use. Very portable, very complete."
—**BOOKLIST**

"Detailed, accurate, and easy-to-read information
for all price ranges."
—**GLAMOUR MAGAZINE**

"Hotel information is close to encyclopedic."
—**DES MOINES SUNDAY REGISTER**

"Frommer's Guides have a way of giving you
a real feel for a place."
—**KNIGHT RIDDER NEWSPAPERS**

WILEY

John Wiley & Sons Canada, Ltd.

Published by:

JOHN WILEY & SONS CANADA, LTD.

6045 Freemont Blvd.
Mississauga, ON L5R 4J3

ISBN 978-0-470-15819-7

Editor: Gene Shannon
Developmental Editor: Melissa Klurman
Project Manager: Elizabeth McCurdy
Editorial Assistant: Katie Wolsley
Project Coordinator: Lynsey Stanford
Cartographer: Lohnes + Wright
Vice President, Publishing Services: Karen Bryan
Production by Wiley Indianapolis Composition Services

Front cover photo: © Henryk T. Kaiser/AGE Fotostock, Inc.
Back cover photo: © Egmont Strigl/AGE Fotostock, Inc.

For reseller information, including discounts and premium sales, please call our sales department: Tel. 416-646-7992. For press review copies, author interviews, or other publicity information, please contact our publicity department: Tel. 416-646-4582; Fax: 416-236-4448.

Wiley also publishes its books in a variety of electronic formats. Some content that appears in print may not be available in electronic formats.

Manufactured in the United States

1   2   3   4   5   RRD   12   11   10   09   08

CONTENTS

4 SUGGESTED POLAND ITINERARIES 49

5 WARSAW 62

6 ŁÓDŹ & SOUTH-CENTRAL POLAND 97

7 KRAKÓW, ZAKOPANE & THE TATRA MOUNTAINS 116

8 LUBLIN & SOUTHEASTERN POLAND 162

9 WROCŁAW & LOWER SILESIA 182

LIST OF MAPS

ABOUT THE AUTHORS

Journalist, photographer, and freelance writer **Mark Baker** has had a deep interest in Central Europe since receiving a degree in International Affairs at Columbia University in the 1980s. He currently lives in Prague, Czech Republic, but is a frequent visitor to, and a big fan of, Poland. In addition to writing guide books, he is a contributor to *The Wall Street Journal Europe* and *National Geographic Traveler,* among other publications.

Kit F. Chung is a Malaysian-born writer who has been based in Warsaw since 2001. Poland is her first encounter with a former "Iron Curtain" country. She appreciates the Poles for tolerating her incessant inquisitive questions on anything and everything Polish. She reckons the best part of writing the guide was eating her way around the country.

AN INVITATION TO THE READER

In researching this book, we discovered many wonderful places—hotels, restaurants, shops, and more. We're sure you'll find others. Please tell us about them, so we can share the information with your fellow travelers in upcoming editions. If you were disappointed with a recommendation, we'd love to know that, too. Please write to:

Frommer's Poland, 1st Edition
John Wiley & Sons Canada, Ltd. • 6045 Freemont Blvd. • Mississauga, ON L5R 4J3

AN ADDITIONAL NOTE

Please be advised that travel information is subject to change at any time—and this is especially true of prices. We therefore suggest that you write or call ahead for confirmation when making your travel plans. The authors, editors, and publisher cannot be held responsible for the experiences of readers while traveling. Your safety is important to us, however, so we encourage you to stay alert and be aware of your surroundings. Keep a close eye on cameras, purses, and wallets, all favorite targets of thieves and pickpockets.

Other Great Guides for Your Trip:

Frommer's Eastern Europe

FROMMER'S STAR RATINGS, ICONS & ABBREVIATIONS

Every hotel, restaurant, and attraction listing in this guide has been ranked for quality, value, service, amenities, and special features using a **star-rating system.** In country, state, and regional guides, we also rate towns and regions to help you narrow down your choices and budget your time accordingly. Hotels and restaurants are rated on a scale of zero (recommended) to three stars (exceptional). Attractions, shopping, nightlife, towns, and regions are rated according to the following scale: zero stars (recommended), one star (highly recommended), two stars (very highly recommended), and three stars (must-see).

In addition to the star-rating system, we also use **seven feature icons** that point you to the great deals, in-the-know advice, and unique experiences that separate travelers from tourists. Throughout the book, look for:

(Finds)	Special finds—those places only insiders know about
(Fun Facts)	Fun facts—details that make travelers more informed and their trips more fun
(Kids)	Best bets for kids, and advice for the whole family
(Moments)	Special moments—those experiences that memories are made of
(Overrated)	Places or experiences not worth your time or money
(Tips)	Insider tips—great ways to save time and money
(Value)	Great values—where to get the best deals
(Warning!)	Warning—traveler's advisories are usually in effect

The following **abbreviations** are used for credit cards:

AE	American Express	DISC	Discover	V	Visa
DC	Diners Club	MC	MasterCard		

FROMMERS.COM

Now that you have this guidebook to help you plan a great trip, visit our website at **www.frommers.com** for additional travel information on more than 4,000 destinations. We update features regularly to give you instant access to the most current trip-planning information available. At Frommers.com, you'll find scoops on the best airfares, lodging rates, and car rental bargains. You can even book your travel online through our reliable travel booking partners. Other popular features include:

- Online updates of our most popular guidebooks
- Vacation sweepstakes and contest giveaways
- Newsletters highlighting the hottest travel trends
- Podcasts, interactive maps, and up-to-the-minute events listings
- Opinionated blog entries by Arthur Frommer himself
- Online travel message boards with featured travel discussions

The Best of Poland

1 THE MOST UNFORGETTABLE TRAVEL EXPERIENCES

- Sip your coffee on Kraków's Main Square (Kraków). Superlatives don't do justice to Kraków's main square, the Rynek Główny. It's said to be Central Europe's largest town square and is reputed to have the most bars and cafes per square meter than any other place in the world. Even if that's not the case, it's still one of the most jaw-droppingly beautiful spaces you'll find and the perfect spot to enjoy a cup of coffee or a glass of beer and watch the world go by. And don't forget to listen for the bugler on top of St. Mary's Church at the top of the hour. See p. 121.

- Reflect on history at the Auschwitz-Birkenau concentration camp (Oświęcim). The word "best" is clearly a misnomer here, yet a visit to the Nazi wartime extermination camp that came to define the Holocaust is one of the most deeply affecting and moving experiences you will have anywhere. Give yourself at least a few hours to take in both camps (just a couple of miles apart). Auschwitz is undeniably horrible, but it is at Birkenau where you really grasp the scale of the tragedy. See p. 146.

- Shop for souvenirs along Gdańsk's Długa Street (Gdańsk). As you stroll Gdańsk's main pedestrian thoroughfare, it's hard to believe this stunning port city was reduced to rubble in World War II, so historically sensitive was the reconstruction. Amber-philes will think they died and went to heaven. It's not

surprising when you consider that the Baltic Sea (where amber comes from) is just a block away. Still, the quality and choice is overwhelming. There's even an amber museum if the shops don't have what you're looking for. See p. 231.

- Look for bison in Białowieża (Białowieża National Park). Better put this under your "Most Unexpected Travel Experiences," too. Who would have imagined that part of Poland's eastern border with Belarus is primeval forest that's home to Europe's largest surviving bison herd? Both children and adults alike will enjoy touring the pristine national park. See p. 275.

- Visit a wooden "Peace" church (Jawor and Świdnica). Few visitors to Poland have heard of these two massive 17th-century wooden Protestant churches in southwest Poland. Congregations had to build the churches from wood because of strictures on Protestant worship at the time by the Catholic Habsburg rulers. The churches' size, grace, and stunning beauty all testify to the builders' faith and their remarkable engineering skills. See p. 193.

- See the miraculous icon of the "Black Madonna" (Częstochowa). The first Pauline monks starting coming here to the Jasna Góra Monastery in the 14th century. Over the years it evolved into Catholic Poland's most important pilgrimage destination and place of worship, drawing millions of Poles and other people from around the world every year. Authorship of the miraculous Black Madonna icon is traditionally attributed to Luke, and the painting is said to have made its way here through the centuries from the Holy Lands, to Constantinople (now Istanbul), to the Ukrainian city of Belz, and finally to Częstochowa in 1382. The monastery allows the painting to be viewed for only a few hours each day, and getting a glimpse of it among the throngs is not unlike trying to see the Mona Lisa at the Louvre. Still, it's very much worth the effort. See p. 106.

2 THE BEST HOTEL SPLURGES

- Królewski (Gdańsk). Rooms to die for just across the canal from Gdańsk's Old Town. Number 310 is a corner room with views over the city in two directions. The breakfast room looks out over the river through little round windows, creating the illusion of being on an ocean cruise. See p. 235.
- Hotel Carska (Białowieża National Park). A hotel fit for a tsar—in this case, Russia's Tsar Nicholas II. A must for fans of unusual hotel design, this hotel/restaurant occupies a refurbished railway station that was built to welcome the tsar and his family in the 19th century. The waiting room has been converted into an upscale restaurant, but you may not want to ever leave your room. See p. 278.
- Palac Bonerowski (Kraków). Kraków's latest entry in the five-star category is a jaw-dropper: a sensitively restored 13th-century town house just off the main square. Many period elements, including original stonework and carvings, have been preserved in the spacious rooms. See p. 134.
- Jaczno Lodge (Suwałki Landscape Park). This lovely cluster of stone and timber houses is hemmed in by woods and the pristine water of Lake Jaczno. The owners are architects who have meticulously designed every space, from the luxurious rooms to the rose bushes and fruit trees in the garden. See p. 272.
- Grand Hotel Stamary (Zakopane). Beautifully restored turn-of-the-century manor hotel that will whisk you away to the stylish 1920s and '30s with its elegant lobby and cocktail bar. The hotel recently added a luxury spa, with indoor pool and Jacuzzi. See p. 153.
- Pałac Paulinum (Jelenia Góra). This elegant 19th-century palais was originally the home of a Silesian textile baron; now it's a stunningly renovated luxury hotel, but thankfully without the ultra-luxury price tag. See p. 199.
- Grand Hotel (Sopot). Step back in time to the Jazz Age 1920s, when summering in Sopot meant you had really arrived. The Grand attempts to recapture some of that glamour with sumptuous period interiors, high-class service, and a location right on the beach. See p. 244.
- Stary (Kraków). Eye-catching, upscale renovation of a former palace just off the Rynek Główny. Amenities include two indoor pools and a salt cave. See p. 135.

3 THE BEST HOTEL BARGAINS

- Hotel Karmel (Kraków). This lovely family-run inn, tucked away on a quiet street in the former Jewish quarter of Kazimierz, is a total surprise. From the warm and smiling receptionist at the front desk to the parquet flooring and the crisp linens on the beds, everything about this place says quality. See p. 137.

- Premiere Classe (Warsaw). This French-run chain came up with the novel idea of offering clean, modern rooms the size of a cubicle for a fraction the price of other hotels. Sure, the rooms are microscopic, but the beds are big and comfortable, the bathrooms are clean, and the hotel location is just a couple of tram stops from the main sights. See p. 74.

- Castle Inn (Warsaw). A restored 16th-century inn that's clean, priced to please, and has a wacky, theatrical side to boot. The effects are created by bold colors and an eclectic blend of antique and modern furnishings. See p. 71.

- Pensjonat Szarotka (Zakopane). This quirky, 1930s mountain chalet is the perfect place to try to tap into Zakopane's funky, artistic past. The squeaky stairways, the cozy little reading room with a fireplace, and the evocative black-and-white photos on the wall will remind you of your grandmother's house. See p. 154.

- U Pana Cogito (Kraków). One of the best hotel bargains in Kraków is a remodeled former rectory about 15 minutes by foot from the city center. The modern rooms don't have loads of personality, but they are spotlessly clean and quiet. See p. 138.

- Wenecki (Częstochowa). A bargain hotel offering inviting, even beautiful, rooms with hardwood floors and big comfortable beds. The reception is welcoming and the overall effect is actually much nicer and more comfortable than the most expensive hotels in town. See p. 108.

- Olimpijski (Katowice). This might be better filed under "most memorable sleeping options" for the hotel's location—in the belly of Katowice's futuristic flying saucer building, the Spodek.

Come here if you've ever wondered what a night on Star Trek's USS Enterprise might be like. See p. 112.

- Liburnia (Cieszyn). A cross between a business hotel and a boutique at prices you'd expect to pay at a pension. The mattresses are thick and comfortable and the cotton-thread count in the sheets is well above the average at this price point. The in-house Italian restaurant is one of the best places in town to eat. See p. 115.

- Hotel Savoy (Łódź). A likeably run-down, turn-of-the-20th-century hotel that feels perfectly in sync with Łódź's "seen better days" aesthetic. Don't expect a charming boutique; this is a pure time-warp property (the kind of hotel that might appear in a 1950s detective novel). See p. 103.

- Tourist Information Office (Tarnów). The Tarnów city tourist information office rents out the rooms above the office at some of the cheapest rates you'll find in the whole country. See p. 160.

- Pensjonat Sioło Budy (Białowieża National Park). This is homestead living for those wanting a taste of rural life but without forsaking clean toilets, hot showers, and espresso. The owners, folk history enthusiasts, have fashioned four traditional chalets around a garden of apple trees, flowers, ferns, and fluttering butterflies. See p. 278.

- Kamienica Gotyk (Gdańsk). Ordinarily, you'd expect to part with a fortune to enjoy the hotel's setting in Gdańsk's oldest house and on its loveliest street. Breakfast on the petite patio in the shadows of St. Mary's Church adds to the sense of history. See p. 237.

- Vincent Pensjonat (Kazimierz Dolny). An enchanting, family-run pension, situated about 5 minutes from the center of town. See p. 180.

4 THE BEST LOCAL DINING EXPERIENCES

- Piwnica Świdnicka (Wrocław). At first glance, this pub looks like a classic tourist trap; but it's actually an excellent traditional Polish restaurant serving big plates of classic dishes. See p. 190.

- U Kucharzy (Warsaw). It's perhaps an ironic comment on Polish cooking that one of the capital's best restaurants is actually in a hotel kitchen. The chefs ladle out their creations straight to your plate from their cast-iron cookware. If you're a kitchen voyeur, book a table in front of the mega-burners to watch the chefs prepare Polish mainstays up close and personal. See p. 75.

- Alfredo (Szklarska Poręba). Proof that in Poland you can never judge a restaurant by its cover. If so, you'd never dream of stopping at this tiny mom-and-pop and you'd end up missing some excellent home-style Polish cooking. See p. 201.

- Pawłowicz (Warsaw). A take-out-only, hole-in-the-wall operation that draws a constant flow of customers looking for the city's best doughnuts (pączki) and pastries at bargain prices. See p. 78.

- Bolków Hotel Restaurant (Bolków/Jawor). The restaurant at the tiny Bolków Hotel specializes in home cooking done well, including big plates of roast meats served with mounds of mashed potatoes. The desserts are homemade, and the throwback atmosphere to the 1920s is fun and inviting. See p. 195.

- Ciągoty i Tęsknoty (Łódź). Perched between two ghastly apartment blocks, this small, unassuming restaurant is an oasis of '50s jazz and fresh flowers. The menu is perched somewhere between home cooking and haute cuisine, with salads, pierogi, and pasta dishes, and some seriously good entrees. Take a taxi to get there or risk never finding it. See p. 104.

- Wierzynek (Kraków). This esteemed eatery has played host to visiting dignitaries, celebs, and heads of state since way back in 1364. The cuisine is an imaginative take on traditional Polish cooking, with an emphasis on local treats such as wild boar, quail, and venison. See p. 140.

- Dawno Temu Na Kazimierzu (Once Upon a Time in Kazimierz) (Kraków-Kazimierz). Finally, a Jewish-themed restaurant in Kazimierz that doesn't feel like a kitschy tourist trap. The interior is relaxed and intimate and the food is great. See p. 140.

- La Rotisserie (Warsaw). For those in the know, this is one of the capital's most inviting splurge options. It helps to be a foodie to know some of the terms on the menu, but everything is great, so just point to an item and relax. For great value, try the 5-course Sunday Linner (a play on "lunch" fused with "dinner"). See p. 74.

- Hacjenda (Poznań). This is rumored to be the best place in Poland to try czernina, a soup made from duck's blood and bits of offal. They also do a good roast duck, if blood soup isn't on your list of must-tries. See p. 213.

- Ke Moro Original Gypsy Restaurant (Tarnów). Quite likely Poland's only restaurant to specialize in Gypsy (or Roma) cuisine. The food is great—mostly spicy versions of roast meats and hearty stews—but the warm atmosphere is the deal maker, with a Gypsy folk band on tap some nights. See p. 161.

- Kawiarnia Naleśnikarnia (Jelenia Góra). What a surprise to find this excellent creperie—with fantastic concoctions of chocolate, nuts, and whipped cream—right on Jelenia Góra's handsome town square. See p. 200.

- Karczma U Zagłoby (Częstochowa). A regional award-winning restaurant and a serious contender for best food in central Poland. The perfect spot for exquisite renditions of beet soup (barszcz), potato pancakes, pierogi, and much more ambitious cooking. See p. 109.
- Fantasmagoria (Katowice). Easily the best restaurant in town and possibly all of this part of Poland. Excellent and inventive home-style cooking that takes equal inspiration from Ukrainian and eastern Polish classics, mixed with more modern notions

of using local ingredients and a fresh presentation. See p. 112.

- Knajpa U Fryzjera (Kazimierz Dolny). Wacky Jewish-themed tavern restaurant with hearty dishes featuring roast meats and stews. The atmosphere is festive, with lots of alcohol to accompany the excellent cooking. In nice weather grab a table out back and drink long into the night. See p. 181.
- Muzealna (Zamość). Handsome and memorable restaurant set in three brick Renaissance cellars that look like they've just stepped out of the 16th century. The traditional Polish cooking is superb. See p. 177.

5 THE BEST PLACES TO GET PIEROGI

- Leniwa (Toruń). Leniwa means "lazy," but the genial folks here are anything but in making some of the best pierogi in the country. Sample the various types of sweet and savory dumplings at bargain-basement prices. Popular with locals, so be prepared to wait. See p. 223.
- Ciepłe Kluchy (Warsaw). Not far from the Royal Castle, a lovely cobblestone lane leads to this vaulted-ceilinged chamber. The menu has all the usual suspects and a bunch of hard-to-find varieties. Dudy, pierogi stuffed with a variety of pork innards, stand out as the connoisseur's choice. See p. 78.
- Pierogarnia U Dzika (Gdańsk). Pierogi used to be widely dismissed as dowdy peasant food, but no longer. Now they are all the rage. This is an upscale pierogarnia—literally, pierogi restaurant—located just a couple minutes'

walk from the town center. The menu includes the usual fillings plus a few inventive variants. Pierogi "Wileński" are padded with delicious buckwheat and bacon. See p. 239.

- Pierożki U Vincenta (Kraków). This tiny and inviting pierogi joint in Kazimierz serves every style of pierogi imaginable. The house special, "Vincent," is stuffed with minced meat and spicy lentils and served with fried onions and bits of bacon. Other concoctions include Moroccan-inspired couscous pierogi and "Górale" (highlander) pierogi stuffed with sheep's cheese. See p. 142.
- Domowy Przysmaki (Kraków). Informal lunch counter, with excellent pierogi (try the fruit-filled varieties). Just a few minutes' walk from the main square and the best-value lunch for miles around. See p. 142.

6 THE BEST GIFTS TO BRING BACK HOME

- Amber (Gdańsk). What is it about this ossified pine tar resin that's so mesmerizing? Gdańsk grew wealthy over the centuries on the amber trade, and the demand today is as strong as ever. Gdańsk, on the Baltic (the source of amber), is the traditional home of the stuff, but you'll find amber at shops all around the country. Just be careful to buy the genuine article—fakes abound. See p. 240.

- Salt from the Wieliczka Salt Mine (Kraków). This might be the most famous salt mine in the world. For years, salt was to Kraków as amber was to Gdańsk: the goose that laid golden eggs, and kept laying and laying. Salt is not nearly so important for Kraków these days, but the resplendent Wieliczka Salt Mine is reminder of how valuable a commodity salt once was. See p. 144.

- Bison grass from Białowieża (Białowieża National Park). This is an especially long, fragrant grass that grows near the Białowieża National Forest. Despite the name, the bison don't actually graze on it. You'll find a blade of bison grass in every bottle of Żubrówka Vodka, which might be the most practical way to buy (or consume) it. You can even make

your own "bison grass" vodka by referring to the instructions on the package the grass is sold in. See p. 277.

- Gingerbread (Toruń). Gingerbread comes in all shapes and sizes, and usually comes well wrapped for the long trip home. Toruń is the country's gingerbread capital, and Toruń gingerbread is sold all around the country. See p. 222.

- Smoked sheep's cheese (Giant Mountains/Zakopane). The closer you get to the mountains, the more likely you are to see mountain people lined up along the road to sell their little rounds of smoked sheep's cheese called Oscypek. It's considered a delicacy and the recipe goes back some 500 years. Buy several different types to see which ones you like best. The salty cheese goes especially well with beer. See p. 156.

- Vodka. Poland is known for the quality of its vodkas. Among the most popular brands, Belvedere and Chopin are considered the highest quality. In addition, you'll find a range of flavored vodkas. Żubrówka is slightly greenish due to a long blade of bison grass in every bottle. Miodówka, honey-flavored and easy to drink in large quantities, is also worth a try. See p. 28.

7 THE BEST COMMUNIST-ERA EXPERIENCES

- Visit the Palace of Culture and Science (Warsaw). Warsaw's landmark Socialist-Realist palace is the granddaddy of all Communist architectural icons. Universally loathed yet at the same time thoroughly riveting, you won't be able to take your eyes off it. Tour the museums inside or take an elevator ride to the top to look out over Warsaw. Part of

the fun are the ever-present guards, ready to bark nie dotykać (do not touch!) the moment you get close to any of the exhibits. See p. 83.

- Eat at a milk bar (all over the country). Every visitor to Poland eventually has to have his or her "milk bar" experience. A milk bar—the milk refers to the fact that no alcohol is served—has no direct

American or Western European equivalent. "Cafeteria" sounds too sterile, and "greasy spoon," well, too greasy. But that's the idea, at any rate: heaping steam tables of mostly meatless Polish specialties that you line up for and point to. Not bad tasting and great value.

- See a concert at the Spodek (Katowice). Katowice's retro futuristic "Flying Saucer" building may be the coolest rock concert venue ever built. It's the city's best representative of the "Brussels Expo '58" style of design inspired by 1950s-era science and science fiction that influenced so many architects behind the Iron Curtain at the time. Performers like Robbie Williams, Pearl Jam, and Sir Elton John have all played here. See p. 111.

8 THE BEST WAYS TO ACT LIKE A LOCAL

- Drink beer from a straw. This inexplicable practice is especially popular among women, but occasionally you'll see Polish guys doing it as well. The idea is to sweeten the beer first with fruit juice, usually raspberry juice, and then sip it leisurely like a cocktail. Watch out for the consequences, though. Polish beer is unusually strong, and drinking through a straw only heightens the effect of the alcohol.

- Get in line for ice cream. Poles are loony for lody (ice cream). Part of the attraction comes from Communist days, when ice cream was one of the few pleasures accessible to most people. Part of the attraction is also, well, because it's ice cream and it tastes great. Each city has its own ice cream stand of choice. The best strategy is to scout around and see where the longest lines are. See p. 27.

- Eat sushi. That doesn't sound Polish at all, yet the country is currently experiencing sushi mania, and some seriously good sushi joints are springing up all over. The Poles' love affair with fish is understandable. After all, Poland is right on the Baltic Sea and dishes such as herring have been part of the local cuisine for centuries. For some of the best sushi in the country, try the Sakana Sushi Bar in Wrocław or Edo Sushi Bar in Kazimierz. See p. 190 and p. 140.

- Feed breadcrumbs to the pigeons. You'll see the young and old alike at nearly every big square in every Polish town tossing breadcrumbs to flocks of pigeons. And they are the bane of city officials around the country trying to fight the onslaught of unwanted fowl. The problem is so serious that officials in Kraków even considered dynamiting the birds. But as the old saying goes—if you can't beat them, might as well join them.

- Go mushroom picking. Mushroom picking is a popular autumn pastime for all Poles. The best strategy for success is to get up early to scour the forest floors for the fungus of choice, usually chanterelle, porcini, and milk caps. One caveat: Don't try this if you're not experienced at sorting out the edible from the poisonous varieties. If you're staying in the countryside, simply ask your host to arrange a mushroom hunt for you. Most likely, they will have an aunt or cousin who knows the best place to land a bagful of mushrooms for your morning omelet.

- Go shopping at a farmer's market. Most Polish cities will have a central market filled with goodies such as fresh fruits and vegetables, cheeses, breads, and meats. Often, these will also have a little pierogi stand for a quick bite. They're the perfect one-stop shop for a picnic lunch. Check out the Hala Mirowska in Warsaw or the Hala Targowa in Wrocław. See p. 90 and p. 187.

- Hang out at a Sphinx restaurant. Poles seem to love chain restaurants, and in nearly every city and town of any size you'll find a Sphinx, usually right at the heart of the main square. It will invariably be packed, although there's no accounting for the restaurant's popularity. The mix of vaguely Middle Eastern entrées, like shish kebab, is only average at best, but the mood is always festive. And your local Sphinx can be a lifesaver if you're starving and there's no other place around.

9 THE BEST DIAMONDS IN THE ROUGH

- Łódź. On the outside, Poland's second-largest city (pronounced "Woodge") appears cold and gray, a former industrial powerhouse that has gone through some tough times and looks it. But the more you find out about the place, the more fascinating it gets: The center of Poland's film industry, enormous pre-war Jewish population, biggest shopping mall in Europe, active culture calendar, great art museum. The list goes on. See p. 97.
- Kazimierz (Kraków). Next to Kraków's glamorous Old Town, Kazimierz, the city's former Jewish ghetto, looks positively derelict. And that appears to be its secret charm. What else could explain Kazimierz's increasing popularity among Kraków's ultra-cool and arty set? After admiring the handsome buildings of the Old Town, come out here to party and let your hair down—and see what really makes Kraków tick. See p. 127.
- Tarnów. The small city of Tarnów east of Kraków came late to the tourism party, but is making up for lost time with the friendliest tourist information office in the country as well as some decent museums and the occasional blockbuster exhibition. If Kraków's crowded streets get a little too much to bear, head to Tarnów for a respite before it too becomes too popular for its own good. One nice surprise is a Western-style horse-riding ranch in the vicinity that's happy to set up greenhorns for the day. See p. 157.
- Katowice. Cool in the way that Cleveland is cool, or in the U.K. maybe the way Glasgow or Manchester is cool. This big industrial city's charms are hard to pin down, but there is definitely something there. Maybe it's the retro-futuristic flying-saucer building—the Spodek—or all of the other Communist-era architecture around. Or the fact that it feels authentic and there are absolutely no other tourists around. The wags at the local office of Katowice, In Your Pocket have tried to carve out a kind of anti-cool image for the city, calling it a needed antidote to overly prettified and touristed Kraków. See p. 109.
- Nowa Huta (Kraków). It's hard to make a Socialist-era housing project next to a steel mill sound like something you might want to see on your vacation. But this planned 1950s community is undeniably cool. Architecture and urban planning buffs will be drawn to the plans and designs of housing designed especially for the workers' state. Irony of ironies, they even named the main square after union-busting, anti-Communist U.S. president Ronald Reagan. See p. 129.
- Praga district (Warsaw). Not too many years ago, Warsaw's rough and tumble Praga district, on the other side of the

Vistula River from the heart of the city, used to be a no-go zone. The low rents, though, attracted the artistic crowd and now it's emerging into the capital's coolest neighborhood. Don't expect anything quite like Kazimierz in Kraków yet, but several good restaurants and clubs are up and running and the future promises to bring more. See p. 86.

10 THE BEST OUTDOOR ACTIVITIES

- Hiking in the Tatras. Zakopane is the jumping-off point for hundreds of miles of gorgeous hiking trails. You can try one of the 2,000m (6,560-ft.) assaults on the peaks, or a more leisurely stroll along breathtaking valleys carved out by tiny mountain streams. For more ambitious climbers, plan a whole-day outing to cross the peaks into Slovakia in summer. See p. 151.
- Biking in the Giant Mountains (Szklarska Poręba). Szklarska Poręba has evolved into the mountain biking capital of southern Poland. More than a dozen decent trails, catering to all skill levels, fan out from the town in every direction. Some of the trails are all-day affairs, while others are shorter and oriented more toward recreational cyclists or families with children. Pick up a free cycling map from the tourist information office. See p. 198.
- Rafting the Dunajec River (near Zakopane). The Dunajec River marks the country's southeastern border with Slovakia. It winds through a picturesque gorge in the Pieniny Mountains east of the Tatras that makes it absolutely perfect for rafting. The season runs from April through October, and on a sunny afternoon this can be a fabulous day out, especially for kids. It's less whitewater rafting and more of a slow, gentle float down the river on group rafts manned by Górale mountain men kitted out in their traditional folk garb. The boating center on the Polish side is at Sromowce Kąty, not far from Zakopane. See p. 152.
- Kayaking in northeastern Poland (near Olsztyn). Rivers and canals crisscross the lake districts of northeastern Poland, allowing you to drift from marshland to woodland, with plenty of bird watching in between. You can paddle for one day or seven; there are plenty of routes—rated from kid-friendly to daredevil—to choose from. See p. 264.
- Downhill skiing (Giant Mountains, Tatras). Poland is not the first country that comes to mind when you think of skiing in Europe. But in the south of the country, in the mountainous areas near the Czech Republic and Slovakia, there are several excellent ski resorts and some very good downhill runs. The country's longest ski run is at Szklarska Poręba in the Giant Mountains. The most popular resort is Zakopane in the Tatras. Both have good infrastructures with lifts and ski rentals. See p. 199 and p. 152.
- Swimming in the Baltic (Sopot). A beach holiday in Poland? It doesn't seem possible, but yet, thousands of people flock to resorts like Sopot in the summer to dip their toes (quite literally, given the temperature of the water) in the Baltic Sea. There are miles of sandy beaches and the water is clean and refreshing. Pity that the surf temp rarely rises to above tolerable, but that's really part of the charm. See p. 243.

11 THE BEST MUSEUMS

- Museum of the Warsaw Uprising (Warsaw). When you're done walking through the exhibitions and watching the startling documentaries filmed during the fighting in 1944 on display here, you'll understand a lot more about the Poles' resolve to preserve their nation. Just the photos alone of Warsaw's total destruction will leave you in awe that a modern city actually exists here. See p. 84.

- Museum of Zakopane Style (Zakopane). This low-key museum is dedicated to the fine woodworking craft of the early Zakopane architects of the late 19th and early 20th century. No stunning high-tech visuals, just beautifully carved furnishings and a wonderful aesthetic feel. They took the log cabin and made it a palace. See p. 151.

- Museum of Technology (Warsaw). Don't expect cutting-edge technology or hands-on interactive exhibits. Instead, you'll find a sprawling collection of dated technology—from bicycles with wooden wheels to early transistors dating from the 1950s. Fans of retro design will be especially engaged. It's a time capsule of sorts you shouldn't miss. See p. 82.

- Galicia Jewish Museum (Kraków-Kazimierz). The main exhibition here features contemporary and often beautiful photographs of important Jewish sites throughout southern Poland taken by the late British photographer Chris Schwarz. Schwarz spent 12 years traveling throughout Poland using photography as a way of trying to preserve the country's rapidly disappearing Jewish heritage. The effect here works beautifully. See p. 128.

- Czartoryski Museum (Kraków). Members of the noble Czartoryski family were gifted art collectors, and this collection is one of the finest in central Europe. Two international masterpieces are on display: Leonardo da Vinci's Lady with an Ermine and Rembrandt's Landscape with the Good Samaritan. See p. 124.

- Gingerbread Museum (Toruń). The town of Toruń is famous for two things: the birthplace of Copernicus and gingerbread cookies. At this privately owned museum, you not only learn the secret ingredients of great gingerbread but get to make your own. Good fun and great for kids. See p. 221.

- Roads to Freedom Exhibition (Gdańsk). An inspiring and sobering history lesson of the anti-Communist struggle in Poland. The mock-up of a typical empty grocery store in late 1970s, grainy news reels, interactive displays, and documentary films keenly capture the atmosphere of the times. See p. 230.

- Łódź Art Museum (Łódź). A must for fans of modern art, the collection includes works by Marc Chagall and Max Ernst. Skip the first two floors and head straight for the museum's prize pieces on the third floor, including several of the young rake Witkacy's amazing society sketches from the 1920s. See p. 102.

- Amber Museum (Gdańsk). A must for all fans of the beautiful ossified pine resin that helped make Gdańsk wealthy. On six floors of exhibits, you'll learn everything you'll ever need to know about amber; if you're thinking of buying some amber while you're in Gdańsk, you might want to stop here first for an educational primer. See p. 229.

- Museum of Cinematography (Łódź). International film fans will want to stop here to pay tribute to Poland's panoply of great directors, including Roman Polański, Andrzej Wajda, and Krzysztof Kieslowski, all of whom studied and worked in Łódź. See p. 102.

- Ethnographic Museum (Tarnów). A rare and fascinating exhibition on the history and culture of Europe's Roma

(Gypsy) population, it traces the emergence of the Roma from parts of modern-day India some 1,000 years ago to their arrival in Europe and subsequent (mostly tragic) history. See p. 159.

- Pharmacy Museum (Kraków). One of the biggest and best old-style pharmacy museums in this part of the world, with fascinating exhibits of potions and leeches and concoctions that show just how far modern medicine has come. See p. 124.

12 THE BEST CASTLES & CHURCHES

- Wawel (Kraków). This remains Poland's pride and joy and the country's number-one tourist attraction. The original castle dates from around the 10th century, when the area was first chosen as the seat of Polish kings. For more than five centuries, the castle stood as the home of Polish royalty. See p. 126.
- Malbork (Malbork). This castle, a UNESCO World Heritage Site and the biggest brick castle in the world, is silent testimony to the power and influence the Teutonic knights once had in this part of Poland. See p. 253.
- Książ Castle (Wałbrzych). The 400-room Książ Castle is the biggest castle in Lower Silesia. It was originally laid out in the 13th century by members of the early Polish nobility but was refurbished and rebuilt several times down through the centuries, resulting in today's baroque-renaissance-rococo-neoclassical mish-mash. See p. 192.
- St. Mary's Cathedral (Kraków). Kraków is a city of churches, and this is its signature house of worship, right on the main square. The elaborately carved 15th-century wooden altarpiece is the biggest of its kind in Europe. The rest of the interior is similarly impressive, but the highlight of the church is not on the inside, it's the forlorn bugler in the high tower, playing his hourly dirge. See p. 125.
- Synagogue (Zamość). An unexpected and beautiful reminder of the size and vitality of the pre–World War II Jewish community in Zamość. Nearly every southern Polish city had a sizable Jewish community before the war, but very few synagogues of this quality have survived. See p. 176.
- St. Mary's Church (Gdańsk). This enormous red-brick church is reputedly the largest of its kind in the world. Its nave and 31 chapels can hold more than 20,000 people. The church endeared itself to the people of Gdańsk in the years after the imposition of martial law in 1981 when members of the Solidarity trade union sheltered here. See p. 232.
- St. Elizabeth Church (Wrocław). Wrocław was so thoroughly rebuilt following World War II that it's only in the city's solemn red-brick churches, like this one on the northwest corner of the main square, that you really see something of pre-war Breslau (and witness the surviving scars of the war). See p. 186.
- Kłodzko Fortress (Kłodzko). This fortress has played an important strategic role for centuries, straddling the traditional borderland first between the Polish and Bohemian kingdoms, and then later Prussia and Austria. The present massive structure dates from the middle of the 18th century. Napoleon, early on, shattered the fortress's illusion of invincibility by capturing the structure in 1807. During World War II, the Nazis used the fortress to hold political prisoners. Today, it is the region's leading tourist attraction for the labyrinth of underground tunnels once used for troop mustering, hiding, and escape if necessary. See p. 202.

Poland in Depth

Poland suddenly finds itself on everyone's hot list for European travel.
That's right, Poland—the land of cabbage, potatoes, and vodka—which not all that long
ago was still trapped behind the Iron Curtain with its own bleak images of strikes and
tanks. All of that seems a world away these days. Poland has gone on a 20-year renovation
project since the Communist government fell in 1989. The hotels and restaurants have
had long-overdue makeovers, the buildings and squares have been spruced up, and
Poland these days is very much open for business.

And while the cabbage and vodka are still great, there are lots of other good reasons to
visit. For some, a trip to Poland is an opportunity to reconnect with their Polish roots, a
chance to sample some of their grandmother's stuffed cabbage and *pierogi* in their natural
setting. Others are attracted to the unique beauty of cities such as Kraków, which
has rightfully joined Prague and Budapest as part of the trinity of must-sees in central
Europe.

Still others are drawn by Poland's dramatic and often tragic history. The horrors of
World War II, followed by decades of Communist rule, have etched painful and moving
memories throughout this land. No country, with the possible exception of Russia, suffered as much as Poland during World War II. Millions of Poles, and nearly the entire
prewar Jewish population of more than 3 million, were killed in fighting or in the concentration camps. The deeply affecting and sobering experience of seeing the extermination camps at Auschwitz and Birkenau, near Kraków, will last a lifetime. Nearly equally
moving are the stories of the Łódź and Warsaw Jewish ghettos, or the tragic story of the
Warsaw uprising of 1944, when the city's residents rose up courageously, but futilely,
against their Nazi oppressors.

There are plenty of triumphant moments from history as well. In Warsaw, which was
85 percent destroyed during World War II, the entire Old Town has been rebuilt brick-
by-brick in an emotional show of a city reclaiming its identity from the rubble. In
Gdańsk, you can visit the shipyards where Lech Wałęsa and his Solidarity trade union
first rose to power to oppose Poland's Communist government in 1980. It was the rise
of Solidarity that helped to bring down Communism in Poland and arguably sparked the
anti-Communist revolutions that swept through all of Eastern Europe in 1989.

And there is plenty of natural beauty here as well. In the south of the country, below
Kraków, rise the majestic High Tatras, one of Europe's most starkly beautiful alpine
ranges. To the north, the Baltic Sea coast, with its pristine beaches, stretches for miles.
The northeast is covered with lakes that run to the borderlands with Lithuania and
Belarus. In the east of the country, you'll find patches of some of Europe's last-remaining
primeval forest and a small herd of the indigenous bison that once covered large parts of
the European continent.

1 POLAND TODAY

Poland these days finds itself a bit like a gangly adolescent on the world stage. With a population of around 40 million people, it is by far the biggest of the mainly former Communist countries that joined the European Union in 2004, and it has slowly grown into a kind of regional leader, though the region in question, Eastern Europe, can seldom agree on anything. It's also one of the biggest EU member states overall, just below the most-populous countries of Germany, France, and Britain, but on par with mid-sized countries like Spain. After 40 years of Communist rule, and with just a few short years to hone its Western diplomatic skills, you'd expect a few blunders, and Poland has made its share. But it's also shown itself willing to oppose bigger states to protect its own interests. It went up against Germany a couple of years ago when the Germans wanted to make a separate natural gas deal with Russia and cut Poland out of the picture. It's also gone up against France several times, most vocally to get France to open up its labor market to Polish workers. And it defied the EU as a whole on several occasions, famously siding with the U.S. in the 2003 Iraq war, over French objections, and agreeing to host part of a U.S. anti-missile battery aimed at defending the U.S. and Europe against rockets fired from Iran. The EU generally frowns on member states cutting separate defense deals with third countries, but that didn't stop the Poles.

DOMESTIC POLITICS

As Poland's international diplomacy continues to mature slowly, the country's domestic politics remains mired in back-biting and scandal. The current right-wing government headed by president Lech Kaczyński and Prime Minister Donald Tusk is famously dysfunctional, and every week seems to bring new rumors of collapse and fresh elections.

As with many of the new Eastern European democracies, Poland has lurched rightward and leftward over the years without really establishing any firm political framework.

In the immediate aftermath of the fall of Communism in 1989, the country was led by former Solidarity leader Lech Wałęsa. Wałęsa's presidency was marked by back-biting, infighting, and a splintering of the party system to such an extent that governing proved practically impossible. Voters then opted for a former Communist, Aleksander Kwaśniewski. Kwaśniewski's rule brought unexpected stability and political progress, though in time gave way to the current right-wing Kaczyński government and renewed bickering. Only time will tell if the country can get its act together.

ECONOMY

Luckily for Poles, this lack of political stability has not seemed to harm economic development. Indeed, until the global economic crisis hit toward the middle of 2008, Poland was a model success story, with strong economic growth and a firm currency, the złoty. Living standards had been rising for more than a decade and Poland—a famously poor country between the two world wars, made even poorer under Communism—could finally see itself catching up with Western Europe. At press time it wasn't possible to say with any certainty what the global economic slowdown would bring, but as 2008 was coming to a close Poland found itself dealing with an expanding banking crisis, a weakening currency, and rapidly slowing growth. As for the euro, the EU's common currency, Prime Minister Tusk announced plans in September 2008 for Poland to join the Eurozone by 2012, though that date is considered by many to be wildly optimistic.

To be sure, in spite of the country's economic progress over the past 20 years, you'll still run across many depressed areas—particularly in industrial cities such as Łódź and in large parts of Warsaw itself. You'll also see greater numbers than you might expect of homeless people, public drunks, beggars, and those who have simply fallen through the cracks. Not everyone has benefited equally from the country's rapid transformation to a democratic political system and a free-market economy. Industrial workers, particularly those over the age of 50 for whom adapting to the changes proved more difficult, have been hardest hit.

Young people, too, have found it difficult to cope with ever-rising living costs on very low wages. Many have left the country for places like the U.K. and Ireland, where they can earn more tending bar than they can working as young professionals at home.

But it's important to put this into perspective. Just a little more than two decades ago, Poland was literally falling apart. The country was $30 billion in debt to international lenders. The air was unbreathable, particularly in Kraków, downwind from the enormous steel mill complex at Nowa Huta. It wasn't unusual for Poles to spend hours standing in line simply to buy a piece of fruit or a bottle of imported shampoo. And membership in the European Union was unthinkable. Worst of all, perhaps, was the feeling of utter hopelessness, as if it were somehow Poland's fate to end up on the wrong side of history every time. That's been replaced by something

better and infectious: a cautious optimism that maybe this time around the good times are here to stay.

CONTACT WITH POLES

In your travels, you'll find that Poles are generally highly educated and cultured, with a firm grasp of their country's long and rich tradition in literature, poetry, performing arts, and film. The strong role of culture in everyday life is not surprising given the country's tragic history. For the 125 years, until 1918, that Poland ceased to exist as a country, it was quite literally a shared culture that held the people together. In modern times, it was this common cultural heritage that helped Poles to weather the Nazi and Soviet occupations, and to endure 40 years of Communist rule after World War II.

You'll sense, too, a strong feeling of national pride. Poles are proud of their history. They're proud of their resistance, however futile, to the Nazi invasion in 1939, and of the tragic Warsaw uprising in 1944. And they're proud of their country's leading role in ending Communism in the 1980s. Today, this pride extends to Poland's membership in the European Union. Americans are likely to feel particularly welcome. Poland's ties to the United States go back all the way to Tadeusz Kościuszko and the Revolutionary War. Poles proudly cite Chicago as the second-biggest Polish city in the world after Warsaw (even though these days more young Poles are emigrating to Ireland and the U.K. than to the U.S.). Just about everyone has a cousin, uncle, or grandparent who lives or used to live in one of the 50 states.

2 LOOKING BACK AT POLAND

Nowhere in Europe will you feel recent history more strongly than in Poland. The country's unenviable physical position through the ages—between Germany in the west and Russia to the east, and without defensible natural borders—has meant

Polish history has been one long struggle for survival. It all reads like a giant novel. And indeed American author James A. Michener did write a giant novel in 1981 called *Poland,* chronicling the trials and tribulations of three Polish families over

1   966: Duke Mieszko I, in Poznań, agrees to be baptized, making Christianity Poland's official religion and creating what would become the modern Polish state.

2   February 19, 1473: Polish astronomer Nicolaus Copernicus is born in the city of Toruń.

3   July 1, 1569: At a signing ceremony in Lublin, the kingdoms of Poland and Lithuania agree to merge, creating for a time Europe's largest country.

4   1596: Poland's capital is shifted from Kraków to Warsaw following the union with Lithuania and the enormous expansion of Polish territory.

5   March 1, 1810: Polish composer Frédéric Chopin is born in the village of Żelazowa Wola in what was then the Duchy of Warsaw.

6   1899: Rail workers extend the line south to the Tatra resort of Zakopane, paving the way for the town to emerge as the cultural center of Polish art and architecture.

7   September 1, 1939: World War II begins as Nazi Germany fires on Polish forces at Westerplatte, across from Gdansk harbor.

8   July 20, 1944: German army officer Claus Schenk Graf von Stauffenberg fails in his attempt to assassinate Adolf Hitler at Hitler's command bunker in the former East Prussia.

9   January 27, 1945: The Soviet Red Army liberates the Auschwitz concentration camp, finding the remains of thousands dead and just around 7,500 survivors.

10   October 16, 1978: The Vatican elevates Kraków cardinal Karol Wojtyła as pope, becoming John Paul II.

11   August 31, 1980: The "Gdańsk Accords" are signed in the port city between Poland's Communist regime and the Solidarity trade union led by Lech Wałęsa, legitimizing Eastern Europe's first non-Communist labor union and paving the way for the end of Communism nine years later.

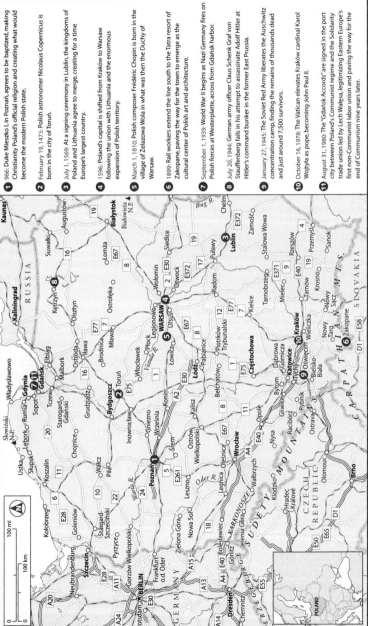

POLAND IN DEPTH

2

LOOKING BACK AT POLAND

It Happened Here: Poznań

While Kraków and Warsaw seem to grab all the glory where Polish history is concerned, Poznań can make a good case for being at the start of it all. It was here that Duke Mieszko I first accepted Catholic baptism in the 10th century. One of the country's most celebrated cathedrals still stands here, and this is also where Mieszko is buried.

eight centuries (see "Books" below). He hardly had to make up a single word.

THE EARLY POLISH KINGS

The Poles first established themselves in the areas to the west of Warsaw around the turn of the first millennium, descendants of migrant Slav tribes that came to Eastern Europe around A.D. 700–800. The first documented Polish dynasty was the Piast dynasty, and the country's first ruler was Duke Mieszko I, who ruled from Poznań's *Ostrów Tumski* (see p. 187). It was Mieszko who made the decision to be baptized in 966, making Christianity Poland's official religion and setting the tone for what would remain to this day one of Europe's most deeply Christian and Catholic countries. Though it had its ups and downs the way that any medieval kingdom would, Poland in the early centuries of its existence was one of Europe's most successful countries. From its capital in Kraków, it prospered under first the Piast and later the Jagiellon dynasties, stretching at one point from the Baltic in the north to the Hungarian kingdom in the south. It was also known as a comparatively tolerant kingdom, and it was at this time that Poland became known as a sanctuary for Jews. In 1410, the Polish king, allied with Lithuania, successfully fought off a challenge by a wayward order of crusaders, the Teutonic knights, at the battle of Grünwald in one of the great epic battles of the late Middle Ages. The knights had originally been brought to Poland from the Holy Lands to try to subdue the pagan Prussians. The problem was that they had gotten too big for their own britches and had to be put down: the Teutonic knights' castle at Malbork (p. 253) is testament to their boundless ambition.

The seat of government was moved from Kraków to Warsaw in the 16th century after a formal political union with Lithuania greatly expanded Poland's territory. The union was signed in 1569 in Lublin (p. 162) and still bears the name "Union of Lublin." To this day, it's probably the most exciting thing to ever happen to Poland's eastern metropolis.

In the 17th century, the Poles are generally credited with saving Europe in another epic battle, this one against the Ottoman Turks. Commander Jan Sobieski saved the day for Christian Europe, repelling the Turks at the gates of Vienna in 1683.

THE RISE OF RIVALS & THE POLISH PARTITIONS

From this point, Polish history runs mostly downhill. A series of wars, first with Sweden and later with Russia, sapped the monarchy's energy and money. Complicated voting rules in Poland's early parliament, the Sejm, completely paralyzed the government. At the same time, both Prussia and tsarist Russia began their long-term rises as great powers. The result was that at the end of the 18th century Poland was divided up like a pie, with big pieces going to both Prussia and Russia, and a smaller piece in the south going to Habsburg Austria. This is known in history textbooks as the Polish partitions. For some 125 years, until the end of World War I, Poland disappeared from the map of Europe.

During the 19th century, various Polish heroes tried valiantly—and fruitlessly—to win back the country's independence. Polish patriots of the time threw in their lot with Napoleon, who was storming Europe and promising to recreate the Polish state. In fact, Napoleon did reconstitute part of old Poland in the Duchy of Warsaw in 1807, but his eventual defeat in Russia meant that Poland was divided again, losing vast tracts of territory to tsarist Russia in the east. In spite of the disappearance of the Polish state, Polish language and culture managed to survive. Kraków, at this point, re-established itself as the center of Polish culture. It was located deep in the Austrian part of Poland, which—compared to the Russian- and Prussian-controlled zones, at least—was a bastion of freedom and free expression.

WORLD WAR I & POLISH INDEPENDENCE

Independent Poland was restored in 1918 after the collapse of Austria-Hungary and Germany in World War I. Indeed, point 13 of U.S. President Woodrow Wilson's famed "14 points," which set the terms for the surrender of Germany, called directly for the reconstitution of Poland:

An independent Polish state should be erected which should include the territories inhabited by indisputably Polish populations, which should be assured a free and secure access to the sea, and whose political and economic independence and territorial integrity should be guaranteed by international covenant.

The first years for the independent Polish state were rocky. The first order of business was to fend off attack by the Soviet Union in the Polish–Soviet war of 1919–21. Polish forces, led by Marshal Józef Piłsudski, succeeded in repelling the Red Army at the 1920 Battle of Warsaw, often called the "Miracle on the Vistula." Victory, though, could not guarantee the success of Poland's fledgling democracy, and in 1926, amid rampant hyperinflation, Piłsudski came to power in a military coup. Piłsudski guided the Poles until his death in 1935, and is widely credited with preserving the Polish state under difficult times. Though in effect a dictator, he is fondly remembered and buried with the Polish kings at Kraków's Wawel Castle (p. 126).

WORLD WAR II & THE HOLOCAUST

If the interwar years were hard, World War II was Poland's worst nightmare come to life. Nazi Germany fired the first shot of the war at Polish forces garrisoned near Gdańsk harbor on September 1, 1939. Soviet Russia, under terms of a nonaggression pact with Germany, then seized the eastern part of the country a few weeks

---

Local Wisdom: Napoleon & the Poles

At the turn of the 19th century, Napoleon and Polish patriots trying to re-establish their country formed what can be seen as a marriage of convenience. The Poles needed Napoleon to defeat the Russians, and Napoleon needed the Poles, well, for the very same thing. Napoleon, in the end, grew quite respectful of Polish fighters, once saying famously that "800 Poles would equal 8,000 enemy soldiers."

It Happened Here: Tarnów

The charming southern Renaissance city of Tarnów has the unenviable distinction of having been the site of the first mass transportation of prisoners to the Auschwitz concentration camp on June 14, 1940. The transport was made up of 728 Poles, mostly political prisoners affiliated with resistance movements. Tarnów's records indicate that 753 prisoners actually left on the transport, but only 728 arrived at Auschwitz. The fate of the missing 25 prisoners has never been solved.

later. In June 1941, the Nazis violated their nonaggression pact and declared war on Russia, initially pushing the Soviet Red Army out of Poland and deep into Russian territory. In the ensuing battle between Fascism and Communism, Poland was literally caught in the middle. Nearly a quarter of all Poles died in the war, including some 3 million Polish Jews.

For Poles, the most poignant memories of the war include the 1940 massacre of Polish army officers by Soviet forces at the Katyń forest. For years, the Soviets denied they had carried out the mass killing, instead blaming the Nazis. Only after the fall of the Soviet Union was the historical record made clear. The story of the massacre was later made into a blockbuster movie by director Andrzej Wajda (*Katyń;* see "Film" below). Poles also recall the ultimately futile uprising of 1944, when the residents of Warsaw rose up against the Nazis. The Soviet Red Army was closing in on German positions from the East, and the Poles expected the Soviets to join in the fight. Instead, the Red Army chose to watch the fighting from across the Vistula River. The Poles scored some initial successes, but the Germans ultimately prevailed and retaliated ruthlessly. Hitler ordered that Warsaw be destroyed, building by building.

The war itself was bad enough, but the Nazis used Polish soil for the worst of their plans to exterminate Europe's Jewish population and to reduce the Polish and Russian residents to slaves. The Nazis established extermination camps around the country. The most famous of these were at Auschwitz-Birkenau (p. 146), Treblinka, and Chełmno near Łódź (p. 101), but smaller or less-well-known extermination camps were established in all parts of the country. In addition, the Nazis set up huge ghettos to forcibly hold Poland's once-enormous Jewish population before they could be sent to the camps. Today, you can tour several of the death camps, as well as walk around the former ghettos at Warsaw (p. 85), Łódź (p. 101), Kraków-Kazimierz (p. 127), and Lublin (p. 166), among others. Though these types of Holocaust visits sound depressing, they will constitute the most moving memories you bring home from your trip to Poland.

Though ethnic Poles were generally spared the organized genocide of the Holocaust, they too suffered greatly under the Nazis. Countless numbers of Polish POWs, resisters, and ordinary citizens, as well as thousands of Russian POWs, died at Auschwitz and at the other camps alongside Jewish Poles.

The destruction of Poland's physical property is hard to exaggerate. Take Warsaw as an example. Following the 1944 failed Warsaw uprising, the Nazis ordered Poland's once-handsome capital razed to the ground. The buildings were dynamited one by one in order of their importance. By the end of the war, 85 percent of the city lay in ruins. The numbers are similar for other large cities. Gdańsk was nearly totally destroyed. Wrocław was a smoking ash heap.

THE COMMUNIST PERIOD & THE RISE OF SOLIDARITY

Poland was reconstituted at the end of the war, but with radically different borders. Bowing to Soviet leader Josef Stalin's demands, the U.S. and U.K. ceded vast tracts of formerly Polish territory in the east to the Soviet Union. In turn, the new Poland was compensated with former German territory in the west. The Polish borders were shifted some 200km (120 miles) westward. The ethnic German population was expelled and replaced by Poles transferred from the east of the country.

But the end of the war brought little relief. Poland fell on the Soviet side of the Iron Curtain, and though Communism as an ideology held little appeal for most Poles, a series of Soviet-backed Communist governments uneasily led the country for the next four decades, until 1989.

The government managed to maintain order through massive borrowing on international financial markets, but mismanagement of the economy led to one crisis after another, including bloody riots in 1970 that killed more than 40 people and shocked the country and the world.

In the end it was the desire for higher living standards—perhaps even more than a desire for political freedom—that led to the creation of the Solidarity trade union and the genesis of the anti-Communist movement. Solidarity began at the shipyards in Gdańsk, but eventually spread to the rest of the country. The union's breakthrough came in 1980, under the leadership of the young, charismatic Lech Wałęsa. The Polish government had been forced to raise food prices in the summer of 1980, sparking nationwide protests and strikes. The workers of the Lenin Shipyard in Gdańsk (p. 227) called a strike and refused to back down, ultimately forcing the government to recognize Solidarity as a free and independent trade union, the first of its kind in Eastern Europe. The strike led to the August 1980 Gdańsk Accords, and the first step in what would be Poland's decade-long struggle to break the bonds of Communism. The low point came a year later, as the Communist authorities—pushed by their Soviet overlords—were forced to declare martial law in December 1981 to prevent a complete loss of control. Thousands of people were arrested and some 100 died in the crackdown.

In 1978, at around the same time that all this was happening, the Catholic Church had elevated another charismatic Pole, a cardinal from Kraków named Karol Woytyła, to be pope. If Solidarity provided the organizational framework for Poles to resist, Pope John Paul, through his visits and sermons, provided the moral inspiration.

In early 1989, the Poles held their first semi-free election—a landmark vote that bolstered anti-Communist activists across Eastern Europe. By the end of that epic year, the entire Eastern bloc was free.

Local Voices: Josef Stalin on Bringing Communism to Poland

"It's like putting a saddle on cow," said former Soviet leader Josef Stalin on the difficulties of imposing Communism on a deeply religious country such as Poland.

Important Historical Events

- 966: Duke Mieszko I, in Poznań, agrees to be baptized, making Christianity Poland's official religion and creating what would become the modern Polish state.
- February 19, 1473: Polish astronomer Nicolaus Copernicus is born in the city of Toruń.
- July 1, 1569: At a signing ceremony in Lublin, the kingdoms of Poland and Lithuania agree to merge, creating Europe's largest country at the time.
- 1596: Poland's capital is shifted from Kraków to Warsaw following the union with Lithuania and the enormous expansion of Polish territory.
- March 1, 1810: Polish composer Frédéric Chopin is born in the village of Żelazowa Wola in what was then the Duchy of Warsaw.
- 1894: Stanisław Witkiewicz finishes the giant wooden Willa Koliba in Zakopane, the first building to use the groundbreaking "Zakopane style" of architecture.
- 1899: Rail workers extend the line south to the Tatra resort of Zakopane, paving the way for the town to emerge as the cultural center of Polish art and architecture.
- November 11, 1918: Poland regains its independence after 125 years with Warsaw to be the country's new capital.
- September 1, 1939: World War II begins as Nazi Germany fires on Polish forces at Westerplatte, across from Gdańsk harbor.
- July 20, 1944: German army officer Claus Schenk Graf von Stauffenberg fails in his attempt to assassinate Adolf Hitler at Hitler's command bunker (the Wolf's Lair) in the former East Prussia.
- January 27, 1945: The Soviet Red Army liberates the Auschwitz concentration camp, finding the remains of thousands dead and just around 7,500 survivors.
- October 16, 1978: The Vatican elevates Kraków cardinal Karol Woytyła to pope, anointing him Pope John Paul II.
- August 31, 1980: The "Gdańsk Accords" are signed in the port city between Poland's Communist regime and the Solidarity trade union led by Lech Wałęsa, legitimizing Eastern Europe's first non-Communist labor union and paving the way for the end of Communism nine years later.
- May 1, 2004: Poland fulfills its long-term foreign policy goal of joining the European Union with celebrations in the capital, Warsaw, and around the country.

THE PERIOD SINCE 1989

The period since 1989 has been hugely chaotic, but the result has been the creation of a stable, democratic Polish state that's a member of both NATO and the European Union. Each of the former Soviet satellite states chose a different path toward democratization and creation of a free market, and Poland's contribution in this regard has been accurately called "shock therapy." Designed by Poland's finance minister at the time, Leszek Balcerowicz, shock therapy essentially meant allowing wages and prices to float freely and indebted Communist companies to go bankrupt. Understandably, it caused massive disruption in the economy, and millions lost their jobs. The jury is still out on whether shock therapy was good or bad, but it's generally credited with promoting high rates of growth, albeit at a high social cost. Politically, however, the country stagnated. Lech Wałęsa's early stint as president (1990–95) proved to be disastrous—he

IPoland in History: 10 Surprising Facts

- Poland has been a Christian country for more than a thousand years; its first ruler, Duke Mieszko I, converted to Christianity in 966.
- The country's first capital was Poznań, before being moved to Krakow for some 500 years, and then to Warsaw around 1600.
- The Polish kingdom was traditionally seen as a safe haven for Jews, so that by the 16th century, Poland was home to some 80 percent of the world's Jewish population.
- The city of Toruń is famous in Poland for two things: for being the birthplace of noted astronomer Nicolaus Copernicus, and for having the country's best gingerbread cookies (p. 222).
- Poland completely disappeared from the map of Europe from around 1800 to 1918, swallowed up by Germany (Prussia), Russia, and Austria-Hungary.
- Noted Polish composer Frédéric Chopin was born in Poland, but had a French father and actually spent most of his adult life in Paris.
- Misery and poverty in the late 19th and early 20th centuries forced some 4 million Poles to emigrate to the United States, around 20 percent of the population at the time.
- World War II began on Polish territory when Nazi units fired on a Polish garrison at Westerplatte, near Gdańsk harbor, on September 1, 1939 (p. 232).
- The 1944 failed assassination attempt on Adolf Hitler—which forms the basis for the 2008 Tom Cruise movie *Valkyrie*—took place at Hitler's bunker in the lake district north of Warsaw (p. 84).
- Prior to World War II, the Polish city of Wrocław was known as the German city of Breslau; Gdańsk was Danzig. The Ukrainian city of Lviv was formerly the Polish city of Lwów.

was a much better labor leader than national leader—and since then Poland has lurched left and right without finding a stable middle. The high point of the post-Communist period came in 2004, when Poland, along with seven other formerly Communist states, joined the European Union.

3 POLAND IN POPULAR CULTURE: FILM, BOOKS & MUSIC

Poland is well-known for its contribution to international cinema, having spawned a generation of world-renowned directors in the immediate aftermath of World War II. Poland's contribution to world literature—at least to English-language readers—is limited by what's available in translation, but the Communist period was particularly rich, and the country has at least two internationally renowned poets to its credit. In music, at least in classical music, the name Chopin rises above all others. Wherever you travel in Poland, you can be certain you won't be far from a Chopin concert.

FILM

Poland's greatest contribution to popular culture, arguably, is in film. No fewer than three of the world's great post-war directors are Polish and learned their craft at the country's school of cinematography in Łódź: Roman Polański, Krzysztof Kieslowski, and Andrzej Wajda. Łódź, incidentally, has the country's only museum devoted to cinematography, and film buffs should certainly seek it out.

Of the three, Polański is probably the best-known abroad (though Kieslowski rates a close second), both for his films and his tragic and stormy personal life, including living through the brutal murder of his pregnant wife, Sharon Tate, in 1969 by members of the Charles Manson gang and by a conviction in the U.S. in 1977 for allegedly having sexual relations with a 13-year-old girl. Polański's films are best known for having a dark and sinister feel. His breakout film was 1962's *Knife in the Water*, made in Poland, concerning a murderous ménage-a-trois. It was received coolly by Poland's Communist authorities but was a big international hit, securing him a filmmaking future in Great Britain and later the United States. In Britain, Polański collaborated with French actress Catherine Deneuve to make the thriller *Repulsion*. Once in the U.S. in the late 1960s he scored a series of blockbusters, including *Rosemary's Baby* with Mia Farrow (1968) and *Chinatown* (1974) with Faye Dunaway and Jack Nicholson. Later hits included *Frantic* (1987), starring Harrison Ford, and 2002's critically acclaimed *The Pianist*, with Adrien Brody in the lead role of Warsaw Jewish ghetto survivor Władysław Szpilman. That movie earned Polański an Oscar for Best Director.

Krzysztof Kieslowski is best-known abroad for his *Three Colors* movies: *Blue* (1993), *White* (1994), and *Red* (1994). Kieslowski made the films—based on the French virtues of liberty, equality, and fraternity—after he had moved to France. However, he had already earned a formidable reputation in Poland for his ironic Socialist Realist movies of the 1970s and '80s, the best of which is probably *Man*

With a Camera (1979). He's also the director of the critically acclaimed *Decalogue* (1988) series (10 movies based on the 10 commandments), and the art-house favorite *The Double Life of Veronique* (1991).

Andrzej Wajda may be less well known to those outside Poland, but within the country he's widely considered the most important director to emerge after World War II. He earned his reputation in the 1950s, with unsparing movies about the war, including *Ashes and Diamonds* (1957). Two films depicting life in Soviet-dominated Poland—1976's *Man of Marble* and 1981's *Man of Iron*—won Wajda widespread international critical acclaim. Though now in his 80s he's still going strong, and 2007's premiere of *Katyń*, which focuses on the mass execution of Polish officers in the Katyń forest by the Soviets in 1940, was Poland's biggest film event in years.

Movies about Poland

In addition to movies made by Poles, there are countless movies about Poland, usually focused on World War II or the Holocaust. The best known of these is Steven Spielberg's 1993 epic *Schindler's List*. The movie depicts the efforts of German industrialist Oskar Schindler to shield his Jewish factory workers from deportation to the concentration camps and his subsequent actions that saved 1,000 people from a certain death at Auschwitz. Much of the movie was filmed in and around Kraków's former Jewish quarter of Kazimierz, and Schindler's factory, now derelict, is still standing (see p. 118). Janusz Kamiński, Spielberg's Polish cameraman for *Schindler's List* and then later for *Saving Private Ryan*, won Oscars for both films.

Another outstanding movie that features wartime Poland is 1982's *Sophie's Choice*, starring Meryl Streep and based on the William Styron novel of the same name. In the movie, Streep plays a Polish immigrant and Auschwitz survivor living in Brooklyn who finds it impossible to

Purely Personal "Top 10" Polish Films

Dozens and dozens of great films were either made by Polish directors or are about Poland. Many of these are now available on DVD. A purely subjective list of the best would include the following:

1. *Schindler's List* (1993), Steven Spielberg
2. *Chinatown* (1976), Roman Polański
3. *Three Colors: Blue, White, and Red* (1993, 1994, 1994), Krzysztof Kieslowski
4. *Rosemary's Baby* (1968), Roman Polański
5. *The Pianist* (2002), Roman Polański
6. *Man of Marble* (1976), Andrzej Wajda
7. *Sophie's Choice* (1982), Alan J. Pakula
8. *Knife in the Water* (1962), Roman Polański
9. *The Double Life of Veronique* (1991), Krzysztof Kieslowski
10. *Man of Iron* (1981), Andrzej Wajda

escape the world she left behind, and the horrific choice she had to make.

It's also worth noting that American cult filmmaker David Lynch reportedly has a love affair with Poland's film capital, Łódź. His most recent film, *Inland Empire,* was apparently inspired by a visit to the city.

BOOKS

Polish literature, with few exceptions, remains largely unknown to people outside the country, due mainly to publishers' reluctance to invest in translating the books into English rather than to a lack of literary merit. Poland, in fact, has no fewer than six Nobel Prize winners for literature: Henryk Sienkiewicz (1905), the author of *Quo Vadis;* Władysław Reymont (1924), a largely forgotten journalist; Jewish writers Shmuel Yosef Agnon (1966) and I. B. Singer (1978); and poets Czesław Miłosz (1980) and Wisława Szymborska (1996) (see "Poetry" below). You can make a case for a seventh Nobel by including German writer Günter Grass, who was born and raised in Gdańsk when the city was part of Germany and known as Danzig.

For Poles, the most fruitful period in literature came during the two world wars, when writers such as Witold Gombrowicz and Stanisław Ignacy Witkiewicz shocked polite society with novels involving previously taboo themes like homosexuality and illicit drugs. Gombrowicz's *Pornografia* and Witkiewicz's *Insatiability* are both available in English translation and are difficult but worthwhile reads.

The Communist Period

The post–World War II period proved to be a surprisingly productive time in Polish literature as writers reacted to the war and life under Communism. Penguin's highly influential 1980s series "Writers from the Other Europe," edited by American writer Philip Roth, exposed several of the most talented Eastern bloc writers to an international audience (you can still find many of these books on bookstore shelves or on the Internet). Writers in the series from Poland include Bruno Schulz (*Street of Crocodiles* and *Sanatorium Under the Sign of the Hourglass*), Jerzy Andrzejewski (*Ashes and Diamonds*), Tadeusz Borowski (*This Way for the Gas, Ladies and Gentlemen;* see "Holocaust Literature," below), and Tadeusz Konwicki (*A Dreambook for Our Time* and *The Polish Complex*). Though Schulz was included in the collection, he wrote mostly about Jewish life in interwar Poland and during World War II.

No doubt the biggest book to come out of Poland in the post-war period was Jerzy Kosinski's *The Painted Bird*, which provoked a firestorm when it was published in 1965. The book tells the story of a young Jewish or Roma orphan who wanders from village to village during World War II, experiencing the anti-Semitism, violence, and frank perversions of the Polish peasantry at the time. The book was banned in Poland on publication, but wowed Western critics in the 1960s. It's since lost some of its luster amid controversy that Kosinski greatly embellished the stories and in fact profited from the book's association with Holocaust literature, but still makes for a gripping read.

Other Writers

Aside from literature, Polish writers are well known in other genres. Fans of science fiction will no doubt know the name Stanisław Lem, the author of the 1961 classic *Solaris* and dozens of other titles.

Journalist Ryszard Kapuściński carved out an immense reputation as a travel writer, focusing particularly on accounts in the developing world. His best-known work remains *Another Day of Life* (1976), about the collapse of Portuguese colonialism in Angola.

American writer Alan Furst, though not a Pole, has written several fun and worthwhile spy and noir novels set in World War II Poland or involving Polish characters. His best is probably 1995's *The Polish Officer*. In 2008, he published the thriller *The Spies of Warsaw*.

For a Polish page-turner that will have you thumbing through eight centuries of Polish history in the course of a long afternoon, try James Michener's epic *Poland* (1981). The novel traces the tortured histories of three families through some eight centuries of war and upheaval. It's a surprisingly gripping read and Michener, as usual, manages to bring to life what might in the hands of another writer be just a dry, historical account.

Holocaust Literature

There's no shortage of great books written about the Holocaust, and bringing a few titles along with you can greatly enhance your experience as you visit former Nazi concentration camps and wartime Jewish ghettos. There are several excellent accounts written by survivors of the camps, but two of the best include Italian writer Primo Levi's *Survival in Auschwitz*, an unvarnished account of Levi's arrival at Auschwitz's Monowitz camp in 1944 and what happened to him after he got there, and Rudolf Vrba's *Escape from Auschwitz: I Cannot Forgive*, the true account of one of the few men to have escaped from Auschwitz and lived to tell the tale: Vrba and a fellow Slovak managed to escape from Auschwitz's Birkenau camp in 1944. This book tells the incredible story of how they did it and how they later tried to tell

Local Voices: An Excerpt from Szymborska's Poem "True Love"

Look at the happy couple.
Couldn't they at least try to hide it,
fake a little depression for their friends' sake?
Listen to them laughing—it's an insult.
The language they use—deceptively clear.
And their little celebrations, rituals,
the elaborate mutual routines—
it's obviously a plot behind the human race's back!
—Wisława Szymborska (translated by Stanisław Baranczak and Clare Cavanagh)

Purely Personal "Top 10" Polish Books

It's a mish-mash (books by Poles, books about Poland, books about events in Poland), but a good reading list in English for anyone contemplating a trip would start with the following:

1. *The Captive Mind*, Czesław Miłosz
2. *The Painted Bird*, Jerzy Kosinski
3. *This Way for the Gas, Ladies and Gentlemen*, Tadeusz Borowski
4. *Survival at Auschwitz*, Primo Levi
5. *Escape from Auschwitz: I Cannot Forgive*, Rudolf Vrba
6. *Poland*, James Michener
7. *Pornografia*, Witold Gombrowicz
8. *The Polish Complex*, Tadeusz Konwicki
9. *The Polish Officer*, Alan Furst
10. *Street of Crocodiles*, Bruno Schulz

the world about the Holocaust but found that few were willing to listen.

Tadeusz Borowski's *This Way for the Gas, Ladies and Gentlemen* tells the Auschwitz story from a different perspective. Borowski was a Polish political prisoner at Auschwitz and worked in the coveted "Kanada" brigade, responsible for cleaning up and storing possessions of new arrivals as they entered the camp. The work was horrific, but day-to-day survival was not usually an issue. Instead, Borowski paints an unsparing picture of desperate prisoners willing to do anything it took—including collaborating with their captors—in order to survive. (Borowski ended up committing suicide after the war.)

Commandant of Auschwitz: The Autobiography of Rudolf Hoess tells the story of the Auschwitz SS commander in his own words. Hoess wrote his autobiography in 1946 after being captured by Allied troops at the end of the war. It's chilling in its coldness and lack of regret. Hoess was hanged by Polish authorities in 1947 at Auschwitz, not far from one of the crematoria he helped to build.

In terms of understanding the Nazis' extermination plans, an excellent if somewhat academic read is Christopher R. Browning's *The Origins of the Final Solution*.

Poetry

Poland has produced two Nobel Prize–winning poets: Czesław Miłosz (1980) and Wisława Szymborska (1996). Miłosz, who died in 2004, spent much of his life as a professor of Slavic literature at the University of California at Berkeley. Aside from numerous volumes of poetry, Miłosz is the author the highly regarded "The Captive Mind" (1953), a long and absorbing essay that attempts to describe intellectuals' acceptance of Stalinism at the end of World War II. He's also the author of a highly regarded textbook on Polish literature, *The History of Polish Literature*.

Szymborska is a Kraków-based poet and essayist, known for short, witty, and humorous poems on life's ironies. See the box for an excerpt from her poem "True Love."

MUSIC

Though Poland has a rich musical tradition going back centuries, it's probably best known for two contributions: the polka and Frédéric Chopin.

Crediting Poland with the polka is actually a common error, probably because of the similarity of the names. Though the

(**Moments**) **"For where thy treasure is, there will thy heart be also"**

Though Chopin spent much of his life in France, his heart—quite literally—belongs to Poland. Shortly before his death, as the story goes, Chopin asked that his heart be moved to the country of his birth. Complying with his wishes, doctors removed the composer's heart after he died, and it was taken to Warsaw by his sister. The heart is preserved in a pillar of the Holy Cross Church (*Kościół Świętego Krzyża*) on Warsaw's Krakówskie Przedmieście, beneath the inscription taken from the Bible, Matthew 6, verse 21 (the title of this box). Chopin's heart is still there. It was removed briefly during the fighting in World War II, and then restored to the church after it was rebuilt.

polka is as popular in Poland as anywhere else in Eastern Europe, it actually comes from Bohemia, in the modern-day Czech Republic.

Poles have a more legitimate claim on Chopin, though another country, France, is involved there too. Though Chopin was born in the village of Żelazowa Wola, not far from Warsaw, to a Polish mother, his father was French and the composer spent much of his short life in Paris and even for a time became a French citizen. And, for a time, he carried on a stormy relationship with French intellectual George Sand (female).

Chopin is generally regarded as one of the foremost composers of the 19th-century Romantic Movement. His music is still wildly popular in Poland, and wherever you travel in the country you're certain to be able to catch a Chopin concert somewhere nearby. Poles say that no matter where they are in the world, when they hear a Chopin piece, such as "Polonaise" Op. 53, they are immediately transported back to the Polish countryside. Chopin is most famous for his *études*, compositions written mainly to help students learn their instruments, but which have become concert pieces in their own right. His best-known piece of music is probably his "Funeral March" (piano sonata no. 2), which nearly everyone will recognize after just a few bars (imagine the somber tones they play on a cartoon when someone has to walk the plank).

Chopin died in Paris at the age of 39 of chronic lung failure brought on by tuberculosis. He is buried at Paris's fabled Père Lachaise Cemetery—everything except his heart, of course, which was carted off to Warsaw shortly after his death and is sealed in a pillar at the Holy Cross Church (*Kościół Świętego Krzyża*) (see p. 81).

4 EATING & DRINKING IN POLAND

Polish food has a hearty, homemade feel, and when it's done well it can be delicious. It's similar to other Central European national cuisines in that it's centered on main courses of mostly meat dishes and features plenty of hearty soups and sides of potatoes and grains. Game dishes, such as venison, boar, and duck, play a more prominent role here than in the United States or Western Europe. Poles also have a mania for mushrooms, the best being those picked in the forest that morning.

Visitors to Poland will be happy to see that traditional **pierogi** are still going strong. These hand-rolled dumplings are stuffed with everything from potato and cottage cheese to cabbage, from ground meat to even plums or strawberries in

Tea vs. Coffee?

Like the English, Poles through the ages have traditionally been tea drinkers, though coffee, increasingly sold as espresso and lattes in trendy coffee shops, is making some inroads. Tea is normally drunk from a glass and flavored with sugar and/or lemon. The quality of the coffee has greatly improved in the past decade, but for some reason the dark, bitter liquid called "coffee" served at hotel and pension breakfasts is still often undrinkable!

season (see the box below for some of the more inventive filling options). *Pierogi* are traditionally prepared by boiling in water, though they can also be baked or fried. *Pierogi* with savory fillings, such as cheese and meat, are traditionally topped with fried onions or bacon bits; fruit *pierogi* are best eaten with butter or cream.

Pierogi have lots to recommend them. For one thing, they're often the cheapest item on the menu, making them tailor-made budget food. They are also extremely flexible, and can be eaten as a snack or as a main course, for lunch or dinner. They also make a great option for vegetarians; just be sure to tell them to hold the bacon bits they sometimes pour on top. *Pierogi* prepared "Ruskie" style are meatless, stuffed with potatoes and cottage cheese.

Placki, potato pancakes, are nearly as ubiquitous and delicious as *pierogi,* and are often cooked with mushrooms or smoked meat.

TRADITIONAL MEAL

Polish meals generally begin with an appetizer, which can be either cold (*przekąski zimne*) or warm (*przekąski gorące*). Among the former, herring (*śledź*), usually served in a sour cream sauce and piled with chopped onions, is invariably a good choice. Other popular cold starters include stuffed fish or pâté (*pasztet*). Hot starters can include *pierogi* or a piece of homemade sausage (*kiełbasa*).

Soups (*zupy*) are a mainstay of a Polish meal. *Żurek* is a filling, sourish rye broth, seasoned with dill and usually served with

sausage and egg. *Barszcz* is based on red beets, but it isn't exactly "borscht." In Poland, it's usually served as a broth, often with a little pastry on the side. *Bigos,* often called "hunter's stew" on English menus, is another national mania and is made from sauerkraut and smoked meat, and often flavored with caraway seeds or juniper berries. Every Polish grandmother has her own version, and local lore says the homemade variety tastes best on the seventh reheating!

Main courses are less original, and often revolve around chicken, pork, or beef, though game (usually venison or boar) and fish (pike and trout) are also common. Sides (*dodatki*) usually involve some form of potato, fried or boiled, or sometimes fried potato dumplings. More creative sides include buckwheat groats (*kasza*) or mashed beets, the latter sometimes flavored with apple. Common desserts include fruit *pierogi*, apple strudel, the ubiquitous ice cream (*lody*), and pancakes, sometimes filled with cottage cheese and served with fruit sauce.

Breakfast is taken early, and is often no more than a cup of tea or instant coffee and a bread roll. Hotels usually lay on the traditional buffet-style breakfast centered on cold cuts, cheeses, yogurts, and cereals, but this is more than what Poles normally eat in the morning. Lunches are served late, around 1 or 2pm, and restaurants don't usually get rolling until about 1pm. Dinner starts around 7pm and can run until 9 or 10pm, though restaurants often claim to stay open "until the last customer." Some

Local Fare: Pierogi Decoder

It used to be that *pierogi*—those hand-rolled dough balls stuffed with good things and boiled—came in three basic flavors: meat (filled with a salty mix of pork and beef); cabbage; and the ever-popular "Ruskie," a mix of cottage cheese and potato. Those are all good, but *pierogi* seem to be going up-market and now there are literally dozens of varieties to choose from. Here's an eclectic list of some of the more unusual (courtesy of "Pierogarnia u Dzika" in Gdańsk; see p. 239):

Pierogi Wigilijne: Cabbage and mushroom
Pierogi Myśliwskie: Venison or game
Pierogi Farmerskie: Chicken, raisins, and nuts
Pierogi Wileńskie: Buckwheat groats and bacon
Pierogi Fantazyjne: Cottage cheese, cinnamon, raisins, and peaches
Pierogi Twarogowe Szaleństwo: Sweetened cream cheese
Pierogi Jarskie: Spinach and tomato
Pierogi Leśne: Forest mushrooms

actually do stay open late, but many kitchens start closing down after 10pm, so get there early to avoid disappointment.

FAST FOOD

Poles are big snackers and the latest mania is for Middle Eastern and Greek snack foods such as chicken and meat shawarma and kebabs. You'll find dozens of stands and windows serving some variation of a sandwich based on shaved meat, tomatoes, onions, and plenty of mayo. Pizza is also ubiquitous, and no self-respecting Polish city or town would be complete without at least half a dozen pizza restaurants of varying quality. Look also for *zapiekanki*—foot-long, open-faced baguettes, topped with sauce and cheese and then baked. It's known affectionately as "Polish pizza."

In addition to the "mom and pop" places, the big international chains have made inroads. The big players in Poland are McDonald's and KFC, and you'll invariably find one or the other (often both) in city centers and train stations. Polish domestic chains are also becoming more common. The best known is probably Sphinx, which seems to have an outlet in every city in the country. The specialty is fairly mediocre Middle Eastern–style food, served in a smoke-free, family-friendly atmosphere. It's easy to criticize the chains, but they can be a lifesaver if you're looking for something fast and reliable.

VODKA & BEER

While Poles may be best known for their vodka, it is in fact beer that's the national drink. You'll find the major beer brands—Okocim, Lech, Tyskie, and Żywiec—just about everywhere. There's little difference among the majors, though Tyskie appears to be the most popular. Men take theirs straight up. Women frequently sweeten their beer with fruit syrup (raspberry is the most common) and drink it through a straw. Among the most popular vodkas, Belvedere and Chopin are considered top-shelf, though imported vodkas are increasingly squeezing out the local brands. In addition, you'll find a range of flavored vodkas. Żubrówka is slightly greenish, owing to the long blade of bison grass in every bottle. Miodówka, honey-flavored and easy to drink, is worth a try. Wine is much less common, and nearly always imported.

Planning Your Trip to Poland

Visiting Poland has never been easier. Travelers from the U.S. and the European Union, including the U.K., don't require visas or need to take any particular health or safety precautions. Indeed, Poland is now a member of the "Schengen Zone" (EU-speak for the European Union's common border area), and if you're arriving from another EU member state, you're unlikely even to have show a passport or ID card at the border.

As far as packing goes, your suitcase or backpack will look pretty much the same as for any other U.S. or Continental destination with four distinct seasons (bearing in mind that a Polish winter might be colder than what you're used to). If you forget anything, rest assured that, just like at home, there's likely to be a shopping mall or drugstore down the street where you can find a suitable substitute.

More challenging might be deciding where to spend your time. Poland is relatively large as European countries go and road and rail connections still leave a lot to be desired. That means you'll have to pick and choose your target destinations carefully, leaving plenty of extra time for getting from here to there. A week in Poland, for example, would leave a comfortable amount of time for seeing Warsaw and the northern half of the country or seeing Kraków and the southern half, but unless you plan on flying from city to city, it would not leave enough time to do it all.

Another factor to consider is *what* you plan to do. Poland is an active destination—depending on what you want to do, you might think about bringing along things like golf clubs, a bicycle, hiking boots, or even skis. Whatever is in the cards, don't forget comfortable walking shoes. Although there's great public transportation within the cities, you're going to do a lot of walking wherever you go.

1 VISITOR INFORMATION

The Polish National Tourist Board (www.poland.travel) maintains offices in major countries around the world to promote Polish tourism and to help prospective visitors plan their trips. The website is an excellent source of general information on Poland, as well as ideas for where to go and what to do.

In the United States and Canada, contact the **Polish National Tourist Office** (5 Marine View Plaza, Hoboken NJ, 07030-5722; © **201/420-9910**). In the U.K., contact the **Polish National Tourist Office** (Level 3, Westgate House, West Gate, London W5 1YY; © **08700-675-010**). Other helpful websites include Poland's Web portal (www.poland.pl); the Polish Ministry of Foreign Affairs (general and visa information) (www.msz.gov.pl); and Polish Rail (www.pkp.pl).

Just about every Polish city of any size will have a tourist information agency that hands out maps and advice on what to see and do. Most of the time, you'll find this office on the town's central square, situated either nearby or inside the town hall building.

2 ENTRY REQUIREMENTS

PASSPORTS & VISAS

All visitors to Poland are required to hold a passport that is valid for at least six months beyond the date of entry into the country. Passport holders from the U.S., Canada, and Australia can enter Poland without a visa and stay for 90 days. Passport holders from EU member countries, including the U.K., do not need a visa. Poland is a member of the EU's "Schengen" common border zone, meaning that—in theory at least—if you are arriving from another EU country, you will not be asked to show a passport. Note that you are still obliged to carry your passport with you and show it if requested. Citizens of other countries should check in with the Polish Ministry of Foreign Affairs website (www.msz.gov.pl) to see whether they are required to have a visa and for any specific instructions necessary for obtaining it.

MEDICAL REQUIREMENTS

There are no unusual health concerns for visiting Poland and visitors are not required to get any special inoculations or show medical documents to enter the country. Medical and hospital standards are generally high. Though there are pharmacies everywhere, you should consider bringing along extra supplies of any prescription drugs you are taking. Tap water is drinkable, but you may want to avoid drinking from taps in old buildings since the pipes may be rusty. Bottled water is widely available.

CUSTOMS

Travelers from outside the European Union, including the U.S., Canada, Australia, and New Zealand, are permitted to bring with them into Poland duty-free: 200 cigarettes, 50 cigars, or 250g of pipe tobacco, 2 liters of wine, and 1 liter of spirits. For travelers coming from within the EU, at least in theory, the duty free limit is 800 cigarettes, 200 cigars, or 1kg of pipe tobacco, 110 liters of beer, 90 liters of wine, and 10 liters of spirits. There are no limits on what you can take out of Poland, but special restrictions apply on exports of certain cultural items, including works of art created before 1950.

WHAT YOU CAN TAKE HOME
U.S. Citizens

Returning U.S. citizens who have been away at least 48 hours are allowed to bring

---

Destination Poland: Pre-Departure Checklist

- Is your passport valid for at least six months after the end of your trip?
- Do you have the address and phone number of your country's embassy or consulate with you?
- Did you notify your credit card issuers that you would be traveling to and using your cards in Poland?
- Do you have your credit card/ATM four-digit PIN?
- If you purchased traveler's checks, have you recorded the check numbers and stored the documentation separately from the checks?
- Did you bring ID cards that might entitle you to discounts, such as AAA and AARP cards, and student IDs?
- Did you leave a copy of your itinerary with someone at home?

Saving Time If You're Flying Out of the U.S.

The U.S. Transportation Security Administration (TSA; www.tsa.gov) has approved a pilot program to help ease the time spent in line for airport security screenings. In exchange for information and a fee, persons can be pre-screened as registered travelers, granting them a front-of-the-line position when they fly. The program is run through private firms—the largest and most well-known is Steven Brill's Clear (www.flyclear.com), and it works like this: travelers complete an online application providing specific points of personal information including name, addresses for the previous five years, birth date, social security number, driver's license number, and a valid credit card (you're not charged the $99 fee until your application is approved). Print out the completed form and take it, along with proper ID, with you to an "enrollment station" (this can be found in over 20 participating airports and in a growing number of American Express offices around the country, for example). It's at this point where it gets seemingly sci-fi. At the enrollment station, a Clear representative will record your biometrics necessary for clearance; in this case, your fingerprints and your irises will be digitally recorded. Once your application has been screened against no-fly lists, outstanding warrants, and other security measures, you'll be issued a clear plastic card that holds a chip containing your information. Each time you fly through participating airports (and the numbers are steadily growing), go to the Clear Pass station located next to the standard TSA screening line. Here you'll insert your card into a slot and place your finger on a scanner to read your print—when the information matches up, you're cleared to cut to the front of the security line. You'll still have to follow all standard procedures such as removing your shoes and walking through the x-ray machine, but Clear promises to cut 30 minutes off your wait time at the airport.

On a personal note: Each time I've used my Clear Pass, my travel companions are still waiting to go through security while I'm already sitting down, reading the paper, and sipping my overpriced smoothie. Granted, registered traveler programs are not for the infrequent traveler, but for those of us who fly on a regular basis, it's a perk I'm willing to pay for.

—David A. Lytle

back, once every 30 days, $800 worth of merchandise duty free. You'll pay a flat rate of duty on the next $1,000 worth of purchases. Any dollar amount beyond that is subject to duties at whatever rates apply. Be sure to keep your receipts or purchases accessible to expedite the declaration process. Note that if you owe duty you are required to pay on your arrival in the United States—either by cash, personal check, money, or in some cases by Visa or MasterCard. Meat products are prohibited.

With some exceptions, you also cannot bring fresh fruits and vegetables into the United States. For specifics on what you can bring back and the corresponding fees, download the invaluable free pamphlet "Know Before You Go!" at www.cbp.gov.

Canadian Citizens
For a clear summary of Canadian rules, write for the booklet "I Declare," issued by the **Canada Border Services Agency** (© **800/461-9999** in Canada, or **204/983-3500**; www.cbsa-asfc.gc.ca).

U.K. Citizens

For information, contact **HM Customs & Excise** at ✆ **0845/010-9000** (from outside the U.K., ✆ **020/8929-0152**), or consult their website at www.hmce.gov.uk.

Australian Citizens

A helpful brochure available from Australian consulates or Customs offices is "Know Before You Go." For more information, call the **Australian Customs Service** (✆ **1300/363-263**), or log on to www.customs.gov.au.

New Zealand Citizens

Most questions are answered in a free pamphlet available at New Zealand consulates and Customs offices: "New Zealand Customs Guide for Travellers, Notice no. 4." For more information, contact **New Zealand Customs** (The Customhouse, 17–21 Whitmore St., Box 2218, Wellington; ✆ **04/473-6099** or **0800/428-786**; www.customs.govt.nz).

3 WHEN TO GO

Poland's climate has four distinct seasons and is characterized by hot summers and dark, cold winters. Unless you're heading to the Tatras to ski, avoid travel from January to March. Many of the attractions are closed for the season, and the cold and snow make getting around difficult. Note that Kraków and Zakopane are both popular Christmas and New Year's destinations and hotel prices rise accordingly. Summer brings good weather, but more crowds as Poles take to the roads on their summer holidays. September and October are ideal, with fewer crowds and usually reliably good weather.

CALENDAR OF EVENTS

The calendar is filled with festivals of all kinds, with the most popular celebrations connected to religious dates or Poland's folk or cultural traditions. The annual Marian pilgrimages culminate in August at the Jasna Góra shrine in Częstochowa for the Feast of the Assumption on Aug 15. Warsaw, Kraków, Wrocław, and Poznań all host jazz, contemporary, and classical

Warsaw Average Temperatures

Temps shown in Fahrenheit/Celsius.

Month	High	Low	Precipitation (mm)
Jan	32/0	21/–6	27
Feb	32/0	21/–6	32
Mar	43/6	28/–2	27
Apr	53/12	37/3	37
May	68/20	48/9	46
Jun	73/23	53/12	69
Jul	75/24	59/15	96
Aug	73/23	57/14	65
Sep	66/19	50/10	43
Oct	55/13	41/5	38
Nov	43/6	34/1	31
Dec	35/2	27/-3	44

music festivals throughout the year. The best idea is to check in with the local tourist information offices when you arrive to see what's going on during the time you're there. Kraków's Kazimierz district hosts the increasingly popular Jewish Cultural Festival every year in late June and July. Klezmer music concerts, films, and cultural discussions highlight the agenda.

Zakopane and the surrounding area is the epicenter of the country's folk fests, with the biggest draw being Zakopane's Mountain Folklore Festival in August.

For an exhaustive list of events beyond those listed here, check http://events. frommers.com, where you'll find a searchable, up-to-the-minute roster of what's happening in cities all over the world.

---

4 GETTING THERE & GETTING AROUND

GETTING TO POLAND
By Plane
Warsaw's Frederic Chopin airport (WAW) is the major air gateway into Poland, with extensive connections throughout Europe, and some nonstop flights to North America. Warsaw is well served by the major European flag carriers, including Poland's LOT, British Airways, CSA, Air France, KLM and Lufthansa, as well as a growing number of budget carriers. See Warsaw, "Getting There" (p. 62), for more details. Kraków's Jan Paweł II Airport (KRK) is the country's second most important airport and is also easy to reach from nearly any large city in Europe, and currently has one nonstop (LOT to Chicago) to North America. The advent of low-cost budget carriers in Europe in recent years has opened up several other major cities to regular and convenient air travel, including Łódź (LCJ), Poznań (POZ), Wrocław (WRO), and Gdańsk (GDN).

IMMIGRATION & CUSTOMS CLEARANCE   Immigrations and customs clearance is relatively straightforward and shouldn't take too long. Incoming passengers will be divided into two groups for passport control: "EU" and "All Others," the latter being where travelers from the U.S., Canada, Australia, and New Zealand must go. Customs is a breeze. If you're an ordinary traveler with nothing to declare, simply sail through the green-marked line

(if you need to declare something, you'll have to go through the red line). You'll rarely even be asked to open your suitcase.

GETTING INTO TOWN THE AIRPORT   Depending on where you fly into, you'll have the option of taking a taxi, shuttle bus, or public bus into town. Kraków airport is even served by an express train that takes you to the center of town. For specific airport arrival information, see Warsaw "Getting There" (p. 62) or Kraków "Getting There" (p. 119).

By Car
Poland is easily accessible by car, and Polish highways are well integrated into the larger EU highway grid. If entering from an EU country (Germany, Czech Republic, Slovakia, and Lithuania) you no longer have to stop to show a passport. Standard border controls are still in effect if traveling to or from Ukraine, Belarus, or the Russian Federation.

Car rental agencies are ubiquitous in Poland and include most of the major international agencies, such as Hertz, as well as locally owned companies. Spot rental rates can be high—much higher than in the United States. It's often cheaper to rent in advance over the Internet. Rentals will usually include the legally required third-party liability insurance, but will not include things like vehicle theft or damage. Be sure to ask what is covered. Most cars will have standard transmissions, but

Staying Comfortable on Long-Haul Flights

- Your choice of airline and airplane will definitely affect your legroom. Find more details about U.S. airlines see www.seatguru.com. For international airlines, the research firm Skytrax has posted a list of average seat pitches at www.airline quality.com.
- Emergency exit seats and bulkhead seats typically have the most legroom. Emergency exit seats are usually left unassigned until the day of a flight (to ensure that someone able-bodied fills the seats); it's worth checking in online at home (if the airline offers that option) or getting to the ticket counter early to snag one of these spots for a long flight. Many passengers find that bulkhead seating offers more legroom, but keep in mind that bulkhead seats have no storage space on the floor in front of you.
- To have two seats for yourself in a three-seat row, try for an aisle seat in a center section toward the back of coach. If you're traveling with a companion, book an aisle and a window seat. Middle seats are usually booked last, so chances are good you'll end up with three seats to yourselves. And in the event that a third passenger is assigned the middle seat, he or she will probably be more than happy to trade for a window or an aisle.
- To sleep, avoid the last row of any section or the row in front of an emergency exit, as these seats are the least likely to recline. Avoid seats near highly trafficked toilet areas. Avoid seats in the back of many jets—these can be narrower than those in the rest of coach. Or reserve a window seat so you can rest your head and avoid being bumped in the aisle.
- Get up, walk around, and stretch every 60 to 90 minutes to keep your blood flowing. This helps avoid deep vein thrombosis, or "economy-class syndrome." See the box "Avoiding 'Economy Class Syndrome,'" p. 39.
- Drink water before, during, and after your flight to combat the lack of humidity in airplane cabins. Avoid caffeine and alcohol, which will dehydrate you.

some agencies may offer cars with automatic transmission at a much higher price. The minimum age to rent a car is usually 21, though higher at some agencies.

For additional major car rental agencies in Poland, see Appendix A, p. 286.

Before setting off, buy a good Polish road atlas (the excellent *Polska Atlas Samochodowy* is available at large service stations). In addition, car satellite navigation systems, such as Garmin, have become very popular in the past couple of years and you might consider bringing yours from home. Check to see whether you have built-in European and Polish maps (many companies now offer these).

By Train

Poland is easy to get to by train. The Polish national rail network, PKP (www.pkp.pl), is well integrated into the Europe-wide rail system. Poznań and Warsaw lie on the main east–west line running from Berlin to Moscow. Kraków is accessible from Prague, Vienna, and points south, though some connections may require a change of trains at Katowice.

By Bus

International bus travel has become less popular in recent years due to the arrival of the budget air carriers, which often match bus ticket prices but get you there much quicker. Nevertheless, the Polish national bus carrier works in cooperation with the trans-European carrier Eurolines, and large Polish cities are easy to reach by bus.

GETTING AROUND POLAND

By Plane

The Polish national carrier **LOT** (© 0801/ 703-703 (in Poland); www.lot.com) offers regularly scheduled flights between major Polish cities, including Warsaw, Kraków, and Gdańsk. These can save time, but tend to be expensive.

By Car

Car travel offers maximum flexibility, but driving in Poland can be a slow and highly frustrating experience. Most Polish highways—even those connecting major cities—are of the narrow, two-lane variety and are usually clogged with trucks, buses, tractors, and even occasionally horse-drawn carts. For most stretches, plan on at least 2 hours' driving time per 100km (60 miles) distance. And drive defensively. Polish

drivers have an abysmal record when it comes to per capita accidents and fatalities.

Poland follows normal Continental rules of the road, with priority given to cars on roundabouts and vehicles coming from the right at unmarked intersections. Note that drivers are required to keep their headlights on at all times. The speed limit on (the few) four-lane freeways is 130kmph (78 mph). This drops to 90kmph (54 mph) on two-lane highways outside urban areas, and 50kmph (30 mph) or slower in built-up areas. Speed checks are common. Random sobriety checks are also frequent. The blood/alcohol limit is 0.02%—approximately one beer.

By Train

The Polish state railroad, **PKP** (www.pkp. pl), has improved its service in recent years, and train travel is usually the quickest and best way to move between big cities or to cover long distances. PKP maintains a useful online timetable (but be sure to use Polish spellings for city names): www.rozklad-pkp.pl.

(Tips) Coping with Jet Lag

Jet lag is a pitfall of traveling across time zones. If you're flying north–south and you feel sluggish when you touch down, your symptoms will be the result of dehydration and the general stress of air travel. When you travel east–west or vice-versa, your body becomes confused about what time it is, and everything from your digestive system to your brain is knocked for a loop. Traveling east is more difficult on your internal clock than traveling west because most peoples' bodies are more inclined to stay up late than to fall asleep early.

- Here are some tips for combating jet lag:
- Reset your watch to your destination time before you board the plane.
- Drink lots of water before, during, and after your flight. Avoid alcohol.
- Exercise and sleep well for a few days before your trip.
- If you have trouble sleeping on planes, fly eastward on morning flights.
- Daylight is the key to resetting your body clock. At the website for Outside In (www.bodyclock.com), you can get a customized plan of when to seek and avoid light.

Sample Driving Times between Major Cities

The times here are only approximate and depend very much on weather and traffic conditions. In general, Polish roads are busy and it's best to travel at off-peak hours.

Prague to Wrocław	3–4 hours
Prague to Kraków	7–8 hours
Kraków to Wrocław	3–4 hours
Kraków to Warsaw	3–4 hours
Kraków to Zakopane	2 hours
Łódź to Warsaw	3 hours
Warsaw to Gdańsk	5–6 hours
Poznań to Warsaw	3 hours
Lublin to Warsaw	3 hours

The best trains are the intercity (IC) trains, which link nearly all the country's biggest cities. You'll see IC trains marked in red on timetables; these are more expensive than regular trains and require an obligatory seat reservation. Next best are express trains (Ex), which also require a reservation. Avoid other types of trains for longer distances.

You can buy tickets at stations or directly from the conductor on the train, though you'll have to pay a surcharge of 8 zł ($3.20/£1.80) for the latter. Fares are relatively low by Western standards. A second-class ticket from Kraków to Warsaw, for example, costs about 85 zł ($34/£19). For overnight trips, you can usually book a couchette in a six-bunk car or a sleeper in a three-bunk car. Sleepers run about 120 zł ($48/£27). Be sure to book these in advance.

By Bus

Poland is well served by myriad public and private bus companies that go everywhere from the biggest cities to the smallest towns. Prices and journey times are often comparable to the trains, and buses can be a highly useful alternative if you can't find a convenient train connection. In fact, within specific regions, buses are often better than

trains for getting to outlying cities and towns. From Kraków, for example, buses are quicker and cheaper than trains for the popular day trip to Zakopane.

One of the best private bus companies is **Polski Express** (© **022/843-30-91;** www.polskiexpress.pl), which maintains an extensive network of routes linking Poland's major cities.

You'll usually find bus stations located beside or behind train stations. Buy tickets in advance from ticket windows at stations or directly from the driver. Watch to have exact change on hand since drivers may not have enough cash to deal with large bills. Try to arrive at the station well before your bus is scheduled to leave. Lines at bus platforms start forming early and the best seats go to those who get there first.

By Public Transportation

Most Polish cities have excellent public transportation systems consisting of buses, trams, trolley buses, and, in Warsaw, a small metro. See separate city listings for public transportation details. Though each city's system differs slightly, the overall idea is the same. Buy single-ride tickets from tobacconists and news agents for about 2.50 zł ($1/55p) per ride, validate the ticket in machines on entering the tram or bus, and keep the ticket until you get off. Once you've mastered public transportation, you'll find there's rarely any need to take a taxi.

On Foot

You'll likely spend a lot of time walking. Since cars and taxis are largely barred from the centers of large cities, and public transportation can get you only so close to where you need to go, walking is often the only alternative. Buy comfortable shoes and break them in before you arrive; you're going to use them.

By Bike

Poland is relatively flat, and depending how much time you have and what kind of shape you're in, you could conceivably cycle around the entire country. There are plenty of cycling trails that crisscross the country. Check out the organization **Bicycles for Poland** (www.rowery.org.pl) for some rules of the road and ideas on good routes. Cycling in cities is not recommended. Though some cities, like Kraków, do have specially marked bike lanes, traffic is heavy and the lanes are not that well maintained.

5 MONEY & COSTS

The main unit of currency is the złoty (zł), which is divided into 100 groszy (gr). Bills come in denominations of 10 zł, 20 zł, 50 zł, 100 zł, and 200 zł. The most useful coins are the 5 zł, 2 zł, and 1 zł. You'll also see less-useful coins of 50 gr, 10 gr, 2 gr, and, rarely, 1 gr. At press time, $1 equaled 2.50 zł, and £1 equaled 4.45 zł. For up-to-date currency conversions, check out the website www.oanda.com.

Though Poland is a member of the European Union, the euro does not circulate in Poland and cannot be used for making purchases. The government recently committed itself to adopting the euro by 2012, but that date is considered by many to be a bit optimistic. For convenience's sake, some hotels will quote their rates in euros and accept euros as payment, but in general it's best to carry local currency.

Poland is not as cheap a destination as it was a few years ago, but remains generally less expensive than Western Europe. Prices for everyday travel expenses such as food and drink, hotels, and museum admissions are substantially less than they would be in Paris or London. The exceptions are rental cars, five-star hotels, and imported clothing and other imported luxury goods, for which prices are as high as anywhere else.

What Things Cost in Poland

	zł	$	£
Decent cup of coffee	8	3.20	1.80
Taxi to the airport	60	24	14
Tram or bus ticket	2.5	1	55p
Museum admission (adult)	7	2.80	1.60
Gallon of gasoline (4 liters)	17	6.80	3.80
3-course dinner w/out alcohol	40	16	9
Hotel room (moderate double)	250	100	60

You can change money at nearly any bank or exchange office, identified in Polish as a *kantor*. You'll see these privately run exchanges everywhere, but be sure to shop around for the best rates and fees, since these differ from office to office.

You'll get a decent, no-hassle exchange rate simply by using your credit or debit card at a bank ATM. In large cities and towns, you'll see an ATM on nearly every block. Before you leave home, be sure to alert your bank or credit card company that you will be traveling abroad. The bank or card company could block your card if security personnel see unusual charges coming through (such as purchases coming from Poland if you don't usually travel here). Also make sure your card has a four-digit PIN code, since some Polish ATMs cannot take longer codes.

Credit cards are gaining in popularity and are now almost universally accepted at hotels and expensive restaurants. The most popular cards are American Express, Diners Club, MasterCard, and Visa. Travelers' checks can still be cashed at large banks, but are almost more of a hassle than they are worth since they aren't usually accepted at shops, hotels, or restaurants.

6 HEALTH

A trip to Poland poses no unusual health concerns aside from the usual bromides of not overindulging in food and, especially, drink, and looking both ways before you cross the streets (especially for trams). Still, there are a few things to keep in mind.

GENERAL AVAILABILITY OF HEALTH CARE

Polish health care is generally good and of high standard. Hospitals and doctors' offices may look shabby on the outside, but they are acceptably clean and well maintained. Travelers do not require any specific shots before a trip to Poland, and aside from vaccinations against tick-bite encephalitis if you plan on doing a lot of hiking or sleeping in the open (see below), none are advised.

Over-the-counter medications, such as aspirin, are not sold in drugstores or convenience stores, but only in pharmacies (though you don't need a prescription to buy them). It's best to bring along extra aspirin or Tylenol (or whatever you're used to) so as to minimize time looking around if you need to buy some. Bring along extra doses of whatever prescription medications you're taking. Polish pharmacies are well-stocked and common prescription drugs are widely available, but the local pharmacist may not recognize your doctor's prescription.

COMMON AILMENTS

DIETARY RED FLAGS Meat is a staple of Polish cooking, and vegetarians will have to pre-plan to avoid seeing it show up on their plate. Even seemingly "safe" options such as *pierogi* "Ruskie" style (stuffed with potato and cheese) may come covered in bacon drippings. (See "Vegetarian Travel," below.)

BUGS & OTHER WILDLIFE CONCERNS Mosquitoes are rampant in Poland, particularly in forested areas and near lakes and rivers, and can be a major nuisance. Be sure to pack strong mosquito repellant and some after-bite cream to reduce itching and swelling when you are inevitably bitten. Most pharmacies will stock these if you forget to bring them.

Tick-bite encephalitis is also a problem, and you're strongly advised to get vaccinated if you plan on spending a lot of time hiking and/or sleeping in woods and fields.

(Tips)   Avoiding "Economy Class Syndrome"

Deep vein thrombosis, or as it's known in the world of flying, "economy-class syndrome," is a blood clot that develops in a deep vein. It's a potentially deadly condition that can be caused by sitting in cramped conditions—such as an airplane cabin—for too long. During a flight (especially a long-haul flight), get up, walk around, and stretch your legs every 60 to 90 minutes to keep your blood flowing. Other preventive measures include frequent flexing of the legs while sitting, drinking lots of water, and avoiding alcohol and sleeping pills. If you have a history of deep vein thrombosis, heart disease, or another condition that puts you at high risk, some experts recommend wearing compression stockings or taking anticoagulants when you fly; always ask your physician about the best course for you. Symptoms of deep vein thrombosis include leg pain or swelling, or even shortness of breath.

In any event, check your body thoroughly for ticks at the end of a long day of hiking and be sure to seek medical attention if you're concerned. Poisonous snakes and spiders are rare and not usually a problem.

RESPIRATORY ILLNESSES   Polish air quality is improving, though during winter you may encounter short periods of poor air quality, particularly in the industrial areas around Katowice and Kraków. Residents are usually advised to stay inside on bad air days.

SUN/ELEMENTS/EXTREME WEATHER EXPOSURE   The sun is a constant danger, so be sure to pack plenty of sunscreen. Choose a higher SPF if you plan to spend a day on the beach or skiing in the mountains. Also don't forget to bring along a hat, sunglasses, a long-sleeved shirt, and good sunscreen on summer mountain hikes, where you may be exposed to the sun for hours at a time.

WHAT TO DO IF YOU GET SICK AWAY FROM HOME

Polish medical care is good, and rest assured that if something bad does happen on your vacation, you'll receive adequate care. In an emergency, immediately call

(C) **112** (general emergency) or (C) **999** (ambulance). Most operators are trained to understand at least a little bit of English. Slowly try to explain the problem and your location, and an ambulance will come as quickly as possible to take you to the nearest hospital. Be sure to take along your passport as well as some means of payment (cash or credit card).

Though Poles have universal medical coverage, foreign visitors are obliged to cover the total costs of any medical care they get in Poland. It's worth checking before you arrive whether your health insurance will cover you while you are abroad and, if not, how to supplement your insurance to get international coverage. Usually, you will have to pay any hospital fees out of pocket and then try to reclaim the costs later through your insurance. Retain all of the hospital paperwork, since you can never be sure what the insurance company might ask for.

Canadians should check with their provincial health plan offices or call **Health Canada** ((C) **866/225-0709;** www.hc-sc.gc.ca) to find out the extent of their coverage and what documentation and receipts they must take home in case they are treated abroad.

Travelers from the U.K. should carry their European Health Insurance Card (EHIC), which covers emergency treatment.

In addition to the publicly financed health system, Poland has several excellent private medical clinics. These often offer higher standards and more personalized care, though they are usually more expensive. Additionally, they may be familiar with your insurance company and be able to bill directly. In Warsaw, the **LIM Medical Center** (Al. Jerozolimskie 65/79; ✆ **022/458-70-00;** www.cmlim.pl) is centrally located in the Marriott complex and staffs a full range of English-speaking doctors and specialists. For other cities, check with your hotel or the local tourist information office.

We list additional emergency numbers in Appendix A, p. 281.

7 SAFETY

STAYING SAFE

Poland is a relatively safe country and travelers should not have any major safety or security concerns. The biggest potential threat is likely to be crime. Petty theft, pick-pocketing, and car break-ins remain a problem. Watch your wallets and purses in crowded areas, particularly those frequented by tourists. Always park your car in a well-lit area and use hotel or guarded parking lots where available. Never leave valuables in the car or packages in plain view, as this may invite a break in. Bike theft is rife. Never leave a bike unattended for more than a few minutes (even if it is securely locked) and always store it inside overnight. Hotels will often have a special area for storing bikes; otherwise simply take it with you to your room.

Though robberies and violent crime are rare, it's best to avoid seedy areas at night (such as Warsaw's Praga neighborhood or parts of Łódź, or around train stations in any city). This is particularly strong advice for single women travelers, though in most other instances women shouldn't encounter difficulties in Poland.

Polish police and law-enforcement agencies are invariably friendly and helpful to tourists, but they take a dim view toward public drunkenness. If you're out drinking, it's best to keep it down and keep your cool, otherwise you might find yourself spending a night in the drunk tank.

Drugs of any kind, including marijuana, are strictly illegal and anti-drug laws are rigorously enforced. If you're caught with illegal drugs, you're best advised to contact your local embassy or consulate immediately, though you're unlikely to find much sympathy there or among law-enforcement agencies.

Prostitution is legal, though it's unregulated and potentially high-risk. While you probably won't see prostitutes standing on street corners in big cities, you may occasionally see them along highways, offering their services to passing truckers and other motorists. The "bars" you see along highways are often little more than brothels for truckers. You'll also find plenty of nightclubs, strip joints, escort agencies, and massage parlors around. Many of these are more or less legitimate businesses, but some are fronts for prostitution or organized crime. If you choose to patronize one of these places, minimize your risk by taking only small sums of money with you and leaving your credit cards back at the hotel. Maintain a high state of awareness and be prepared to leave at the slightest sign that something's not right.

While Poland is ethnically and racially homogenous, travelers from other countries and of different races are not likely to encounter overt discrimination. Homosexuality is publicly frowned on, but openly gay travelers are not likely to experience specific problems. Gay couples should probably avoid open displays of affection so as not to offend local sensibilities, though it's unlikely anything bad would happen.

Remember to be respectful around churches, particularly during masses. Make sure to wear appropriate dress. The rules aren't too strict on this, but in practice, women should cover their shoulders and avoid too-short skirts; both sexes should wear shoes. Also be sure to heed any prohibitions against making noise or taking photos, videos, or using flash photography.

Finally, be sure to donate something, however small, at the entrance if the church is not taking an admission fee. Many churches wouldn't be able to survive without visitor donations.

8 SPECIALIZED TRAVEL RESOURCES

TRAVELERS WITH DISABILITIES

Sadly, Poland is decades behind the United States and other countries in making its buildings and sidewalks more easily accessible to people in wheelchairs or with disabilities. The only exceptions are likely to be newly built hotels, which will usually have at least one room set aside for wheelchair access. The leading Polish group promoting the elimination of architectural barriers in Poland is **Integracja** (© 022/635-13-30; www.integracja.org).

For more on organizations that offer resources to disabled travelers, go to www.frommers.com/planning.

GAY & LESBIAN TRAVELERS

Poland is not particularly gay-friendly, and the country's center-right government has recently spoken out against granting homosexuals legal rights or even discussing homosexuality in the public schools. That said, traveling gays and lesbians are not likely to encounter overt discrimination or have trouble booking rooms. There are active gay populations in both Warsaw and Kraków, and several gay-friendly bars and clubs. **GayGuide.net** (http://warsaw.gayguide.net) publishes a useful list of gay clubs in the capital.

For more gay and lesbian travel resources visit www.frommers.com/planning.

SENIOR TRAVEL

Senior citizens can qualify for a 50% discount on Polish rail tickets if they buy a PKP Senior Citizen ID *(Legitymacja Seniora)*. The card costs 75 zł ($30/£17) and is available to anyone over 60 (bring along a passport-sized photo). Museums will sometimes grant senior discounts for over 65. Try showing your passport or an AARP card.

For more information and resources on travel for seniors, see www.frommers.com/planning.

FAMILY TRAVEL

Poland is not particularly well suited to traveling with small children. Distances between cities are relatively far and kid-friendly sights are few on the ground. To make things worse, museum exhibits tend to be static rather than interactive. So, it pays to read up a bit in order to entertain the kids with tidbits of historic tales. Among Polish cities, Toruń (see p. 220) is compact and easy to manage, with tales like the Teutonic knights and Copernicus and rewards like a trip to the Gingerbread Museum to keep children motivated. Malbork Castle (see p. 253) will certainly set a benchmark for kids in sizing up any castle they are likely to see in the future. For real interactive family fun, try kayaking in Mazury and Suwałki (see p. 152), or rafting down the Dunajec river (see p. 152).

To locate accommodations, restaurants, and attractions that are particularly kid-friendly, refer to the "Kids" icon throughout this guide. For a list of more family-friendly travel resources, visit www.frommers.com/planning.

WOMEN TRAVELERS

Solo women travelers will face no extraordinary safety or security issues in Poland. Women should avoid walking alone in unsavory areas at night, but at most other times there are no special dangers.

For general travel resources for women, go to www.frommers.com/planning.

STUDENT TRAVEL

Polish organizations frequently offer considerable discounts for students and young people. Check out the International Student Travel Confederation (ISTC) (www.istc.org) website for comprehensive travel services information and details on how to get an International Student Identity Card (ISIC), which qualifies students for substantial savings on rail passes, plane tickets, entrance fees, and more. It also provides students with basic health and life insurance and a 24-hour helpline. The card is valid for a maximum of 18 months. You can apply for the card online or in person at **STA Travel** (© **800/781-4040** in North America; © **132-782** in Australia; © **0871/2-300-040** in the U.K.; www.statravel.com), the biggest student travel agency in the world; check out the website to locate STA Travel offices worldwide.

If you're no longer a student but are still under 26, you can get an International Youth Travel Card (IYTC) from the same people, that entitles you to some discounts. **Travel CUTS** (© **800/592-2887**; www.travelcuts.com) offers similar services for both Canadians and U.S. residents. Irish students may prefer to turn to **USIT** (© **01/602-1904**; www.usit.ie), an Irish-based specialist in student, youth, and independent travel.

SINGLE TRAVELERS

Single travelers will encounter no specific problems in Poland. Most hotels set aside at least a few rooms for single occupancy, though prices are often nearly as high as for double occupancy. Single diners at restaurants may have to work a little harder to get a waiter's attention, but face no unique difficulties.

For more information on traveling single, go to www.frommers.com/planning.

VEGETARIAN TRAVEL

Polish food, built as it is around pork and game, is not particularly vegetarian-friendly, though there are plenty of meat-less items on menus that you can build a meal around. *Pierogi* "Ruskie," for example, are stuffed with potato and cheese, but be sure to have them hold the bacon bits they sometimes throw on top. Other popular meatless *pierogi* fillings include cabbage and wild mushroom.

Green Way (www.greenway.pl) is an inexpensive and excellent chain of vegetarian restaurants with branches around the country, including in Warsaw, Kraków, Katowice, Gdańsk, Poznań, and Łódź.

For more vegetarian-friendly travel resources, go to www.frommers.com/planning.

Sustainable tourism is conscientious travel. It means being careful with the environments you explore, and respecting the communities you visit. Two overlapping components of sustainable travel are ecotourism and ethical tourism. The International Ecotourism Society (TIES) defines ecotourism as responsible travel to natural areas that conserves the environment and improves the well-being of local people. TIES suggests that ecotourists follow these principles:

- Minimize environmental impact.
- Build environmental and cultural awareness and respect.
- Provide positive experiences for both visitors and hosts.
- Provide direct financial benefits for conservation and for local people.
- Raise sensitivity to host countries' political, environmental, and social climates.
- Support international human rights and labor agreements.

You can find some eco-friendly travel tips and statistics, as well as touring companies and associations—listed by destination under "Travel Choice"—at the TIES website, www.ecotourism.org. Also check out Ecotravel.com, which lets you search for sustainable touring companies in several categories (water-based, land-based, spiritually oriented, and so on).

While much of the focus of eco-tourism is about reducing impacts on the natural environment, ethical tourism concentrates on ways to preserve and enhance local economies and communities regardless of location. You can embrace ethical tourism by staying at a locally owned hotel or shopping at a store that employs local workers and sells locally produced goods. Responsible Travel (www.responsible travel.com) is a great source of sustainable

travel ideas; the site is run by a spokesperson for ethical tourism in the travel industry. Sustainable Travel International (www. sustainabletravelinternational.org) promotes ethical tourism practices, and manages an extensive directory of sustainable properties and tour operators around the world.

In the U.K., Tourism Concern (www. tourismconcern.org.uk) works to reduce social and environmental problems connected to tourism. The Association of Independent Tour Operators (AITO) (www. aito.co.uk) is a group of specialist operators leading the field in making holidays sustainable.

Volunteer travel has become increasingly popular among those who want to venture beyond the standard group-tour experience to learn languages, interact with locals, and make a positive difference while on vacation. Volunteer travel usually doesn't require special skills—just a willingness to work hard—and programs vary in length from a few days to a number of weeks. Some programs provide free housing and food, but many require volunteers to pay for travel expenses, which can add up quickly. For general info on volunteer travel, visit www.volunteerabroad.org and www.idealist.org.

Before you commit to a volunteer program, it's important to make sure any money you're giving is truly going back to the local community, and that the work you'll be doing will be a good fit for you. Volunteer International (www.volunteer international.org) has a helpful list of questions to ask to determine the intentions and the nature of a volunteer program.

ANIMAL-RIGHTS ISSUES

Animal-rights issues are making slow progress in Poland, a largely agrarian

Tips **It's Easy Being Green**

Here are a few simple ways you can help conserve fuel and energy when you travel:

- Each time you take a flight or drive a car, greenhouse gases release into the atmosphere. You can help neutralize this danger to the planet through "carbon offsetting"—paying someone to invest your money in programs that reduce your greenhouse gas emissions by the same amount you've added. Before buying carbon offset credits, just make sure that you're using a reputable company, one with a proven program that invests in renewable energy. Reliable carbon offset companies include Carbonfund (www.carbonfund.org), TerraPass (www.terrapass.org), and Carbon Neutral (www.carbonneutral.org).

- Whenever possible, choose nonstop flights; they generally require less fuel than indirect flights that stop and take off again. Try to fly during the day—some scientists estimate that nighttime flights are twice as harmful to the environment. And pack light—each 15 pounds of luggage on a 5,000-mile flight adds up to 50 pounds of carbon dioxide emitted.

- Where you stay during your travels can have a major environmental impact. To determine the green credentials of a property, ask about trash disposal and recycling, water conservation, and energy use; also question if sustainable materials were used in the construction of the property. The website www.greenhotels.com recommends green-rated member hotels around the world that fulfill the company's stringent environmental requirements. Also consult www.environmentally friendlyhotels.com for more green accommodation ratings.

- At hotels, request that your sheets and towels not be changed daily. (Many hotels already have programs like this in place.) Turn off the lights and air-conditioner (or heater) when you leave your room.

- Use public transport where possible—trains, buses and even taxis are more energy-efficient forms of transport than driving. Even better is to walk or cycle; you'll produce zero emissions and stay fit and healthy on your travels.

- If renting a car is necessary, ask the rental agent for a hybrid, or rent the most fuel-efficient car available. You'll use less gas and save money at the tank.

- Eat at locally owned and operated restaurants that use produce grown in the area. This contributes to the local economy and cuts down on greenhouse gas emissions by supporting restaurants where the food is not flown or trucked in across long distances. Visit SustainLane (www.sustainlane.com) to find sustainable eating and drinking choices around the U.S.; also check out www.eatwellguide.org for tips on eating sustainably in the U.S. and Canada.

country that still depends on animals, in some cases, for farm labor. Some may take issue with the horse-drawn carriages that line up along Kraków's main square, the Rynek Główny, where the horses stand in the hot sun and occasionally suffer the whips of their master.

For information on animal-friendly issues throughout the world, visit Tread Lightly (www.treadlightly.org). For information about the ethics of swimming with dolphins, visit the Whale and Dolphin Conservation Society (www.wdcs.org).

10 PACKAGES FOR THE INDEPENDENT TRAVELER

Several international travel agencies offer travel packages that focus exclusively on Poland or offer Polish destinations as part of a "Central European" or "Eastern European" tour. A few of the best are described below:

U.S.-based **Kensington Tours** (300 Delaware Ave., Suite 1704, Wilmington, DE 19801; © **888/903-2001;** Fax 866/613-7599; www.kensingtontours.com) offers a signature "Eight Days in Poland" tour that starts in Gdańsk and makes its way across the country to Warsaw and Kraków.

U.S. operator **Tauck's** (© **800/788-7885;** www.tauck.com) two-week Eastern European and Poland tour includes Kraków, Auschwitz, and a private Chopin recital in Warsaw on a regional getaway that includes stops in Budapest, Vienna, and Prague. Tauck also offers a 5-day, 4-night extension package to lengthen your stay in Poland.

The Polish operator **Almatur-Opole** (Ozimska 26/2, 45-058 Opole; © **077/423-28-48;** Fax 077/423-28-40; www.excitingpoland.com) offers several highly rated Polish packages, including "Poland in One Week," the "Pearls of Northern Poland," and "Polish-Jewish Heritage."

For more information on package tours and for tips on booking your trip, see www.frommers.com/planning.

11 STAYING CONNECTED

TELEPHONES

Poland's country code is 48. To dial Poland from abroad, dial the international access code (011 in the U.S.) plus 48 and then the local Poland area code (minus the zero). The area code for Warsaw, for example, is 022, so a call from the U.S. to Warsaw would begin 011-48-22 plus the local number. To call long distance within Poland, dial the city's area code (retaining the zero) plus the number. To dial a number in Warsaw from another city in Poland, for example, you would dial 022 plus the local number. To dial abroad from within Poland, dial 00 and then the country code and area code to where you are calling. The country code for the U.S. and Canada is 1, meaning that a call to the U.S. from Poland would begin 00-1, plus the area code and local number.

CELL PHONES

Polish cell phones operate on a GSM band of 900/1800MHz. This is the same standard in use throughout Europe, but different from the one used in the United States. U.S. mobiles will work here provided they are tri-band phones (not all phones are tri-band) and that you've contacted your service provider to allow for international roaming. Keep calls to a minimum, however, since roaming charges can be steep.

U.K. mobiles should work without any problem provided that you've contacted your service provider to activate international roaming (the same precautions about steep prices apply to U.K. mobiles.)

One way of avoiding international roaming charges is to purchase a pay-as-you-go SIM card for your cell phone and

Online Traveler's Toolbox

Veteran travelers usually carry some essential items to make their trips easier. Following is a selection of handy online tools to bookmark and use.

- Address finder (Warsaw, Kraków, and other large cities) (www.euroave.com)
- Airplane food (www.airlinemeals.net)
- Airplane seating (www.seatguru.com; www.airlinequality.com)
- English–Polish Language Converter (www.poltran.com)
- Kraków Calendar of Events (www.krakow-info.com)
- Maps (www.mapquest.com)
- Metric converter (www.convert-me.com)
- Polish train timetable (http://rozklad-pkp.pl)
- Polski Express national bus service (www.polskiexpress.pl)
- Time and date (www.timeanddate.com)
- Travel warnings (http://travel.state.gov; www.fco.gov.uk/travel; www.voyage.gc.ca; www.smartraveller.gov.au)
- Universal currency converter (www.oanda.com)
- Warsaw calendar of events (www.multifest.pl)
- Weather (www.intellicast.com; www.weather.com)

a pre-paid calling card. This provides you with a local number and allows you to make calls and send text messages at local rates. All the major local telephone operators offer this service.

VOICE OVER INTERNET PROTOCOL (VOIP)

If you have Web access while traveling, consider a broadband-based telephone service (in technical terms, Voice over Internet protocol, or VoIP) such as **Skype** (www.skype.com) or **Vonage** (www.vonage.com), which allow you to make free international calls from your laptop or in a cybercafe. Neither service requires the people you're calling to also have that service (though there are fees if they do not). Check the websites for details.

INTERNET & E-MAIL
With Your Own Computer

Nearly every hotel from a two-star property on up will offer some kind of free in-room Internet access. Most often these days this will be wireless, though occasionally it will

be a LAN (dataport) connection. If the hotel offers LAN connections, they usually also loan out Ethernet cables for guests to use during their stay. Check with the reception desk. If having a good in-room Internet connection is important to you, make this clear when you register for your room. Wi-Fi signal strength drops off considerably the farther your room is from the router. Though the hotel may generally offer Wi-Fi, some rooms may not be close enough to make this practical.

Also be sure to ask before you check in whether the Internet is working that day. The hotel may advertise in-room Internet access knowing full well the Internet is on the blink and is not likely to be fixed anytime soon.

Even if your hotel doesn't offer in-room Internet, there are usually lots of options for logging on with your own laptop. A surprising number of cafes, restaurants, and bars now offer free Wi-Fi to customers with a purchase. You may have to finagle a bit with the password (particularly if it uses Polish letters), but you'll normally be able to get it to work. Look out particularly for Costa Coffee outlets, which—in addition to having excellent coffee—also usually offer reliably good, free Wi-Fi connections.

To locate Wi-Fi hotspots in Poland (and around the world), go to www.jiwire.com; its Hotspot Finder holds the world's largest directory of public wireless hotspots.

Without Your Own Computer

Many hotels will have a public computer or a business center for guests to use. If your hotel doesn't and you just want to check e-mail, it's sometimes worth asking at the reception desk whether you can use the hotel's computer for a few minutes.

The answer is likely to be yes if it's a small place and the reception desk is not busy at the time.

Your hotel receptionist will certainly know the location of the nearest Internet cafe. The number of Internet cafes has stagnated in recent years as more and more people have gotten their own home computers, but most towns and cities will have at least a couple of cyber hangouts, usually stuffed to the gills with teens playing video games. Internet cafe rates are reasonable at around 6 zł ($2.40/£1.35) per hour.

For help locating cybercafes and other establishments where you can go for Internet access, see "Internet Access" in Appendix A (p. 282).

12 TIPS ON ACCOMMODATIONS

Decent hotels in Poland tend to be expensive. The past decade has seen a boom in hotel construction, but most of that has come in the high and high-middle ends of the market in order to cater to the growing amount of business travel to Poland. That means rates will probably be higher than you expect. On the plus side, however, this

Popular Polish Hotel Chains

Many international hotel chains, including Holiday Inn, InterContinental, Sheraton, Best Western, Marriott, and Radisson, own or operate at least one property in Poland. The following companies maintain chains in Poland with properties around the country.

- **Campanile** (✆ **331/64-62-59-70** (France); www.campanile.com.pl): French-owned chain that runs hotels under the Kyriad Prestige, Campanile, and Premiere Classe brands. The mid-market Campanile hotels are particularly good value, invariably cheerful, clean, and well-run.
- **Orbis** (✆ **0801/606-606** (in Poland); www.orbis.pl): The former state-owned Polish hotel operator Orbis has hooked up with a French group and now operates hotels under the Novotel, Mercure, IBIS, and Etap brands. Novotels and Mercures tend to be upmarket (and occasionally overpriced) affairs, while IBIS hotels are short on personality but big on value.
- **Qubus** (✆ **071/782-87-65** (in Poland); www.qubus.pl): A relatively young Polish chain that aims for the upscale business traveler and has properties in major cities around the country. Qubus hotels invariably have a high standard and are an excellent choice.

dependence on business travelers means that hotels often cut rates on the weekends to fill beds; it never hurts to ask at reception if the rate they are quoting is the best one available. Rates are often also lower if you pre-book over a hotel's website.

"Standard double rooms" are usually understood to mean twin beds; rooms with queen-size beds are often classified as "deluxe" and cost more. Most places now have nonsmoking accommodations, and a growing number of hotels are now mostly or entirely smoke-free.

If you're traveling by car, note that parking is often not included in the price. Hotels will frequently offer guarded parking for a fee, usually for around 30 zł ($13/£7.10). This is probably a good idea, especially in urban areas where there's a small but definite chance of a break-in.

In addition to hotels and pensions (*pensjonaty*), there's no shortage of people offering private accommodations in their homes or flats. This is more common in heavily touristed areas away from larger cities—in places like Zakopane, for example. Look for the signs saying *wolny pokój* (free room) or *noclegi* (lodging) hanging from a house. Prices are lower than hotels, but standards vary considerably. Always take a look at the room first before accepting.

For tips on surfing for hotel deals online, visit www.frommers.com/planning.

Suggested Poland Itineraries

Poland is a deceptively large country, so it's best to scale down your geographic ambitions from the outset. One week in Poland is ideal if your goal is to get in two big cities—say, Warsaw and Kraków—and a little bit in between. For anything more comprehensive, give yourself 10 days or, ideally, two weeks.

The problem isn't so much Poland's size, but the transportation infrastructure. Train travel in Poland continues to improve, and an express train can now get you from Warsaw to Kraków in around three hours, but most trains still move aggravatingly slowly, and you can literally spend a whole day on the train going from, say, Kraków to Gdańsk or from Lublin to Wrocław. Bus travel is similar; buses can only travel as fast as the roads allow. That said, buses are often a better bet than trains for travel within regions and along selected city-to-city routes.

And then there are the roads. Poland's antiquated network of two-lane highways is the butt of national jokes and a real bottleneck to the country's economic growth. The country has launched a massive road-building effort funded by the European Union, but for the foreseeable future (certainly the lifetime of this book), be prepared to put up with huge traffic jams, crowded and impassable roads, and frustrating detours that always seem to pop up just as you approach your destination. As a rule of thumb, figure on 2 hours of car travel for every 100km (60 miles). One notable exception is the excellent A4 superhighway (*autobahn* might be a more apt term, given the speeds people drive), linking Kraków with the German border in the west and passing through Wrocław. The EU's involvement has a darkly comic dimension. Invariably when you see a sign saying something like "This road brought to you by the European Union," expect to find traffic backed up for miles in both directions ("This traffic jam brought to you by the EU," might be more appropriate). Even with the hassles and inconveniences, car travel might still be the best way to explore smaller towns and off-the-beaten-track destinations otherwise accessible only by sporadic bus service.

Depending on the length of your stay, there are several ways you could focus your itinerary to get the most out of your trip. One logical choice is to divide the country into north and south, including Warsaw in both, but making Gdańsk (north) or Kraków (south) the focal point of your travel. Another way would be to focus on a particular interest—World War II, or Jewish heritage—or on an activity such as hiking, biking, boating, or, yes, even sunbathing on the beach.

1 POLAND IN ONE WEEK

There's no way to cover the entire country in just one week, so this itinerary is divided into two itineraries for you to choose between depending on how you want to spend your time: Warsaw plus Kraków and southern Poland; or Warsaw plus Gdańsk and northern Poland.

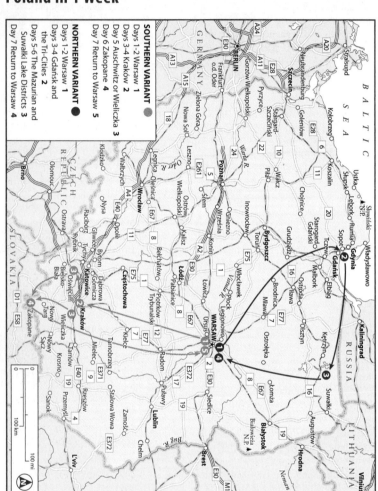

SOUTHERN VARIANT ●
Days 1-2 Warsaw **1**
Days 3-4 Kraków **2**
Day 5 Auschwitz or Wieliczka **3**
Day 6 Zakopane **4**
Day 7 Return to Warsaw **5**

NORTHERN VARIANT ●
Days 1-2 Warsaw **1**
Days 3-4 Gdańsk and the Tri-Cities **2**
Days 5-6 The Mazurian and Suwałki Lake Districts **3**
Day 7 Return to Warsaw **4**

SOUTHERN POLAND ITINERARY: WARSAW & SOUTH

Days ❶–❷: Warsaw

Get settled in, and if you've got the energy try to arrange for an organized city tour by bus in the afternoon. Warsaw is sprawling, and even if you're not an "organized tour" type of person, this is one place where a bus tour makes sense. Spend the second day with a more leisurely stroll of the Old Town, admiring the old look of the place, even though it's barely 25 years old. Warsaw's Old Town was totally destroyed in World War II and rebuilt brick by brick.

Don't pass up the chance to see the Museum of the Warsaw Uprising ★★★, which will help you to understand that spirit of the city. If it's a nice day, try to get out to Łazienki Park ★★. On Sunday, you might even catch the weekly open-air Chopin concert.

Days ❸–❹: Kraków

Drive or take the train to Kraków—either way it will take about 3 to 4 hours. Give yourself plenty of time to enjoy Poland's most popular travel destination. Dedicate at least one full day to the Old Town and the Wawel Castle area, and don't miss either the Czartoryski Museum ★★ with an original Leonardo da Vinci to its credit or the castle Cathedral ★★★, whose crypt is filled with tombs of Polish kings. Leave another full day for Kazimierz and the sights of the former Jewish quarter.

Day ❺: Kraków Daytrip: Auschwitz or Wieliczka

The former Nazi extermination camp at Auschwitz-Birkenau ★★★ lies about 90 minutes west of Kraków by car; alternatively, you can go by train or bus or book one of several Auschwitz day tours through the tourist information office. It's a must, particularly if you've never had the chance to visit a Holocaust site in the past. Plan to sleep back in Kraków; after a day of touring the camps, you'll want to come back to a place full of life. If you're traveling with small children and looking for a more cheerful day trip, try the Wieliczka Salt Mines ★★★, easily reachable from Kraków by bus or train.

Day ❻: Zakopane

If you've got time and energy for more travel, hit the bus and head down to the Tatra resort of Zakopane. If you get an early enough start, you'll have enough time for a bit of a mountain walk; otherwise, you'll have to content yourself with a stroll around town and a maybe a cable-car ride to the top of one of the peaks. For an offbeat, old-style villa that really captures old Zakopane, book a room at the Pensjonat Szarotka ★★.

Day ❼: Return to Warsaw

If you're leaving from Zakopane, take the bus back to Kraków and the train back to Warsaw. Leave at least two hours for the journey to Kraków and three more for the trip back to Warsaw.

NORTHERN POLAND ITINERARY: WARSAW & NORTH

Days ❶–❷: Warsaw

See the "Poland in One Week" tour above.

Days ❸–❹: Gdańsk & the Tri-Cities

This Baltic Sea port is one of the real highlights of any trip to Poland: a beautifully restored city, rich with history and natural beauty. Don't miss stunning ul. Długa, Gdańsk's main shopping thoroughfare; also take in the Amber Museum ★ and a walk along the pier. For good old-fashioned cooking with an updated flair, try the *pierogi* at Pierogarnia U Dzika ★★. If the weather is warm, be sure to try to spend some time on the beach and greet the sunset from Sopot's long and lively pier; after sunset, Sopot comes alive with drinking and dancing spots.

Days ❺–❻: The Mazurian & Suwałki Lake Districts

Head south and east to visit a nature lover's paradise: The Mazurian Lake district. This area is famous in Poland for its ample sailing and kayaking opportunities. While you're in the area, stop in at the Wolf's Lair ★★, the site of the 1944 assassination attempt on Hitler's life made by his own officers (an episode recently explored in the movie *Valkyrie*.) In the Suwałki Landscape

Park, try getting a room at the Jaczno Lodge ★★★, a lovely cluster of stone and timber houses hemmed in by woods and the pristine water of Lake Jaczno.

Day ❼: Return to Warsaw

Catch the train or bus back to the capital. Depending on where you start off from, the trip back could take the better part of a day. If you're driving, allow time to hit plenty of traffic on your way into Warsaw.

2 POLAND IN TWO WEEKS

In two weeks you can cover a lot of ground, even in Poland. While you'll still have to pick and choose, you'll at least have a chance to relax at the major sites and hit some out-of-the-way places. One way to approach Poland in two weeks would be to simply combine the two one-week tours, using one of your weeks for the south of the country and the second week for the north. The tour below is a modified version of this, heading to Gdańsk first after Warsaw and then moving around Poland in a clockwise circle. It could also be done quite easily by going to Kraków first after Warsaw and moving, again, clockwise.

Days ❶–❷: Warsaw
See "Poland in One Week" tour above.

Days ❸–❹: Gdańsk & the Tri-Cities
The first stop after Warsaw is the Baltic port city. Stroll the Old Town, hit the beaches, and try to get out for a day on the Hel peninsula ★★. You may opt to spend an extra day in Gdańsk (especially in hot weather) and skip the day at Malbork (see below). Alternatively, you can keep heading west to Słowiński National Park ★ and its amazing and enormous sand dunes.

Day ❺: Malbork
If you've got the time, don't pass up the chance to see the enormous Teutonic knights' castle at Malbork ★★★. You can use Gdańsk as your base or treat Malbork as a stopover en route to the Mazurian Lakes. The knights once schemed to control the rich Baltic amber trade, but ultimately their ambition did them in. This massive castle is silent testimony to the size

of those ambitions. If you're looking to give your feet a rest, hop on a one-of-a-kind in Europe boat-and-rail ride on the Elbląg-Ostróda Canal.

Days ❻–❼: The Mazurian & Suwałki Lake Districts
See "Poland in One Week" tour above. If the weather is good, you may want to add an extra day canoeing and skip the trip to the Białowieża National Forest or Lublin (see below).

Day ❽: Białowieża National Forest ★★★
Now for something completely unexpected: Who would have thought that Poland would have some of Europe's last pieces of primeval forest, untouched by man over the centuries. Hire a guide and take a long walk through the woods, admiring the old growth and the interaction of flora and fauna (but don't forget your mosquito repellent—some interactions with nature are better than others). At Białowieża, the Hotel Carska ★★ was

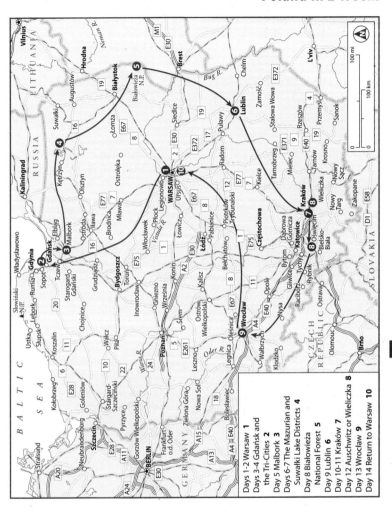

Days 1–2 Warsaw **1**

Days 3–4 Gdańsk and
the Tri-Cities **2**

Day 5 Malbork **3**

Days 6–7 The Mazurian and
Suwałki Lake Districts **4**

Day 8 Białowieża
National Forest **5**

Day 9 Lublin **6**

Days 10–11 Kraków **7**

Day 12 Auschwitz or Wieliczka **8**

Day 13 Wrocław **9**

Day 14 Return to Warsaw **10**

literally built for a tsar, in this case, Russia's Tsar Nicholas II. A real splurge and a must for fans of unusual hotel design.

Day **9**: Lublin

Continue south to the city of Lublin, with its great hotels and restaurants and big-city diversions that you may have been missing when you were at the lakes and Białowieża. Be sure to walk through the Old Town, chock full of pubs and restaurants and home to lively open-air concerts in summer. Lublin has a clutch of great hotels and some of the best restaurants in this part of Poland. If you aren't going to Auschwitz but would like to visit a Holocaust site, the infamous Majdanek ★★★ camp is just a short walk or city bus ride from the center of town.

Days ⑩–⑪: Kraków
See "Poland in One Week" tour above.

Day ⑫: Kraków Daytrip: Auschwitz or Wieliczka
See "Poland in One Week" tour above.

Day ⑨: Wrocław
Wrocław is Poland's hidden gem. Find a place to stay—if you're up for a bit of a splurge try the classy Qubus ★★—and then head for the Rynek and a traditional Polish dinner at the fabled pub Piwnica Świdnicka ★★★. Stroll along the river and unwind from your long trip around the country. If you're up for a night of carousing on the town, try the strip of bars along Kiełbaśnicza.

Day ⑭: Return to Warsaw
See "Poland in One Week" tour above.

3 POLAND FOR FAMILIES

Poland isn't the easiest of destinations for families with children. Walking with younger children can prove strenuous, and even older kids may not have an appreciation of the historic sites. It doesn't help that most of the museums are of the old-school variety, more static than interactive. However, there are a number of unique spots that are captivating for kids of all ages.

Day ❶: Kraków
Krakow is definitely the most kid-friendly of Poland's big cities. The Old Town Square is a natural draw, not to mention the city's zoo, with its big collection of exotic hippos, and the country's largest water park.

Day ❷: Toruń
The central Polish city of Toruń is compact and easy to manage, and is laced with tales about the Teutonic knights and Copernicus and rewards such as gingerbread to keep the kids motivated. Be sure to visit the Gingerbread Museum, where you get to not only look at the confections but make them and eat them, too.

Day ❸: Malbork Castle ★★★
The massive former Teutonic knights' castle at Malbork will certainly set the

benchmark for children when sizing up other castles in the future. Tales of the knights will likely keep them enthralled longer than other sites, as well.

Day ❹: The Mazurian & Suwałki Lake Districts
If the kids are suffering from overexposure to "Old Towns," try a day of kayaking in Mazury and Suwałki. The Krutynia route in Mazury, and the lower section of the Czarna Hańcza route, are an easy and enjoyable introduction to rafting.

Day ❺: Rafting Down the Dunajec
In the south of the country, take the kids for a great day of rafting down the Dunajec. See the tour "Five-Day Outdoor Vacation" below.

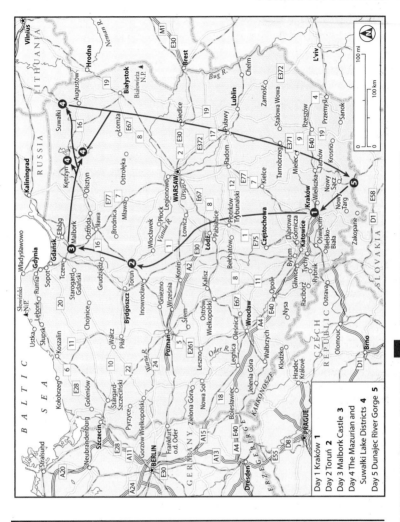

Day 1 Kraków **1**
Day 2 Toruń **2**
Day 3 Malbork Castle **3**
Day 4 The Mazurian and
   Suwałki Lake Districts **4**
Day 5 Dunajec River Gorge **5**

4 FIVE-DAY FOCUS ON JEWISH HERITAGE

Five days is just enough time to begin to scratch the surface of Poland's immense and important Jewish history. This tour assumes you're beginning in Warsaw and includes a stop in the industrial city of Łódź, which was made wealthy by Jewish industrialists in the 19th and 20th centuries, as well as stops in Kraków's former Jewish quarter, Kazimierz, and at the Nazi extermination camps of Auschwitz and Birkenau.

Day 1 Warsaw **1**
Day 2 Łódź **2**
Day 3 Kraków **3**
Day 4 Auschwitz **4**
Day 5 Return to Warsaw **5**

Day ❶: Warsaw

Arrive in Warsaw and find your feet. Spend the afternoon walking Warsaw's former Jewish ghetto, taking in sites such as the Monument to the Ghetto Heroes, which recalls the heroic Jewish uprising in 1943, and a concrete-bunker-type memorial at the "Umschlagplatz." Warsaw was home to the largest wartime ghetto in Poland and it deserves better than this, but sadly not much remains to be seen. A major Jewish museum is in the works, but at press time was not yet open.

Day ❷: Łódź

Get an early start and drive or take the train to the former industrial powerhouse of Łódź. Before World War II, Łódź's Jewish population numbered more than 200,000—the largest concentration of

Jews in Europe after Warsaw. Today, just a handful remain. The Jewish sites here, however, are some of the best in the country. A tour of the former wartime ghetto is an absolute must, as is a stop at the former Jewish cemetery and the Radegast train station, where trains to the concentration camps left from. Be sure, too, to stop by the History of Łódź Museum, housed in the former residence of Jewish industrialist par excellence, Izrael Kalmanowicz Poznański. Have dinner at Anatewka ★★, an informal Jewish restaurant.

Days ❸–❹: Kraków & Auschwitz

From Łódź, take the bus to Kraków, once one of the most important centers of Jewish life and scholarship in Europe. Save plenty of time for an enthralling walking tour of Kazimierz and the adjoining wartime ghetto of Podgórze across the river. Try to get a room in Kazimierz and experience its new lease on life in the evening as one of Poland's liveliest clubbing districts. For dinner book a table at Dawno Temu Na Kazimierzu ★★★, a great mix of excellent food and just enough kitsch to keep it interesting. On your second day, plan an all-day trip to visit the Auschwitz-Birkenau concentration camps ★★★. Spend the night back in Kraków.

Day ❺: Return to Warsaw

The trip to Warsaw will take around 3 hours by train, leaving you a little time left in the morning to explore Kraków's Old Town and Wawel Castle ★★★ if you've not already seen it.

5 FIVE-DAY SCENIC DRIVE THROUGH POLAND

There are plenty of scenic road trips through Poland. This particular trip focuses on the Giant Mountains and the province of Lower Silesia, south of Wrocław. But the lakes north of Warsaw and the coastal areas to the west of Gdańsk are all spectacular; even if they're just seen from the car window.

Day ❶: Wrocław

The capital of Lower Silesia makes a good base for starting this exploration of Poland's scenic southwest. Once you've had a chance to walk around Wrocław's Old Town square, the Rynek, take the train, bus, or your own wheels to the nearby city of Wałbrzych, home to one of Poland's most spectacular castles, Książ Castle ★★. Wrocław is also a great base for exploring Poland's two wooden "Peace" churches, one at Świdnica ★★ and the other at Jawor ★★. Plan on spending the night at one of Książ Castle's very nice hotels or at the Bolków Hotel ★ near Jawor, with its excellent restaurant ★★★.

Day ❷: Jelenia Góra

The regional capital of Jelenia Góra is a natural stopping off point for exploring Karkonosze National Park and Poland's Giant Mountains. But before heading for the hills, stop to admire the town's nearly perfect baroque town square and be sure, too, to have a nut and chocolate pancake at the little cafe Kawiarnia Naleśnikarnia ★ on the square. There's a museum here to help you bone up on your Karkonosze history before venturing onward. Spend the night at the Pałac Paulinum, a renovated villa deep in the forest that surrounds the town.

4

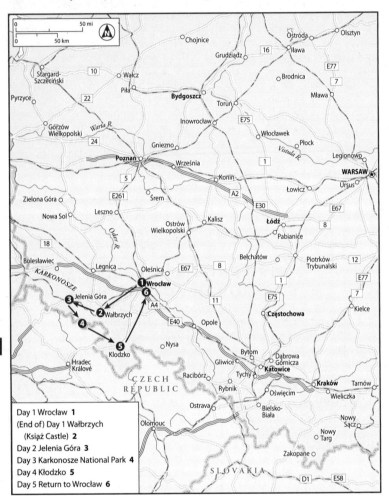

Day 1 Wrocław **1**
(End of) Day 1 Wałbrzych
    (Książ Castle) **2**
Day 2 Jelenia Góra **3**
Day 3 Karkonosze National Park **4**
Day 4 Kłodzko **5**
Day 5 Return to Wrocław **6**

Day ❸: Karkonosze National Park

Get an early start and head for one of the park's main resorts of Szklarska Poręba or Karpacz. Both are more or less the same: Ramshackle collections of old mountain lodges, hotels, cafes, ticky-tacky gift shops, and plenty of bike and ski rental outlets. The drive along the main road between the two towns is absolutely jaw-dropping,

cutting through tiny mountain villages, green fields, and, here and there, rocky peaks. The drive is fun, but if you've got the time and energy, try one of Szklarska Poręba's mountain bike trails. Around a dozen trails fan out from the town, catering to all levels of ability. You may want to extend your visit here and skip the trip to Kłodzko (below).

Day ❹: Kłodzko

Get another early start and begin the journey east to the town of Kłodzko. A trip here feels like a journey back in time; not long ago the towns and villages along the route were part of Germany and the area retains a strong Teutonic feel. Kłodzko itself feels like one of the most remote towns in Poland, stuck in the center of a sliver of land that extends deep into the Czech Republic. Don't miss a tour of the Kłodzko fortress, and, if you have time, check out the picturesque village of Międzygórze, another Alpine village on the lip of the mountains. Book a room or at least have a meal at the Hotel Korona ★, a good value hotel/motel on the edge of Kłodzko.

Day ❺: Back to Wrocław

The drive back to Wrocław is a straight shot north on the E67 highway about 120km (75 miles), or an easy bus ride. Leave about 2 to 3 hours for the journey. On the other hand, if you've got the time, keep pushing east toward Zakopane and the Tatras and more mountain splendor (see below).

6 FIVE-DAY OUTDOOR VACATION IN POLAND

In Poland, an "outdoor" vacation invariably boils down to either mountains or seashore. That means having to choose between the Baltic Sea and Mazurian Lakes far in the north, or the Giant Mountains and the Tatras far to the south. Unless you've got lots of time to travel, you'll have to make the same choice too. Below are two five-day itineraries, depending on whether you're a "seashore" or a "mountain" person.

SEASHORE ITINERARY

Days ❶–❷: Gdańsk & the Tri-Cities

This is the center of Poland's beach scene, and a surprisingly lively beach scene it is. Most of the best beaches are in Sopot or on the Hel Peninsula, reachable by boat from Gdańsk. You'll find all the usual beach diversions in Sopot, including a long pier, a "boardwalk"—actually a sidewalk—that runs for miles on both sides of the pier, and a late-night disco scene. If you're traveling in July or August and you get a patch of hot weather, this is where you'll find a good percentage of the Polish population.

Days ❸–❹: The Mazurian & Suwałki Lake Districts

From Gdańsk, make your way over to the Mazurian lakes for some long-distance canoeing. See "Poland in One Week" above.

Day ❺: Białowieża National Forest

From the lakes, head south and east to the Belarusian border from some unspoiled forest and gorgeous hiking territory. See "Poland in Two Weeks" above.

MOUNTAIN ITINERARY

Day ❶: Warsaw or Kraków to Zakopane

Depending on your base, make your way to the Tatra resort of Zakopane, one of the country's most popular hiking centers in summer and a leading ski resort in winter. In summer, pick up some hiking maps once you hit town and plot your assault on the peaks. There are hundreds of kilometers of marked trails for all skill levels. Check our hiking suggestions (p. 152) or consult the tourist information office for some ideas.

SEA ●
Days 1 and 2: Gdańsk and the Tri-Cities **1**
Days 3 and 4: The Mazurian and Suwałki Lake Districts **2**
Day 5: Białowieża National Forest **3**

MOUNTAIN ●
Day 1 Warsaw or Kraków **1**
Day 2 Zakopane **2**
Day 3 Dunajec River Gorge **3**
Day 4 Jelenia Góra **4**
Day 5 Szklarska Poręba **5**

Day ❷: Hiking in the Tatras ★★★

Hit the mountains early and remember to wear sturdy shoes and bring plenty of water, sunscreen, a rain slicker, sunglasses, a bite to eat, and the map. The trails may be well-marked, but believe me, you're going to need the map anyway. With luck, you'll get a clear, sunny day, but remember to start heading back down the hill the

moment it starts to look like afternoon showers. In keeping with the mountain theme, celebrate your outdoor adventure with dinner at Mała Szwajcaria (Little Switzerland) ★★ when you return.

Day ❸: Boating Down the Dunajec ★★

After an exhausting hike, take it easy today with a relaxing float down the scenic

Dunajec River. Several travel agencies in Zakopane book rafting trips down the Dunajec. Each raft holds around a dozen people and the guides are decked out in mountain garb. The float takes a couple of hours and you have the option of walking back to the parking lot or renting and riding bikes. It's a great day out and perfect for kids.

Day ❹: Travel to the Giant Mountains

There's no easy way to get from the Tatras to the Giant Mountains in the southwest. The easiest is to drive down the A4 highway from Kraków to Wrocław (3–4 hours), or alternatively take a bus. From Wrocław, make your way by car or bus to one of the Giant Mountain resorts or the regional capital of Jelenia Góra. Plan on traveling most of the day. Reward yourself with an excellent Polish meal at Metafora ★★ in Szklarska Poręba.

Day ❺: Cycling in the Giant Mountains ★★

Find your way to the resort town of Szklarska Poręba for a day of heaven in the open air. Stop by the tourist information office to pick up some cycling maps and good advice on rentals and trails. Szklarska Poręba has cast itself as southern Poland's biking capital, and some of the best mountain trails in the country—including plenty for novice riders and families—are here. Some of the most rewarding and longest trails dip into the Czech side of the mountains, but be sure not to go overboard on your first ride. These are mountains, and you'll have to work hard uphill for every easy downhill (but it's worth it!).

Warsaw

Poland's capital city, not often included on tourist itineraries, deserves a fresh look. While it may not be a place you'll fall in love with instantly, there's an energetic spirit of rebirth here that's immediately contagious. Get to know the city and you could very well develop a soft spot for it. Visiting Warsaw is about seeing a capital city getting back on its feet time and time again after military and ideological occupations. With some 85% of the city demolished in World War II, nearly everything you see, including the charming and very "old" looking Old Town *(Stare Miasto),* has been around only for a few decades. The Old Town was so faithfully rebuilt that it earned a place on the UNESCO list of World Cultural Heritage Sites. Much of the city center was propped up by the workers' power philosophy of Communism, creating the Eastern Bloc look of imposing Socialist Realism structures and sculptures as well as dreary and drab housing blocks. In the post-Communism years, modern skyscrapers—both beautiful and ugly—jostle for space in the city's skyline. The changes are every bit as dramatic on the cultural front. New clubs, theaters, performance spaces, and restaurants have opened their doors, and the city feels like it's in a hurry to make up for time lost in the Communist years.

To understand this city, a visit to the **Warsaw Uprising Museum** is a must. The museum gives a full-blown account of the single event in World War II that was largely accountable for the scarred cityscape. And as you trace the former Jewish quarter, you'll sense the void left by a community that made up one-third of the city's population before the war. Top on most sightseeing agendas are the **Old Town,** the **Royal Route,** and the sprawling **Łazienki Park.** While these enclaves of beauty and history are well deserving of your time, recently more attention has been shifting to the leftover relics of Communism as the younger generation comes to accept the quirks of that era as part of the city's heritage. Also gaining limelight is the rundown district of Praga—relatively undamaged during the war, it has some of the oldest original buildings in the city.

You'll want to budget at least two days to get the most out of Warsaw's diverse daytime and after-dark activities.

1 ESSENTIALS

GETTING THERE

BY PLANE   Warsaw's **Okęcie Airport** (Żwirki i Wigury 1; © **022/650-42-20;** www. lotnisko-chopina.pl), sometimes called by its formal name, Fryderyk Chopin Airport, is 10km (6 miles) from the city center. Most major international carriers use the new Terminal 2, while budget airlines arrive and depart from **Etiuda,** a separate but nearby terminal. The main terminal is well served by a tourist information office, automated teller machines, car rental booths, and kiosks for tram and bus tickets. By bus or taxi, it takes approximately 20 to 30 minutes to get to the city center. During the day, take bus no. 175. The night bus is no. N32. Tickets cost 2.80 zł ($1.10/63p). Taxis, operated by SAWA, Merc, and MPT, make the run to the center for around 40 zł ($16/£9). Watch out for unlicensed drivers. There are fewer of them these days but they still manage to nab unwary travelers, charging 3 to 4 times the going rate.

BY TRAIN   Major international and domestic trains arrive and depart from Warsaw's **Central Station (Warszawa Centralna;** Al. Jerozolimskie 54; ✆ **022/620-45-12**; www. pkp.com.pl), located in the heart of the city in Śródmieście (just across the street from the Marriott Hotel). Centralna is, to put it mildly, confusing. It's a vast 1970s concrete jungle, filled with underground passageways that seemingly lead nowhere and misleadingly marked stairways that will have you coming and going, and getting no place at all. Fortunately, the officials at Polish Rail have cleaned up the station. Centralna is well served by tramlines and buses; the only trick is finding which stairway to use to locate the tram going in the direction you want to travel. Taxis stationed here have a higher rate, it's worth calling for an independent taxi (see "Getting Around").

BY BUS   Warsaw's main **bus station (Dworzec Autobusowy Warszawa Zachodnia;** Al. Jerozolimskie 144; ✆ **0300/300-130**; www.pks.warszawa.pl) is situated in the city center, about 1km (½ mile) to the west of the Centralna train station. The station handles all of the bus traffic to and from Western Europe as well as most major Polish routes. The station is well served by tram, bus, or taxi to anywhere in the city. Bus no. 127 and 130 and night bus no. N35 and N85 run to the Centralna train station. Journey time is about 15 minutes. A 2 zł (80¢/45p) ticket, valid for 20 minutes, will suffice. Validate your ticket upon boarding.

BY CAR   As Poland's capital city, all roads lead to Warsaw. You'll have no problem finding your way here. You may be surprised, though, by how long it takes to get here, and once you're here, by the sheer volume of traffic. After you've found your hotel, stow the car and use public transportation and taxis.

VISITOR INFORMATION

The main tourist information office is the **MUFA Warsaw Tourist Information Center,** at the entrance to the Old Town, near to the Royal Castle (Zamkowy 1/3; ✆ **022/635-18-81;** www.wcit.waw.pl). The **Warsaw Tourist Office** (✆ **022/94-31, 022/474-11-42;** www.warsawtour.pl) also maintains a helpful network of tourist information agencies at entry points to the city, including the airport, central train station, and Old Town. All are open daily; operating hours are as follows: **Warszawa Centralna Train Station** (May–Sept 8am–8pm; Oct–Apr 8am–6pm); **Fryderyk Chopin Airport** (May–Sept 8am–8pm; Oct–Apr 8am–6pm); **Krakowskie Przedmieście 39** (Old Town) (May–Sept 9am–8pm; Oct–Apr 9am–6pm).

You can pick up walking-tour itineraries such as *Warsaw City Breaks* and *Jewish Warsaw* at any tourist office. You'll almost always find an English speaker on hand to help with general directions and hotel advice, and provide maps and brochures. If you're planning to use public transportation, get the free ZTM (www.ztm.waw.pl) map of tram and bus routes. Warsaw is blessed with a number of English-language publications that include cultural listings, restaurant reviews, and general information. Look out particularly for the comprehensive *Warsaw, In Your Pocket* (5 zł/$2/£1.10), which is free of charge in most hotels.

CITY LAYOUT

Warsaw is cut in two by the Vistula River (Wisła), but nearly all the interesting things to see and do lie on the river's western side. The heart of the city, and where you'll find most of the hotels, restaurants, and nightlife, is the central district known as Śródmieście. With its huge avenues and acres of space between buildings, it's not particularly pedestrian-friendly. But trams scoot down the rails at an impressive speed and can whisk you around in a few minutes. The center of Śródmieście is the intersection of Al. Jerozolimskie (Jerusalem Avenue) and Marszałkowska Street. The Old Town *(Stare Miasto)* lies about 1km (½ mile) to the north. The best way to find it on foot is to follow the "Royal Route," which intersects with Al. Jerozolimskie. The Royal Route was the journey taken by Polish royalty to travel from the Royal Castle in the Old Town to the Wilanów Palace in the south. This stretch passes along Krakowskie Przedmieście, Nowy Świat, Plac Trzech Krzyży, and Al. Ujazdowskie. To the south of Jerozolimskie, along the Al. Ujazdowskie, beginning at Plac Trzech Krzyży, you'll find Warsaw's embassy district, and some of the city's swankiest shops, cafes, restaurants, and nightclubs. Farther to the south lie the enormous residential districts of Mokotów and Ursynów, home to half of the city's 2 million people. Across the Vistula from the Old Town is the up-and-coming district of Praga. This area has long been one of the poorest districts in Warsaw, but is starting to see something of a revival, primarily led by artists attracted by Praga's rock-bottom rents.

2 GETTING AROUND

ON FOOT   Warsaw is a big city, so walking is an option only within specific areas, such as the Old Town or in Śródmieście. For longer distances, you'll want to use public transportation or taxis.

BY TRAM   Trams trundle down Warsaw's enormous avenues regularly from about 4:30am to 11pm, and are the best means for covering large distances quickly and cheaply. The tram network will look highly confusing at first, but once you have learned the names of major roads and intersections, you'll get the hang of it. You can also get the free map of the tram and bus routes (www.ztm.waw.pl) from the tourist information centers. Warsaw Transport Authority (© **022/94-84**) has public transportation information and usually has English-speaking operators.

Tickets costs 2.80 zł ($1.10/63p) per ride, and you can buy them from Ruch kiosks around town or almost any place near a tram stop that sells newspapers and cigarettes. You may have a hard time finding a place to buy a ticket in the evening, so buy several during the day and stock up. You can also buy reasonably priced long-term tickets: for 1 day (9 zł/$3.60/£2.03), 3 days (16 zł/$6.40/£3.60), and 1 week (32 zł/$12.80/£7.20).

DIY Sightseeing: Hop-On-Hop-Off

You can easily see the top sights in town using public transportation. Public bus no. **180,** a daily service, runs from the Powązki Cemetery to Wilanów and passes by the Old Town and Royal Route in its 1-hour north–south traverse. The weekend bus no. **100** is a loop service starting from the Old Town on Podwale Street, near King Sigismund's Column. It passes places like the Warsaw Uprising Museum and Praga, taking about 90 minutes to complete the loop. **Tram T,** a restored historical tram, covers similar ground as bus no. 100 and also operates on weekends only. For all three options, a day ticket is all you need.

The **Warsaw Tourist Card** (www.warsawtour.pl), available at various places including tourist information centers, gives access to public transportation, and free or discounted rates for attractions, restaurants, and hotels. A 24-hour card costs 35 zł ($14/£7.90); a 3-day card is 65 zł ($26/£14.60).

BY BUS   Buses supplement the tram network and run pretty much the same hours and use the same ticketing and information system. The bus layout is even more confusing than the trams, so get specific directions to your destination.

BY METRO   Warsaw has a small subway (metro) system, but most likely you'll not need it. There's only one line and it connects the center of town to the districts in the north and south of the city. Tickets are the same as for the buses and trams, and must be validated before boarding the train.

BY TAXI   Taxis are a cheap and reliable way of getting from point A to point B. The meter starts at 6 zł ($2.40/£1.40). The rates vary depending on the company. Expect to pay about 25 zł ($10/£5.60) for in-town destinations. Dishonest drivers have been a problem in the past, but the situation is improving. Nevertheless, **use only clearly marked cabs,** and always make sure the driver has switched on the meter. It is also common to book by phone even when there's a taxi rank nearby. Most of the time, there are English-speaking operators who can help you. Good choices include **Merc Taxi** (✆ 022/ 677-77-77), Super Taxi (✆ 022/96-22), and MPT (✆ 022/91-91).

BY BIKE   Cycling in the city is getting more common, but it's still viewed by many as a suicidal undertaking. The bike rental shop **Wygodny Rower** (Al. Jerozolimskie 49; ✆ 0888/498-498; www.wygodnyrower.pl) is open all week and also has a weekend outlet at Nowiniarska 10. The **Oki Doki Hostel** (see "Where to Stay") also has a fleet of bikes for hire.

(*Fast Facts*)   **Warsaw**

American Express   The office is located in Warsaw Lim Center, al. Jerozolimskie 65/79 (✆ 022/630-69-52). It's open weekdays 9am to 7pm and Saturday 10am to 6pm.

Business Hours   Stores and offices are generally open Monday to Friday 9am to 6pm. Banks are open Monday to Friday 9am to 4pm. Some larger stores have limited Saturday hours, usually 9am to noon. Museums and other tourist attractions are often closed on Mondays.

Camera Repair   **Adam Bieniek** (Al. Jerozolimskie 113/115; ✆ 022/629-99-59) can handle repair work for most camera models. The shop is on the second floor and the staircase is by the kebab stall. It's opens on weekdays from 9am to 6pm.

Car Rental   At the airport, you'll find global chains such as **Avis** (✆ 022/650-48-72; www.avis.pl), **Budget** (✆ 022/650-40-62; www.budget.pl), and **Hertz** (✆ 022/ 650-28-96; www.hertz.com.pl). **Joka**, in the city at Okopowa 47 (✆ 022/636-63-93; www.joka.com.pl), offer cars with GPS. For luxury cars, contact **Limocars Executive Services** at Al. Jana Pawła II 15 (✆ 022/697-73-77; www.limocars.pl).

Currency Exchange   Most banks and some hotels have currency exchange counters. The airport and train station also have *kantor* (currency exchange) booths, but you'll find better rates in the city's malls and streets. A 24-hour *kantor* is at Piękna 11 (📞 **022/625-14-24**).

Doctors & Dentists The **LIM Medical Center** (al. Jerozolimskie 65/79; 📞 **022/458-70-00;** www.cmlim.pl) has several facilities in the city. A centrally located option is located in the Marriott Hotel tower and staffs a full range of English-speaking doctors and specialists. For dentists, the **Austrian Dental Center** (Zelazna 54; 📞 **022/654-21-16**) is highly recommended.

Drugstores Independent *"apteka"* are everywhere. **Apteka Grabowskiego** (Al. Jerozolimskie 54; 📞 **022/825-69-86;** www.doz.pl), at the Central Station, is open 24 hours. So is **Apteka Beata** at al. Solidarności 149 (entrance from al. Jana Pawła; 📞 **022/620-08-18**). **Super Pharm** is a chain found in most malls.

Embassies **U.S.:** Al. Ujazdowskie 29/31, 📞 **022/502-20-00; Canada:** Matejki 1/5, 📞 **022/584-31-00; U.K.:** al. Róż 1, 📞 **022/311-00-00.**

Emergencies In an emergency, dial the following numbers: police 📞 **997,** fire 📞 **998,** ambulance 📞 **999,** road assistance 📞 **981** or 9637 (Polish motoring association/PZM). The general emergency number if using a cell phone is 📞 **112.**

Internet Access If you have a laptop, Wi-Fi access is complimentary in many cafes and restaurants. Nearly all hotels either have Wi-Fi or Internet terminals. Internet cafes around town charge about 6 zł ($2.40/£1.35) per hour. **Arena 2** at pl. Konstytucji 5 (📞 **022/629-07-76**) is a smoke-free 24-hour facility. **Incognito**, in the underground maze of the Central Station, is also a 24-hour service. The dingy office is located near McDonald's and not in the basement level of the Marriott's as the outdated posters say.

Laundry Laundry chains with same-day service, such as **5 à Sec** (www.5asec.pl), can be found in most malls including Złote Tarasy and Arkadia.

Maps City and regional maps are widely available in bookshops, roadside kiosks, and petrol stations. One of the most popular brands is **Copernicus.**

Newspapers & Magazines Local news in English is carried in the *Poland Monthly* and *Warsaw Voice* available in bookshops such as Empik and the American Bookstore (see "Shopping"). The *Warsaw Business Journal* is a weekly publication on market news. The *New Warsaw Express* is a weekly electronic publication you can subscribe to on www.nwe.pl.

Post Offices The **Central Post Office** is at Świętokrzyska 31/33 (📞 **022/505-33-16**; www.poczta-polska.pl) and it is open 24 hours. There is also a post office at the Central Station on the ground floor.

Safety Violent crime is relatively rare, but theft is a serious problem. Don't leave valuables in cars overnight. Watch your pockets and purses carefully. If you're traveling with a bike, don't leave it outside unattended (even if it's firmly locked). Many hotels and pensions will allow you to take your bicycle in with you to your room.

Telephones & Fax The area code for Warsaw is 022. To call long distance within Poland, dial the area code (retaining the zero) plus the number.

Global chains like the **Radisson SAS Centrum** (Grzybowska 24; ☏ 022/321-88-88; www.radissonsas.com), **Sheraton** (ul. B. Prusa 2; ☏ 022/450-61-00; www.sheraton.com.pl), and **Westin** (Jana Pawła II 21; ☏ 022/450-88-44; http://westin.com/warsaw) are all centrally located. These high-end four- and five-star places thrive on business travel and can be frightfully expensive. April, May, September, and October are the months when the business pace picks up. The good news is, once the business community goes home, many hotels slash rates by as much as 40%. So hunt around, especially for weekend rates.

Very Expensive

InterContinental Hotel ★★   Just about all the luxury and professionalism you'd expect from the InterContinental chain can be found in this postmodern glass skyscraper. Its next-door neighbor is the iconic Palace of Culture; if you can't keep your eyes off this piece of Socialist Realism even when you're freshening up, ask for room no. 11 on any floor where bathrooms have windows looking out to the Palace. Do splash in the pool on the 43rd floor for the city view. The breakfast buffet is one of the very few in the city catering to a wide palate, including Asian options like *miso* soup and *nori* salad. **Frida** restaurant, noted for its Nuevo Latino fare, has expanded the menu to cover rare cuts, making it the only place in Warsaw where you get Wagyu beef, Argentinean beef, and crocodile escalope all under one roof.

Emilii Plater 49. ☏ **022/328-88-88.** Fax 022/328-88-89. www.warsaw.intercontinental.com. 404 units. 324 zł–1,044 zł ($130–$418/£73–£235) double. AE, DC, MC, V. Parking 100 zł ($40/£23). **Amenities:** 3 restaurants; bar; cafe; concierge; club floor; business center; 24-hr. room service; same-day dry cleaning; club floor; club lounge; health club w/indoor pool, sauna, gym; beauty salon w/massages, facials, hair dresser; shoe shine service; golf stimulator; nonsmoking rooms. *In room:* A/C, TV, dataport, Wi-Fi (complimentary in deluxe rooms), bathrobe, rain shower (deluxe rooms), minibar, kettle, hair dryer, iron, safe, anti-allergy pillows.

Le Meridien Bristol ★   Regarded as Warsaw's most prestigious address, the Bristol is the custodian of the quintessential old world charm. The sensitively restored Art Nouveau building is part of the city's architectural heritage. Through the years, Picasso, Jackie Onassis, Queen Elizabeth II, and Bob Dylan have been among the luminaries who graced the premises. The ornate period details, location on the Royal Route, and history are compelling reasons for checking in. But for the asking price, they could update the well-trampled carpet, file off the random bits of chipping paint, and liven up the somber gray marble bathrooms. If you're a history buff, you'll want to stay in the Paderewski Suite, named after the former prime minister of Poland who was also a world-class composer. Breakfast in the inner courtyard is quite memorable. So are drinks at the aptly named **Column Bar** and fine dining at the Michelin-recommended **Malinowa Restaurant.**

Krakowskie Przedmieście 42/44. ☏ **022/551-10-00.** Fax 022/625-25-77. www.lemeridien.com/warsaw. 205 units. 1040 zł–1220 zł ($416–$488/£234–£275) double; 7,200 zł ($2,880/£1,620) Paderewski suite. Children 12 and under stay free in parent's room. Extra person 126 zł ($50/£28). AE, DC, MC, V. Limited free parking. **Amenities:** 2 restaurants; bar; cafe; pool; health club; sauna; concierge; courtesy car; business center; 24-hr. room service; dry cleaning; executive floor; nonsmoking rooms; currency exchange. *In room:* A/C, plasma TV, fax (business rooms), dataport, minibar, hair dryer, iron, safe.

Le Régina ★★ (Value)   Converted from a restored 18th-century palace, this boutique hotel is stashed in the serenely quiet far end of the New Town. All rooms have a slightly

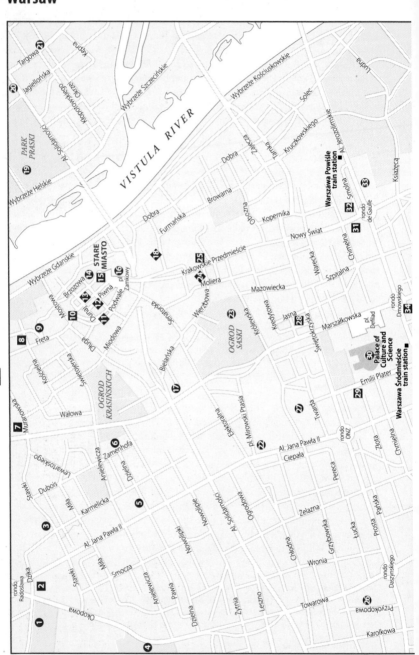

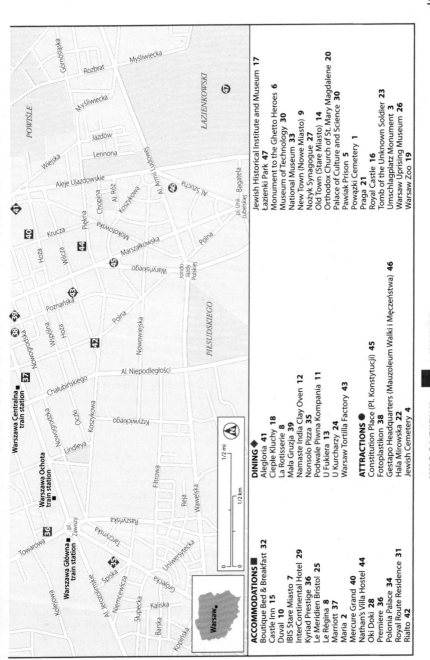

ACCOMMODATIONS ■
Boutique Bed & Breakfast **32**
Castle Inn **15**
Duval **10**
IBIS Stare Miasto **7**
InterContinental Hotel **29**
Kyriad Prestige **36**
Le Meridien Bristol **25**
Le Régina **8**
Marriott **37**
Maria **2**
Mercure Grand **40**
Nathan's Villa Hostel **44**
Oki Doki **28**
Premiere **36**
Polonia Palace **34**
Royal Route Residence **31**
Rialto **42**

DINING ◆
Alegloria **41**
Cieple Kluchy **18**
La Rotisserie **8**
Mała Gruzja **39**
Namaste India Clay Oven **12**
Nonsolo Pizza **35**
Podwale Piwna Kompania **11**
U Fukiera **13**
U Kurcharzy **24**
Warsaw Tortilla Factory **43**

ATTRACTIONS ●
Constitution Place (Pl. Konstytucji) **45**
Fotoplastikon **38**
Gestapo Headquarters (Mauzoleum Walki i Męczeństwa) **46**
Hala Mirowska **22**
Jewish Cemetery **4**

Jewish Historical Institute and Museum **17**
Łazienki Park **47**
Monument to the Ghetto Heroes **6**
Museum of Technology **30**
National Museum **33**
New Town (Nowe Miasto) **9**
Nożyk Synagogue **27**
Old Town (Stare Miasto) **14**
Orthodox Church of St. Mary Magdalene **20**
Palace of Culture and Science **30**
Pawiak Prison **5**
Powązki Cemetery **1**
Praga **21**
Royal Castle **16**
Tomb of the Unknown Soldier **23**
Umschlagplatz Monument **3**
Warsaw Uprising Museum **26**
Warsaw Zoo **19**

different configuration, but share the sleek furnishings in shades of brown and champagne. Hand-painted frescos act as headboards or accents on creamy walls. The Zebra room stands out with a different color scheme. Two rooms on the ground floor have access to a sun-kissed private patio, and several rooms on the attic floor have private rooftop terraces. Staff here is some of the best-trained in town. Rooms are modestly sized. If you want more stretching space, look into the full-service apartments of their associated property, **Residence Diana** (Chmielna 13A; ✆ **022/505-91-00;** www.residence diana.com), which has similar upscale minimalistic decor in a prime location in the city center.

Kościelna 12. ✆ **022/531-60-00.** Fax 022/531-60-01. www.leregina.com. 61 units. 1,188 zł ($457/£267) double; 5,760 zł ($2,304/£1,296) presidential suite. Breakfast 72 zł ($29/£16). Extra person 216 zł ($86/£49). Children 12 and under 108 zł ($43.20/£24.30). AE, DC, MC, V. Valet parking 100 zł ($40/£23). **Amenities:** Restaurant (p. 74); bar; lounge; business center; same-day dry cleaning; gym; indoor pool; 24-hr. room service; baby cot; babysitting. *In room:* A/C, plasma TV, paid movies, dataport, complimentary Wi-Fi, minibar, bathrobes, hair dryer, safe.

Expensive

Marriott ★★ Of the big chains in town, this one offers arguably the best location and the best value. Previous guests include former U.S. President George W. Bush. Directly opposite the Central Station and the Palace of Culture, it's popular with business travelers; the lobby has all the hubbub of a busy airport. The hotel completed major refurbishment works two years ago and the results are visible in the luxurious and comfortable bedding, new carpets, and updated bathrooms.

Al. Jerozolimskie 65/79. ✆ **022/630-63-06.** Fax 022/630-03-11. www.marriott.com/wawpl. 518 units. 739 zł ($296/£166) double. Breakfast 75 zł ($30/£17). Extra person free. AE, DC, MC, V. Public parking. **Amenities:** 3 restaurants; 2 cafes; bar; indoor basement pool; health club and spa; concierge; business center; 24-hr. room service; dry cleaning; nonsmoking rooms; 8 rooms for those w/limited mobility. *In room:* A/C, plasma TV, dataport, minibar, coffeemaker, hair dryer, iron, safe.

Polonia Palace ★★ Originally built in 1913, it recently underwent two years of a thorough top to bottom spruce up. The result is a winning merge of Old World charm and plush contemporary appeal. Two blocks away from the Marriott, it also shares the view of the Palace of Culture, but it is right by the crossroads of two major arteries. Step beyond busy street and the grand facade, however, and it's all peace and quiet inside. Watch for excellent weekend deals that tumble prices by as much as 40%.

Al. Jerozolimskie 45. ✆ **022/318-28-00.** Fax 022/318-28-89. www.poloniapalace.com. 206 units. 594 zł ($238/£134) double. Breakfast 64 zł ($26/£14). Extra bed 198 zł ($79/£45). Children 14 and under stay free in parent's room. AE, DC, MC, V. Parking 45 zł ($18/£10). **Amenities:** Restaurant; bar; 24-hr. room service; same-day laundry service; health center; business center; conference room; currency exchange; nonsmoking rooms. *In room:* A/C, TV, dataport, hair dryer, safe.

Rialto ★★ A high-style boutique hotel for those who demand original Thonet chairs and William Morris furniture. The inspiration here is Art Deco, using a mix of authentic furnishings and new creations or reproductions. The meticulous attention to detail is reflected by touches like Honeywell's retro air-conditioning control panels. And the bathrooms—reminiscent of the Great Gatsby's heyday—are an antidote for those jaded by modern minimalism. The only small detraction is the lack of a garden/patio. But the location, a 10-minute walk from pl. Konstytucji, is atmospheric. From the 6th-floor gym and some of the rooms you can see neighborhood buildings with pockmarked walls, left by bullets from the Warsaw Uprising.

Wilcza 73. ℂ **022/584-87-00.** Fax 022/584-87-01. www.rialto.pl. 44 units. 810 zł ($423/£182) single; 900 zł ($360/£203) double; 1,764 zł ($706/£370) suite. Rates do not include 7% tax. Extra person 126 zł ($50/£28). Children 12 and under stay free in parent's room. Breakfast 87 zł ($35/£19). AE, DC, MC, V. Valet parking 100 zł ($40/£23). **Amenities:** Restaurant; lounge; bar; business center; laundry service; same-day dry cleaning; nonsmoking rooms; gym; 24-hr. room service; cigar room w/fireplace; sauna and steam rooms; access to Sinnet racquet club for indoor tennis, squash, and pool; library w/CD and DVD. *In room:* A/C, plasma TV, movies, Wi-Fi, coffeemaker (suites), minibar, hair dryer, safe, CD/DVD player.

Mercure Grand ★★   A hotel from Communist times that has been transformed by a thorough overhaul. What remains from the past are the Social Realism facade and the marble and granite staircase. Everything else is brand new, including the service-oriented crew. The room count was reduced from 355 to fewer than 300 rooms, creating larger rooms all with the comforts of a high-end hotel. Bathrooms have heated floors and most feature showers with glass walls between the bathroom and bedroom (privacy curtains available)—great for exhibitionists. The location is ideal: some of the city's best restaurants, cafes, and shops are within walking distance.

Krucza 28. ℂ **022/583-21-00.** Fax 022/583-21-21. www.mercure.com. 299 units. Weekdays 700 zł–800 zł ($280–$320/£158–£180) double. Weekends 250 zł ($100/£56) double. Breakfast 70 zł ($28/£16). Extra person 70 zł ($28/£16). Children 12 and under stay free in parent's room. AE, DC, MC, V. Parking 70 zł ($28/£16). **Amenities:** Restaurant; bar; 24-hr. room service; nonsmoking rooms; health center; sauna; 3 rooms for those w/limited mobility; business center; conference room; same-day dry cleaning; laundry service. *In room:* A/C, plasma TV, dataport, minibar, kettle, bathrobe, hair dryer, safe.

Moderate
Boutique Bed & Breakfast ★★   A unique B&B in the city center aiming to create the best small hotel experience in the city. Located in a pre-war town house, each of the high-ceilinged rooms is done up differently, but the emphasis is on top-quality traditional furniture and Art Deco highlights. It has a decidedly pre-war ambience of a well-to-do family. Five studio apartments are in a separate building across the street. If Jarek, the owner, is in town, you'll find him at breakfast, waxing enthusiastically about his hometown while you enjoy a fine organic spread. They also organize music festivals, and the dining room and hallway double as galleries for young Polish artists.

Smolna 14/7. ℂ **022/829-48-01.** www.bedandbreakfast.pl. 12 units. 260 zł–390 zł ($128–$156/£59–£88) single, 320 zł–420 zł ($128–$168/£72–£95) double. Rates include breakfast. Children 8 and under stay free in parent's room. Extra person 30 zł ($12/£7). DC, MC, V. Public parking. **Amenities:** Kitchen; conference room; nonsmoking rooms; laundry service. *In room:* TV, kitchen (some rooms), fridge (some rooms), coffeemaker (some rooms), hair dryer, complimentary Wi-Fi.

Castle Inn ★★ (Finds (Value   Occupying a restored 16th-century building in the Old Town opposite the Royal Castle, the inn is well-priced, spick and span, and has a bit of a theatrical feel to boot. Unique room adornments range from the hearts and spades in the "Alice in Wonderland" room to an 800kg four-poster bed in the "Maharaja" room to blown-up cartoons in the "Comic" sanctum. The effects are created by bold colors, plus an eclectic blend of antique and modern furnishings. Deluxe rooms have supersized bathrooms completed with claw-foot baths. It's quiet in general, but there are complimentary earplugs for you to filter out the 6am church bell peals or the evening music from the concerts in the castle. The management is professional, having graduated from Oki Doki (see below). Everything promises to be a memorable stay. *Note:* No elevators.

Świętojańska 2 (entrance from Pl. Zamkowy). ℂ **022/425-01-00.** Fax 022/635-04-25. www.castleinn.pl. 22 units. 250 zł ($100/£57) single; 260 zł–280 zł ($104–$112/£59–£63) double w/castle view; 240 zł–420 zł ($96–$168/£54–£95) triple. Breakfast 20 zł ($8/£5). Children under 3 stay free in parent's room. MC, V.

Amenities: Common room w/microwave, kettle; water-cooler. *In room:* Plasma TV, bathrobe, complimentary Wi-Fi, minibar, hair dryer.

Duval ★ (Finds)   Along the lane merging the Old Town and the New Town are these four individually furnished apartments. The themes are loosely based on "Japanese," "Glass," "Polish," and "Retro." The Japanese room has the most natural light. Two rooms look out to a courtyard and the others to the thoroughfare on Nowomiejska Street. This section of the Old Town hushes up after dark, so you'll have a quiet sleep. There are no stoves for you to whip up a meal, but restaurants of all price brackets are within walking distance. Duval has been in operation for four years, but everything is still spanking new. *Note:* No elevators.

Nowomiejska 10. ✆ **0608/679-346.** Fax 022/831-91-04. www.duval.net.pl. 4 units. 250 zł–330 zł ($100–$132/£56–£74.) apt. Breakfast 35 zł ($14/£9). Extra person 110 zł ($44/£25). Weekly and monthly rates available. AE, MC, V. Street parking. **Amenities:** Restaurant; cafe; nonsmoking rooms. *In room:* TV, kitchenette w/fridge and kettle, hair dryer, complimentary Wi-Fi.

IBIS Stare Miasto ★★   Sometimes, the IBIS hotel chain is a real lifesaver. The philosophy of a clean, modern, stripped-down business hotel at tourist rates is especially welcome in a city like Warsaw, where every other place seems to assume that Expense Account is footing the bill. The rooms and public areas are stark in keeping with the IBIS idea, but you won't find a nicer room at this price so close to the Old Town (a 5-minute walk). Another alternative is **IBIS Warszawa Centrum** (al. Solidarności 165; ✆ **022/530-30-30**) located near a tram stop, just a 10-minute hop to Old Town. For comparable standards at lower rates, **IBIS Ostrobramska** (Ostrobramska 36; ✆ **022/515-78-00**) is in the heartlands of Praga.

Muranowska 2. ✆ **022/310-10-00.** Fax 022/310-10-10. www.ibishotel.com. 333 units. Weekdays 289 zł ($116/£65) double. Weekends 219 zł ($88/£49) double. Breakfast 29 zł ($12/£7). Children 12 and under stay free in parent's room. AE, MC, V. Underground parking 40 zł ($16/£9). **Amenities:** Restaurant; bar; business center; nonsmoking rooms; dry cleaning; water cooler; 5 rooms for those w/limited mobility. *In room:* A/C, TV, Wi-Fi.

Kyriad Prestige ★★   This hotel is owned by the same chain as the Premiere Classe (see below), but the philosophy here is to offer top-end business services at moderate prices. Travelers accustomed to four-star luxuries can save substantial cash over the likes of the Marriott. The neighborhood is on the gray side, but a nearby tram can get you to the center in about 5 minutes. The rooms are large and comfortably furnished in contemporary styles. **Campanile** (Towarowa 2; ✆ **022/582-72-00**), run by the same folks, is next door in the same complex. Their rooms are just as comfortable, but smaller and the furnishings simpler to be in line with the lower price tag.

Towarowa 2. ✆ **022/582-75-00.** Fax 022/582-75-01. www.kyriadprestige.com.pl. 133 units. Sun–Thurs 359 zł ($144/£81) double. Fri–Sat 299 zł ($120/£67) double. Breakfast 37 zł ($15/£8). AE, DC, MC, V. Parking 40 zł ($16/£9). **Amenities:** Restaurant; health club; limited room service; conference room; nonsmoking rooms; 6 rooms for those w/limited mobility. *In room:* A/C, TV, safe, dataport, kettle, minibar, hair dryer, trouser press, complimentary Wi-Fi.

Maria ★   Arguably the best of the smaller, family-run hotels in town. The rooms are on the austere side of modern, but several have hardwood floors and these tend to be smarter looking and more comfortable. Rooms at the back, peering at McDonald's, are quieter. The restaurant is old-fashioned but cheerful and the staff couldn't be more welcoming. The in-town location is convenient to get to the sights, especially to the former Jewish ghetto. The Old Town is about a 20-minute walk.

Jana Pawła II 71. ✆ **022/838-40-62.** Fax 022/838-38-40. www.hotelmaria.pl. 24 units. Weekdays 250 zł–320 zł ($100–$128/£56–£72) single; 380 zł ($152/£86) double. Weekends 220 zł ($88/£50) single; 280

zł ($112/£63) double. Rates include breakfast. Children 10 and under stay free in parent's room. Extra person 90 zł ($36/£20). AE, DC, MC, V. Free parking. **Amenities:** Restaurant; bar; limited room service; laundry service; nonsmoking rooms. *In room:* A/C, TV, dataport, hair dryer, complimentary Wi-Fi.

Royal Route Residence ★ These comfortable, full-service apartments are located on the trendy Nowy Świat and Chmielna streets. The apartments come in various sizes; some have two bedrooms, a spacious living room, and good-size kitchen, while others are only big enough for a double bed and a closet-size kitchen. The furnishing is mainly sourced from IKEA. The fixtures and walls get spruced up annually. Most guests are long-term business travelers. The **Old Town Apartments** (Rynek Starego Miasta 12/14; *②* **022/887-98-00;** www.warsawshotel.com), owned by the same company, offer 36 apartments scattered in various buildings in the Old Town. Although these rooms are modern, the standards are not as high as at the Royal Route Residence.

Nowy Świat 29/3 (entrance from Nowy Świat 27). *②* **022/692-84-95.** Fax 022/831-49-56. www.warsaw-apartments.net. 15 units. 216 zł–575 zł ($86–$230/£47–£130) apt. Extra person 54 zł ($22/£12). Children 6 and under stay free in parent's room. AE, DC, MC, V. Limited parking 18 zł ($7/£4). *In room:* Fully equipped kitchen; dishwasher (some apt.); complimentary Wi-Fi.

Inexpensive

Etap ★ (**Value**) Opened in 2006, this budget cousin of IBIS (see above) has the same dependable concept: cheap, clean, and modern. Pared-down means the basin and shower cubicle are next to the beds, but a sturdy door separates the toilet. The family room sleeps three. To spare yourself the clatter from the busy road, request a room facing the courtyard. Etap is on the quiet side of town near the river, so it's an uphill workout to get to the happening places. Buses 171 and 155 from nearby Rozbrat Street will get you to the center. Taxis to town cost roughly 20 zł ($8/£4.50).

Zagórna 1. *②* **022/745-36-60.** Fax 022/622-55-01. www.orbisonline.pl. 176 units. 179 zł ($72/£40) single, 189 zł ($76/£43) double. Breakfast 20 zł ($8/£5). AE, MC, V. Parking 15 zł ($6/£3). **Amenities:** 24-hr. warm snacks; Internet terminal; nonsmoking rooms; 5 rooms for those w/limited mobility. *In room:* A/C, TV, Wi-Fi.

Nathan's Villa Hostel ★★ The same owner as the Nathan's hostel in Kraków uses the same popular formula here: combining some of the amenities of a decent hotel with the sociability of a hostel. Several private double rooms are on offer, so you don't have to sleep *en groupe*. The dorms, which sleep 4 to 12, are neat and clean. Free laundry is one of several perks that you wouldn't normally expect at a hostel. The fully equipped kitchen, cleaned three times daily, is a great place to swap travel tales with your hostelmates, most of whom are usually the young, arty, savvy backpacker types. The location is central, but still quiet enough for you to catch 40 winks.

Piękna 24/26. *②* **022/622-29-46.** Fax 022/622-29-46. www.nathansvilla.com. 13 units. 160 zł–200 zł ($64–$80/£36–£45) double, 45 zł–60 zł ($18–$24/£10–£14) dorm bed. Rates include breakfast. DC, MC, V. **Amenities:** Laundry; kitchen; TV room; Internet terminal; complimentary Wi-Fi; nonsmoking rooms. *In room:* lockers (dorm).

Oki Doki ★★ Opened by backpackers (with a penchant for art and antiques) for backpackers, this is not your typical hostel where the central location is the only frill. Located in a reconstructed pre-war building, each of the high-ceilinged rooms is in a different theme, from "Mexico" to "the Communist Dorm." The kitchen here is not as functional as at Nathan's, but the vibe is more vibrant. The bar's happy hour, from 7pm to 8pm, claims to have the cheapest beer in town. The front desk's tips on getting the best out of Warsaw are more creative than at the city's tourist information centers. In 2006, they snatched the Hoscar award as one of the top 10 hostels in the world. *Note:* No elevators.

Pl Dąbrowskiego 3. ℂ **022/826-51-12.** Fax 022/826-83-57. www.okidoki.pl. 82 units. 120 zł–140 zł ($48–$56/£27–£32) single w/shared bathroom; 150 zł–175 zł ($60–$70/£34–£40) double w/shared bathroom; 190 zł–220 zł ($76–$88/£43–£50) double w/bathroom; 42 zł–70 zł ($17–$28/£9–£16) dorm bed. Rates for private rooms include breakfast. Breakfast 10 zł ($4/£2). M, V. Street parking. Pets accepted (in private rooms only). **Amenities:** Kitchen; Internet terminals; complimentary Wi-Fi; nonsmoking rooms; women-only dorm; laundry; bike rental. *In room:* TV, kettle (private rooms only), lockers.

Premiere Classe ★ (Value)   The theory behind this French hotel chain is to offer spotless, modern rooms with absolutely no frills at cut-rate prices. It's found a real niche in Warsaw, where decent, affordable rooms in the center are in short supply. The rooms themselves are microscopic—we've seen Winnebagos with bigger bathrooms—but they're very clean and comfortable. The breakfast buffet is rather miserable; the cafes on al. Jerozolimskie can be your salvation.

Towarowa 2. ℂ **022/624-08-00.** Fax 022/620-2629. www.premiereclasse.com.pl. 126 units. 189 zł ($76/£42) double. Breakfast 20 zł ($8/£5). AE, DC, MC, V. Parking 40 zł ($16/£9). **Amenities:** Bar; Internet terminals; complimentary Wi-Fi; nonsmoking rooms; 6 rooms for those w/limited mobility. *In room:* TV.

4 WHERE TO DINE

While in Warsaw, take the chance to branch out—culinarily speaking—to non-Polish cuisine. Once you get to the smaller towns, it's mainly Polish or Italian staples. The budget Vietnamese-Chinese eateries here are deft with the sizzling hotplates. As for Indian, the no-frills joints do just as good a job, if not better, than their up-market cousins. And you'll no doubt notice the sushi rage. Locals tend to avoid eating in the Old Town Square due to the inflated price tag. But you don't have to wander far from the square to find reasonably priced meals. And the New Town *(Nowe Miasto)* is also strewn with eating options. Most restaurants, even the formal ones, welcome kids.

Very Expensive & Expensive

AleGloria ★★★ MODERN POLISH   AleGloria's decor takes Polish folk art as the underlining motif, but updates it with a magical wand to create a cheerful and fairytale feel. Get the waiter to give you a tour of the strawberry, crystal, and hunting rooms and point out the Malczewski reproductions. The menu, saturated with posh noshes like lobster, foie gras, and truffles, shares the same spirit as the decor: a Polish repertoire with flights of fancy whipped in. The "carp ribbons" are fillets twirled to mimic *faworki,* a traditional festive treat. The herring tartare with nuts and ginger may sound odd, but tastes heavenly. Most dishes pair fruits with meat, like roasted figs with pork tenderloin. Save room for the pavlova with strawberry sauce, which can be shared by two. The top-notch service wraps up an evening that will leave you reminiscing about AleGloria for quite a while.

Plac Trzech Krzyży 3. ℂ **022/584-70-80.** www.alegloria.pl. Reservations recommended. Main courses 54 zł–89 zł ($21.60–$35.60/£12.15–£20). Daily 11am–11pm.

La Rotisserie ★★★ INTERNATIONAL   Although it's one of the best fine-dining experiences in Poland, the restaurant of Le Régina's boutique hotel (see above) has largely stayed under the mainstream radar. However, it's the splurge option of those in the know. Chef Paweł Oszczyk stands among the country's top talents, and his short menu changes regularly. At times it seems like you need to be a true foodie to know all the terms on the menu, such as partridge with boletus and fresh lovage risotto, or for dessert, chestnut

24/7 Snacks

The shabby chic **Przekąski Zakąski** (Ossolińskich 7, entrance from Krakowskie Przedmieście; ☎ **022/826-79-36;** www.gessler.pl) is in the Europejski Building on the Royal Route. As part of the take-us-as-we-are spirit of the place, not all of the nine Polish snacks on the menu are available at the same time. But, the 4 zł ($1.60/90p) vodka shots are perennially popular. **Szpilka** (pl. Trzech Krzyży 18; ☎ **022/628-91-32**) is good for a cup of morning brew. It's a trendy hangout, but the food is not as exciting as it could be.

bavarois with coffee and cognac "milk glass." There is a compact Polish section of the menu if you want to sample strictly traditional flavors. The wine list also changes to keep pace with the menu. The upscale setting is one of understated elegance and the mood is approachable and relaxed. It doesn't get as many large groups of business diners as the other upscale places, so it's great for an intimate dinner. For the value deal, try the Sunday Linner (no, that's not a typo, but a play on fusing Lunch with Dinner). From 1pm to 6pm, 175 zł ($70/£39) gets you a 5-course tasting menu and two glasses of wine.

Kościelna 12. ☎ **022/531-60-00.** www.leregina.com. Reservations recommended. Main courses 74 zł–112 zł ($29.60–$44.80/£16.65–£25.20). AE, DC, MC, V. Daily 6:30am–11pm.

Różana ★ POLISH   Slightly out of the way, but worth the taxi ride to get to this double-story villa that has all the refined touches of aristocratic country manors. The compact menu, in the same vein, is "noble" food. Calves' brains on toast are a traditional morsel that has become a rare find. Familiar fillers come in forms of roast duck, baked salmon, and braised pork tenderloin. You'll be sharing space with the Expense Account people, treating themselves to caviar and pancakes with crayfish and bantering up the noise level and thus chipping away the romantic ambience. If you don't feel like having a full meal, it's a treat just to have their coffee and meringue cakes. **Tradycja** (Belwederska 18a; ☎ **022/840-09-01**), with the same taste and feel, is their outpost in the south of Park Łazienki.

Chocimska 7. ☎ **022/848-12-25.** www.restauracjatradycja.com.pl. Reservations required. Main courses 34 zł–79 zł ($13.60–$31.60/£7.65–£17.80). AE, DC, MC, V. Daily noon–1pm.

U Fukiera ★ POLISH   A Warsaw institution and one of the fanciest spots for a meal in the city, served in an overwrought but undeniably romantic space in the Old Town's main square. The guest list reads like an international Who's Who, for this used to be *the* place to wine and dine visiting dignitaries. These days, with rampant competition, it has to do more to stay on the top of the game. The menu doesn't razzle and dazzle you with recherché items, but instead takes everyday Polish classics like *żurek, kołduny,* and pork and delivers them in sheer perfection. It does a fabulous *nóżki* (jellied pork trotters). If you're a petite eater, two can share the generous main course portions so as to leave space for the tempting desserts. Despite the romantic accents, U Fukiera is more suited for groups rather than a party of two. The competent service is at times a bit stiff and somber.

Rynek Starego Miasto 27. ☎ **022/831-10-13.** www.ufukiera.pl. Reservation recommended. Main course items 41 zł–99 zł ($16.40–$39.60/£9.20–£22.30). AE, DC, MC, V. Daily noon–11pm.

U Kucharzy ★★ POLISH   "At the Chefs," you eat in the kitchen of the former Europejski Hotel, spruced up to look at once Spartan and luxurious. The chefs come to

WARSAW

5

WHERE TO DINE

76

Biting into the Past

For a glimpse of the dining scene during the Communist era, a visit to a milk bar is a must. **Bar Mleczny Prasowy** (Marszałkowska 10/16; ✆ **022/628-44-27**) is particularly quaint and the place to go if you have only have time to visit one. The coffee is awful, but where else can you get scrambled eggs for 1.28 zł (50¢/29p) at 7am on a weekday? Go soon; these old diner-like digs are dwindling fast in a gentrifying city. Also dying are the likes of **Lotos** (Belwederska 2; ✆ **022/481-13-01;** www.restauracjalotos.pl), located to the south of the Łazienki Park. Not milk bars, but "elegant" restaurants that were originally for bigwigs and those who had scrimped and saved up for a special occasion. At Lotos the clock is stuck in the '80s, from the cloakroom to the dinner clientele, who all sport a bottle of vodka on the table to go with the traditional Polish food. Service, though, has moved on and is quite friendly.

---

your table and ladle the meats and sides straight to your plate from their cast-iron pots and skillets, and they'll even slice and dice your steak tartare in front of you. Book a table in front of the mega-burners to watch the men-in-uniform prepare Polish mainstays such as roast boar and venison. These "front row" seats have become so popular that you almost rub elbows with other diners. Other tables are quieter, but you miss out on the kitchen buzz that generates the fun and magical experience of dining here. Although the staff fusses over guests, service is not the most efficient. The owner, who bears a passing resemblance to Van Gogh, often hobnobs with the diners, making everyone feel like a special guest.

Ossolińskich 7. ✆ **022/826-79-36**. www.gessler.pl. Reservations recommended. Main courses 40 zł–80 zł ($16–$32/£9–£18). AE, DC, MC, V. Daily noon–midnight.

Moderate

Podwale Piwna Kompania ★★ (Value) EUROPEAN   The good-value-for-money meat platters keep this Bavarian/Czech-inspired beer hall constantly abuzz with merry locals and visitors. It's ideal for groups; tables for two are squeezed into leftover corners or along corridors. The most popular order is the chunky stump of *golonka* (pork knuckles), weighing at least a kilo. Mind you, the crispy crust is very salty and will leave you parched long after the meal is over. The menu also offers Polish staples like *bigos* (hunter's stew), *pierogi*, and blood sausages. If want something a bit lighter, a hearty *żurek* soup supplemented with the freebie bread basket and cream cheese will fill you up. Complimentary *nalewka* (fruit-infused vodka) comes with the bill. **U Szwejka** (Pl. Konstytucji 1; ✆ **022/339-17-10**) is the city center cousin with the same successful partnership of meat and beer.

Podwale 25. ✆ **022/635-63-14.** www.podwale25.pl. Reservations recommended. Main courses 21 zł–49 zł ($8.40–$19.60/£4.73–£11). DC, MC, V. Mon–Fri 11am–1am, Sat–Sun noon–1am.

Żywiciel ★ (Kids) POLISH   Had enough of the peasant theme, aristocratic platter, rustic spread, or knights' table? And you just want a casual and reasonably priced neighborhood restaurant? This is one of the best in town, equally popular with local families and an occasional celebratory party of 12. Had Seinfeld lived in Warsaw, he and his buddies would have hung out here. Although the menu has well-executed Polish staples like

WARSAW

5

WHERE TO DINE

pierogi, pork cutlets, and pancakes, there are also traditional delicacies such as calves' kidneys and sweetbreads on toast, ox tongue, and jellied pork's trotters on the menu. Some of the main courses come without veggies, so factor in another 5 zł ($2/£1.10) for sides. There's also a simple breakfast menu. Throughout the day, it doubles as a cafe.

Pl. Inwalidów 10. ℰ **022/322-82-28.** www.zywiciel.pl. Main courses 24 zł–43 zł ($9.60–$17.20/£5.40–£9.70). AE, DC, MC, V. Daily 9am–11pm. Tram: 36.

Mała Gruzja ★★ GEORGIAN   Georgian cuisine is edging its way into the city center. And "Little Georgia" is a welcome addition. Like Polish cuisine it focuses on carbs galore, but there's more lamb, and eggplant, and an unbridled use of garlic. The semi-basement space seats about 10 tables of 2 to 4 people. The exposed brickwork and a smattering of Georgian emblems give it a more sophisticated feel. The *chaczpuri* is translated on the English menu as "cheese cake," but it's a kind of savory puffy quesadilla. *Mcwady* isn't a Scottish chap, but a traditional oven for roasting skewers of meat. What come out from the *Mcwady* are tender and tasty morsels.

Nowogrodzka 40. ℰ **0600/880-724.** Main courses 16 zł–28 zł ($6.40–$11.20/£3.60–£6.30). MC, V. Daily noon–11pm.

Namaste India Clay Oven ★★ INDIAN   Thankfully, over-the-top praises from the local press haven't resulted in a deterioration in quality or a bumping up of prices at this popular Indian spot. This petite grotto is on a side lane in the Old Town, where the Indian chefs rustle up a good coverage of the usual suspects. The firepower is toned down for local palates, but you can ask the kitchen to up the game. Treats that won't singe your tongue include *murgh malai kebab* (creamy grilled chicken) and *palak paneer* (spinach and cottage cheese) that you can sop up with warm *naan* bread. No beer here, but you can chill out with a mango *lassi* to the tune of Bollywood beats. The even smaller maiden outlet is on Nowogrodzka 15 (ℰ 022/357-09-39), where the take-out queues can be unbearably long.

Piwna 46/1. ℰ **022/635-77-66.** www.namasteindia.pl. Main courses 14 zł–30 zł ($5.60–$12/£3.15–£6.75). No credit cards. Mon–Sun noon–10pm.

Nonsolo Pizza ★ ITALIAN   These pizzas, made in a wood-fired oven, are some of the best in town. And the folks here are proud to have the real deal—there's a none-too-subtle sign here saying that folks in Italy don't dollop ketchup on pizzas. The functional, austere decor is offset by the merry buzz of locals breaking bread here. The house specialty is the "Nonsolo" pizza, topped with tomato, mozzarella, ham, mushroom, and garlic. If you're after pasta, try the fettuccine *arrabiata* (with spicy tomato sauce). In the evenings, you may have to queue for a table.

Weekday Lunch Crunch

Milk bars are not the only places for budget meals. The staff canteen of the **Ministry of Culture and National Heritage** (Krakowskie Przedmieście 15/17; no phone) is open to the public on weekdays from 8am to 4pm. It serves a decent Polish spread. The menu is chalked up in Polish only but the genial staff will help you along. **Restaurant & Club Vena** (Nowogrodzka 31; ℰ **022/628-24-02**) has a different set lunch every weekday from noon to 5pm. For a mere 12.90 zł ($5.15/£2.90), the soup and main course are probably the best value (and taste) in town.

Sweet Spots

Batida (Krakowskie Przedmieście 13; ℂ **022/826-44-74**) has a dessert selection that includes tangy lemon meringue tarts and the Warsaw's best French pastry. Another outlet is on pl. Konstytucji (ℂ **022/621-53-15**).

Blikle (Nowy Świat 35; ℂ **022/826-66-19**) has been in business since 1869 and is famous for its *pączki* (donuts).

Pawłowicz (Chmielna 13; no phone) is a take-out-only, hole-in-the-wall operation catering to a constant queue looking for fresh, made-on-the-premises donuts and sweet bread for only about 2 zł (80¢/45p) a pop.

Słony i Słodki (Mokotowska 45; ℂ **022/622-49-34**) serves fancy, mouth-watering cake in a Laura Ashley-esque rustic milieu.

Smaki Warszawy (Żurawia 47/49; ℂ **022/621-82-68**) is the place for pretty parcels of "pepper and vanilla" and *kajmak* (Polish toffee) tarts.

To Lubię (Freta 10; ℂ **022/635-90-23**) is a smoke-free cafe converted from a belfry in New Town. Tuck in to hot chocolate and homemade desserts like pumpkin cake and then pick up some cookies for the road.

Wedel (Szpitalna 8; ℂ **022/827-29-16**) "chocolate drinking house" has become a nationwide franchise, but the original store is still *the* place to lap up Old World charm. A must-do.

Wróble (Noakowskiego 10; ℂ **022/825-55-29**) has been in the business of baking standard Polish sweet snacks since 1921. It's low-key and offers an inexpensive selection.

Grójecka 110. ℂ **022/824-12-73**. www.nonsolo.pl. Pizza 14 zł–27 zł ($5.60–$10.80/£3.15–£6). Pasta 13 zł–28 zł ($5.20–$11.20/£2.93–£6.30). MC, V. Daily noon–11pm. Tram: 7, 9, 25.

Warsaw Tortilla Factory ★ TEX-MEX A Tex-Mex joint that delivers the goods, elevating burritos, enchiladas, and fajitas to as much a Warsaw staple as *pierogi*. The atmosphere is casual, and the clientele is mostly young professionals and expats out for a fun night of beer, strong cocktails, and chain smoking. Live music on Wednesday and Saturday nights pulls in large crowds.

Wilcza 46. ℂ **022/621-86-22**. Lunch and dinner items 18 zł–79 zł ($7.20–$31.60/£4.05–£17.80). AE, DC, MC, V. Daily noon–10pm.

Inexpensive

Ciepłe Kluchy ★★ (Value) POLISH Not far from the Royal Castle, a lovely cobblestone lane leads you to this vaulted ceiling chamber. It's just the place for a dependably satisfying *pierogi* fix. A self-service setup, it has the usual parade of sweet and savory varieties. *Dudy*, made with a pork lung stuffing, stands out as a true foodie item. If you want to continue in discovery mode, try the sour vegetable juices. Lunchtime sets of soup, salad, and dumplings are only 14 zł ($5.60/£3.15). If you're not too hungry, get the kid's size for 6 zł ($2.40/£1.35).

Bednarska 28/30. ℂ **022/828-28-30**. www.pierogarnianabednarskiej.pl. *Pierogi* 12 zł ($4.80/£2.70). No credit cards. Daily 11am–9pm.

5 EXPLORING WARSAW

Warsaw is a large city, so plan your exploration to utilize trams or taxis to move between areas. A good place to start a walking tour of the city is the **Old Town** *(Stare Miasto)* and the adjacent **New Town** *(Nowe Miasto)*. Just as the Old Town isn't old (but reconstructed), the New Town isn't new but a settlement dating back to the 15th century. Aside from churches and museums, the New Town has scores of lovely cafes and restaurants. In the same itinerary, you can also bundle in part of the **Royal Route.** As you stroll along the swanky, cafe-lined streets of **Krakowskie Przedmieście** and **Nowy Świat,** bear in the mind that these streets once saw intense fighting during World War II and were rebuilt from rubble after the war. Much of Krakowskie Przedmieście is dominated by Warsaw University, and the streets are often filled with students. Set aside half a day for tracing the remnants of Jewish Warsaw. And if time permits, the streets of Praga are definitely worth half a day's time as well.

In addition to the major sights listed below, there are small museums to suit every interest, including one dedicated to Polish Romantic poet **Adam Mickiewicz** (Rynek Starego Miasta; (*C*) **022/831-76-91**; www.muzeum-literatury.pl); one to the Nobel Prize–winning scientist **Maria Skłodowksa-Curie** (Freta 16; (*C*) **022/831-08-95;** www.ptchem.lodz.pl/en/museum.html); and one to the horrific **Katyń** massacre in which an entire generation of Polish army officers—some 20,000 in all—were shot and killed by the Soviet Red Army in the Katyń woods (ul. Powsińska 13; (*C*) **022/842-66-11;** www.muzeumwp.pl).

TOP ATTRACTIONS
Old Town & Royal Route
The beautiful baroque and Renaissance-style burghers' houses of the Old Town would be remarkable in their own right for their period detailing, but what makes these buildings truly astounding is that they're only a few decades old. As one of the main centers of the 1944 Warsaw Uprising (see below), the Old Town bore the brunt of German reprisal attacks and the entire area, save for one building, was blown to bits at the end of 1944. After the war, to reclaim their heritage, the Polish people launched an enormous project to rebuild the Old Town, exactly as it was, brick by brick. Many of the original architectural sketches were destroyed in the war, so the town was rebuilt from paintings, photographs, drawings, and people's memories. The reconstruction was so authentic that UNESCO in 1980 listed the Old Town as a World Heritage Site. Today, the Old Town is given over mostly to touts and tourists, but still rewards a couple of hours of strolling.

Royal Castle (Zamek Królewski) ★★   The original residence of Polish kings and later the seat of the Polish parliament, the 14th-century castle was completely destroyed in the Warsaw uprising and its aftermath. What you see today is a painstaking reconstruction that was finished only in 1984. Two tours are offered: "Route I" and "Route II." The latter is more interesting, passing through the regal apartments of Poland's last monarch, King Stanisław August Poniatowski, and to the Canaletto room, where the famed cityscapes of Warsaw by the Italian painter Bernardo Bellotto hang. These paintings, and others not on display, were of extreme value in rebuilding the Old Town from scratch after the war. The tour ends in the lavish ballroom, the largest room in the castle. It is also a magical experience to attend the classical music concerts held in the castle's courtyard. The concerts usually start at 6pm. The repertoire is on the Castle's website and

History in Brief

Warsaw started life as a relatively small river town in the 14th century, but within a century it had become the capital city of the Duchy of Mazovia, ruling over small fiefdoms in central Poland. The city's fortunes steadily improved in the 16th century after the duchy was incorporated into the Polish crown and Poland formed a union with Lithuania. The union greatly expanded the amount of territory under Polish influence. In 1596, King Sigismund III moved the capital to Warsaw from Kraków. The city remembers his efforts with the King Sigismund's Column outside the Royal Castle. The Polish partitions at the end of the 18th century relegated Warsaw to the status of a provincial town for the next 125 years. Initially, the Prussians ruled over the city, but the Congress of Vienna, in 1815, placed tsarist Russia in firm control. Despite the occupation, Warsaw thrived in the 19th century as a western outpost of the Russian empire. Finally, in 1918, after Germany's defeat and Russia's collapse in World War I, Warsaw was reconstituted as the capital of newly independent Poland. The brief period of optimism ended when Nazis occupied the city in 1939 and held it for nearly the entire course of the war. The occupation was brutal. Warsaw lost almost its entire Jewish population (see "Exploring Jewish Warsaw"). The August 1944 Warsaw Uprising (see "Uprising Awareness") is another significant turning point that still haunts the city. By the end of the war, 85% of Warsaw lay in ruins, and two out of every three residents—nearly 900,000 people—had died or were missing. The postwar years were bleak ones. Reconstruction was in the hands of Socialist-inspired planners (see "Socialist Realism"). One notable exception is the Old Town. Warsaw residents overwhelmingly chose to reconstruct exactly what they had lost. It's a moving story of reclaiming identity from history, and the results are phenomenal, even earning it a place on the UNESCO list of World Cultural Heritage sites.

concert tickets can be bought at the Castle's information desk an hour before the start of the concert.

Pl. Zamkowy 4. (℡ **022/657-21-70** or **022/355-51-78** (to book guides). www.zamek-krolewski.pl. Admission 14 zł ($5.60/£3.15) Route I; 22 zł ($8.80/£4.95) Route II. Free Sun (May, June & Sept), Mon (June 30, July & Aug). Guided tour in English 85 zł ($34/£19.10). Tues–Sat 10am–6pm; Sun 11am–6pm. May, June & Sept Mon 11am–6pm. Jul–Aug Mon 11am–4pm. Last entry 1 hour before closing.

The Citadel (Cytadela) ★ A mid-19th-century brick fortress that was commissioned by Russian Tsar Nicholas I following the 1830 November Uprising. The sprawling fortress, along Vistula River, is located off the beaten track to the north of the New Town. Most of the compound is now used by the Polish military. The section opened to the public is the grounds of the Museum Pavilion-X, formerly the prison for Polish insurgents. Stenciled on the wall by the cell entrances are names of famous inmates, such as Józef Piłsudski, the man credited as responsible for Poland regaining independence in 1918. The exhibits include farewell letters to loved ones. There is hardly any information in English, but the brooding paintings relay the oppressive mood of the times. The Gate of Execution (*Brama Straceń*) was the site where Polish patriots were publicly executed.

Skazańców 25 (entrance from Wybrzeże Gdyńskie, corner of Czujna street or Brama Straceń). (℡ **022/ 839-12-68**. www.muzeumniepodleglosci.art.pl. Free admission. Wed–Sun 9am–4pm. Bus: 118. On foot:

Chopin 'R' Ours

Born to a French father and a Polish mother, Fryderyk Chopin (1810–49) is Poland's most famous composer. His birthplace in **Żelazowa Wola** (see below) is the pilgrimage point for fans worldwide. In November 1830, Chopin left to perform in Vienna, not knowing that he would never again return to Poland. Later that month, the November Uprising against the Russians broke out. However, Chopin left his heart in Warsaw, in the literal as well as the emotional sense. As was his wish, upon his death his heart was sealed in an urn and returned to Warsaw. The urn is in the **Holy Cross Church** (Krakowskie Przedmieście 3; ℭ **022/556-88-20;** www.swkrzyz.pl). Unfortunately, the **Chopin Museum** (Okólnik 1) is closed for refurbishment and will reopen in March 2010. The **Chopin Salon** (Salonik Chopina; Krakowskie Przedmieście 5; ℭ **022/320-02-75**), the living room used by the family when they were residing in Warsaw, is a modest consolation. It has a copy of the piano Chopin played on. The salon is poorly signposted: you'll find it through the second door on the left side of the courtyard. The room is on the second floor.

25 min from the New Town Square; go north on Zakroczymska St. and turn right at Krajewskiego St. to get to Wybrzeże Gdyńskie.

Tomb of the Unknown Soldier   Located in the Saxon Garden *(Ogród Saski),* the three arches of a colonnade are the remains of the Saxon Palace, destroyed in World War II. There are plans to eventually rebuild the palace. The monument honors the soldiers who perished in World War I, the subsequent Polish-Soviet Wars, and World War II. The main ceremonial changing of the guards is at noon on Sunday. At other times, there is an hourly small-scale guard change.

Pl. Piłsudskiego.

Łazienki Park ★★   The 76 hectares (188 acres) classicist-style "Royal Baths" along the Royal Route is where the city's residents go for a stroll in good weather. Established in the 17th century, the park got its moniker from a bathhouse located here. King Stanisław Poniatowski, the last king of Poland, acquired the property in 1764. No matter which entrance you take, the footpaths will lead you to the neoclassical **Palace on the Water** (Agrykoli 1; ℭ **022/506-01-01;** www.lazienki-krolewski.pl), a royal summer residence and now a museum where you can view the king's private chambers and opulent baroque-style ballrooms. Or it's great just to spend time in the park and coax "Basia" (Barbara; the local pet name for squirrels) into nipping walnuts from your hands. Don't miss the summertime piano recitals in the rose garden, where a larger-than-life sculpture of Chopin is the centerpiece. The 45-minute free recitals are held Sunday at noon and 4pm. It's a great place to slow down, but keep off the grass.

Al. Ujazdowskie. Free admission. Daily dawn to dusk. Palace on the Water: Tues–Sa 9am–4pm. 12 zł ($4.80/£2.70). Bus: 180.

Exploring the City Center

Fotoplastikon ★★   Fotoplastikon, or stereoscopy, is an invention of the mid-19th century and the precursor of the movie world. Through these lenses, you see 3D images of anything from the streets of pre-war Warsaw where the shops' signs are in Russian to

Socialist Realism

In the postwar years, Poland was cut off from Marshall Plan aid and the bulk of the reconstruction funds initially came from the Soviet Union. With 85% of the city in ruins, the Soviet-inspired planners could start from scratch. They knocked down pre-war tenement houses that had survived the war to make way for the wide avenues you see today, and then stacked the roads with drab Socialist-Realist style offices and apartment blocks. To be fair, some of these buildings aren't so awful. The unmissable **Palace of Culture and Science** is the granddaddy of them all. **Pl. Konstytucji,** the focal point of the MDM (Marszałkowska Housing Estate), has impressive Socialist reliefs of miners, farmhands, and the women's work force. The KFC at the northeast corner gives an ironic juxtaposition of Socialism vs. Capitalism. From the square, stretching along **Marszałkowska Street** all the way south to **pl. Unii Lubelskiej,** are some handsome postwar buildings. Make a detour to the **Ministry of Agriculture** (Wspólna 30) to witness how classic Greek colonnades were incorporated into the extravagance of workers' power. At the crossing of al. Jerozolimskie and Nowy Świat is the **former headquarters of the Communist Party**. After the fall of communism, it housed the Warsaw Stock Exchange from 1991 to 2000. Now, you'll find luxury boutiques occupying the ground level. For Communism tours, see "Guided Tours."

the postwar construction of the Palace of Culture. With more than 3,000 images in its archives, the show changes monthly. Since the Warsaw Uprising Museum took over the operation, the selection leans on visuals from the autumn 1944 insurgency. However, there are thematic exhibitions allowing you to time travel to the *fin de siècle* epoch of Paris, Beijing, and Moscow. A stop here won't take more than 20 minutes, so it's a great way to make a quick journey into the past.

Al. Jerozolimskie 51. ✆ **022/539-79-05.** www.1944.pl. Admission 1 zł (40¢/20p) adult. Wed–Mon 10am–6pm.

Gestapo Headquarters (Mauzoleum Walki i Męczeństwa) Currently the home of the Ministry of Education, from 1939 to 1945 this was the one place in town you absolutely didn't want to visit. A small museum in the building's lower reaches holds the cells and interrogation rooms that are nearly untouched from how they were at the end of the war. The displays paint a vivid picture of the torture and killing that went on here—and the lengths to which the Nazis went to break the Polish opposition.

Szucha 25. ✆ **022/629-49-19.** www.muzeum-niepodleglosci.art.pl. Free admission. Tues, Thurs, Sat 9am–4pm, Wed 9am–5pm, Fri 10am–5pm, Sun 10am–4pm.

Museum of Technology (Muzeum Techniki) ★ Don't come expecting to see cutting-edge technology and hands-on interactive exhibits. Instead, there's a sprawling collection of dated technology, from bicycles with wooden wheels to the first transistor differential analyzer built in 1959—it's really more of a History of Technology Museum, and therein lies the quirky fun of the place. Fans of retro designs will enjoy the home appliances and motorbike sections. Even the items not meant as exhibits, such as the dustbins, the lamps, and the cafe, are steeped in Socialist-era design. Adding to the throw-back-to-Communism experience is the posse of "guards" ever ready to bark *nie* *dotykać* (do not touch!) should your nose or digits hover too close to the artifacts. It's a time capsule of sorts that you shouldn't miss.

Pl. Defilad 1 (Palace of Culture). ℭ **022/656-67-47.** www.muzeum-techniki.waw.pl. Admission 8 zł ($3.20/£1.80) adult; 5 zł ($2/£1.10) children and seniors. Apr–Sept, Tues–Fri 9am–5pm; Sat–Sun 10am–5pm. Nov–March Tues–Fri 8:30am–4:30pm; Sat–Sun 10am–5pm.

National Museum (Muzeum Narodowe) ★ This 1930s oversized bunker houses a collection ranging from archaeology to early Christian art and 15th-century Flemish paintings. The star attraction from the Polish masters is the Jan Matejko collection. Look for *Stańczyk* (1862), depicting a 16th-century court jester mulling over the grave content of a letter while behind him the royal household partied on in oblivion. And don't miss *The Battle of Grünwald* (1878), another of Matejko's masterpieces chronicling the Teutonic knights' downfall in 1410. The postwar section covers painting and sculptures glorifying the workers' utopia. Well worth a stopover even if you have only an hour to spare.

Al. Jerozolimskie 3. ℭ **022/621-10-31.** www.mnw.art.pl. Admission 17 zł ($6.80/£3.80) temporary & permanent exhibitions; 12 zł ($4.80/£2.70) permanent exhibition only; free entry to permanent exhibition Sat. Tues–Fri 10am–4pm; Sat–Sun 10am–6pm.

Palace of Culture and Science (Palac Kultury i Nauki) ★ Warsaw's landmark tower is a building many residents would like to see knocked down. The 1950s Socialist-Realist wedding cake was commissioned by Josef Stalin as "a gift from the Soviet people." The symbolic intention was clear from the start: Stalin was marking his turf and Poland was part of the Eastern bloc. After the fall of Communism, there were heated talks of pulling it down. However, public attitudes toward the "palace" have softened somewhat. You can ride to the top—30 stories—for a fine view over the city (but let's be honest here—30 stories is not really that dramatic). The building continues in its role as a cultural and trade venue. One way of seeing some of the grand halls, Socialist-Realist reliefs, and wacky chandeliers is to buy a ticket to the trade fairs (from books to pet food) being held during your visit or go to one of the many museums housed within. Better still, catch a concert at the Sala Kongresowa. (Also see "Specialty Tours.")

Pl Defilad. ℭ **022/656-76-00.** www.pkin.pl. Daily 9am–8pm. Admission to viewing terrace 20 zł ($8/£4.50).

Pawiak Prison ★ Another frightening reminder of the horrific times of World War II. Something like 100,000 prisoners passed through the gates here during the years of the Nazi occupation, when the prison was run by the Gestapo. Among the prisoners were political activists, members of the clergy, university professors, or simply anyone suspected of opposing the Germans. Very few of the people imprisoned here got out alive. Most were sent to extermination camps, while around 40,000 people were actually executed on the grounds.

Sign of Resistance

You'll soon notice the symbol of a "P" fused to a "W" on monuments and buildings in Warsaw and all over Poland. "PW" stands for "Polska Walczy" (Poland Fights) and represented the Polish Resistance Army during World War II. It also stands for "Powstanie Warszawskie," Warsaw Uprising (see below).

The Warsaw Uprising

On August 1, 1944, at precisely 5pm, the commander of the Polish insurgent Home Army, loyal to Poland's government-in-exile based in London, called for a general uprising throughout Nazi-occupied Warsaw. The Nazis were in retreat on all sides, having suffered reversals on the Western fronts, in France and Italy, and in the East, at the hands of the Soviet Red Army. By the end of July that year, the Red Army had moved to within the city limits of Warsaw and was camped on the eastern bank of the Vistula in the district of Praga. With the combined forces of the Home Army and the Red Army, it seemed the right moment to drive the Germans out and liberate Warsaw. Alas, it was not to be. The first few happy days of the uprising saw the Polish insurgents capture pockets of the city, including the Old Town and adjacent districts. But the Nazis resisted fiercely, and the Red Army, with its own agenda, never stepped in to help. The resistance lasted weeks before Polish commanders were forced to capitulate in the face of rapidly escalating civilian casualties. The uprising so infuriated Hitler that he ordered the complete annihilation of the city. In the weeks following the uprising, Warsaw's buildings were listed in terms of their cultural significance and dynamited one by one. Some 85% of the city was eventually destroyed. The **Monument to the Warsaw Uprising** (pl. Krasińskich), in the New Town, commemorates the thousands of residents who died in the fighting.

Dzielna 24/26. ℂ **022/831-92-89.** www.muzeum-niepodleglosci.art.pl. Free admission. Wed 9am–5pm; Thurs & Sat 9am–4pm; Fri 10am–5pm; Sun 10am–4pm.

Powązki Cemetery ★★   Established in 1790, it is one of the oldest cemeteries in Warsaw. The 43-hectare (106-acre) ground is filled with ornate and grand tombs, topped with elaborate sculptures from the 18th and 19th centuries. A mausoleum holds the ashes of those who perished in concentration camps and the "Avenue of Merit" has the tombs of famous citizens. Among those buried here are Nobel Prize winner Władysław Reymont and the second President of the Republic of Poland, Stanisław Wojciechowski. At all times of the year the cemetery is well-kept, but on All Saints' Day (November 1), the traditional day for Poles to visit cemeteries, the compound is ablaze with candlelight and filled with visitors until way past midnight. The Jewish Cemetery (see below) is within walking distance from the Powązki Cemetery and can be covered in one visit.

Powązkowska 14. Free admission. Dawn to dusk. Bus: 180.

Warsaw Uprising Museum (Muzeum Powstania Warszawskiego) ★★   Within the walls of this museum lies the answer to why Warsaw is nowhere as pretty as Kraków. And, some say, to understand Poland's political stance on the world stage, a visit here is a must. The majestic red-brick building is a spruced-up former tramway power station. Along the self-guided path, historical posters, flyers, photos, newsreels, radio broadcasts, and replicas give a blow-by-blow account of the social-political events prior to, during, and after the autumn 1944 uprising against the Nazis. The replicas include an impressive life-sized B-24 plane and the underground sewage tunnels used by the insurgents. The occupiers hit back hard, taking a toll on lives and the city's architectural heritage. All the details can be information overload for newcomers to Polish history. If so, rest your feet in the museum's cafe decked out to resemble cafes from the inter-war period, right down to the cakes and music. This award-winning museum doubles as a memorial. In an adjacent park, a wall is inscribed with the names of over 6,000 casualties. There is a chapel for those in need of quiet contemplation. With advanced booking, guides in almost every European language are available. However, even without knowing a word of Polish, you can manage on your own. Free babysitting is available and there is also a children's museum area. This museum is one of the most interactive and visitor-friendly in Poland.

Grzybowska 79. (℃) 022/539-79-05. www.1944.pl. Admission 4 zł ($1.60/90p) adult; 2 zł (80¢/45p) children and seniors, free Sunday. Mon, Wed, Fri 8am–8pm; Thurs 8am–6pm; Sat, Sun 10am–6pm. Bus: 100.

Exploring Jewish Warsaw

Before World War II, the Jewish community in Warsaw stood at about 350,000. That was almost one-third of the city's population and the second-largest Jewish community outside of New York. Toward the end of 1940, the Nazis herded the city's entire Jewish population, as well as around 100,000 Jews from elsewhere in Poland, into a small ghetto area west of the Old Town. Walls went up and an elaborate system of gates and staircases was built to allow Jews to move within the ghetto, but no one was permitted to enter or leave. The first deportations and mass killings began at the end of 1941. In the 1943 Ghetto Uprising (not to be confused with the 1944 Warsaw Uprising), the Jews heroically rose up against their oppressors. The uprising was quickly put down and what remained of the ghetto was liquidated.

In postwar reconstruction, the area was planted with cheap housing blocks. The **Monument to the Ghetto Heroes (Pomnik Bohaterów Getta)** (Al. Zamenhofa) is amid these Communist-era buildings. You can still see some examples of the derelict 19th-century tenement houses riddled with bullets on **Próżna Street ★★**. At the courtyard of **no. 55 Sienna Street,** you'll find fragments of a ghetto wall and a simple plaque. Long narrow metal plaques have been installed on pavements to mark the places where some of the ghetto walls stood. You'll find these plaques at the crossing of Żelazna and Chłodna streets and also at the crossing of Żelazna Street and Solidarności Avenue.

Today, hardly any of the Jewish culture remains. But in recent years there has been a growing interest in the lost heritage. The **Jewish Theater** (see "Venues") maintains a year-round repertoire of Jewish cultural plays and musical performances. The **Museum of the History of Polish Jews** (www.jewishmuseum.org.pl) is scheduled to open in 2010.

Most of the city's tourist agencies have tours of Jewish Warsaw (see "Guided Tours"). For a self-guided tour, pick up the *Jewish Warsaw* walking itinerary designed by the Warsaw Tourist Office.

Jewish Historical Institute and Museum (Żydowski Instytut Historyczny) ★

A must for anyone tracing the history of Jews in Poland. Brace yourself for the emotional impact from the photos and news reels chronicling the dire conditions of life within the ghetto walls. On the second level of the museum there is a small segment of religious and secular Jewish art, some dating to the late 19th century. Between the levels, you'll find the mock-up of a synagogue. The institute's library has a depository of Jewish-related documents, books, and journals. It's a game of hide-and-seek to locate this museum: It's hidden from view by a glass-fronted modern office tower. This modern tower was once the site of the Great Synagogue, the largest temple in Warsaw, which was blown up in the aftermath of the May 1943 Ghetto Uprising.

Tłomackie 3/5. (℃) 022/827-92-21. www.jewishinstitute.org.pl. Admission 10 zł ($4/£2.25) adult, 5 zł ($1.60/£1.10) children and seniors. Guided tours 130 zł ($52). Mon–Wed, Fri 9am–4pm; Thurs 11am–6pm.

The Pianist's Warsaw

Roman Polański's Oscar-winning film *The Pianist* (2002) recounts life in Warsaw during World War II through the eyes of Władysław Szpilman, an accomplished pianist and composer and one of the Warsaw ghetto's best-known survivors. Adrien Brody starred as the protagonist in the production that garnered three Oscars and numerous international awards. Based on Szpilman's autobiography, the film shows the horrific conditions of life within the perimeters of the ghetto, one of the largest of the Jewish ghettos in Poland during the war. The concrete-bunker style **Umschlagplatz Monument** (Stawki 10, near the corner with Dzika Street) marks the place where the Jews boarded cattle wagons to the Treblinka extermination camp (see below). Although Szpilman narrowly escaped deportation to Treblinka here, this scene for the movie was filmed in a military compound in the outskirts of the city. To capture the mood of war-torn Warsaw, part of the filming took place in Praga (see below), with its scores of dilapidated pre-war buildings. After the war, Szpilman returned to his job at the Polish Radio. He passed away in July 2000, and is buried in the **Powązki Cemetery** (see above).

Jewish Cemetery (Cmentarz Żydowski) ★★ Established in 1806, it holds more than 150,000 tombs on 83 acres, making it one of the largest Jewish cemeteries in Europe. Ludwik Zamenhof, the creator of the Esperanto language, was among those buried here. Although the site was relatively unscathed during the war, many of the headstones are now barely legible or crumbling and the grounds are overgrown. It is a poignant "memorial" and not to be missed.

Okopowa 49/51. www.beisolam.jewish.org.pl. Admission 8 zł ($3.20/£1.80). Mon–Thurs 10am–5pm, Fri 9am–1pm, Sat 9am–4pm. Bus: 180.

Nożyk Synagogue (Synagog Nożyków) The only synagogue in Warsaw to survive World War II. Named after its founders, it opened its doors to worshipers in 1902. The facade is in neo-Romanesque style, and the interior can hold up to 600 people. It is closed to tourists during prayers and special events. Access to the synagogue is not via the front door, but from the far end. The ticket includes a guide service, but you must call in advance to book. There are no guides on Sundays.

Twarda 6. ℂ 022/620-43-24 ext 121. www.warszawa.jewish.org.pl. Admission 6 zł ($2.40/£1.35). Mon–Thurs 10am–5pm, Fri 9am–2pm, Sun 9am–4pm.

Exploring Praga

Praga, on the right bank of the river, is often regarded as Warsaw's poor cousin and the haunt of criminals. The district wasn't damaged much during World War II, but fell into disrepair in the postwar years. The streets, lined with derelict, plaster-bared, pre-war tenement blocks, served as the set for Roman Polański's *The Pianist*. Recently, however, Praga has been enjoying a slow rejuvenation as artists and businesses move in, searching for cheaper real estate. Though it is no longer strictly off-limits, care should still be taken when visiting, especially when flashing cameras or camcorders. Most explorations of the area are centered along Targowa (see "Shopping") and Ząbkowska streets. It's advisable not to wander about alone after dark. At all times, it's best to avoid Brzeska Street,

WARSAW

5

EXPLORING WARSAW

reputed as the most dangerous street in Praga. With the increasing interest in this district, tourist agencies are offering Praga tours (see "Organized Tours").

Koneser Vodka Factory (Wytwórnia Wódek Koneser) ★   Listed on the Polish Architectural Heritage list (a protected status that prohibits tearing down a building), this red-brick complex was built in 1895 specifically to supply 1 liter of vodka per day to the 120,000 Russian soldiers based at this outpost. Aside from its own labels, the plant also had contracts with brands like Finlandia. Production halted in 2007 and the facility is still grappling for a new identity. It leases space to shops, art galleries (see "Shopping"), theaters, and a restaurant. You're free to kick about the forlorn grounds and the storage area now used as exhibition halls. To access the bottling section, book a day in advance for a weekday tour that includes vodka sampling and snacks of cold cuts and bread.

Ząbkowska 27/31. ✆ **022/619-90-21** ext. 202. monopol@data.pl for guided tour in English. Free admission. Guided tour 50 zł ($20/£11.25). Daily 8am–7pm.

Orthodox Church of St. Mary Magdalene (Cerkiew Św. Marii Magdaleny)
Built in the 1860s to serve Russians arriving from St. Petersburg at the nearby Wileńska train station, the golden chapel retains its original Byzantine portraits. The impressive building sports five onion domes and is in Russo-Byzantine style. It is one of the two Orthodox churches that survived demolition in the 1920s. Across the street is the Soviet War Memorial commemorating the soldiers who "liberated" Warsaw in 1945. It is often smothered in graffiti, reflecting what the city thinks of it.

Al. Solidarności 52. ✆ **022/619-84-67.** Free admission. Tues–Fri 11am–4pm. Sun noon–4pm. Tram: 4. Bus: 100.

Warsaw Zoo (Kids)   Dating from 1928, the 40-hectare compound is home to more than 280 species of animals from all corners of the globe. The most famous inhabitants are the bears, who look jaded from years of being the zoo's live advertisement in a concrete enclosure by the busy Solidarności Road. If you're not going to northeastern Poland, this is the place to see the European bison.

Ratuszowa 1/3. ✆ **022/619-40-41.** Admission 14 zł ($5.60/£3.15) adult, 8 zł ($3.20/£1.80) children and seniors, children 3 and under free. Daily 9am–7pm. Tram no. 4, 13. Bus: 100.

Outdoor Activities

GOLF   First Warsaw Golf & Country Club (Rajszew 70, Jabłonna; ✆ **022/782-45-55;** www.warsawgolf.pl), located 29km (17 miles) from the city, is an 18-hole facility, complete with a driving range, equipment rental, and English-speaking staff. The greens fees are 225 zł ($90/£51) on weekdays and 375 zł ($150/£84) on weekends. Rates are reduced after 3pm. Taxis from the city cost about 150 zł ($60/£34).

PLAYGROUNDS   Warsaw has woefully few attractions targeted at kids, but the saving grace is there's always a playground at hand. In and around the Old Town, the swings and slides are in the **Saxon Garden** (Ogród Saski, near the Tomb of the Unknown Soldier) and in **Krasińkich Garden** (near the Monument to the Warsaw Uprising). Along the Royal Route, the play area in **Ujazdowski Park** (al. Ujazdowskie) is often crowded. There's also a sandy play corner in the southern section of **Łazienki Park.** In the Żoliborz district in the north, **Park S. Żeromskiego** (pl. Wilsona) has a large playground, and the nearby **Kalimba i Kofifi** cafe and shop (see "Shopping") is very family-friendly. One of the largest rumble and tumble terrains is the **Jordanowski Garden** (corner of al. Niepodległości and Odyńca street) in the Mokotów district; the nearest subway station is Racławicka.

GUIDED TOURS   You can hire guides fluent in almost any language from the tourist information offices. The going rate is about 450 zł ($180/£101) for 4 hours, with every subsequent hour an additional 95 zł ($38/£21). It's best to call a day ahead to book.

Most tourist agencies have city tours and day excursions to Żelazowa Wola, Kraków, Auschwitz, the Wieliczka Salt Mines, Gdańsk, and Malbork. **Mazurkas Travel** (Wojska Polskiego 27; ✆ **0668/121-455;** www.mazurkas.com.pl) and the **LRCompany** (140 Marszałkowska St; ✆ **22/826-71-00;** www.lrc.com.pl) offer several different daily city tours and will pick up guests from most hotels. They cover the essentials like the Old Town, the Royal Route, Jewish points of interest, and the Łazienki Park in about 3 hours. Both have comparable rates: 140 zł ($56/£31.50) for adults, 70 zł ($28/£15.80) for children 4 to 12. *Note:* The pickups from hotel to hotel can add an extra hour. **Warsaw Adventure** ★ (✆ **0664/702-755;** www.warsawtraveltours.com) is a smaller operation and will deliver you directly to the starting point at the Royal Castle from your hotel. It has a similar 3^1/$_2$-hour city highlights tour, but also ventures into Praga for 120 zł ($48/£27) per person. If you want to be chauffeured around in a BMW 7 Series, Mercedes S-Series, or Mercedes Viano for a 3-hour city tour, contact **Limocars Executive Services** (see "Fast Facts").

SPECIALTY TOURS   For a 1^1/$_2$-hour fact-filled tour of the Palace of Culture's inner sanctums, contact **Trakt** (Kredytowa 6; ✆ **022/827-80-68;** www.trakt.com.pl). No two tours are the same, since some chambers are closed when there are special events. The price for the English narration is steep: 350 zł ($180/£79) for a group of 10, and that excludes the ticket to the viewing terrace. If you just want to look but not understand the narrative, join the Polish tour for 18 zł ($7.20/£4) per person. The schedule changes monthly.

One of the most interesting ways to connect the Warsaw you see today with the Warsaw that was lost in World War II is to play **Enigma Warsaw** ★★, a 3- to 4-hour outdoor quiz-cracking game designed by **StayPoland** (Miła 2; ✆ **022/351-22-22;** www.enigmawarsaw.com). Supplied with a map of Warsaw in 1939, and a set of clues, you hunt for streets and buildings that no longer exist. Be sure to book in advance for this unusual outing.

The **Misguides** (✆ **0721/721-166;** www.misguides.pl) ferry you around in a Nysa, a retro van designed in Poland in the '60s. The 3-hour tours are based on topics such as Communist Warsaw, Old Praga, Postwar Industrial Warsaw, and Crime in the Interwar Years. Expect liberal anecdotes from the chirpy, young band of "misguides," supplemented by old propaganda films and Communist paraphernalia. It's 144 zł ($58/£32) per person and the minimum group size is 2. Book a day ahead.

Warsaw Adventure (see above) has guided tours of the Koneser Vodka Factory in Praga. The tour starts at 1pm on Tuesday, Thursday, and Saturday, and lasts about 2^1/$_2$ hours. The 130 zł ($52/£29) ticket includes a traditional Polish meal, vodka-tasting session, and T-shirt.

The **Night Guides** ★ (✆ **0501/226-939;** www.night-guides.com) specialize in dusk-to-dawn pub-and-club crawls, tailored to your personal preferences. They even have a special program for those with limited mobility. For bachelor parties and boys' nights out, get your party plans from the **Warsaw Pissup Tours** (✆ **0693/778-802;** www.pissup.com/warsaw). They also organize adrenaline-packed daytime activities like firing off Kalashnikov rifles and spins in tanks on military compound.

While in the vicinity of the Wilanów Palace, pop in to the **Poster Museum (Muzeum Plakatu)** (Potockiego 10/16; ☎ 022/842-48-48; www.postermuseum.pl), which has an impressive collection of posters from around the globe. It's open on Monday noon to 4pm, Tuesday to Friday 10am to 4pm, and weekends 10am to 6pm.

Wilanów Palace   Poles are rightfully proud of this baroque-era palace built to honor King Jan Sobieski (although it's not as grand as some other sites in the country). The 45-hectare (111-acre) property sports a palace with no fewer than 60 rooms, most stuffed with royal memorabilia and portraits of Polish monarchs and heavyweights. Some rooms, like the Etruscan Room, display oddities such as vases dating from the 4th century B.C. The palace can be seen only with a guided tour. Take the hourly Polish tour if you're not particularly interested in all the details of all the portraits; otherwise book an English tour (90 zł/$36/£20.25) in advance by calling the number below, or once there try to piggyback on any English-speaking group you happen to see. It's best to visit in good weather so that you can also explore the park, which comprises a neo-Renaissance rose garden, a split-level baroque garden, an English landscaped park, a Chinese-English park, and a lake. *Note:* In summer, the Sunday free tickets to the palace are all snapped up as early as 1pm.

Potockiego 10/16. ☎ **022/842-25-09** (to book guides). www.wilanow-palac.art.pl. Admission to palace 16 zł ($6.40/£3.60), free Sun. Admission to the park 5 zł ($2/£1.10); free Thurs. Mid-may to mid-Sept, Mon, Wed, Sat 9:30am–6:30pm; Tues, Thurs–Fri 9:30am–4:30pm; Sun 10:30am–6:30pm. Mid-Sept to mid-May, Mon, Wed–Sat 9:30am–4:30pm; Sun 10:30am–4:30pm. Last entry to palace 1¹/₂ hours before closing. Park daily 9am–dusk. Bus: 116, 180.

Day Trips from Warsaw

Treblinka ★★   From July 1942 to August 1943, an estimated 850,000 people, mainly those of Jewish descent, perished in the Treblinka II extermination camp and the Treblinka I labor camp. It's the second largest of such Nazi camps after Auschwitz. Unlike Auschwitz, Treblinka is often described as "not much to see" since much of it was razed by the Nazis. The whole site now operates under the name of the **Museum of Fighting and Martyrdom.** By the information office, you'll find the visitors' books filled with touching messages in all languages including English, Yiddish, and Spanish. The memorial standing in Treblinka II consists of hauntingly silent islets of jagged stones and boulders, a symbolic cremation pit, and a stretch of symbolic railway track. Surrounded by pinewoods and in the middle of nowhere, the impact is surreal and powerfully poignant. Another 10-minute walk takes you to Treblinka I and another execution site.

Strictly speaking, Treblinka is in Northeastern Poland. From Warsaw, by car it should take about 2 hours, but factor in another hour for ongoing road work. There are regular trains from Warsaw to Małkinia, taking about 90 minutes. It's 8km (5 miles) to Treblinka from the Małkinia station. Your options are a 1¹/₂-hour walk or the taxi. A round trip by taxi is from 100 zł to 150 zł ($40–$60/£22.50–£33.75), depending on how much time the driver waits for you at Treblinka. Most visitors spend 1 to 2 hours here.

☎ **025/781-16-58.** Daily sunrise to sunset.

Żelazowa Wola   A petite manor house and park whose claim to fame is being Chopin's birthplace, thus a key pilgrimage point for Chopin fans. It is one of three places in Poland (the other two are in Kraków) listed in Patricia Schultz's *1,000 Places to See Before You Die.* That is a debatable accolade. Looted in World War II, the interior has no original fixtures. The family portraits are reproductions of the ones on display at the Chopin Salon in Warsaw. The Chopin memorabilia is sparse, and the 7-hectare park is nothing sensational. Having said all that, the property truly sparkles during the Sunday piano recitals when you can bask in the sunshine while listening to renditions of Chopin's *polonaise* and *mazurkas* by international pianists.

Żelazowa Wola is 50km (30 miles) west of Warsaw. The travel time is about 1 hour. There are regular buses and guided tours from Warsaw. From May to September, the **Chopin Academy** (Okólnik 2; ✆ 022/826-81-80; hwrzesiak@nifc.pl) organizes mini-buses departing on Saturdays at 10:30am and Sundays at 1:30pm. Return tickets are 26 zł ($10.40/£5.85). Seats are limited, so book early.

Żelazowa Wola. ✆ 046/863-33-00. Concerts May–Sept, Sun noon and 3pm. Admission to museum and park 12 zł ($4.80/£2.70), 6 zł ($2.40/£1.35) children and seniors; park only 4 zł ($1.60/90p) adult, 2 zł (80¢/45p) children and seniors, 4 zł ($1.60/90p) dog. Concert 30 zł ($12/£6.75) indoors, free outdoors.

---

6 SHOPPING

Warsaw is not an obvious shopping haven, but it has a blend of familiar malls, quirky old-style bazaars, and plenty of creative local crafts to sate your shopping appetite. Those looking for global heavyweights like Burberry, Escada, and Gant will find them in the trendy enclave of **Plac Trzech Krzyży** and the malls around the city. Along nearby **Mokotowska Street,** there are interesting small boutiques. In the past, Nowy Świat and Chmielna streets were the places for luxury goods; today there are several antiques shops here, but cafes and restaurants have taken up most of the floor space.

Most shops in the city are open Monday through Friday 11am to 7pm, and Saturday 10am to 2pm. Malls are open Monday through Saturday 10am to 10pm, and Sunday 10am to 8pm.

Shopping Malls

The hippest mall in town is the new **Złote Tarasy** (Złota 59; ✆ 022/222-22-00; www.zlotetarasy.pl). It's also well stocked with restaurants—including a branch of the Hard Rock Café—and cafes. Even if you're not after retail therapy, pop in to see the perspective of the city from beneath the wavy, glass domes. **Arkadia** (Jana Pawła II; ✆ 022/331-34-00; www.arkadia.com.pl) and **Galeria Mokotów** (Wołoska 12; ✆ 022/541-30-00; www.galeriamokotow.com.pl) are two larger malls outside the city center.

Outdoor & Street Markets

For time traveling to the past, hop across the eastern bank to the legendary 103-year-old **Russian Bazaar *(Bazar Różyckiego)*** (Ząbkowska Street) in Praga. During the Communist days, the rows of wooden stalls were the prime source for foreign goods such as Coca-Cola, jeans, and radios. It is a shadow of its former self, but still musters up some life on Saturdays. Don't confuse this bazaar with the **Russian Market (Dziesięciolecia Stadium)**—the outdoor market infamous for counterfeit Tommy Hilfiger, pirated DVDs, and pick-pockets—which has closed shop to be transformed into a sports stadium for Euro 2012 football championship. The **central train station *(Dworzec Centralny)*** is also earmarked for a Euro 2012 facelift. The burrow of shops occupying the tunnels of the station has everything from donuts to dowdy lingerie.

Hala Mirowska ★★ One of the oldest food markets in the center of Warsaw; though it is not quite as spectacular as Barcelona's Boqueteira, it buzzes with life and clues you in on the feeding habits of typical Poles. Within the ochre brick walls, the warren of

stalls sells everything from beetroot and blood sausages to pig's head. Walk around to the
outside wall and you'll find traders proffering honey, pickled mushrooms, and German
chocolates from the backs of their beat-up cars. Pl. Mirowski 1 (main entrance from Al. Jana
Pawła II). No phone. Tram: 16, 17, 19.

Koło Bazaar (Bazar Na Kole) ★★ An open-air antiques bazaar that's a history
museum of sorts: You can rummage through Socialist-era tableware, obsolete surgical
equipment, fur coats, period furniture, and somewhat morbid World War II paraphernalia. Few traders here speak English. Come with a local and you might pick up a 6-piece
set of silver cutlery for a reasonable 100 zł ($40/£22.50). On your own, traders will flog
made-yesterday-in-China Ming vases for an indecent 250 zł ($100/£56). Saturday early
mornings are best for bargains. By afternoon, some goods have changed hands several
times among the traders and each such transaction sees a price mark-up. Sunday at
around 1pm is also good for bargains, when the traders are keen to offload their stock.
It opens on weekends from dawn to early afternoon. Obozowa 99. No phone. Tram: 13.

The Goods A to Z
Antiques & Art
Available at tourist information points, the "What's On in Warsaw Galleries" and "Warsaw Art" pamphlets list the current exhibitions at the galleries around town. To take art
objects (including jewelry) out of the country, you need legal paperwork for items that
are older than 55 years or produced by an artist that is no longer living.

Desa Unicum The biggest auction house and gallery in Poland, with several branches
including one in the Old Town Square. The English-speaking staff can advise you on the
art and antique market scene, but they do not assist with the legal paperwork required
for exports. Marszałkowska 34/50. ✆ 022/584-95-25. www.desa.pl.

Galeria Sztuki Katarzyny Napiórkowskiej A noted gallery for Polish contemporary art. It has several outlets including one in the Old Town. Świętokrzyska 32. ✆ 022/652-
19-39. www.napiorkowska.pl.

Galeria Farbiarnia Another well-regarded gallery for contemporary art showcasing
Polish and international works. Piękna 28/34. ✆ 022/621-72-35. www.galeriafarbiarnia.pl.

Galeria Autorska Andrzeja Mleczki The store of Polish caricaturist Andrzej
Mleczko is stocked with socio-political humor cartoons in the form of reprints, calen-
dars, mugs, postcards, and T-shirts. Originals sketches can be purchased, too.
Marszałkowska 140. ✆ 022/829-57-60. www.mleczko.pl.

Galeria Plakatu ★ An impressive collection of Polish placards, the most eye-catching of which are the Communist-era posters in the "political and propaganda" section.
Rynek Starego Miasta 23. ✆ 022/831-93-06. www.poster.com.pl.

Luksfera Located in the compound of the Koneser Vodka Factory, this spot showcases
a modern interplay of photography and painting. Ząbkowska 27/31. ✆ 022/619-91-63. www.
luksfera.pl.

Ostoya Not much English is spoken in this art and antique store, but the friendly staff
will assist you with the export paperwork. They also hold regular auctions. Freta 25.
✆ 022/635-55-78. www.aukcjeostoya.pl.

Yours Gallery ★ Enthralling documentary snapshots by Polish photographers. Krakowskie Przedmieście 33. ✆ 022/890-95-00. www.yoursgallery.pl.

Books & CDs

American Bookstore   This English-language chain, with a central location as well as outlets in the malls, has a range of Polish authors in translation and books on the Holocaust, World War II, the Warsaw Uprising, and other Poland-centric topics. Nowy Świat 61. ℂ 022/827-48-52. www.americanbookstore.pl.

Empik   This major national chain is good for maps, coffee table books of Poland, and international newspapers. Nowy Świat 15/17. ℂ 022/627-06-50. www.empik.com.

Sawart   A small store near the Grand Theater with plenty to offer for classical music lovers, including music scores published by Edition Peters and Chopin CD recordings by labels like Decca and Deutsche Grammophon. Moliera 8. ℂ 022/826-23-78. www.sawart. com.pl.

Ceramics, Glass & Pottery

Banasik   A sizeable two-story store stacked with Polish and European tableware. Representing the host nation are names like Bolesławic, Włocławek, and Krosno. If needed, the store will bubble wrap items for you. Piękna 28/34. ℂ 022/621-83-37. www.dhbanasik.pl.

Bolesławiec Company Store   A warehouse-style store with an extensive choice of Bolesławiec stoneware, from mugs to casserole dishes, in prints ranging from the classic blue-and-white peacock to special edition stars-and-stripes. Prosta 2/14. ℂ 022/624-84-08. www.ceramicboleslawiec.com.pl.

Krosno   Glass, dining sets, and vases by Krosno, a renowned Polish brand. Al. Jana Pawła II 82 (Arkadia Mall). ℂ 022/331-25-55.

Crafts, Linens & Souvenirs

Abonda Gallery ★   Enjoy the rustic ambience as you peruse the embroidered linen, pottery, lamps, and jewelry on display here, all hand made by Polish craftsmen based on traditional design. Śniadeckich 12/16. ℂ 022/628-89-95. www.abonda.com.pl.

Bracia Łopieńscy ★   A humble workshop with an impressive history behind it. Since 1862, the Łopieński family has produced a number of the bronze monuments in Poland. You may not need a monument, but take a look at the pitchers, sugar bowls, lamps, and small sculptures hand made from four generations of expertise. Poznańska 24. ℂ 022/629-20-45. www.b.lopienscy.webpark.pl.

Cepelia   Goods in this nationwide chain are slightly overpriced, but handy for last-minute souvenir shopping since most of the traditional Polish crafts—from ceramics to sculptures, jewelry to paintings—are under one roof. Marszałkowska 99/101. ℂ 022/628-77-57. www.cepelia.pl.

Galeria Lnu   A pokey shop offering table cloths, napkins, bedding, and tunics and other items, all made from linen. There are also bundles of fabric to choose from should you opt for custom-made tablecloths. Senatorska 20. ℂ 022/827-54-18. www.galerialnu.pl.

Khaja Brush Workshop ★   Such shops are a rarity these days. It's brushes galore, from common hairbrushes and shaving brushes to unusual face brushes, mostly hand-made from natural bristles. The owner learned the craft from his brush maker grandfather. Poznańska 26. ℂ 022/621-76-56. www.kjhaja.g03.pl.

Magazyn Praga ★   A creative and quirky depository of fashion, home accessories and furniture, electronics and paintings by young Polish talents in a warehouse located in the old Koneser Vodka Factory. Ząbkowska 27/31. ℂ 022/670-11-85. www.magazynpraga.pl.

Manufaktura Królewska ★ A unique tapestry workshop inside a converted greenhouse at Łazienki Park (next to the Belvedere Restaurant). The tapestries, tablecloths, and scarves are hand-woven with tradition wooden looms and using linen, silk, or woolen threads. Agrykoli 1. ✆ **0519/795-493.**

Fashion

Andrzej Jedynak If fur coats and hats are your thing, you'll find a wide selection of made-in-Poland designs here. Al. Jerozolimskie 23. ✆ **022/628-62-56.** www.andrzejjedynak.pl.

Maciej Zień A young Polish talent who dresses the A-list of Polish celebrities. Get sized up for bespoke layers or pick from the ready-to-wear for men and women. The boutique is located in a mall on the right bank of the river. Ostrobramska 75C. ✆ **022/611-73-37.** www.zien.pl.

Food & Drinks

Chopin Luxury Alcohol bottles are stacked from floor to ceiling here. Among the bottles are more than 20 types of vodka, mostly made from potato or rye. Goldwasser, vodka with gold flakes, is also available. Złota 59 (Złote Tarasy). ✆ **022/222-01-03.**

Krakowski Kredens Stacked full with Polish larder staples such as jams and pickles in pretty jars. The most portable item is the *krówki* (similar to fudge) in a tin ox. Nowy Świat 22.✆ no phone.

Wedel Although it is now part of the Cadbury Schweppes group, Wedel (founded in 1851) is still very much a Polish icon. The circular *Torcik* (chocolate-coated wafer) is an instantly recognizable Polish treat. Szpitalna 8. ✆ **022/827-29-16.** www.wedel.pl.

Jewelry

W. Kruk ★ Poland's best-known family-run jeweler was founded in 1840. The fourth-generation owners take pride in using local material, designers, and craftsmen. You'll find amber, but look out for the *krzemień pasiasty* series, which is made from banded flint found only in the Sandomierz area of southern Poland. Pl Konstytucji 6. ✆ **022/628-75-34.** http://wkruk.pl.

Leather

Wittchen A Polish high-end brand known for its handbags, it also produces shoes, jackets, gloves, belts, and other leathery accessories. You can also find them in most malls. Marszałkowska 72. ✆ **022/628-11-36.** www.wittchen.pl.

Tableware

Platerland The shop carries silver and silver-plated tableware and cutlery made by Hefra, a Polish brand known for its ornate, period designs. You'll find chafing dishes, water pitchers, trays, candelabras, and all the trimmings for a formal dining table. Jana Pawła II 35. ✆ **022/624-26-23.** www.platerland.pl.

Szlif A small shop carrying cutlery and knives produced by Grelach, a renowned Polish brand. Książęca 6. ✆ **022/621-75-00.**

Toys

Kalimba i Kofifi A cafe-cum-shop noted for its unique toys designed by the owner. Mierosławskiego 19. ✆ **022/839-75-60.** www.kalimba.pl.

7 AFTER DARK

THE PERFORMING ARTS

The city's opera and classical music offerings are some of the best in the country, and the availability of relatively cheap tickets means the performances are accessible to just about anyone. Aside from the box office, you can also buy tickets at most Empik stores (see "Shopping") or online from www.ebilet.pl.

CLASSICAL MUSIC The **Filharmonia Narodowa** is the home of the National Philharmonic (Jasna 5; ✆ **022/551-71-30;** www.filharmonia.pl). The box office is located at Sienkiewicza 10 and is open Monday to Saturday 10am to 2pm and 3pm to 7pm. They are closed from June to mid-August. Tickets are from 20 zł to 40 zł ($8–$16/£4.50–£9). Arrive just before show time to get cheaper last-minutes tickets.

OPERA The grand opera venue is the **Teatr Wielki** (Grand Theater) (pl. Teatralny 1; ✆ **022/692-02-00;** www.teatrwielki.pl). Here you'll find everything from the Italian classics to bolder works featuring Polish avant-garde composers. The box office is open Monday to Friday 9am to 7pm, Saturday and Sunday 10am to 7pm. Tickets are from 18 zł to 120 zł ($7.20–$48/£4.05–£27). The **Warsaw Chamber of Opera** (Solidarności 76B; ✆ **022/831-22-40;** www.operakameralna.pl) stages performances in several venues around town including the Great Ballroom of the Royal Castle. The box office is open daily from 9am to 6pm.

VENUES The **Museum of Modern Art** at the **Ujazdowski Castle** (Jazdów 2; ✆ **022/628-12-71** ext. 135; www.csw.art.pl) not only holds exhibitions, but also has concerts of contemporary music and screenings of indie films. **Sala Kongresowa** (pl. Defilad 1, entrance from E. Plater; ✆ **022/656-72-99)**, in the Palace of Culture is an atmospheric rotund concert hall used by a range of stars, from the Rolling Stones to Goran Bregovic. The box office, by entrance C, is open on weekdays 11am to 6pm and on weekends 11am to 3pm. The **Jewish Theater (Teatr Żydowski)** (pl. Grzybowski 12/16; ✆ **022/620-62-81**; www.teatr-zydowski.art.pl) has cultural productions in Yiddish. The box office is open weekdays 11am to 2pm and 3pm to 6pm; Saturday 12:30pm to 7pm and Sunday 2:30pm to 6pm. Experimental dance is on offer at **Teatr Wytwórnia** (Ząbkowska 27/31; ✆ **0602/771-112;** www.teatrwytwornia.pl), which occupies a disused mint factory in the Koneser Vodka Factory compound.

THE BAR & WINE BAR SCENE

BrowArmia ★ A lively pub-cum-restaurant with the capacity to seat more than 200 people. The microbrewery dispenses four types of light and dark concoctions that carry a bitter note. Best views of the copper vats and giant tubes are in the subterranean level. Królewska 1. ✆ **022/826-54-55.** www.browarmia.pl.

Champions Sports Bar ★ An American-style sports bar, run by the Marriott, offering hearty burgers and ribs and beer by the pitcher. It gets filled up by expats and sports fans catching the live telecasts on the big-screen TVs. Al. Jerozolimskie 65/79. ✆ **022/630-51-19.**

Lolek A BBQ pit and pub under giant marquees in the middle of the Pole Mokotowskie Park, it is swarmed by youngish residents especially on nights when there's live music or sports on the big screens. Rokitnicka 20. ✆ **022/825-62-02.** www.lolekpub.pl.

Mielżyński Wine Bar ★★★   Absolutely peerless in Warsaw, it's a wine bar with bistro fare and a shop attached. Converted from a disused lace factory, the chic industrial-warehouse mood works well for the buffed and glossed society clientele. Book a table in advance or risk a 2-hour wait. Burakowska 5/7. ✆ **022/636-87-09.**

Panorama Bar ★   A dual-level bar offering stunning night views of the city from the 40th floor of the Marriott hotel. Al. Jerozolimskie 65/79. ✆ **022/630-50-74.**

Pewex ★   Pewex stores, in the bad old days, were state-run hard-currency stores, where imported goods—everything from "Lee Cooper" jeans to "Fa" shampoo—were priced in dollars and available only to the lucky few. This Pewex is filled with kitschy '70s memorabilia and lots of good-natured irony. Since it closes at 11pm, it's a place to start an evening. Nowy Świat 22/28. ✆ **022/826-54-81.**

THE CLUB SCENE

Most of the action is still in the central part of the city, though some of the trendier places are pioneering areas farther afield, like the still-dingy but cool district of Praga. The pace is fairly lethargic on weekday nights but goes into overdrive on weekends. Most places are open Tuesday to Thursday until midnight. On Friday and Saturday, it's party till you drop at dawn. Drinks on average cost 20 zł ($8/£4.50). Some clubs have covers ranging from 5 zł to 30 zł ($2–$12/£1.10–£6.80). There's also the somewhat sexist practice of letting in women for free and charging the men. The door policy (or "door selection" in local lingo) is quirky.

Balsam ★   Out of way in the Mokotów district, this plain but atmospheric place was once a military fort and now is the hideout of those in the know who don't care for glitz and kitsch. Racławicka 99. ✆ **022/898-28-24.** www.balsam.net.pl.

Café Kulturalna   Not really a cafe or a typical club either, this bar in the Palace of Culture is happening on most nights of the week. With imperialist-style decor and occasional live jazz concerts, it hits the spot for those who are not fans of typical clubs. Pl. Defilad 1. ✆ **022/656-54-55.** www.kulturalna.pl.

The Cinnamon   High-powered disco/dance club, complete with velvet ropes and doormen. The good-looking 20s to 40s crowd is posh bordering on kitsch, with thick wallets (for him) and slinky dresses (for her). Pl. Piłsudskiego 1. ✆ **022/323-76-00.** www.the cinnamon.com.pl.

Enklawa   A two-story club staffed by female bartenders, dispensing easy but a varied range of commercial music. Tuesday is ladies' night, with an occasional stripper thrown in. Wednesdays are '80s in spirit, and live acts are booked on weekends. Mazowiecka 12. ✆ **022/827-31-51.** www.enklawa.com.

Fabryka Trzciny ★   Funky performance art space in a rundown old factory in Praga. There's no regular program, and the opening hours are spotty, but Friday and Saturday nights usually offer some interesting DJs or live music. Otwocka 14. ✆ **022/619-05-13.** www. fabrykatrzciny.pl.

Klubokawiarnia ★   A Communist-themed club that's difficult to locate and equally difficult to get into. But once you're in, the kitschy props are good for a laugh and the electro/house music good for all-night dancing. Czackiego 8 (at the corner of Świętokrzyska Street). No phone. www.klubokawiarnia.pl.

Obiekt Znaleziony ★   Eclectic, rough, and ready minimalism in a sprawling Gothic-like subterranean chambers of the Zachęta National Gallery. Popular with the young crowd. Małachowskiego 3. ℂ **022/828-05-84.** www.obiekt.blog.pl.

Platinium Club   The latest addition to the glitzy night scene; dress up or you won't be let in to play show-off with the expat regulars, business travelers, and well-heeled Poles. Fredry 6. ℂ **022/596-46-66.** www.platiniumclub.pl.

Tygmont   Low-key in terms of decor, but the best venue for live jazz with both veterans and rookies taking the stage nightly. Mazowiecka 6/8. ℂ **022/823-34-09.** www.tygmont.com.pl.

GAY & LESBIAN

Warsaw still has a long way to go before the gay and lesbian way of life becomes as open as in Western European cities.

Rasko   One of the least snobbish gay clubs where you can watch drag queen shows and karaoke contests. It's more of a warm-up point for an evening out and empties out at around 10pm. Krochmalna 32a. ℂ **022/890-02-99.** www.klubrasko.pl.

Tomba Tomba   Multi-level, lots of rooms, and one good-sized Jacuzzi to lose yourself in. Brzozowa 37. ℂ **022/831-95-39.** www.tomba-tomba.pl.

Toro   A two-level dance club where the basement is for men only. They bring in shows and striptease acts from abroad. Marszałkowska 3/5 (entrance from Emila Zoli Street). ℂ **022/825-60-14.** www.toro.waw.pl.

Utopia   This is like the gay counterpart of the Cinnamon Club. Finicky door policy grants entry only to those with super hot (or super cool) clothing and war paint, but charm the doorman and he might relent. The dance floor is small but the DJs and live acts never fail to deliver great music. Jasna 1. ℂ **022/827-15-40.** www.utopiaclub.eu.

Łódź & South-Central Poland

The big swath of territory that lies southwest of Warsaw and between the popular cities of Wrocław and Kraków is mostly, unfortunately, unvisited by visitors to Poland. Łódź (pronounced "Woodge"), Poland's second-largest city, is a 19th-century boom town that, like parts of the industrial Midwest of the United States or the Midlands in the U.K., fell on hard times in the modern era and has had to reinvent itself. The results, so far, have been mostly positive, but the city hasn't quite yet broken into the top tier of tourist destinations.

Farther south, the Upper Silesian heartland (not to be confused with Lower Silesia near Wrocław) has long been Poland's main industrialized region. The smokestack-laden metropolis centered on Katowice and including the cities of Bytom and Gliwice is home to some 3 million people, but largely devoid of traditional tourist sites.

Still, there are several good reasons you may want to schedule a stop in either Łódź or Katowice (or both). Łódź—sometimes called *HollyŁódź*—is home to Poland's famed film industry, and was the early stomping ground for Poland's trilogy of world leading film directors: Andrzej Wajda, Krzysztof Kieslowski, and Roman Polański. It was also the site of Poland's second-largest wartime Jewish ghetto, after Warsaw, and parts of the former ghetto still look very much as they did during

World War II. If you're interested in Jewish or Holocaust history, you can walk the old streets and take in the story of the Łódź ghetto at your own pace. It's deeply moving in a way that more highly polished memorials or museums often are not.

Katowice is an important transportation hub, lying on the main rail line between Prague and Kraków and the highway between Wrocław and Kraków. It's got some great restaurants and some offbeat attractions that can feel like a much-needed antidote to sometimes overly touristy Kraków.

The pilgrimage city of Częstochowa is the region's true must-see. The **Jasna Góra Monastery,** home to the fabled painting of the "Black Madonna," has drawn believers and miracle-seekers for centuries, and retains an aura of hushed holiness into the modern age. History buffs may want to push farther south to the city of Cieszyn, which straddles the border between Poland and the Czech Republic. This once-independent duchy in the Middle Ages proved a sore point between Poland and then-Czechoslovakia in the run-up to World War II, when Poland annexed territory on both sides of the border just as Adolf Hitler was making his own Czech land grab. Polish–Czech relations are much improved since then, and you can leisurely stroll both sides of the border by crossing a small footbridge over the charming Olza River.

---

1 ŁÓDŹ

Poland's second-largest city has traditionally been called the "Manchester of Poland," a reference to its rise in the 19th century as an industrial powerhouse, and to the vast

Starry Eyed

It's not exactly Sunset and Vine in Hollywood, but Łódź has its own sidewalk Walk of Stars located along a stretch of Piotrkowska in front of the Grand Hotel (see "Where to Stay.") Like in Hollywood, the names of Poland's most prominent film stars and directors are etched in concrete, with a big star around the name. Not surprisingly, you'll find stars for Polish greats like Andrzej Wajda and Roman Polański, but you're not likely to recognize many other names. One Polish favorite is Zbigniew Cybulski, a handsome young star from the late 1950s and '60s who is often compared to American actor James Dean. Like Dean, Cybulski was tragically killed in his prime (in his case, run over by a train). One possible celeb we may see someday on the Łódź Walk of Fame is American cult film director David Lynch. Łódź is one of Lynch's favorite cities and may even have inspired the story for his most recent film, *Inland Empire.*

textile mills that employed tens of thousands of workers at the turn of the 20th century. For Americans, the hulking relics and depressed building stock of a bygone era may bring to mind Detroit or Cleveland. Still, there's an energy and vitality here that many Polish cities lack, and, if you're passing by, Łódź merits at least a day of exploration. The city can be visited as a long daytrip from Warsaw, but it's better approached as a destination in its own right. The prospect of some excellent restaurants and a couple of nice hotels sweetens the deal.

Łódź is relatively young as Polish cities go. It came into its own only in the 19th century, when German and later Jewish industrialists built large textile mills to exploit access to the vast Russian and Chinese markets to the east. Unlike Kraków or Wrocław, you'll search in vain here for a large market square, a Rynek, surrounded by gabled baroque and Renaissance houses. Instead, you'll find—amid the tenements and badly neglected housing stock—fine examples of the sumptuous neo-baroque and neoclassical mansions and town palaces favored by the wealthy 19th-century bourgeoisie.

By the start of the 20th century, Łódź had grown from a village just a few decades earlier to a city of more than 300,000 people, and its factories, mansions, and civic institutions were among the finest in the country. It was a magnet for poor Poles from around the country, but above all it attracted Jews, drawn here by the relatively tolerant social climate and economic opportunity. At its height, the Jewish community numbered some 230,000 people, around a third of the city's immediate pre–World War II population.

But if the city's economic rise was rapid, its decline was precipitous as well. At the end of World War I, with the establishment of independent Poland, the city lost its privileged access to the Russian and Far Eastern markets. World War II, and the Nazi occupation, was an unmitigated disaster. While many of the buildings survived the war intact, nearly the entire Jewish population was wiped out—first herded into a massive ghetto north of the city center, and then shipped off train by train to the death camps at Chełmno and Auschwitz-Birkenau. For decades after the war, the story of the "Litzmannstadt" ghetto, as it was known at the time, was little known outside of Poland. Now, Jewish groups from around the world are getting the word out. You can tour much of the former ghetto as well as visit the Jewish cemetery, the largest of its kind in Europe.

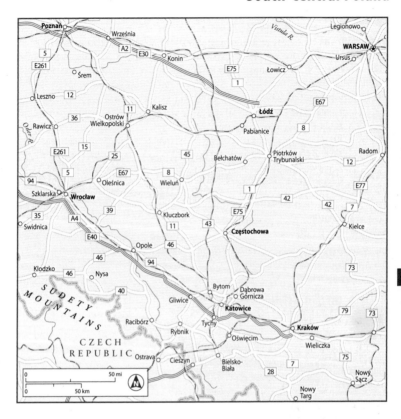

The Communist period brought more ruin to the city. The once-profitable mills were run into the ground by inept state ownership. The city was blighted by some of the most insensitive Communist-era planning to ever come off the drawing board. The period since 1989 has seen a massive effort to transform the bleak postindustrial cityscape into a lively cultural center. And that effort is partially succeeding. The heart of the transformation is the city's main drag, **Piotrkowska,** a nearly 4km-long (2.5-mile) pedestrian strip lined with restaurants, cafes, bars, clubs, and shops. By day, it's a place to stroll, window-shop, and have an open-air coffee. By night, it's arguably Poland's most intense street party, filled with raucous revelers swilling beer as club music blares from behind nearly every door. Just to the north of the city center, the huge complex of former textile mills has now been transformed into Europe's biggest shopping and entertainment complex, Manufaktura.

Łódź also boasts one of Poland's best museums of modern art, and a clutch of other interesting museums, many housed in the mansions of the old industrial elite. For fans of international film, Łódź is home to the Poland's most highly regarded film school and the country's only Museum of Cinematography. Legendary Polish film directors Andrzej Wajda, Krzysztof Kieslowski, and Roman Polański, among others, all learned their craft here.

Getting There

BY PLANE Łódź's Władysław Reymont Airport (Gen. Stanisława Maczka 35; ✆ **042/688–84–14;** www.airport.lodz.pl) is a 10- to 15-minute drive southwest of the center. On arriving, take bus no. 55 to get to the main street Piotrkowska. A 30-minute bus ticket costs 2.40 zł ($1/66p). A taxi into town will run about 30 to 40 zł ($12–$16/£6.75–£9).

BY TRAIN Most trains arrive and depart from the main station: Fabryczna (Pl. Salacińskiego 1; ✆ **042/94-36;** www.pkp.pl). Fabryczna is a 10-minute walk from the center of town. A taxi to the center will cost 10 zł ($4/£2.25). Some trains also arrive at and depart from suburban Kaliska station (ul. Unii Lubelskiej 3/5; ✆ **042/94-36**) or Widzew station (Słozbowa 8; ✆ **042/94-36**), so be sure to check your ticket.

BY BUS The main bus station (Pl. Salacińskiego 1; ✆ **042/631-97-06;** www.pks.lodz.pl) is situated just behind Fabryczna train station. This is also where Polski Express buses arrive. Several budget air carriers now fly to Łódź from various cities in the U.K. and continental Europe.

BY CAR Łódź lies at the geographic center of Poland and at the crossroads of several major highways, including the main E75 highway that runs from Gdańsk to the Czech border. Figure on about a 3-hour drive from Warsaw and Wrocław and about 4 hours south from Gdańsk.

Visitor Information

The city of Łódź **Tourist Information Center** (Piotrkowska 87; ✆ **042/638-59-55;** www.cityoflodz.pl) is one-stop shopping for all you'll ever need to know. Here you'll find two helpful pamphlets for negotiating the city: *Łódź Tourist Attractions* and the *Łódź City Guide,* as well as the essential *Jewish Landmarks in Łódź.* The latter includes a (long) self-guided walking tour of the Łódź (Litzmannstadt) ghetto. The staff maintains a complete list of hotels and can help arrange transportation and restaurant reservations.

City Layout

Łódź is a sprawling city situated on a loose grid around the main pedestrian walk Piotrkowska. Try to stay as close to the center as possible. Most of the better places to eat as well as the main tourist sites and the Manufaktura shopping center are within walking distance.

Getting Around

Distances are vast in Łódź, so you'll probably find yourself mixing walking with taking trams, taxis, and the occasional pedicab.

ON FOOT The center of the action is a mainly pedestrian avenue called Piotrkowska. It's a good 45-minute walk end to end. Walking is also the best way to see the former Jewish ghetto. Elsewhere, going on foot is not much fun. The distances are too long and there's not much to see along the way.

BY PEDICAB/RICKSHAW Pedicabs whisk you from one end of Piotrkowska to the other in about 10 minutes for about 5 zł ($2/£1.10) with tip. Rates tend to go up sharply for destinations away from Piotrkowska; in these cases be sure to negotiate the fare in advance.

BY TRAM/BUS Łódź has an excellent public transportation system of buses and trams. Tickets cost 2.40 zł ($1/60p) for a standard 30-minute trip and are available from newsagents.

BY TAXI Taxis are cheap and plentiful. Figure on fares of 15 zł to 20 zł around town. Reputable firms include **Merc Radio Taxi** (© **042/650-50-50**) and **MPT Taxi** (© **042/ 91-91**).

BY BIKE Łódź is flat as a pancake and Piotrkowska is fun to cycle, but rentals are few and far between; your best bet is to consult with the tourist information office.

TOP ATTRACTIONS

To get your bearings, start out at one end of Piotrkowska (it doesn't matter which) and walk to the other end. Piotrkowska is where it all happens in Łódź. Meander down the various side streets. You'll find houses and buildings in all states of repair and disrepair. It's an urban-rehabber's dream, and someday this all might be trendy shops and boutiques. In addition to the numerous pubs, restaurants, and coffee bars, Piotrkowska is lined up and down with turn-of-the-last-century *neo*-this, *neo*-that architectural gems. The house at no. 78 marks the birthplace of renowned pianist Artur Rubinstein, the city's most famous local son.

The former textile mills, now the Manufaktura shopping mall, as well as the History of Łódź Museum and the former Jewish ghetto all lie to the north of the city center, beyond the terminus of Piotrkowska at the Plac Wolności, identified by the statue of Polish national hero Tadeusz Kościuszko at the center. At the other end of Piotrkowska is the highly recommended Cinematography Museum, situated in another sumptuous former industrialist's mansion.

The Łódź Ghetto (Litzmannstadt) ★★ If one of your reasons for visiting Poland is to trace Jewish heritage, then you'll certainly want to explore what remains of the Łódź ghetto (known by its German name of Litzmannstadt), once the second-biggest urban concentration of Jews in Europe after the Warsaw ghetto. But be forewarned: Although spending time here is highly worthwhile, not all of the former ghetto survived World War II and some of the area has been rebuilt with mostly prefab Communist housing blocks and shops. Much of the walking tour of the ghetto consists of weaving through drab and depressed streets, looking for hard-to-find memorial plaques and trying to imagine what life must have been like during what was a much different era.

The Litzmannstadt ghetto is one of the saddest and least-well-known stories of the war. The Germans first formed the ghetto in 1940, after invading Poland and incorporating the Łódź area into the German Reich. In all, some 200,000 Jews from Łódź and around Europe were moved here to live in cramped, appalling conditions. Next to the Jewish ghetto, the Nazis formed a second camp for several thousand Gypsies *(Roma)* brought here from Austria's Burgenland province. High fences and a system of heavily guarded steps and pathways allowed the detainees to move between various parts of the ghetto, but prevented anyone from entering or leaving. For a time, the ghetto functioned as a quasi-normal city, with the Jews more or less allowed to administer their own affairs in exchange for forced labor that contributed to the Nazi war effort. In 1944, with the coming of the end of the war, the Nazis stepped up their extermination campaign and began regular large-scale transports to death camps at Chełmno and Auschwitz. By the end of the war there were just a handful of survivors left.

Begin the tour by picking up a copy of the brochure *Jewish Landmarks in Łódź,* available at the tourist information office on Piotrkowska. The walk starts north of the city center at the **Bałucki Rynek,** once the city's main market and the site of the German administration of the ghetto. You can find it by walking north along Piotrkowski, crossing the Plac Wolności, and continuing on through the park. From here the trail snakes along about 10km (6 miles), ending at the **Jewish Cemetery (Cmentarz Złydowski) ★★**, the largest of its kind in Europe, and the **Radegast ★★★** train station, from where the transports to the extermination camps departed. (If you want to skip the trail you can go directly to the cemetery and the Radegast station.) The cemetery is open daily except Saturdays and has a small exhibition of photographs of Jewish life in Łódź and the ghetto. The Radegast station (about a 15-min. walk north of the Jewish cemetery) has been restored to its appearance during the war, with three Deutsche Reichsbahn transport railcars ominously left standing on the tracks, the doors wide open.

After the war, a scattering of Jews returned to the city to try to rebuild a fraction of what they lost. Today, the Jewish population numbers just a few hundred from a pre–World War II population of nearly a quarter million.

Jewish Cemetery (Cmentarz Złydowski). Ul. Bracka. Free admission. Sun–Fri 10am–4pm.

History of Łódź Museum ★   If you're intrigued by the industrial history of the city and want to know more, this is where to come. Information about textiles, the history of the city's barons, a bit about Artur Rubinstein, and even background on Jewish Łódź, is all housed in the sumptuous neo-baroque palace of Łódź industrialist par excellence, Izrael Kalmanowicz Poznański.

Ogrodowa 15. ✆ **042/633-97-90.** www.poznanskipalace.muzeum-lodz.pl. Admission 7 zł ($2.80/£1.60). Sat–Mon 10am–2pm; Tues, Thurs 10am–2pm; Wed 2–6pm.

Łódź Art Museum (Muzeum Sztuki w Łódźi) ★★   A must for fans of modern art, from the functionalist, constructivist 1920s to the abstract 1950s and pop-art, op-art 1960s. The collection includes works by Marc Chagall and Max Ernst. Skip the first two floors and head straight for the museum's prize pieces on the third floor, including several of the young rake Witkacy's amazing society sketches from the 1920s.

Więckowskiego 36. ✆ **042/633-97-90.** Admission 7 zł ($2.80/£1.60). Tues–Wed, Fri 11am–5pm; Thurs noon–7pm; Sat–Sun 10am–4pm.

Museum of Cinematography ★★   If you're a fan of international film, you'll want to stop by to pay tribute to Poland's panoply of great directors, including Roman Polański, Andrzej Wajda, and Krzysztof Kieslowski, all of whom studied and worked in Łódź. The museum's annual rotating exhibitions highlight the work of one of the directors, including stills and posters from the films and various memorabilia. The museum is housed in the former residence of one of the city's great capitalist barons, Karol Scheibler, and part of the fun is just poking around this incredible neo-baroque mansion.

Pl. Zwycięstwa 1. ✆ **042/674-09-57.** www.kinomuzeum.pl. Admission 5 zł ($2/£1.10) Tues 10am–5pm; Wed, Fri–Sun 9am–4pm; Thurs 11am–6pm.

Radogoszcz Prison ★   This former wartime Nazi detention and torture center for political prisoners today holds fascinating exhibitions on Łódź during the German occupation, as well as photos and displays of the Litzmannstadt ghetto.

Zgierska 147. ✆ **042/655-36-66.** www.muzeumtradycji.pl/muzeum_tnr. Admission 7 zł ($2.80/£1.60). Tues, Thurs 10am–6pm; Wed, Fri 9am–4pm; Sat, Sun 10am–3pm.

Shopping

Łódź offers one of the most unusual shopping opportunities in Poland and possibly all of Europe. In an effort to revitalize the city, the former textile mills have been converted into an enormous shopping mall and entertainment facility, **Manufaktura** (Jana Karskiego 5; $\textcircled{C}$ **042/664-92-60;** www.manufaktura.com; open daily 10am–9pm), complete with a 15-screen multiplex, a climbing wall, Europe's longest fountain at 300m (984 ft.), and an on-site sandpit for beach volleyball. The 19th-century red-brick factory architecture is stunning and the restoration work a model for similar reconstruction efforts around the country. If you're a fan of urban rehab or just want to spend the day at the mall, stop by and take a look.

WHERE TO STAY

The better hotels are clustered around the center at Piotrkowska, but the area can get noisy at night. Ask for a room away from the main street. Rates are generally high for what's offered, but many hotels offer steep discounts on weekends.

Expensive

Grand Hotel   A faded, turn-of-the-20th-century *grande dame* of a hotel that has suffered from the somewhat negligent management of the former state-owned Orbis hotel chain. If you love those period Art Nouveau details, wide sweeping corridors, and generously sized rooms with high ceilings—and don't mind antiquated plumbing, indifferent service, and an inedible breakfast—then this is your place. The location is a major plus, right at the heart of the pedestrian zone.

Piotrkowska 72. $\textcircled{C}$ **042/633-99-20.** Fax 042/633-78-76. www.orbis.pl. 161 units. 360 zł ($144/£80) double. AE, DC, MC, V. **Amenities:** Restaurant; limited room service; nonsmoking rooms. *In room:* TV, dataport, minibar, hair dryer.

Moderate

Campanile ★★   A French chain that aims for the high middle market and delivers with well-designed, clean, stylish rooms and a professional, hospitable staff. It's similar to the IBIS down the street, but a step up in quality. Good location, just a couple of tram stops from Piotrkowska (or a 15-minute walk). There's a decent on-site restaurant and an excellent breakfast buffet (not included in the room price).

Piłsudskiego 11. $\textcircled{C}$ **042/664-26-00.** Fax 042/664-26-01. www.campanile.com. 104 units. Weekdays 270 zł ($108/£60) double; weekends 175 zł ($70/£40) double. AE, DC, MC, V. **Amenities:** Restaurant; limited room service; nonsmoking rooms. *In room:* A/C, TV, dataport, minibar, hair dryer.

IBIS ★   Similar to the Campanile and a good option whether you're here for business or pleasure. The hotel offers relatively rare local amenities like full conference facilities, in-room Internet access, and a dedicated business center. It's also a good choice in midsummer, since it's one of a handful of hotels in town to offer in-room air-conditioning. Big weekend discounts.

Piłsudskiego 11. $\textcircled{C}$ **042/638-67-00.** Fax 042/638-67-77. www.ibishotel.com. 208 units. Weekdays 270 zł ($108/£60) double; weekends 175 zł ($70/£40) double. AE, DC, MC, V. **Amenities:** Restaurant; limited room service; nonsmoking rooms. *In room:* A/C, TV, dataport, minibar, hair dryer.

Inexpensive

Hotel Savoy ★   This likeably run-down turn-of-the-20th-century hotel is just down the street from the similar but more expensive Grand Hotel. The Savoy feels smaller than the Grand and more intimate, though it's much plainer. Many of the older period elements have been stripped away through countless, often thoughtless, renovations. Ask to see several rooms, since they all differ slightly in furnishings. Ask for a room away from the deceptively quiet-looking courtyard; at 6am, it becomes a veritable beehive of construction work. For fans of Austrian writer Josef Roth, this is the "Hotel Savoy" of Roth's novel of the same name.

Traugutta 6. ℂ **042/632-93-60.** Fax 042/632-93-68. www.hotelsavoy.com.pl. 70 units. 250 zł ($100/£55) double. AE, DC, MC, V. **Amenities:** Restaurant; limited room service; nonsmoking rooms. *In room:* Some A/C, TV, hair dryer.

WHERE TO DINE

You'll find most of the restaurants, including all of the big Polish chains such as Rooster, Sphinx, and Sioux, grouped along Piotrkowska. Skip the big chains and try one of the places listed below.

Very Expensive

Anatewka ★★ JEWISH   Fun, informal Jewish-themed restaurant; the kind of place where the chef comes out halfway through the meal to pour you a shot of kosher vodka on the house. The two tiny, crowded dining rooms feel more like the parlor of an old Jewish aunt, with overstuffed chairs and walls crammed with bric-a-brac. A fiddler, while not quite on the roof, plays some nights from a little perch just below the ceiling. The food is very good. The signature "Duck Rubenstein" comes served in a tart sauce of cherries, seasoned with clove.

Ul. 6 Sierpnia 2/4. ℂ **042/630-36-35.** Lunch and dinner items 22 zł–50 zł ($9–$20/£5–£11). AE, DC, MC, V. Daily noon–11pm.

Expensive

Ciągoty i Tęsknoty ★★★ (Finds) INTERNATIONAL   Don't despair as your taxi heads out of town past row after row of falling-down, Socialist-era housing projects. You're heading to one of the best meals in Łódź. Perched between two ghastly apartment blocks is a little oasis of '50s jazz and fresh flowers. The menu is perched somewhere between home cooking and *haute cuisine*, with salads, *pierogi*, pasta dishes, and some seriously good mains centered on pork, chicken, and boiled beef. The tagliatelle with brie and fresh tomatoes is a creative vegetarian option. It's about 3km (2 miles) from the center of town but well worth the taxi fare (15 zł/$6/£3.40) to get there.

Wojska Polskiego 144a. ℂ **042/650-87-94.** Lunch and dinner items 20 zł–40 zł ($8–$16/£4.50–£9). AE, DC, MC, V. Mon–Fri noon–10pm; Sat–Sun 1–10pm.

Moderate

Varoska ★ HUNGARIAN   What could be better—or weirder—than having an authentic Hungarian stew or a chicken *paprika* while sitting in the geographic center of Poland? If your taste buds need re-awakening after all of those *pierogi*, this spicy Hungarian cooking built around hot red peppers might be just the ticket. The Hungarian potato pancake is a great and filling mix of pork goulash, sour cream, and snips of red pepper wrapped up in a fresh-baked potato pancake. The service is friendly, and the atmosphere somewhere between homey and intimate.

Traugutta 4. ℂ **042/632-45-46.** Lunch and dinner items 18 zł–30 zł ($7–$12/£4–£6.75). No credit cards. Daily noon–10pm.

Ganesh ★★ INDIAN   Polish food is good, but sometimes you need a change of pace. This is excellent Indian cuisine, prepared here informally in an open kitchen. The menu lists the usual mix of curry and tandoori dishes, with fresh naan bread and delicious lassi drinks. Tell the server if you'd like your food on the spicy side or it could turn out bland. The restaurant is small, so book ahead to be on the safe side.

Piotrkowska 69 (in the passageway). ✆ **042/632-23-20.** Lunch and dinner items 15 zł–30 zł ($6–$12/ £3.40–£6.80). No credit cards. Reservations suggested. Daily noon–10pm.

Inexpensive
Presto ITALIAN   Much better than the average pizzeria. The doughy pies here are topped with a slightly sweetish red sauce and cooked in a traditional wood-fired oven. The menu includes the usual suspects, but pizza "San Francisco" breaks new ground with banana, pineapple, and curry sauce. A more reliable choice might be "Sparare," with bacon, mushrooms, and onions. Also on offer are a good range of salads and pasta dishes. It's especially popular on Friday and Saturday nights because of its location in a little passageway just off Łódź's main pedestrian walk. Service can be slow, so plan on a long evening.

Piotrkowska 67 (in the passageway). ✆ **042/630-88-83.** Lunch and dinner items 12 zł–21 zł ($5–$8.40/ £2.70–£4.75). No credit cards. Daily noon–10pm.

AFTER DARK
Łódź has a lively cultural calendar jammed with art and film festivals. Check with the tourist information office to see if something big is happening while you are there. The highlight is November's "Camerimage" (www.pluscamerimage.pl) international film festival. The "Four Cultures" festival (www.4kultury.pl) in September celebrates the city's Polish, Jewish, German, and Russian roots.

Cafes, Pubs & Clubs
Łódź is a shot-and-a-beer town in the best sense of the term, and if you're looking for a spot to drink, carouse, and club, you needn't go any farther than Piotrkowska: 4km (2¹/₂ miles) of restaurants, cafes, and bars that open early and close late. One reliable suggestion is **Łódź Kaliska** (Piotrkowska 102; ✆ **042/630-69-55**), filled with inventive photography on the walls and packed with university students and other revelers.

---

2 CZĘSTOCHOWA

The south-central city of Częstochowa provides an unremarkable setting for one of the country's leading attractions for visitors, particularly devout Catholics: the **Jasna Góra Monastery.** For Catholics, Częstochowa occupies a rung on par with Lourdes in France, and just below the Vatican itself. Every year, millions of pilgrims come here to see the monastery's miracle-working pride and joy: an icon of Mary holding the infant Jesus, known as the *Miraculous Painting of Our Lady* (usually shortened to the "Black Madonna"). Not surprisingly, negotiating the crowds and actually getting close enough to see the painting is no small feat (comparable on some days to seeing the *Mona Lisa* at the Louvre in Paris). The best strategy for seeing the painting is to plan an overnight stop and get an early start. The painting is open to the public throughout the morning, but then only once an hour during the afternoon. Aside from the monastery, there's not much else to do in town. Nevertheless, the town center, built around an enormous pedestrian boulevard, the Aleja Najświętszej Maryi Panny (often shortened to Al. NMP), is a pleasant enough place to pass the time. At least the city has a couple of good hotels and a number of excellent places to eat.

Getting There

BY TRAIN   Częstochowa lies on main train lines, with several fast connections a day to Warsaw and Kraków. The train station, the **Dworzec PKP** (Al. Wolności 21/23; ℂ **034/ 376-14-00**), is situated in the center of town, about 20 minutes on foot to the Jasna Góra monastery.

BY BUS   The main bus station, the **Dworzec PKS** (Al. Wolności 45; ℂ **034/379-11-49**), is just down from the train station, close to the center and a 20-minute walk to the Jasna Góra monastery.

BY CAR   Częstochowa is easy to reach by car. From Kraków, take the E40 west to Katowice and then the E75 north to Częstochowa; from Warsaw, first follow the E67 south out of town then the E75 to Częstochowa.

Visitor Information

Częstochowa's helpful **City Information Center** is located in the center of town (Al. Najświętszej Maryi Panny 65; ℂ **034/368-22-50;** www.czestochowa.pl). This office tends to have more information in English on the town and the Jasna Góra monastery than the smaller **Jasna Góra Information Center** located in the monastery itself (Kordeckiego 2; ℂ **034/365-38-88**). If you plan on doing a thorough tour of the monastery, consider renting audio headphones from the Jasna Góra info center (14 zł each/$6/£3.85), which takes you on a long but helpful tour of the monastery and its many rooms and chapels.

Getting Around

The Jasna Góra Monastery is situated just off Aleja Najświętszej Maryi Panny, about a 15-minute walk from the tourist information center. Unless you're staying far from the center, you'll be able to walk everywhere you want to go.

ON FOOT   The monastery lies atop a smallish hill, so you'll have to climb a little. Otherwise, Częstochowa is mostly flat and easy to negotiate.

BY BUS   Częstochowa has a good public bus system, but you'll probably never have to use it. Tickets are available from newsagents.

BY TAXI   Taxis are easy to find and relatively cheap. Use only cabs that are clearly marked.

TOP ATTRACTIONS

Though there are a few attractions in Częstochowa itself, including a city museum and a match museum (the kind you light), the overwhelming number of visitors come here to see the Jasna Góra Monastery and, more particularly, the painting of the Black Madonna. Even if you intend to see some of the city's other sights, be sure to get to the monastery first since it's hard to predict in advance how crowded it will be.

Jasna Góra Monastery ★★★   Even if it weren't for the icon of the Black Madonna, the fabled Jasna Góra monastery would still be an impressive sight. The first Pauline monks starting coming here from the territory of modern-day Hungary in the 14th century, and over the years the monastery was gradually built up and fortified. On several occasions throughout the centuries, the monastery successfully fought off attacks from Swedish and Austrian invaders (attributed in large part to what are believed to be the powers of the Black Madonna), before succumbing for a time to the forces of tsarist Russia. Even today, the monastery retains the appearance of a fortress.

The layout is confusing for first-time visitors. The best approach is to visit the small Jasna Góra Information Center (see "Visitor Information") within the monastery for an orientation map and an optional audio headset (if you want to take a complete tour of the buildings). The main entrance to the Cathedral and the chapels, including the Chapel of the Holy Virgin Mary where the Black Madonna is displayed, is just to the right of the information center. The Cathedral is dazzling, with each room and chapel meticulously decorated in a mix of Gothic, Renaissance and baroque styles. Particularly impressive is the 46m-long (140-ft.) basilica. The mood throughout is hushed and holy, and even non-believers will be touched by a feeling of something sacred. The crowds will naturally lead you to the icon of the Black Madonna. The icon's setting, the ornate Chapel of the Holy Virgin Mary, is in Gothic style, including a richly carved wooden altar of the crucifix from 1400, but has been given a rich baroque overlay. The Black Madonna painting resembles a Byzantine icon and depicts the Virgin Mary holding the infant Jesus. Authorship of the painting is traditionally attributed to Luke, and the painting is said to have made its way here through the centuries from the Holy Lands to Constantinople (now Istanbul), to the Ukrainian city Belz, and finally to Częstochowa in 1382. The painting was partially damaged by Hussite (Protestant) fighters in the 15th century, but this doesn't appear to have diminished its miraculous appeal. The icon is open to the public throughout the morning hours, but a protective screen is lowered at noon, and then it's displayed just once an hour throughout the afternoon. Get there early in the morning to maximize your chances of seeing it. You're free to tour the monastery at will, taking in the various chapels as well as the museum of the 600th anniversary, the Bastion of St. Roch (where Lech Wałęsa's Nobel Peace Prize is displayed), the Tower (at 106m—516 steps—one of the highest in the country), and the Treasury, where the most valuable votive offerings to the Black Madonna are exhibited.

Kordeckiego 2. (☏ **034/377-77-77** (monastery), **034/365-38-88** (tourist information). www.jasnagora.pl. Free admission. Open daily 5am–9:30pm (monastery and chapels), 9am–5pm (Treasury, 600th anniversary museum, Bastion of St. Roch), 8am–4pm (Tower).

Match Production Museum ★ (Kids) Poles know Częstochowa for two things: the holy icon of the Black Madonna and wooden matches for lighting pipes and stoves. This is a mildly diverting rainy-day event, where you get to see how matches were once made using steam technology from the 19th century. The factory is still in use today.

Ogrodowa 68. (☏ **034/365-12-69.** www.zapalki.pl. Admission 7 zł ($2.80/£1.60) adults; Mon–Fri 8am–1pm.

Częstochowa Museum A nice overview of the history of the city and region, with more information on the monastery as well as collections of old coins, medals, paintings, and coats of arms. The main collection is situated here in the Old Town Hall, but various other exhibitions related to the main museum are scattered around the city.

Al. NMP 45 (Old Town Hall). (☏ **034/360-56-31.** www.muzeumczestochowa.pl. Admission 5 zł ($2/£1.10). Tues–Sun 9:30am–5:30pm (closes earlier in winter).

WHERE TO STAY

Częstochowa gets millions of visitors every year, so be sure to book well in advance and try to avoid travel on major Catholic holidays, especially the Feast of the Assumption on August 15, when something like 500,000 people crowd into town for the festivities.

Mercure Patria ★ One of the best hotels in town, with smart, well-appointed rooms done out in a traditional style that have in-room Internet and air-conditioning. The location is excellent: a 10-minute walk to the monastery and within easy walking distance of other main sights in town.

Ks. J. Popiełuszki 2. ℂ **034/360-31-00.** Fax 034/360-32-00. www.accorhotels.com. 102 units. 399 zł ($160/£90) double. AE, DC, MC, V. **Amenities:** Restaurant; nonsmoking rooms. *In room:* A/C, TV, dataport, hair dryer.

Sekwana The kind of hotel that will do in a pinch, but that's really only good for a night. On the plus side, it's cheap and within easy walking distance of the Jasna Góra monastery. There's in-room Wi-Fi and free parking, and several good restaurants nearby. On the minus side, the rooms can be stiflingly hot in summer, freezing in winter, and the beds and hallways all have a worn-out feel. The in-house French restaurant is decent, but the morning breakfast (10 zł extra per person) is only basic: bread, butter, cheese, and a cup of instant coffee.

Wieluńska 24. ℂ **034/324-89-54.** Fax 034/324-63-67. www.sekwana.pl. 20 units. 140 zł ($56/£30) double. AE, DC, MC, V. **Amenities:** Restaurant; nonsmoking rooms. *In room:* TV, dataport, hair dryer.

Wenecki ★★ (Finds) A better choice than the similarly priced Sekwana, offering warmly colored, even beautiful rooms with hardwood floors and big comfortable beds for the same rack rate. Each room is slightly different, so ask to see a couple before choosing. Free guarded parking and in-room Internet. The breakfast (not included) is excellent. The only drawback is location: it's on the opposite end of town from the monastery, meaning you'll have to walk 20 minutes or take the bus. Close to the Karczma u Zagłoby (see "Where to Dine").

Berka Joselewicza 12. ℂ **034/324-33-03.** Fax 034/324-28-07. www.hotelwenecki.pl. 33 units. 140 zł ($56/£30) double. AE, DC, MC, V. **Amenities:** Restaurant; nonsmoking rooms. *In room:* TV, dataport, hair dryer.

WHERE TO DINE

Most of the better restaurants are clustered along a side street just next to the Jasna Góra monastery, close to the Hotel Sekwana, so if you're staying there you need only step outside your hotel door to find a great Polish tavern, decent Greek food, and even acceptably good pizza.

Cafe Skrzynka ★ CAFE Stylish cafe that serves excellent Lavazza espressos, with ample nonsmoking spaces. Good cakes, including excellent cheesecake, plus small entrees and salads that make for a perfect light lunch. To find it, walk along the main boulevard, Aleja Najświętszej Maryi Panny, away from the monastery about 450m (1,500 ft.) and then turn left.

Dąbrowskiego 1. ℂ **034/324-30-98.** www.cafeskrzynka.pl. Lunch and dinner items 10 zł–25 zł ($4–$10/£2.25–£5.60). AE, DC, MC, V. Daily 9am–10pm.

Diavolo ITALIAN/MEXICAN Family-friendly pizzeria conveniently located near the Jasna Góra monastery. Kids will love the interior, done up as something between an Italian trattoria and a Mexican theme park. A giant cactus is engraved into the ceiling, reflecting the restaurant's dabbling in (only so-so) Mexican food. The pizzas are sized sensibly as S, M, and XL, with the "small" at 24cm (9.5 inches) across—big enough to satisfy most appetites. The staff is friendly and the place doubles as a neighborhood bar in the evenings, making it one of the few places around to have an after-dinner drink.

Wieluńska 17. © **034/361-00-07.** www.diavolo.xt.pl. Lunch and dinner items 15 zł–25 zł ($6–$10/£3.30–£5.60). AE, DC, MC, V. Daily noon–11pm.

Karczma u Braci Kiemliczów★ POLISH   Warm and inviting Polish tavern along Częstochowa's restaurant row, next to the Hotel Sekwana along Wieluńska. Ample-portioned Polish favorites such as *bigos, pierogi,* and pork dishes are served here. It's popular with families.

Wieluńska 16. © **034/372-62-64.** www.karczma.bigduo.pl. Lunch and dinner items 25 zł–40 zł ($10–$16/£5.60–£9). AE, DC, MC, V. Daily noon–10pm.

Karczma u Zagłoby ★★★ (Finds) POLISH   Some of the best traditional Polish cooking in this part of the country, and a regional award winner. The perfect spot for exquisite renditions of beet soup (*barszcz*), potato pancakes, *pierogi,* and much more ambitious cooking. The interior is traditional, with lots of wood on the walls, but still refined.

Stary Rynek 13. © **034/324-46-86.** www.uzagloby.pl. Lunch and dinner items 25 zł–40 zł ($10–$16/£5.60–£9). AE, DC, MC, V. Daily noon–11pm.

Pireus ★ GREEK   Upscale Greek restaurant near the Hotel Sekwana and just down from the monastery. Excellent and authentic Greek dishes, including a delicious lemon chicken soup, Greek salad, and favorites like moussaka combined with friendly service make this a good stop for lunch or dinner.

Wieluńska 12. © **034/368-06-80.** www.restauracja-pireus.com.pl. 25 zł–40 zł ($10–$16/£5.60–£9). AE, DC, MC, V. Daily noon–11pm.

3 KATOWICE

Upper Silesia's smoggy, industrial metropolis attracts lots of business travelers, but relatively few tourists. The reasons are obvious once you exit the train station or drive into town. It's an undeniably homely city; the historical center was ravaged by insensitive post–World War II planning that left hulking modernist structures next to dilapidated historical buildings. You'll look in vain for that touristic mainstay of Polish towns: a handsome square, ringed with shops and cafes. Katowice was born in the 19th-century industrial age and thrived on mining and heavy industry (which continues to this day). That doesn't mean, however, it's not interesting in its own way, and the local wags at the offices of *Katowice, In Your Pocket* have even crafted a kind of wacky, anti-tourist image for the city: "If you want pealing cathedral bells and horse-drawn carriages . . . check out Kraków instead. If, however, you want to explore a completely bizarre, unexplored, and some would say unexplainable, corner of Poland, then you've hit the bulls-eye." Maybe. Even if you don't choose to come here, there's a good chance you'll pass through anyway. Katowice lies on the main rail line that connects Prague with Kraków, so it sits astride the modern-day Central European equivalent of the Silk Road. It's also on the main A4 superhighway, making it an easy car jog from Kraków or Wrocław. If you've got a couple hours to kill between trains or need to squeeze in an overnight stop, there's enough to see and do to make a stop here worthwhile.

ESSENTIALS
Getting There
BY PLANE   Katowice International Airport (Wolności 90; © **032/392-72-00;** www. katowice-airport.com) is located 35km (20 miles) northeast of Katowice near the village

of Pyrzowice. The small airport has two terminals, with most services for incoming visitors, including a small tourist information office, situated in terminal A. You have two options for getting into town: a special airport shuttle bus leaves every hour and costs 20 zł ($8/£4.5) per person each way (buy tickets directly from the driver). The bus drops you at Katowice's train station. Catch the bus here for getting to the airport as well. The second option, a taxi, costs around 120 zł ($48/£27) to destinations in the center, but be careful to use only clearly marked taxis.

BY TRAIN Most trains arrive and depart from Katowice's central station **Katowice Dworzec Kolejowy** (Pl. Szewczyka 1; ✆ **032/710-14-00;** www.pkp.pl). The station is conveniently located in the middle of the city, with hotels, restaurants, and sights just a short walk away. Departures to Kraków are frequent and the journey takes 90 minutes, making a day trip feasible.

BY BUS Katowice's bus station, **Dworzec Autobusowy Katowice** (Skargi 1 ✆ **032/ 258-94-65;** www.pkskatowice.internetdsl.pl), isn't much of a station, more of a drop-off and pick-up point. It's served by both Polski Express and Eurolines. Bus destinations are displayed on the front end of the bus above the driver. In most cases, simply signal the bus to stop and buy the ticket from the driver.

BY CAR Katowice lies at the center of Poland's best superhighway, the A4, connecting Wrocław in the west with Kraków in the southeast. Kraków is about an hour away, and Wrocław 2 to 3 hours by car.

Visitor Information

Despite not drawing many tourists, Katowice does have a useful, centrally located **tourist information office** (Rynek 13; ✆ **032/259-38-08;** www.umkatowice.pl; Mon–Fri 9am–6pm, Sat 9am–4pm). The office doesn't book rooms, but is a one-stop source for maps and info about eating, what to see, and what's going on in town.

Getting Around

Katowice is a large city, but just about everything you'll want to see or do is situated in the compact city center. Walking is usually the best option.

ON FOOT Much of the immediate area around the central train station is a pedestrian zone, with lots of shops and restaurants (including maybe the city's only decent coffee at Costa Coffee; see "Where to Eat") situated along Stawowa.

BY TRAM/BUS As you would expect from a Polish city of this size, Katowice has an excellent public transportation system of buses and trams: **Katowice Public Transport Company** (✆ **032/251-78-62;** www.kzkgop.com.pl). Tickets cost 2.40 zł ($1/60p) for a standard trip within the center and are available from newsagents.

BY TAXI Taxis are easy to find and relatively cheap. The meter starts at 5 zł ($2/£1.10) and heads north from there. Use only well-known companies. Two reputable firms are **Hallo Taxi** (✆ **032/203-77-77**) and **MPT Taxi** (✆ **032/259-92-11**).

TOP ATTRACTIONS

In the past 100 years or so, Katowice—a relatively prosperous industrial city without a very long history—has served as a kind of laboratory for modern architects working in whatever style was in fashion at the time. The city has two undeniable masterpieces, one from the crazy retro-futuristic 1960s and the other from the funky-functional 1920s. Other modern styles abound: everything from pieces of Art Nouveau, to Art Deco, from postwar Socialist–Realist to the sort of kitschy "Communist" style that came to dominate much of Polish design in the 1960s and '70s. Just take a walk and look around.

Spodek ★★   This eye-opening concert venue is called the "Flying Saucer"—it really does look like Martians have landed in the middle of Katowice. It's the city's best representative of the "Brussels Expo '58" style of design inspired by 1950s-era science and science fiction that influenced so many architects behind the Iron Curtain at the time. Though the building was designed in the 1950s, delays and safety concerns postponed the opening until 1971. Today, it hosts sporting events and big-time rock concerts, drawing performers such as Robbie Williams, Pearl Jam, and Sir Elton John, among countless others. The Spodek has a futuristic hotel attached (see "Where to Stay") that's great value and lots of fun if you like the architecture and want to experience it first-hand.

Al. Korfantego 35. ✆ **032/258-32-61.** www.spodek.com.pl. Sometimes it's possible to take a peek inside, but it's usually open to visitors only during performances.

Cloud Scraper (Drapacz Chmur) ★   An early skyscraper dating from the golden years between World Wars I and II, when modern architecture, particularly that unadorned style known as Bauhaus, was all the rage. When it was finished in 1934, it was the tallest building in the country, measuring 60m (185 ft.) in height. Now it's often overlooked, but a must for fans of functionalist architecture.

Żwirki i Wigury 15. Open normal office hours.

Katowice Historical Museum (Muzeum Historii Katowic) ★   A much better than average museum dedicated to Katowice's tumultuous history, first under Prussian rule, then Polish, then German, then under Soviet domination—when Katowice for a time was called "Stalinogrod" (Stalin's city)—and today. Unfortunately, most of the commentary is in Polish only, but the exhibits are straightforward enough to make the point.

Szafranka 9. ✆ **032/256-18-10.** www.mhk.katowice.pl. Open Tues–Fri 10am–3pm, Sat–Sun 11am–2pm. Admission 6 zł ($2.40/£1.35) adults.

WHERE TO STAY

Katowice attracts an abundance of business travelers; hence, prices tend to be higher than the facilities might otherwise warrant, and getting a room is much harder on a weekday than a weekend. On the plus side, hotels occasionally discount on weekends. The Hotel Katowice (see below) is a Communist-era mega hotel, but because of its size you can almost always count on getting a room.

Campanile ★★   You can't go wrong with this French mid-market chain, which has succeeded in Poland by offering higher-end amenities, like in-room Internet and air-conditioning, at competitive prices. Count on clean if unimaginative rooms, with attentive service and an excellent breakfast buffet. It's much more comfortable than either the Katowice or the Olimpijski, if lacking somewhat in atmosphere.

Sowińskiego 48. ✆ **032/205-50-50.** Fax 032/209-06-06. www.campanile.com.pl. 76 units. 280 zł ($112/ £63) double. AE, DC, MC, V. **Amenities:** Restaurant; limited room service; nonsmoking rooms. *In room:* A/C, TV, dataport, minibar, hair dryer.

Katowice   An abomination of a hotel in almost every respect. Its 1970s Communist-era panel construction features threadbare floors and paper-thin walls. It's the kind of place where the chambermaids are banging—not knocking—at the door at 7am to clean the rooms. Still, in overpriced Katowice, it's a decent value for the money and the central location is excellent. The large size means it's rarely full to capacity, even on weekdays when getting a room elsewhere is tough. There's Internet access in the lobby.

Al. Korfantego 9. ☎ **032/258-82-81.** Fax 032/259-7526. www.hotel-katowice.com.pl. 230 units. 270 zł ($108/£60) double; rates discounted on weekends. Parking 25 zł ($10/£5.60). AE, DC, MC, V. **Amenities:** Restaurant; limited room service; nonsmoking rooms. *In room:* TV, dataport, minibar, hair dryer.

Olimpijski ★ Just in case you ever wondered what a night on the *USS Enterprise* might be like on an episode of *Star Trek*, the Olimpijski is located within Katowice's landmark "Spodek" (see "Top Attractions"), the flying saucer building that was the height of futuristic chic in the 1970s. It's still incredibly cool, but in a retro kind of way; in fact, the future didn't turn out anything like this. The rooms are Spartan: the beds are no more than glorified cots, with particleboard desks and chairs. But the atmosphere is cheery and clean. If you're looking for cheap, one-of-a-kind lodging, consider a night here.

Al. Korfantego 35. ☎ **032/258-22-82.** Fax 032/258-12-33. www.hotelspodek.katowice.pl. 30 units. 220 zł ($90/£50) double. AE, DC, MC, V. **Amenities:** Restaurant; limited room service; nonsmoking rooms. *In room:* TV, dataport.

WHERE TO DINE

Costa Coffee ★★ CAFE   Keep this in mind if you have to change trains in Katowice and have a couple hours to kill: It's just a short walk out of the train station for some excellent coffee as well as good pre-made sandwiches and sweets like muffins and brownies. Free Wi-Fi on the premises. It's an oasis in a city where "coffee" still usually means the instant variety.

Stawowa 8. ☎ **032/444-72-48.** www.costacoffee.pl. Coffee drinks and small sandwiches 7 zł–15 zł ($2.80–$6/£1.50–£3.40). AE, DC, M, V. Daily 9am–10pm.

Fantasmagoria ★★★ (Finds) POLISH/UKRAINIAN   Easily the best restaurant in Katowice and possibly all of this part of Poland. Excellent and inventive home-style cooking that takes equal inspiration from Ukrainian and eastern Polish classics like grilled meats, soups, and dumplings and mixes it with more modern notions of using local ingredients and a fresh presentation. The mixed beef and lamb kebabs, served with fresh-baked bread and baked potato, is a classic. Worth a trip out of your way.

Gliwicka 51. ☎ **032/253-00-59.** Lunch and dinner items 20 zł–40 zł ($8–$16/£4.50–£9). AE, DC, M, V. Daily 11am–11pm.

AFTER DARK

As the leading city in Upper Silesia, Katowice has an active cultural life, with excellent classical concerts and a good experimental scene. The center of the action is the **Upper Silesian Cultural Center** (Pl. Sejmu Śląskiego 2; ☎ 032/251-79-25; www.gck.org.pl). For popular music and visiting rock stars, don't forget the **Spodek** (see "Top Attractions"). The tourist information office can let you know if anyone big is visiting while you are there. For opera, the **Silesian Opera** *(Opera Śląska)* in the nearby city of Bytom is one of the most celebrated houses in the country (Moniuszki 21–23, Bytom; ☎ 032/281-34-31; www.opera-slaska.pl).

Cafes, Pubs & Clubs

Not surprisingly, there are tons of places to drink in Katowice. Two of the best include **Archibar** (Dyrekčyjna 9; ☎ 032/206-83-50; www.archibar.pl) and **Bohema** (Słowackiego intellectual set; the latter is more a garden-variety pub and conveniently close to the train station if you don't have much time to lose.

4 CIESZYN

The southern border town of Cieszyn is one of Silesia's oldest settlements. According to legend it was founded in 810 by three brothers, Bolko, Leszko, and Cieszko, to celebrate their reunion. More likely, the city dates from around 1200, first emerging as a defense post along the traditional border between the Polish and Bohemian kingdoms, and then later developing into a trading center. Cieszyn served as the capital of the independent Duchy of Cieszyn from the end of the 13th century to the middle of the 17th century, before falling under the domination of the Habsburg Empire. Today, it's interesting for two reasons. One is that it's a nicely preserved medieval market town, with the original street plan intact, a handsome square, and—naturally—an impressive castle. The second is more geopolitical. In more modern times, Cieszyn proved to be a thorn in the side of Polish–Czechoslovak—later, Czech—relations. The town's roots are Polish, but the competing dynastic claims through the ages muddied the waters. At the end of World War I, the town was split down the middle, along the Olza River, with one side going to newly independent Poland and the other side, known as *Český Těšín,* to the newly founded Czechoslovak state. The darkest moment arguably came ahead of World War II, in 1939. Just as Hitler was grabbing Czechoslovakia's German-speaking border regions, Poland forcibly annexed the Czech side of town. At the end of the war, the original borders were restored, but the memory soured bilateral relations for decades. Now, with both countries in the European Union, all seems forgiven, and Cieszyn/Český Těšín has been officially declared an EU "Euroregion." Indeed, you're free to walk at will from one bank of the Olza to the other, enjoying the oddity of a town that is literally half-Polish and half-Czech.

ESSENTIALS
Getting There

BY TRAIN   Cieszyn has two train stations, one on each side of the border. The most useful station is on the Czech side in Český Těšín, with good Eurocity train connections to Prague (5 hours) in one direction and Katowice (2.5 hours) and Kraków (4 hours) in the other. The Polish station has decent connections to other Polish destinations. On the Czech side, the **station** is located in the center of town, across from the Piast Hotel, at Nádražní 1133 (ℂ **420-840-112-113**). On the Polish side, Cieszyn's **train station PKP** is at Hajduka 10 (ℂ **033/852-01-08**), about a 10-minute walk from the center.

BY BUS   Cieszyn has good bus connections to Wrocław and throughout southern Poland, and the tourist office can advise whether you're better off taking a bus or a train for your destination. The bus station PKS is near the train station at Korfantego 23 (ℂ **033/852-02-79;** www.pkscieszyn.pl).

BY CAR   Cieszyn is located on the main north–south E75 highway and is well-signposted for miles around. It's a major road border crossing between Poland and the Czech Republic.

Cieszyn has two helpful tourist information centers, one on each side of the border. Both are useful for hotel and restaurant recommendations, planning outings, and figuring out transport options, but each is much stronger on its respective part of town. Don't expect the Poles to have much info on the Czech side or vice-versa (in spite of the towns' shared EU "Euroregion" designation). On the Polish side, visit the **Cieszyn Information Center** (Rynek 1; ⓒ 033/479-42-49; www.cieszyn.pl). On the Czech side, try the **Český Těšín Regional Information Center** (Hlavní Třída 15; ⓒ 420/558-711-866; www. info.tesin.cz).

Getting Around

Cieszyn is a small city, and walking is the best way to get around. The center of the Polish side is the charming main square, the Rynek. From there it's a short walk to the castle and then across the river to the Czech side. There is a modest city bus system, but you're not likely to use it. Taxis are around, but it's best to ask your hotel or restaurant to call one for you. **Halo Taxi** (ⓒ 033/852-19-19) is a reliable company.

TOP ATTRACTIONS

Begin your exploration on the Polish side at the main square, the Rynek, the center of town life since the 14th century and where you'll find the tourist information office. Most of the buildings on the square date from the 19th century, following several fires through the ages, including a devastating inferno in 1789 that destroyed the original Gothic and Renaissance houses. From here, walk down the town's main drag, Głębocka, that leads past the town hall and the old market, the Stary Targ, to the castle and eventually to the **Most Przyjaźni/Most Družby (Friendship Bridge)** that connects the town's Polish and Czech sides. Once on the Czech side, you can meander along the Olza River or walk down Hlavní Třída to the second tourist information office. From Hlavní, make a left down Pražská to find the Nám. ČSA (ČSA Square) is the center of the Czech side and home to its own town hall.

Castle Hill (Góra Zamkowa) ★★   The seat of power during the time of Duchy of Cieszyn and a site of human habitation since something like the 5th century BC. In the 14th century, at the start of the duchy, a Gothic castle was built here. It was made over time and again through the ages as architectural fashions changed. The current appearance is neoclassical from the 19th century. The highlights include a beautifully preserved Romanesque rotunda from the 11th century—one of Poland's earliest Christian churches (and duly recognized on the 20 zł bank note)—and a 14th-century Gothic tower that you can scramble up for views over the surrounding countryside.

Zamkowa 3. ⓒ 033/851-08-21. www.zamekcieszyn.pl. Admission fee. Tues–Sun 9am–5pm (summer), Tues–Sun 10am–4pm (winter).

The Museum of Cieszyn Silesia (Muzeum Śląska Cieszyńskiego) ★   Regional museum loaded with historical curiosities from the period when Cieszyn was an independent duchy with its own coins and coats of arms, as well as household artifacts, old photos, and preserved interior pieces from the castle and the rotunda.

Regera 6. ⓒ 033/851-29-33. www.muzeumcieszyn.pl. Admission 10 zł adult. Tues–Sun 10am–4pm.

Since passport formalities no longer exist on the border, it doesn't matter which side of town you stay on. Most of the main tourist sights are on the Polish side, but the most useful railway station is on the Czech side.

Hotel Central ★   The nicer of the two main hotels in Český Těšín, on the Czech side of the border. This early-20th-century property that's been renovated in a non-descript 1970s style is nevertheless an excellent value and convenient to the train station (on the Czech side), if that's where you're arriving. The Polish side is 10 minutes by foot across the bridge. Free parking and free in-room Wi-Fi help to make it a good budget pick. 28 rooms, restaurant, bar.

Nádražní 16/10, Český Těšín. ✆ **420/558-713-113**. www.hotel-central.cz. 28 units. 990 Kč/135 zł ($54/£30) double. AE, DC, MC, V. **Amenities:** Restaurant; nonsmoking rooms. *In room:* TV, dataport.

Hotel Piast   Also in Český Těšín, though not quite as pleasant as the nearby Hotel Central. Judging from the handsome 1920s building, this must have been a great hotel in its day. Now it's badly faded, with a sterile 1980s makeover, but still clean and with all the basic amenities you'd need for an overnight stay. The main dining room on the ground floor is an absolute photo-worthy time capsule of life in 1960s Czechoslovakia, with its worn carpets and long, heavy curtains, and yet buzzing with city life.

Nádražní 18, Český Těšín. ✆ **420/558-711-560**. Fax 420/558-711-564. www.hotelpiast.cz. 29 units. 850 Kč/120 zł ($48/£27) double. AE, DC, MC, V. **Amenities:** Restaurant; nonsmoking rooms. *In room:* TV, dataport.

Liburnia ★★ (Value)   On the Polish side—it's a little hard to find, beside and behind a hypermarket outside of town, but worth the effort. A cross between a business hotel and a boutique at prices you'd expect to pay at a pension. The stylish contemporary rooms come with card keys and individual climate control settings. The mattresses are thick and comfortable; the cotton thread count in the sheets is well above the average at this price point. The only obvious amenity missing is in-room Internet (but there's free public Wi-Fi in the restaurant). Take a taxi here if you arrive by bus or train; if you're driving, there's plenty of free parking out front. The in-house restaurant features Italian cooking and is one of the best places in town to eat.

Liburnia 10, Cieszyn. ✆ **033/852-05-31**. www.liburniahotel.pl. 30 units. 180 zł ($72/£40) double. AE, DC, MC, V. **Amenities:** Restaurant; limited room service; nonsmoking rooms. *In room:* A/C, TV, minibar, hair dryer.

Gospoda Targowa ★ POLISH   Reliably good Polish tavern/restaurant on the Polish side of town, with all the chicken and pork classics you'd expect in this part of the world in a fun and inviting atmosphere. One of the few in-town options for breakfast. Offers live jazz some evenings, so be sure to ask.

Stary Targ 1, Cieszyn. ✆ **033/852-18-54**. Lunch and dinner items 15 zł–30 zł ($6–$12/£3.40–£6.80). No credit cards. Daily 9am–10pm.

LODZ & SOUTH-CENTRAL POLAND

6

CIESZYN

Kraków, Zakopane & the Tatra Mountains

Kraków, the capital of the Polish region of Małopolska, is one of the most beautiful cities in central Europe and a highlight of any visit to Poland. The city escaped serious damage during World War II and its only real regional rival for pure drop-dead beauty is the Czech capital, Prague. The size and formal perfection of its enormous central square, the Rynek Główny, is breathtaking and the little lanes that fan off it in all directions ooze with charm. Kraków is one of those places you start plotting to move to nearly the moment you arrive. In addition to the Old Town, there's ancient Wawel Castle, home to Poland's earliest royal rulers and the country's capital until the end of the 16th century. The former Jewish ghetto of Kazimierz is also coming into its own, not just as a fascinating step back into the city's estimable Jewish past, but also as the emerging center of Kraków's booming nightlife.

Kraków's charms have always been known to Poles (and Kraków remains far and away the number-one domestic tourist destination), but now the word is spreading far and wide. The city is firmly (and justifiably) established on the main central European tourism axis that includes Vienna, Budapest, and Prague. All of this is good news for visitors. It means decent plane, rail, and bus connections from any point north, south, or west of the city. It also means that Kraków has some of the best restaurants and hotels in Poland and is fully accustomed to catering to the needs of visitors.

Outside of Kraków, several excursions merit a few hours or a full day of sightseeing. The most important of these is the former Nazi extermination camp at **Auschwitz-Birkenau** (in the town of Oświęcim, about 80km/50 miles west of the city). Also recommended is a trip to the unusual and unforgettable **Wieliczka Salt Mines.** If you've got the time and a penchant for modern architecture, check out the **Nowa Huta Steelworks** and the amazing post–World War II Socialist–Realist housing projects built around the mills.

To the south of Kraków, the High Tatra Mountains begin their rise toward the border with Slovakia. This is prime hiking and skiing country, centered on the main mountain resort of Zakopane. Dozens of hiking trails cover the hills south of town, with some of the most adventurous walks crossing the peaks and ending up in Slovakia. But Zakopane is more than just a hiking and ski resort. A hundred years ago Poland's best young painters, poets, and architects decamped here in a bid to reinvent Polish culture. To this day, Zakopane retains a whiff of arty exclusivity.

The highlands around Zakopane and to the east of Kraków are less breathtaking, but lovely in their own right. If you have extra time, check out the budding tourist town of **Tarnów**—"Little Kraków"—with its nicely preserved Renaissance town square and its own moving history of Polish and Jewish cultures living side by side for centuries, only to be destroyed by Nazi barbarism.

1 KRAKÓW

Kraków's precise origins are unclear, but the city first rose to prominence at the turn of the first millennium as a thriving market town (see the box below for one entertaining version of the city's founding). The enormous size of the Rynek attests to Kraków's early importance, even if the city's early history is more than a little bit cloudy.

As befitting any medieval metropolis, Kraków suffered the usual ups and downs related to religious strife, wars, natural disasters, plagues, and the occasional raid from the Mongol hordes coming from the East. In the 13th century, the city was razed to the ground by Tatars sweeping in from Central Asia, but it was quickly rebuilt (and parts remain remarkably unchanged to this day). Kraków's heyday came arguably in the mid-14th century, when King Kazimierz the Great commissioned many of the city's finest buildings and established Jagiellonian University, the second university to be founded in central Europe after Prague's Charles University. For more than five centuries, Kraków served as the seat of the Polish kingdom (it only lost out to the usurper Warsaw in 1596 after a political union with Lithuania made the new Polish–Lithuanian kingdom so large that it became difficult for noblemen from the north to travel here).

Kraków began a long, slow decline around this time. Following the Polish partitions at the end of the 18th century, Kraków eventually fell under the domination of Austria-Hungary, and was ruled from Vienna. It became the main city in the new Austrian province of Galicia, but had to share some of the administrative duties with the eastern city of Lwów (which must have been quite a climb down for a former Polish capital!).

Viennese rule proved to be a boon in its own right. The Habsburgs were far more liberal in their views than either the Prussians or tsarist Russia, and the relative tolerance here fostered a Polish cultural renaissance that lasted well into the 20th century. Kraków was the base of the late-19th and early-20th-century *Młoda Polska* (Young Poland) movement encompassing a revival of literature, art, and architecture (often likened to "Art Nouveau") that is fondly remembered to this day.

Kraków had traditionally been viewed as a haven for Jews ever since the 14th century, when King Kazimierz first opened Poland to Jewish settlement. The Kraków district named for the king, Kazimierz, began life as a separate Polish town, but through the centuries slowly acquired the characteristics of a traditional Jewish quarter. By the 19th and early 20th centuries, Kazimierz was one of the leading Jewish settlements in central Europe, lending Kraków a unique dimension as a center of both Catholic and Jewish scholarship.

World War II drastically altered the religious composition of the city and for all intents and purposes ended this Jewish cultural legacy. The Nazis made Kraków the nominal capital of their rump Polish state: the "General Gouvernement." The Nazi governor, and war criminal, Hans Frank ruled brutally from atop Wawel Castle. One of the first Nazi atrocities was to arrest and eventually execute the Polish faculty of Jagiellonian University. Not long after the start of the war the Nazis expelled the Jews from Kazimierz, first forcing them into a confined ghetto space at Podgórze, about a half-mile south of Kazimierz across the river, and later deporting nearly all of them to death camps. (As a historical aside: Frank was prosecuted at the Nuremburg trials and executed in 1946.)

Kraków's architecture luckily escaped major destruction at the end of the war, but fared poorly in the postwar decades under Poland's Communist leadership. The Communists never liked the city, probably because of its royal roots and intellectual and

That Dragon Story Sounds a Little Familiar . . .

Like all worthy medieval cities, Kraków's origins are steeped in legend, but it seems as if the more of these legends you hear, the more they all begin to sound alike. An oft-told tale of Kraków's early days involves a dragon that was terrorizing the ancient Polish kingdom. This forced the king to offer any man who could slay the dragon great wealth and his own city. A man named "Krak" took up the challenge. Krak reasoned it would be foolish to try to confront the monster directly, so—legend has it—he filled a lamb carcass with lye or sulfur (these stories always differ a little on the details) and tricked the dragon into eating it. When the dragon later took a drink, the water mixed with the lye and burst a hole in the creature's stomach. The king was naturally overjoyed and offered to Krak what eventually became the city of "Krak-ów."

Well, *maybe,* but the city of Brno, not that far to the south in the Czech Republic, also has a similar myth about *its* early days. In that version, the animal was a giant crocodile, and the same cunning mix of brave prince, lye, and water solved that scourge, too. Frankly, it's hard to imagine there were that many giant creatures—dragon or otherwise—running around, as well as clever men with bags of sulfur on hand to finish the job. At any rate, what is clear is that by the time of the early Piast dynasty in the 11th century, Kraków was booming, and Wawel Hill, with its commanding view of the Vistula River, was a natural setting for a capital city.

Catholic pretensions. For whatever reason, they decided to place their biggest postwar industrial project, the enormous Nowa Huta Steelworks, just a couple of miles upwind from the Old Town. Many argue the intention was to win over the skeptical Kraków intellectuals to the Communist side, but the noise, dirt, and smoke from the mills, not surprisingly, had the opposite effect. The new workers were slow to embrace Communism, and during those wretched days of the 1970s, when a series of food price hikes galvanized workers around the country, the city was suddenly transformed into a hotbed of anti-Communist activism.

Kraków will be forever linked with its most famous favorite son, Pope John Paul II. The pope, Karol Woytyła, was born not far from Kraków, in the town of Wadowice, and rose up through the church hierarchy here, serving for many years as the archbishop of the Kraków diocese before being elevated to pope in 1978. If Gdańsk and the Solidarity trade union provided the industrial might of the anti-Communist movement, then Kraków and Pope John Paul II were the movement's spiritual heart. The pope's landmark trip to Poland in 1979, shortly after he was elected pontiff, ignited a long-dormant Polish spirit and united the country in opposition to the Soviet-imposed government.

Kraków's charms are multidimensional. In addition to the beautifully restored Old Town, complete with its fairytale castle, there's the former Jewish quarter of Kazimierz. If you've seen Steven Spielberg's Oscar-winning movie *Schindler's List,* you'll recognize many of the film locations as you walk around Kazimierz (see the box on p. 130). For anyone unfamiliar with the film (or the book on which it was based, Thomas Keneally's *Schindler's Ark*), Oskar Schindler was a German industrialist who operated an enamel factory during World War II. By employing Jews from the nearby ghetto, he managed to spare the lives of around 1,100 people who otherwise would have gone to the death camps at Auschwitz. Schindler's factory, now closed down, is still standing (there are

plans afoot eventually to open a museum). At the moment it's derelict—and perhaps all the more fascinating for that.

ESSENTIALS
Getting There

BY PLANE **John Paul II International Airport** (📞 012/295-58-00; www.lotnisko-balice.pl) is located in the suburb of Balice, about 10km (6 miles) from town. The airport has two terminals, a larger international terminal and a smaller domestic terminal at the back to handle flights within Poland. Most of the services, including rental-car outlets, ATMs, and restaurants, are located at the international terminal. The best way to get into town from the airport is to take Polish Railways' **"Balice Express,"** regular train service to and from Kraków's main train station with regular departures on the half hour. (The "express" part of the name must be some sort of inside joke at Polish Rail, since the train seems to chug along at about 20 miles per hour, but it gets the job done.) The price is 6 zł ($2.40/£1.35) each way. To reach the small station from where the express train departs, you need to take a blue shuttle bus that departs from outside both terminals. You can also take a taxi into town, but be sure to use only clearly marked cabs and refuse any offers of a ride you might get from individuals inside the terminal or just outside the door: These are likely to be scams. Expect to pay about 70 zł ($28/£15.70) to destinations in the center.

BY TRAIN   Kraków's main train station, the **Dworzec Główny** (pl. Kolejowy 1; ✆ 012/ 393-11-11; www.pkp.krakow.pl) is about a 15-minute walk from the center of the city. Kraków is well served by rail, and departures for Warsaw and other major cities are frequent. The rail distance from Warsaw is about 3 hours. Note that travel to popular international destinations like Prague sometimes requires a change of trains in Katowice.

BY BUS   Kraków's **Central Bus Station** (ul. Bosacka; ✆ 012/393-52-52) is located just behind the main train station and is an easy walk or relatively cheap taxi ride to the center of town. Nearly all buses—international and domestic—use this station. This is also where buses to Zakopane and Oświęcim (Auschwitz) depart from. The station has two levels, so make sure you know which level your bus is using. There's a bank of ticket windows, but often times you'll simply buy your ticket from the bus driver.

BY CAR   Kraków lies on the main east–west highway, the A4, running through southern Poland. It's nearly a straight 3- to 4-hour shot on mostly 4-lane highway from the German border, through the cities of Wrocław and Katowice. You'll have to pay a small toll covering the distance to and from Katowice, but for the speed and convenience (compared to other roads in Poland) it's a bargain. From other directions, including coming in from Warsaw to the north, you'll have to contend with much smaller roads and longer drive times. Once in Kraków, find a place to park the car and leave it. The city's small, tram-clogged streets are no fun to drive on.

Visitor Information

The city of Kraków maintains an extensive and helpful network of tourist information offices around town in all of the tourist hot spots, including an office in the former Jewish quarter of Kazimierz. Here you'll find some excellent brochures, including one called the *Tourist Information Compendium* and another called *Two Days in Kraków*. They also have excellent free maps, a wealth of suggestions, and can help find and book hotel rooms. Note that the Kazimierz office is (inexplicably) closed on weekends. The main offices are located at the following addresses:

> **Town Hall Tower** (Main Square) (✆ 012/433-73-10; daily 9am–7pm)
> **Św. Jana 2** (Old Town) (✆ 012/421-77-87; Mon–Sat 10am–6pm)
> **John Paul II International Airport/Balice** (✆ 012/285-53-41; daily 10am–6pm)
> **Szpitalna 25** (Old Town) (✆ 012/432-01-10; Mon–Sat 9am–7pm, Sun 9am–5pm)
> **Józefa 7** (Kazimierz) (✆ 012/422-04-71; Mon–Fri 10am–4pm)

City Layout

Kraków's Old Town is relatively compact and comprised of the main square *(Rynek Główny)* and the streets that radiate from it in all directions (bordered by what remains of the medieval town walls and the circular park, the Planty). Most of the main tourist sites are situated within a 10- or 15-minute walk from the square.

The Wawel Castle district comprises a second major tourist destination and is a 15-minute walk south of the main square, following Grodzka Street.

The former Jewish ghetto of Kazimierz lies about a 25-minute walk south of the main square beyond the castle. To save time, it's possible to take a taxi from the Old Town to Kazimierz. Expect to pay about 15 zł ($6/£3.40). A number of trams also make the run between the two.

Getting Around

ON FOOT   Much of Kraków is closed to traffic, so walking is often the only option. Distances are manageable.

BY TRAM   Kraków is well served by a comprehensive tram network, and this is a quick and easy way to reach more far-flung destinations. Try to avoid tram travel at rush hour unless you enjoy getting pressed up against the doors like you're in the Tokyo subway. A ticket costs 2.50 zł ($1/60p) and can be bought at newspaper kiosks around town. Validate your ticket on entering the tram and hold on to it until the end of the ride.

BY BUS   Like trams, buses ply Kraków's streets from early morning until after 11pm or so and are a vital part of the city's transit network. You probably won't need to use the buses unless your hotel is well outside the city center. A ticket costs 2.50 zł ($1/60p) and can be bought at newspaper kiosks around town. Validate your ticket on entering the bus and hold on to it until the end of the ride.

BY TAXI   Taxis are relatively cheap and a dependable means of getting around. You can hail taxis directly on the street or at taxi stands around town. The fare for a typical hop, such as from the Old Town to Kazimierz, will average about 15 zł ($6/£3.40).

BY BIKE   Biking is becoming increasingly popular, and there are now bike lanes scattered around town, including a nice run along the Vistula river and through the park, the Planty, that rings the main square. That said, biking is a better bet for an hour or two of sightseeing rather than as a practical means for getting around. **Cruising Kraków bike tours** (Basztowa 17; ✆ **0514/556-017**) offers fun and instructional 2-hour bike tours in season in the afternoon and evening. They also rent bikes and conduct longer trips in summer.

TOP ATTRACTIONS

A sensible plan for sightseeing in Kraków is to divide the city into three basic areas: the Old Town, including the Rynek Główny; the Wawel Castle compound (with its many rooms and museums); and Jewish Kraków, including the former Jewish quarter of Kazimierz and the wartime Jewish ghetto of Podgórze farther south. Ideally, leave a day devoted to each. If you're pressed for time, you could conceivably link the Old Town and Wawel in one day, while leaving Kazimierz and a possible day trip to the Wieliczka Salt Mine for the next.

The Old Town & the Rynek Główny

Kraków's Old Town is a pedestrian's paradise. It's hard to imagine a more attractive town core. It's a powerful argument for historical preservation and the value of vital urban spaces. The **Rynek Główny** by all accounts is a remarkable public space. Measuring some 200m (600 ft.) square and ringed by stately buildings, it creates a natural arena for public performances of all stripes. The square is bordered on all sides by wonderfully restored noblemen's houses, many of which go back nearly 800 years, though they've been remodeled and refurbished throughout the centuries depending on the style of the day.

The most striking building on the square is the beautiful Gothic cathedral of **St. Mary's**—its uneven towers evoking for Poles the very essence of the city. You can go inside to see an intricately carved wooden altar from the 15th century. Be sure to stop here at some point precisely on the hour to hear a lone bugler play from the open window of the highest tower (see box).

At the center of the square is the **Cloth Hall** *(Sukiennice),* which dates from the 14th century and served as the stalls of the town's original merchants. The original Cloth Hall burned down in the 16th century, and what you see today is a mostly Renaissance building,

7

The Bugler's Call

The most popular tourist attraction in Kraków isn't a church, building, or even a museum. It's actually a real-live bugler, who blows his bugle every day, every hour on the hour, from high atop **St. Mary's Church (Kościół Mariacki)** (see "Top Attractions") just off the main square, the Rynek Główny. It's a strange sight and even a more surreal sound to hear the plaintive wail of the bugle call drift down into the modern square, usually filled with its own cacophony, from the clip-clop of horses' hooves to the murmur of the thousands strolling below or taking a drink at a square-side cafe. The tradition of the bugle call, or *hejnal* as it's known in Polish, goes back hundreds of years—to the 13th and 14th centuries—when Central European cities such as Kraków faced the ever-present threat of invasion by Tatar barbarians from the East. The buglers, the town's watchmen, would stand guard and alert the citizens of any threat of invasion. If you listen closely as Kraków's bugler plays, you'll hear him cut short his final note. Legend has it that in 1240, the sentry in the watchtower saw a band of Tatars approaching and began sounding the alarm. One of the invaders let fly an arrow that sliced the bugler in the throat mid-note, and ever since, buglers have continued to make an abrupt ending in his memory. (Judging from the height and size of the window, that Tatar must have been an excellent shot!) To hear the bugler today, find an unobstructed view to St. Mary's close to the top of the hour. The bugler begins just after the clock chimes the hour. You'll see him lift his window, and if it's a sunny day you'll probably catch a glint of sunshine off the bugle. When he's done, it's customary for you to wave—a gesture of thanks for keeping Kraków safe from the barbarians. If you'd like to see the bugler up close, in summer it's possible to climb the 239 steps to the top of the tower. If you time your climb right, you might even get to see the bugler in action.

with neo-Gothic flourishes added in the 19th century. Today, it's still filled with marketers, hawking good-value Polish souvenirs to throngs of visitors.

Just near the Cloth Hall stands the enormous **Town Hall Tower.** It's the last surviving piece of Kraków's original town hall, which was demolished in the early 19th century in an apparent bid to clean up the square. Today the tower houses a branch of the tourist information office, and you can climb to the top for a view over the Old Town.

Streets and alleys lead off the square in all directions. Of these the most important are **Floriańska** and **Grodzka,** both part of the famed Royal Route of Polish kings. Floriańska leads to the Floriańska Gate, dating back to the start of the 14th century. The gate was once the main entryway to the Old Town and part of the original medieval fortification system. Grodzka flows out of the square at the square's southern end and leads to ancient Wawel Castle.

Archdiocesan Museum ★   This is essential viewing for fans of the late Pope John Paul II. John Paul lived here as the archbishop of the Kraków diocese until his elevation to pope in 1978. Today, the museum has largely been given over to his legacy, with a fine collection of gifts presented to the pope by heads of state from around the world. There's also a nice collection of sacral paintings and sculpture dating from the 13th century. Kanonicza 19–21. ⓒ **012/421-89-63.** Admission: 5 zł ($2/£1.10). Tues–Fri 10am–4pm; Sat–Sun 10am–3pm.

KRAKOW, ZAKOPANE & THE TATRA MOUNTAINS

7 KRAKOW

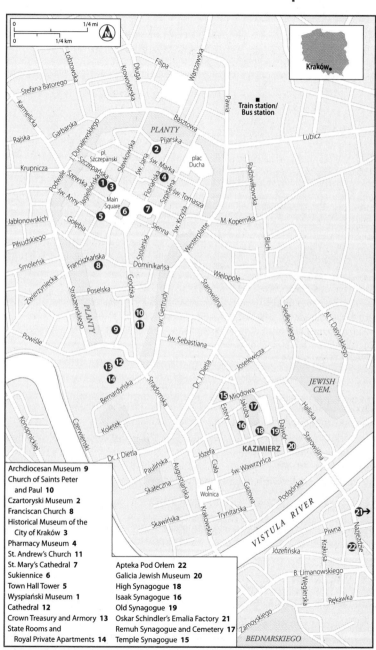

Kraków

Archdiocesan Museum 9
Church of Saints Peter
  and Paul 10
Czartoryski Museum 2
Franciscan Church 8
Historical Museum of the
  City of Kraków 3
Pharmacy Museum 4
St. Andrew's Church 11
St. Mary's Cathedral 7
Sukiennice 6
Town Hall Tower 5
Wyspiański Museum 1
Cathedral 12
Crown Treasury and Armory 13
State Rooms and
  Royal Private Apartments 14

Apteka Pod Orłem 22
Galicia Jewish Museum 20
High Synagogue 18
Isaak Synagogue 16
Old Synagogue 19
Oskar Schindler's Emalia Factory 21
Remuh Synagogue and Cemetery 17
Temple Synagogue 15

Church of Saints Peter and Paul (Kościół Św. Piotra i Pawla) ★★ One of the most evocative of Kraków's many churches, chiefly because of the statues of the 12 disciples lining the front entrance. It's said that the Jesuits spent so much money building the front and the facade that they ran out of money to finish the rest of the building (which, if you look behind the facade, you'll see is constructed from ordinary brick). The interior is less impressive, though still worth a peek in. One of the highlights is a model of Foucault's Pendulum, which demonstrates the rotation of the earth. It's also a great spot for church concerts.

Grodzka 54. ℂ **012/422-65-73.** Daily 7am–7pm.

Czartoryski Museum (Muzeum Książąt Czartorzyskich) ★★ The Czartoryski family members were gifted art collectors, and this collection is one of the finest in central Europe. Two international masterpieces are on display: Leonardo da Vinci's *Lady with an Ermine* and Rembrandt's *Landscape with the Good Samaritan.* A third masterpiece, Raphael's *Portrait of a Young Man,* was stolen by the Nazis during World War II and never recovered. An empty frame hangs in the museum awaiting the painting's return. The museum also houses a sizable collection of ancient art from the Middle East, Greece, and Egypt, as well as a display of Turkish weapons and armor captured by Polish soldiers during the siege of Vienna in 1683.

Św. Jana 19. ℂ **012/422-55-66.** www.muzeum-czartoryskich.krakow.pl. Admission 10 zł ($4£2.25); free Thurs. Tues, Thurs, Sun 10am–3:30pm; Wed, Fri, Sat 10am–6pm. Closed Mon.

Franciscan Church (Kościół Franciszkanow) ★ Another must-visit for fans of the late Pope John Paul II, who used to greet the faithful from the window across the street from this church when he was bishop of Kraków. On news of the Pope's death in 2005, this entire area was filled with mourners and candles. Inside the church, the paintings of flowers and stars on the ceiling, as well as the stained glass window over the entrance, are the work of Polish Art Nouveau master Stanisław Wyspiański.

Pl. Wszystkich Swiętych 5. ℂ **012/422-53-76.** Daily 6am–7:45pm.

Historical Museum of the City of Kraków (Historia Muzeum Historyczne Miasta Krakowa) ★ Worth a look for two reasons: the excellent overview of Kraków's development though the ages, and for the building itself, the Palac Krzysztofory, a 17th-century Renaissance *palais,* built from Italian designs and complete with an arcaded Tuscan courtyard. In addition to the standard exhibits, the Fontana room hosts classical concerts, and in December the museum holds a popular display of handmade nativity scenes in the days leading up to Christmas.

Rynek Główny 35. ℂ **012/619-23-00.** www.mhk.pl. Admission: 7 zł ($2.80/£1.60). Wed–Fri 10am–5pm; Sat–Sun 10am–3pm.

Pharmacy Museum (Muzeum Farmacji) ★ One of the biggest and best old-style pharmacy museums in this part of the world, with fascinating exhibits of potions and leeches and concoctions that show just how far modern medicine has come. Just getting a peek inside this beautiful 15th-century house is almost worth the price of admission itself.

Floriańska 25. ℂ **012/421-92-79.** www.muzeumfarmacji.pl. Admission: 7 zł ($2.80/£1.60). Tues noon–6:30pm; Wed–Sun noon–2:30pm.

St. Andrew's Church (Kościół Św. Andrzeja) It's hard to imagine a more perfect foil to the attention-grabbing Church of Saints Peter and Paul next door. This humble, handsome church dates from the 11th century and has been part of the city's history for some 900 years. Allegedly it was the only church to survive the Tatar onslaught of 1241. The church's simple Romanesque exterior is a tonic to the eyes. The interior, on the other hand, borders on the jarring, remodeled in baroque style in the 18th century.

Grodzka 56. ⟨C⟩ **012/422-16-12.** Open 7:30am–5pm.

St. Mary's Cathedral (Kościół Mariacki) ★★★ The original church was destroyed in the Tatar raids of the 13th century, and rebuilding began relatively soon after. The hushed interior makes for essential viewing. The elaborately carved 15th-century wooden altarpiece, by the master carver Veit Stoss, is the immediate crowd-pleaser. The altar, carved from limewood, measures some 11m by 13m (36 ft. by 43 ft.) and is the biggest of its kind in Europe. The faces on the carvings are intended to depict biblical figures, but—as was the fashion of the day—Stoss used ordinary townspeople as models. The interior is impressive, but the highlight of the church is not on the inside, it's the forlorn trumpeter in the high tower, playing his hourly dirge to the defenders of Kraków from the Tatar hordes, in order that the people below know the correct time.

Rynek Główny 4. ⟨C⟩ **012/422-55-18.** Admission 6 zł ($2.40/£1.35). Mon–Sat 11:30am–6pm; Sun 2–6pm (visits prohibited during mass).

Cloth Hall (Sukiennice) ★★ In the Middle Ages, town squares such as the Rynek Główny were built to support commerce. Kraków's Cloth Hall, which occupies a chunk of valuable real estate in the middle of the square, harks back to this original purpose. The first market stalls on this site date from before the 14th century. This ancient cloth hall burned down in a fire in the 16th century and was replaced by the current Renaissance building. Today, the Sukiennice plays the invaluable role of providing one-stop shopping for all those souvenirs you'll need to buy for the folks back home. The Polish crafts on display here, including carved wooden boxes, chess sets, lace, linens, and, naturally, amber, are all of good quality and priced competitively with other shops around town. Even if you're not in the market for a souvenir, it's a beautifully evocative space, lined with the symbols of Polish towns on the walls.

Rynek Główny 1–3. No phone. Stalls open daily 10am–8pm.

Town Hall Tower (Wieża Ratuszowa) ★ Kraków's forlorn-looking Town Hall Tower, part of the much larger Town Hall (Ratusz) that was pulled down by the Austrians in 1820, houses a branch of the Tourist Information Office, so you'll likely end up here even if you're not interested in climbing to the top for views over the square and out to Wawel Castle in the distance. The tower dates from 1316, though it was destroyed, remodeled, and repaired countless times through the centuries. In the 19th century, when Kraków came under the domination of the Habsburgs, the Town Hall was pulled down as part of an effort to tidy up the square. The tower was spared that fate by an apparent change of heart.

Rynek Główny 1. ⟨C⟩ **012/619-23-18.** www.mhk.pl. May–Oct 10:30am–6pm (tower closed in winter).

Wyspiański Museum ★ Fans of Polish art will have heard of Stanisław Wyspiański, one of the originators of a turn-of-the-20th-century art movement known as *Młoda Polska* (Young Poland). The Młoda Polska movement, based largely here in Kraków and in Zakopane, reinvigorated Polish culture in the years before World War I. You'll note parallels between Wyspiański's paintings and drawings and the Art Nouveau movements in Paris and Brussels, and *Jugendstil* in Vienna.

Szczepańska 11. ⟨C⟩ **012/422-70-21.** www.muzeum.krakow.pl. Admission 8 zł ($3.20/£1.80). Wed, Thurs 10am–3pm; Fri–Sun 10am–6pm. Closed Mon, Tues.

Wawel Castle (www.wawel.krakow.pl) is Poland's pride and joy. With Warsaw having been flattened by the Nazis, this ancient castle and former capital, rising 45m (150 ft.) above the Vistula, has become something of a symbol of the survival of the Polish nation. Understandably, for non-Poles Wawel has less significance, but it's still a handsome castle in its own right and worth an extended visit.

The original castle dates from around the 10th century, when the area was first chosen as the seat of Polish kings. For more than 5 centuries, the castle stood as the home of Polish royalty. The original castle was built in Romanesque style, and subsequently remodeled over the centuries depending on the architectural fashions of the day. What you see today is a mix of Romanesque, Gothic, Renaissance, and baroque.

The castle fell into disrepair after the Polish capital was moved to Warsaw at the end of the 16th century, but its darkest days came during World War II, when it was occupied by Hans Frank, the Nazi governor of the wartime rump Polish state, and came to symbolize the humiliation of the Polish nation. On the plus side, the castle escaped serious damage during the war, and despite languishing under the Communist government has now made a remarkable comeback, looking as beautiful and impressive as ever.

Aside from the castle, the complex comprises the **Royal Cathedral,** including the **Royal Tombs** and the **Cathedral Museum,** the **State Rooms,** with their impressive collection of tapestries, the **Royal Private Apartments,** and the **Crown Treasury and Armory.** (There are several other attractions, but these are the highlights.) It's a lot to see and the tourist office will recommend putting in a whole day, but this is likely to be too much time if your knowledge of Polish history leaves something to be desired or castles aren't really your thing. Two to three hours, depending on the crowds, is usually enough to see the main castle attractions and the cathedral complex.

The grounds and cathedral are open to the public free of charge, but entry to the individual sites, including the Royal Private Apartments and the Crown Treasury and Armory, requires queuing at the castle and buying separate tickets for each. During the high season in mid-summer the number of visitors is restricted, so you're best off phoning ahead to the main ticket office (© **012/422-16-97;** www.wawel.krakow.pl) a day in advance to reserve tickets. Individual guides are also available if you're particularly interested in one or more of the attractions and want more in-depth knowledge. Contact the **Guide Office** (Biuro Przewodnickie; (© **012/429-33-36;** www.przewodnicy.krakow.pl) to ask about availability and prices. Guides are priced by attraction and start at 70 zł ($28/£16) for one attraction to up to 230 zł ($92/£51) for five.

Wawel Cathedral and Cathedral Museum (Katedra Wawelska) ★★★

This is the spiritual home of the Polish state, testifying to the strong historical link between the Polish royalty and the Catholic Church. There's been a church here since around 1000, and the present, mostly Gothic church dates from around the mid-14th century. The chapels here and the Royal Tombs below hold the remains of all but four of Poland's 45 rulers (King Kazimierz the Great's tomb is in red marble to the right of the main altar) as well as a clutch of national heroes, including Polish and U.S. Revolutionary War hero Tadeusz Kościuszko and Polish romantic poet Adam Mickiewicz. Admission includes the tombs and the climb to the top of the Zygmunt Bell, which dates from the early 16th century. The bell is rung only occasionally to mark highly significant moments, such as the death of Pope John Paul II in 2005. Audio headphones are available for a nominal fee and, while the text is long and laborious, the headsets do make it much easier to negotiate the main sights.

State Rooms and Royal Private Apartments ★   The highlight of a visit to the State Rooms are the 136 Flemish tapestries from the 16th century commissioned by King Sigismund August. The rooms hold vast collections of paintings, sketches, frescoes, and period furnishings. One of the more memorable rooms, on the top floor, is the Deputies' Hall, complete with the king's throne and a wooden ceiling carved with the likenesses of Kraków residents of the time. The splendor continues in the Royal Private Apartments (separate admission), with more tapestries and Renaissance decorations as well as paintings by Titian, Raphael, and Botticelli.

Wawel Hill. ℂ **012/422-51-55.** www.wawel.krakow.pl. Admission to the State Rooms: 14 zł ($5.60/£3.10), royal chambers 19 zł ($7.60/£4.25), Sun free. Tues–Sat 9:30am–4pm; Sun 10am–4pm. Closed Mon.

Crown Treasury and Armory ★★   Exhibitions here include what's left of the Polish royal jewels, including the *Szczerbiec,* the ancient coronation sword. There's also an impressive show of medieval fighting instruments, including swords and full complements of knights' armor.

Wawel Hill. ℂ **012/422-51-55.** www.wawel.krakow.pl. Admission: 14 zł ($5.60/£3.10). Sun free. Tues–Sat 9:30am–4pm; Sun 10am–4pm. Closed Mon.

Kazimierz, Podgórze & Jewish Kraków

Kazimierz, the former Jewish quarter, is an absolute must that defies easy description. It's at once a tumbled-down, decrepit former ghetto, filled with the haunting artifacts of a culture that was brutally uprooted and destroyed a generation ago. It also happens to be Kraków's coolest nightclub district, filled with cafes, cocktail bars, and trendy eateries that would not be out of place in New York's SoHo or East Village. The juxtaposition is enlivening and jarring at the same time. To their credit, Kraków city authorities have resisted the temptation to clean up the area to make it more presentable to visitors. Don't expect an easy, tourist-friendly experience. It's dirty, down at the heel, and at the same time thoroughly engaging.

Kazimierz began life as a Polish city in the 14th century, but starting from around 1500 onward it took on an increasingly Jewish character as Jews first decided to live here, and then were forced to by edict. The original Jewish ghetto incorporated the northern half of modern-day Kazimierz, bounded by a stone wall along today's Józefa Street. In the 19th century, the Jews won the right of abode and the walls were eventually torn down. Many elected to stay in Kazimierz, and the 19th century through World War I and the start of World War II is regarded as the quarter's heyday.

The Nazi invasion in 1939 put an end to centuries of Jewish life here. The Nazis first imposed a series of harsh measures on Jewish life, and in 1941 forcibly expelled the residents across the river to the newly constructed ghetto at Podgórze. By 1943, with the liquidation of the Podgórze ghetto, nearly all of Kazimierz's pre-war Jewish population of 60,000 had been killed or died of starvation or exhaustion.

There's no prescribed plan for visiting the former Jewish quarter. The natural point of departure is the central **Plac Nowy,** once the quarter's main market and now given over to a depressing combination of fruit and flea market (no doubt with real fleas). The **Tourist Information Center** maintains an office at Józefa 7 (ℂ **012/422-04-71;** Mon–Fri 10am–4pm), and can provide maps and information. Look, too, for signposted routes marked **"Trasa zabytków żydowskich,"** which includes all the major Jewish sites.

Visit the synagogues individually; each costs around 7 zł ($2.80/£1.60) to enter. Don't expect to find gorgeous interiors; it's fortunate enough that these buildings are still standing.

After you've toured the major sites, don't overlook the **Galicia Jewish Museum** on Dajwór Street, just beyond the main ghetto area. Also check out the **New Cemetery (Nowy Cmentarz)** at the far end of Miodowa Street; you have to walk below a railroad underpass to get to it. This became the main Jewish cemetery in the 19th century, and the thousands of headstones are silent testimony to the former size of this community (Mon–Fri 10am–2pm).

Note: When entering all synagogues, men should cover their heads and women their shoulders.

High Synagogue (Synagoga Wysoka) ★ An only partially restored synagogue dating from the late 1500s, the name refers to the prayer hall, which was traditionally situated on the second floor above street level. Even if you don't choose to go in, check out the ground floor bookshop, which has the city's best collection of books on Judaica, Jewish history, and the Holocaust (See "Where to Shop"). There's also an excellent collection of music CDs with traditional Jewish and Klezmer music. A real treat.

Józefa 38. ☎ **012/430-68-89.** www.austeria.eu. Admission 7 zł ($2.80/£1.60). Sun–Fri 9am–7pm.

Galicia Jewish Museum (Żydowskiego Muzeum Galicja) ★★ This often-overlooked museum, in a far corner of Kazimierz, is almost a must-see. The main exhibition features contemporary and often very beautiful photographs of important Jewish sites throughout southern Poland taken by the late British photographer Chris Schwarz. Schwarz and a colleague spent 12 years traveling throughout Poland using photography as a way of trying to preserve the country's rapidly disappearing Jewish heritage. The effect works beautifully. So much of the experience of visiting Poland is running across sites very much like the ones in these pictures and trying to piece together the histories behind them. The lesson here, sadly, seems to be that nearly every place has a tragic story to tell. There's also an excellent on-site bookshop, with books on Jewish history in Kazimierz and the Holocaust.

Dajwór 18. ☎ **012/421-68-42.** www.galiciajewishmuseum.org. Admission 12 zł ($4.80/£2.70). Daily 10am–6pm.

Isaak Synagogue ★ Even though it was badly damaged during Nazi occupation, this is still considered the most beautiful synagogue structure in Kazimierz. Dating from 1664, it has been only partially restored but still sometimes holds exhibitions on Jewish life in Kazimierz.

Kupa 16. ☎ **012/430-55-77.** Admission 5 zł ($2/£1.10). Sun–Fri 9am–7pm.

Old Synagogue (Stara Synagoga) ★ This stern-looking Renaissance building dating from the 15th century (and the recipient of an architectural makeover a century later) is the oldest surviving Jewish structure in the country. Today, it's home to a rather dry permanent exhibition on Jewish traditions and rituals as well as a more interesting set of drawings and photos of Jewish life in Kazimierz.

Szeroka 24. ☎ **012/422-09-62.** www.mhk.pl. Admission 7 zł ($2.80/£1.60). Tues–Sun 9am–4pm; Mon 10am–2pm.

Remuh Synagogue and Cemetery (Synagoga i Cmentarz Remuh) ★★ This synagogue dates from the middle of the 16th century and is still in active use. You can walk through the cemetery, which was used until 1800 when the New Cemetery was opened, and contains some of the country's oldest surviving tombstones.

Szeroka 40. ☎ **012/429-57-35.** www.krakow.jewish.org. Admission 7 zł ($2.80/£1.60). Sun–Fri 9am–4pm.

Temple Synagogue ★   The 19th century, when this progressive synagogue was built, was a period of great experimentation in Jewish architecture. This synagogue's exterior reflects the influence of Sephardic Jews. The interior has been partly restored, making it the most attractive inside of any of Kazimierz's surviving synagogues.

Miodowa 24. (✆ **012/429-57-35.** www.krakow.jewish.org.pl. Sun–Fri 10am–6pm.

Podgórze

South of Kazimierz, across the Vistula River, lies the wartime Jewish ghetto of Podgórze. It was here, at today's **Plac Bohaterów Getta,** where thousands of the city's Jews were forcibly moved and incarcerated in March 1941. Much of the area has since been rebuilt, and walking the modern street plan today you'll be hard-pressed to imagine what it must have been like for thousands of Jews to be pent up here with only the prospect of eventually being sent to the camps at Auschwitz or, more nearby, Płaszów. The ghetto was eventually razed in 1943 and the inhabitants murdered. Look for the **Apteka Pod Orłem** on the Plac Bohaterów Getta, which today houses a small but fascinating museum on the history of the ghetto.

This part of Kraków is sometimes called "Schindler's Kraków" (see box) since the enamel factory where German industrialist **Oskar Schindler** employed his Jewish workforce is a 10- to 15-minute walk away (follow Lipowa Street, which leads away from the Plac Bohaterów Getta). At press time, the factory was abandoned but occasionally still open to the public to walk around (this may change soon if plans go forward to open a museum here).

Apteka Pod Orłem (Pharmacy Under the Eagle) ★★   You'll find a riveting collection of photographs and documents from life in the Podgórze ghetto here, from its inception in 1941 to its eventual liquidation 2 years later. During the war, the pharmacy was operated by Pole Tadeusz Pankiewicz, who provided medicine to Jews and helped at least some to escape. The exhibition here includes two excellent films. The first, an American documentary from the 1930s, shows typical Jewish life in Kazimierz. The second, a haunting, silent film taken by the Germans, shows the deportation process itself in 1941, as Jewish families are forced to move their belongings across the river amid hopes for a new life (but as we, the viewers, know, the move resulted in a certain death).

Plac Bohaterów Getta 18. (✆ **012/656-56-25.** www.mhk.pl. Admission 4 zł ($1.60/90p); free Mon. Mon 10am–2pm; Tues–Thurs, Sat 9am–4pm; Fri 10am–5pm. Closed Sun.

Oskar Schindler's Emalia Factory ★   An essential stop for anyone interested in the history of the Podgórze ghetto or in the film *Schindler's List.* Some of the scenes were filmed here, and you'll have a distinct sense of déjà vu just arriving at the depressing site. The factory is closed down, but occasionally the gates are open for an impromptu look in. If you can get in, be sure to get a look at the guest book. More than once you'll see the signature of a former Jewish worker here, along with the words "because of Oskar Schindler I am still alive." Gripping.

Lipowa 4. No phone. Hours vary.

Nowa Huta

In the 1950s, the Communist authorities decided to try to win over the hearts and minds of skeptical Cracovians by building this model Socialist community, just a tram ride away from the Rynek Główny. They built an enormous steel mill (*Nowa Huta* means "new mill"), as well as rows of carefully constructed workers' houses, shops, and recreational

Schindler's Kraków

The tragic story of Poland's Jews and of life in the Nazi wartime ghettos has inspired fewer two Oscar-winning movies: Roman Polański's *The Pianist* (2002) is set in Warsaw's wartime ghetto (see the box on p. 86). Even bigger may be Steven Spielberg's *Schindler's List* (1993), starring Liam Neeson, Ben Kingsley, and Ralph Fiennes. The film won seven Oscars, including Best Picture and Best Director. The film was based on the novel *Schindler's Ark,* by Thomas Keneally, and recounts the true story of German industrialist Oskar Schindler, who comes to Kraków at the start of World War II to make his fortune selling war goods to the German army. Though Schindler is a member of the Nazi party, he slowly comes to recognize the evil nature of the destruction of the Jewish community. By arguing to the Nazi hierarchy that he needs his Jewish workers to continue output for the German war effort, Schindler eventually manages to save some 1,100 Jewish people from certain death at Auschwitz. Much of the filming was done on location at various points around Kazimierz and Schindler's former enamel factory in Podgórze across the river, as well as at the former Płaszów labor camp and Auschwitz itself. If you've recently watched the movie, you'll recognize several shots as you walk through Kazimierz. The best-known location is the still highly evocative courtyard running between Józefa and Meiselsa streets (now home to a bunch of cafes and restaurants). Several travel agencies offer full-length tours of "Schindler's Kraków" (see "Customized Tours," below). The movie was not without its criticisms, chief among them that Spielberg somehow managed to diminish the inherently evil nature of Nazism by portraying Nazis merely as crazies and lunatics. Others said he had commercialized the atrocities or that he'd managed somehow to exaggerate Schindler's goodness. Be that as it may, the movie continues to rise in the eyes of film critics. The American Film Institute recently ranked it number 8 on its list of the 100 best American films.

facilities for what was conceived of as the city of the future. It didn't quite work out as planned: Kraków intellectuals were never impressed by having a steel mill so nearby, and the workers never really cottoned on to the Communist cause. But Nowa Huta is still standing and in its own way looks better than ever. Any fan of urban design or anyone with a penchant for Communist history will enjoy a couple hours of walking around, admiring the buildings, the broad avenues, and the parks and squares. There's even a small museum here, **the Museum of the History of Nowa Huta,** to tell the story. The structures have held up remarkably well, and indeed the area looks better now than it ever has. Part of the reason for this is that the mills are no longer running at anywhere near capacity, so the air is cleaner. And, ironically, capitalism has added a touch of badly needed prosperity, meaning the residents now have a little extra money to maintain the buildings. Still, there's something undeniably sad, too; this grandiose project in social engineering has been reduced to little more than a curiosity (though more than 100,000 people still call Nowa Huta home). The shops that line the magnificent boulevards—once conceived to sell everything a typical family would need (even if the shops rarely had anything worth buying)—look forlorn; many of them are empty. You'll also search in vain for a decent restaurant, so plan on eating back in Kraków. The easiest way to reach

Nowa Huta is to take tram nos. 4 or 15 from the train station about 20 minutes to the stop "Plac Centralny." From here it's a short walk to the main square, renamed to honor former U.S. President Ronald Reagan. If you'd like a more in-depth tour, **Crazy Guides** (see "Customized Tours," below) offers guided visits to Nowa Huta, including travel in a Communist-era Trabant car for about 120 zł ($48/£27) per person.

Museum of the History of Nowa Huta ★ A must for fans of urban design or readers of trendy design magazines such as *Wallpaper* or *Dwell*. Others may want to skip it. The museum itself occupies a typical housing block built in 1958 and contains the history of the Nowa Huta quarter in documents, designs, and photos.

Os. Słoneczne 16. ✆ **012/425-97-55.** www.mhk.pl. Admission 4 zł ($1.60/90p). Tues–Sun 9am–4pm.

CUSTOMIZED TOURS

Several private companies offer walking and bus tours of the city, as well as themed tours, such as Jewish Kraków or Communist Kraków, and longer excursions to Zakopane, the Wieliczka Salt Mines, and Auschwitz-Birkenau. The tourist information office has details about tours. **Cracow City Tours** (Pl. Matejki 2; ✆ **012/421-13-33;** www.cracowcity tours.pl) offers possibly the fullest range of options, including, among others, a John Paul II tour, a *Schindler's List* tour, and a Polish vodka-tasting night. They also offer excursions to Czę-nortowa and Zakopane, and a river-rafting trip on the Dunajec River. **Classic Travel** (Grodzka 38; ✆ **0607/884-488**) offers guided tours to both Auschwitz-Birkenau and the Wieliczka Salt Mines. Both tours start at around 90 zł ($36/£20) per person and include all expenses. **Crazy Guides** (Floriańska 38; ✆ **0500/091–200;** www.crazyguides. com) specializes in Communist theme tours, and offers both a "Communism" and a "Communism Deluxe" tour—the latter includes lunch in a Communist-era milk bar.

SHOPPING

The main shopping areas are around the Rynek Główny in the Old Town, the Royal Route leading to Wawel Castle, and the former Jewish quarter of Kazimierz. While Warsaw may be better for high fashion and Gdańsk better for amber, there's no shortage of things to buy in Kraków. Traditional gifts include carved wooden boxes and chess sets, lace, traditional Polish clothing, vodka, chocolates, and, yes, amber.

Art & Antiques

Kraków is crammed with art, antiques, and junk shops. Most of the better stores are concentrated in the Old Town along the streets that radiate from the Main Square, especially Św. Jana. Poke your nose in at the ancient books, maps, and old postcards at Stefan Kamiński (Św. Jana 3; ✆ **012/422-39-65**). Sławkowska Street also has a nice grouping of art and antiques stores. **Atest** (Sławkowska 14; ✆ **012/421-95-19**) is one of the best. For some unusual modern Polish painting and sculpture, stop by **Galeria AG** (Dominikański 2; ✆ **012/429-51-78;** www.galeriaag.art.pl).

Kazimierz has emerged as a second shopping mecca; here, the emphasis understandably is on Judaica, but the little streets are filled with shops selling everything from trendy art and design to out-and-out junk. **Antyki Józefa** (Kupa 3; ✆ **012/422-01-27**) is typical for Kazimierz, an antique store offering both genuine antiques and junk, but it's not always easy to tell one from the other.

Books, Prints & Maps

For English-language books, Kraków is blessed with at least two treasures. The first is undeniably **Massolit Books** (Felicjanek 4; ✆ **012/432-41-50;** www.massolit.com), easily one of the best new and used English bookshops in Europe. Massolit is especially strong on Polish authors in translation, but has thousands of titles under all conceivable categories (plus a very cute cafe and a quiet, contemplative ambience highly conducive to reading and thinking). The other is **Austeria** in Kazimierz (Józefa 38; © 012/430-68-89), next to the High Synagogue. Here you'll find dozens of titles on Judaica, Polish history, and the Holocaust, as well as some incredibly beautiful photographs, posters, CDs, and reproductions of old maps. **Empik** (Rynek Główny 5; © 012/423-81-90; www.empik. com) is a kind of Polish version of Borders or Barnes and Noble, with huge shelves filled with (mostly Polish) books, but also a good selection of magazines (including some English titles), CDs, and DVDs. **Cracow Poster Gallery** (Stolarska 8–10; © 012/421-26-40; www.cracowpostergallery.com) is one-stop shopping for vintage film and exhibition posters, an art form Poles are known for around the world.

Gourmet Food & Vodka

Kraków is a good place to find that exclusive bottle of Polish vodka. Two stores stand out. **Szambelan** (Gołębia 2; © 012/430-24-09; www.szambelan.com.pl) and **F. H. Herbert** (Grodzka 59; no phone). Szambelan is best known for its exotic bottle shapes, but both stores carry a nice range of the best straight and flavored vodkas, as well as an excellent selection of wines and other beverages. **Krakowski Kredens** (Grodzka 7; © 012/423-81-59; www.krakowskikredens.pl) is a relative newcomer in the food segment, offering beautifully wrapped and packaged jams, jellies, teas, fruit syrups, and chocolates as well as a huge deli case of mouthwatering sausages and cheeses. Come here to grab a gift food set or a picnic lunch. **Ciasteczka z Krakowa** (Św. Tomasza 21; © 012/423-22-27) specializes in homemade cookies, cakes, and chocolates all wrapped up in fancy boxes. No discussion of Polish food shops would be complete with mentioning **Wawel Chocolates** (Rynek Główny 33; © 012/423-12-47; www.wawel-sklep.com.pl), where mouth-watering pralines, fruit-filled chocolates, and nuts are sold by the gram and packaged in cute little boxes.

Shopping Centers

Galeria Kazimierz (Podgórska 34; © 433-01-01; www.galeriakazimierz.pl) is an upscale shopping mall within easy walking distance of the Plac Nowy in Kazimierz. It boasts more than 130 boutiques, shops, stores, and cafes of all kinds. Handy if you need to pick up something you forgot at home.

Traditional Handicrafts & Jewelry

For classic Polish souvenirs, including handicrafts, woodcarving, and (naturally) amber, first try the stalls at the **Cloth Hall (Sukiennice)** in the middle of the Rynek Główny. Hidden among the "Poland" T-shirts and mass-produced icons, you'll find some beautifully carved wood and amber chess sets, as well as locally produced cloth, lace, and leather goods. **Galeria Ora** (Św. Anny 3/1a; © 012/426-89-20; www.galeria-ora.com) is a cut above the average amber place, with a group of young jewelry designers working with more contemporary settings. For amber, amber, and more amber, check out **Boruni** (www.boruni.pl), with shops in the Sukiennice (© 012/430-24-01), at Kanonicza 22 (© 012/422-36-96), and Grodzka 60 (© 012/428-50-86), for high-quality, eye-catching stones in contemporary and traditional settings.

WHERE TO STAY

Kraków has some beautiful hotels, and if you've got the cash and want to splurge you can do so in real style. Most of the stunning properties are located in the Old Town, along

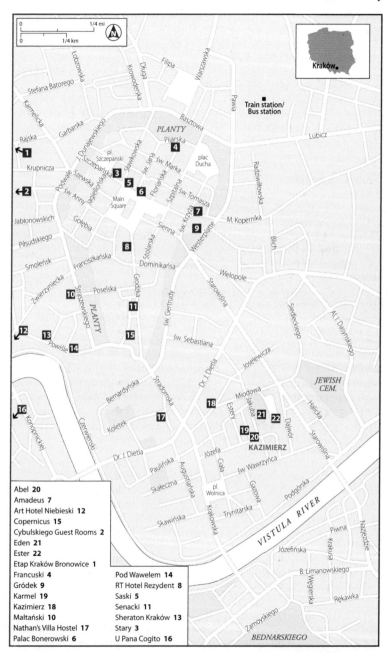

Kraków

Abel **20**
Amadeus **7**
Art Hotel Niebieski **12**
Copernicus **15**
Cybulskiego Guest Rooms **2**
Eden **21**
Ester **22**
Etap Kraków Bronowice **1**
Francuski **4**
Gródek **9**
Karmel **19**
Kazimierz **18**
Maltański **10**
Nathan's Villa Hostel **17**
Palac Bonerowski **6**

Pod Wawelem **14**
RT Hotel Rezydent **8**
Saski **5**
Senacki **11**
Sheraton Kraków **13**
Stary **3**
U Pana Cogito **16**

the streets running off the Main Square or tucked in a quiet park location off the Planty. A second cluster of decent places to stay is in Kazimierz. You won't find the 5-star luxury class here like in the Old Town, but there are a number of nice 3- and 4-star properties that are, on balance, a little cheaper and quieter than their Old Town counterparts. As for location, both are excellent. An Old Town property puts you just a few steps away from the restaurants and cafes around the square, as well as Kraków's main museums and sites. On the other hand, if you're into bars, clubs, and trendy restaurants, then Kazimierz is where you want to be. Either way, the distances between the two are not great, just a 15-minute walk or short cab ride.

Rates are generally highest between April 1 and October 31, as well as over the Christmas and New Year holidays. Room prices drop by 20% or more from November through March. The prices below are for a standard double room (twin beds) in high season (outside of the Christmas and New Year holiday season).

Very Expensive

Amadeus ★   A fully modern hotel that is working hard—and succeeding—at recreating an authentic 18th-century feel. For the room interiors, think Colonial Williamsburg, with intricately carved white woodworking for the beds and nightstands, chandeliers, and floor-to-ceiling floral print drapes. Mozart could drop by and actually feel quite at home. The service is top-notch and the location, just a couple yards off the main square, is ideal. A perfect choice if you want a hotel that will stick in your mind as long as Kraków's main square does.

Mikołajska 20. ⓒ 012/429-60-70. Fax 012/429-60-72. www.hotel-amadeus.pl. 22 units. 700 zł ($280/£157) double. AE, DC, MC, V. **Amenities:** Restaurant; fitness club; sauna; limited room service; nonsmoking rooms. *In room:* A/C, TV, dataport, minibar, hair dryer.

Copernicus ★★   Managed by the international Relais & Châteaux group, this is certainly the best of the boutique-size properties—and possibly of all the hotels—in town. You'll be charmed immediately by the enormous Renaissance atrium shooting to the ceiling, and the period detailing from the 16th century that extends throughout the hotel and to the wood-beamed ceilings in the rooms on the first and second floors. A fresco dating from the year 1500, the *Four Fathers of the Church,* covers the wall in room no. 101.

Kanonicza 16. ⓒ 012/424-34-00. Fax 012/424-34-05. www.hotel.com.pl. 29 units. 900 zł ($360/£200) double. AE, DC, MC, V. **Amenities:** Restaurant; indoor pool; sauna; room service; nonsmoking rooms. *In room:* A/C, TV, dataport, minibar, hair dryer, safe.

Gródek ★★   A good choice if your taste runs to more traditional furnishings such as frilly bedspreads, thick carpets, and patterned drapes. The setting couldn't be more romantic, in a beautifully restored 16th-century townhouse in a quiet spot of the Old Town near a Dominican convent. There's an excellent in-house spa and a restaurant—serving upscale international entrées such as cinnamon-marinated duck breast and curry-flavored lamb chops—rounds out the charm. It's slightly cheaper than the competition, making it a relatively good value in this category.

Na Gródku 4. ⓒ 012/431-90-30. Fax 012/378-93-15. www.donimirski.com. 23 units. 650 zł ($260/£146) standard double. AE, DC, MC, V. **Amenities:** Restaurant; sauna; room service; nonsmoking rooms. *In room:* A/C, TV, dataport, minibar, hair dryer, safe.

Palac Bonerowski ★★★   Kraków's latest entry in the 5-star category is a jaw-dropper: a sensitively restored 13th-century townhouse just off the main square. Many period elements, including some original stonework and carvings, have been preserved in the spacious rooms. The furnishings are tasteful and traditional, with cream-leather sofas and armchairs, and hardwood tables and chairs. The floors are polished parquet accented with Oriental carpets. You can't miss the 15m-high (50-ft.) crystal chandelier running down the main staircase.

Św. Jana 1. ℂ **012/374-13-00.** Fax 012/374-13-05. www.palacbonerowski.pl. 8 units. 900 zł ($360/£200) double. AE, DC, MC, V. **Amenities:** 2 restaurants; courtesy car; 24-hr. room service; nonsmoking rooms. *In room:* A/C, TV, dataport, minibar, hair dryer, safe.

Sheraton Kraków ★   This is a relatively recent addition to the high-end corporate market, but is already setting standards as arguably the best business hotel in the city. Everything is conceived with comfort and convenience in mind all the way down to the high-tech fitness center's special "Cracow Experience" massage ("ideal after long sightseeing, travel, or work"). Unlike many Sheratons around the world, this one is actually in a good location for sightseeing, close to the river and within an easy walk of the Old Town or Wawel Castle. Ask for a room with a view toward the Wawel.

Powiśle 7. ℂ **012/662-10-00.** Fax 012/662-11-00. www.sheraton.com/krakow. 232 units. 680 zł ($272/£150) double. AE, DC, MC, V. **Amenities:** 3 restaurants; health club; sauna; concierge; courtesy car; business center; salon; 24-hr. room service; dry cleaning; executive-level rooms; nonsmoking rooms. *In room:* A/C, TV, fax, dataport, minibar, hair dryer, iron, safe.

Stary ★★   Eye-catching, upmarket renovation of a former *palais* just off the Rynek Główny, complete with silk fabrics, exotic hardwoods, and high-quality marble. Some of the rooms have maintained their period details, showing off the building's original frescoes; others have a brushed-steel contemporary look that's right out of New York's East Village. Ask to see several and choose your mood. Luscious amenities include two indoor pools and a salt cave.

Szczepańska 5. ℂ **012/384-08-08.** Fax 012/384-08-09. www.stary.hotel.com.pl. 53 units. 850 zł ($340/£190) double Jan–Mar; 900 zł ($360/£200) double Apr–Dec. AE, DC, MC, V. **Amenities:** Restaurant; indoor pool; sauna; room service; nonsmoking rooms. *In room:* A/C, TV, dataport, minibar, hair dryer, safe.

Expensive

Ester ★   One of a handful of 4-star hotels in Kazimierz, the Ester is probably the nicest overall property in the former Jewish quarter. The hotel was renovated a couple years ago, and the rooms have an understated, white-linen feel synonymous with a good boutique property. The hotel's Wi-Fi access extends to the public areas and onto the outdoor terrace (so even if you're not staying here you can bring your laptop and surreptitiously check your email). The location, at the heart of the former ghetto, is just a short walk away from the synagogues and major sights.

Szeroka 20. ℂ **012/429-11-88.** Fax 012/429-12-33. www.hotel-ester.krakow.pl. 32 units. 450 zł ($180/£100) double. AE, DC, MC, V. **Amenities:** Restaurant; limited room service; dry cleaning; nonsmoking rooms. *In room:* A/C, TV, dataport, minibar, hair dryer, safe.

Francuski ★   Lovely Art Nouveau–style hotel dating from 1912 and perched just beside St. Florian's Gate, near the traditional royal entryway to the Old Town. The rooms are on the small side, but nicely appointed in a mix of contemporary and period furnishings. The romantic setting makes this a popular honeymoon hotel for Polish newlyweds. You may need to contact the hotel directly to book, since the hotel's Orbis-run website is a disaster to try to negotiate.

Pijarska 13. ℂ **012/627-37-77.** Fax 012/627-37-00. www.orbis.pl. 42 units. 450 zł ($180/£100) double. MC, V. **Amenities:** Nonsmoking rooms. *In room:* Some A/C, TV, dataport, minibar, trouser press, hair dryer.

Maltański ★★ Beautifully renovated boutique with a crisp linens and fresh flowers kind of feel. Under the same management as the similar but more expensive Gródek (see above). The location is excellent, within easy walking distance of both the Wawel Castle and the Rynek. The rooms are small, but beautifully outfitted in a traditional Laura Ashley look.

Straszewskiego 14. ✆ **012/431-00-10.** Fax 012/378-93-12. www.donimirski.com. 16 units. 420 zł ($168/ £94) standard double. AE, DC, MC, V. **Amenities:** Restaurant; room service; nonsmoking rooms. *In room:* A/C, TV, dataport, minibar, hair dryer.

Pod Wawelem ★★ This was the first of what it is hoped will become a Kraków lodging trend: an unfussy, simple, yet stylish boutique hotel. The location is a big draw: a short walk from the Wawel Castle and the river and about a 10-minute walk from the main square. Be sure to request a room with a view on the Wawel. The rooms are outfitted in a high-quality minimalist style, with cheery light-colored walls and dark woods. In-room amenities include free Wi-Fi.

Na Groblach 22. ✆ **012/426-26-26.** Fax 012/422-33-99. www.hotelpodwawelem.pl. 47 units. 450 zł ($180/£100) double. AE, DC, MC, V. **Amenities:** Restaurant; room service; sauna; nonsmoking rooms. *In room:* A/C, TV, dataport, minibar, hair dryer, safe.

RT Hotel Rezydent ★ Not quite the upscale boutique hotel that this place markets itself as, but a nice choice nevertheless, given the absolutely top-notch location just off the main square and on the Royal Route that leads to Wawel and beyond. The rooms are relatively small, but with sturdy, stylishly modern furniture and hardwood floors.

Grodzka 9. ✆ **012/429-54-10.** Fax 012/429-55-76. www.rezydent.krakow.pl. 59 units. 380 zł ($152/£85) double. AE, DC, MC, V. **Amenities:** Restaurant; nonsmoking rooms. *In room:* Some A/C, TV, dataport, minibar, hair dryer.

Senacki ★★ Another sensitive restoration of an older townhouse. This popular hotel sports an excellent location, between the Wawel Castle and the Old Town along the former coronation route, and tastefully decorated rooms, many with views over the Old Town.

Grodzka 51. ✆ **012/422-76-86.** Fax 012/422-79-34. www.senacki.krakow.pl. 20 units. 380 zł ($152/£85) double. AE, DC, MC, V. **Amenities:** Restaurant; nonsmoking rooms. *In room:* Some A/C, TV, dataport.

Moderate

Art Hotel Niebieski ★★ Comfortable, good value hotel situated in a renovated villa in the suburb of Salwator, about a 20-minute walk from the Old Town. The rooms are spotlessly clean and done out in handsome, traditional furnishings. It's easiest to take a taxi here when you first arrive. Good on-site Italian restaurant.

Flisacka 3. ✆ **012/431-18-58.** Fax 012/431-18-28. http://niebieski.com.pl. 13 units. 320 zł ($128/£72) double. AE, DC, MC, V. **Amenities:** Restaurant; limited room service; nonsmoking rooms. *In room:* Some A/C, TV, dataport, minibar, hair dryer.

Eden ★ A good second choice in Kazimierz at this price level if you can't get in at the Karmel (see below). It's similar in many ways and well maintained and quiet, but not quite as immediately charming. The rooms are modestly furnished and on the plain side, more functional than inspiring. Uniquely, the Eden has a "salt grotto" spa in the basement. The idea is for you to sit in the special saline air for 45 minutes to reduce stress and heal a multitude of ills, ranging from asthma to tonsillitis to acne. Once you've cured whatever ails you, head around the corner to the local pub called (not kidding): "Ye Olde Goat."

Ciemna 15. ☏ **012/430-65-65.** Fax 012/430-67-67. www.hoteleden.pl. 25 units. 300 zł ($120/£67) double. AE, DC, MC, V. **Amenities:** Restaurant; spa; room service; nonsmoking rooms. *In room:* A/C, TV, dataport, minibar, hair dryer.

Karmel ★★★ (Finds) The most charming and inviting of Kazimierz's hotels and pensions. Maybe it's the quiet location, in a forgotten spot in the former ghetto, or the flowers hanging off the house windows, or the cute Italian restaurant on the ground floor. Something about the hotel says "home." Parquet flooring throughout. Splurge on a "comfort" room, with a big double bed and a couple of sofas in the room.

Kupa 15. ☏ **012/430-67-00.** Fax 012/430-67-26. www.karmel.com.pl. 11 units. 300 zł ($120/£67) double. AE, DC, MC, V. **Amenities:** Restaurant; room service; nonsmoking rooms. *In room:* A/C, TV, dataport, minibar, hair dryer.

Kazimierz Probably the most popular hotel in Kraków's former Jewish quarter, but not necessarily the best. The plain lobby and public areas are redeemed somewhat by a beautiful, enclosed inner courtyard. The rooms, too, are nothing special, but are clean and comfortable. The location is superb, near the entrance to the former Jewish quarter and also not far from Wawel Castle and the Old Town. They sometimes lower the rates on weekends, so ask when you book.

Miodowa 16. ☏ **012/421-66-29.** Fax 012/422-28-84. www.hk.com.pl. 35 units. 300 zł ($120/£67) double. AE, DC, MC, V. **Amenities:** Restaurant; room service; nonsmoking rooms. *In room:* Some A/C, TV, dataport, minibar, hair dryer.

Saski ★ (Finds) Kraków residents might laugh at this hotel being labeled a "find" since it's one of the best-known hotels in the city, right off the main square. But what many don't realize is that it's at least 100 zł a night less than other hotels in its class and location (especially if you go for a double with a shared bath). So if you're looking for a glorious old hotel, with a tiled-floor lobby and chandeliers, and don't want to shell out major cash, this is your place. Ask to see several rooms, since they're all different—some are quite modern and border on the plain, while others are in high period style with quaint, old-fashioned beds and tables.

Sławkowska 3. ☏ **012/421-42-22.** Fax 012/421-48-30. www.hotel-saski.com.pl. 20 units. 300 zł ($120/£67) double without bathroom; 410 zł ($164/£92) with bathroom. AE, DC, MC, V. **Amenities:** Restaurant; room service; nonsmoking rooms. *In room:* Some A/C, TV, dataport, minibar, hair dryer.

Inexpensive

Abel ★ There are lots of good reasons to stay in Kazimierz. Admittedly the location is not as beautiful as the Old Town, but Kazimierz is much cheaper and somehow feels closer to what makes Kraków tick these days, with all the clubs, restaurants, and party spots popping up. This small, plain hotel is in the heart of the former ghetto. Don't expect much at this price point other than a clean bed and a private bath. No in-room Internet.

Józefa 30. ☏ **012/411-87-36.** Fax 012/411-87-36. www.hotelabel.pl. 15 units. 240 zł ($90/£54) double. AE, DC, MC, V. **Amenities:** Nonsmoking rooms. *In room:* TV.

Cybulskiego Guest Rooms ★★ Not a hotel *per se*, but a series of efficiency apartments with private showers and shared kitchen facilities that offers more privacy than a hostel. The rooms are clean and have good Wi-Fi access. The location is just outside the center, about a 10- to 15-minute walk to the central square. A big plus is the laundry service for about 25 zł ($10/£6) per load, a life-saver in laundromat-deprived Poland.

Cybulskiego 6. ☎ 012/423-05-32. www.freerooms.pl. 14 units. 144 zł ($58/£32) double with bath and shared kitchen; 126 zł ($50/£28) double without bath. AE, DC, MC, V. **Amenities:** Nonsmoking rooms. *In room:* TV, dataport, fridge.

Etap Kraków Bronowice ★ Something Kraków sorely needed: a big, budget hotel that offers clean beds at a fair price, without unnecessary amenities you're unlikely to use on a short stay and that only pad the bill. The major drawback is location, about 5km (3 miles) from the center of town. (Though if you're traveling by car, it's convenient to both the A4 freeway to Wrocław and the E77 to Warsaw.) There's limited Wi-Fi access in the lobby and breakfast room.

Armii Krajowej 11a. ☎ 012/626-11-45. Fax 012/626-20-60. www.orbis.pl. 120 units. 179 zł ($72/£40) double, breakfast 18 zł ($8/£5). AE, DC, MC, V. **Amenities:** Restaurant; nonsmoking rooms. *In room:* A/C, TV.

Nathan's Villa Hostel ★ The American owner of this well-run and highly regarded hostel just across from Wawel Castle says his aim is to combine the social aspects of a hostel with the amenities you'd expect from a hotel. And at this price he definitely gets it right. In addition to the standard 8- and 10-bed rooms typical for a hostel, Nathan's rents out private doubles. In summer most of the guests are backpackers, but during the rest of the year the hostel fills up with people of all age groups looking to save money while not sacrificing on location or cleanliness. Perks include free laundry, an Internet room, and a DVD movie room for rainy days.

Św. Agnieszki 1. ☎ 012/422-35-45. www.nathansvilla.com. 20 units. 180 zł ($72/£40) double. MC, V. **Amenities:** Bar; laundry service; nonsmoking rooms.

U Pana Cogito ★★ (Value) If you don't mind walking, this renovated villa complex, about 15 minutes by foot from the city center, represents real value. The modern rooms, done up in neutral beige and gold, have all the personality of a standard Holiday Inn, but they're clean and quiet, with nicely done bathrooms and unexpected touches at this price point like air-conditioning in the rooms and full Internet access (both Wi-Fi and LAN connections).

Bałuckiego 6. ☎ 012/269-72-00. Fax 012/269-72-02. www.pcogito.pl. 14 units. 250 zł ($100/£56) double. AE, DC, MC, V. **Amenities:** Restaurant; nonsmoking rooms. *In room:* A/C, TV, dataport, minibar, hair dryer.

WHERE TO DINE

Most of the fancier and more established restaurants are in the Old Town on the main square or along the streets running off the square, particularly to the south. The newer, trendier, and sometimes better places are located in Kazimierz. One area in the former ghetto to look is along Plac Nowy; the other dining cluster, including most of the Jewish-themed restaurants, is along Szeroka. Except for the very pricey places in the Old Town, dress is mostly casual. That's particularly true of the Kazimierz locales, which cater to a largely student and young professional crowd. Note that though many restaurants will claim to stay open until 11pm or "until the last guest," on slow nights kitchens often start closing down at 10pm. Go early to avoid disappointment.

Very Expensive

Cyrano de Bergerac ★★★ FRENCH It's such a pleasure to taste Polish food with a French twist when it's done this well. That means staples like game, pork, and duck, but with a nuance. The duck, for example, isn't served with apple or cranberry, but caramelized peach and cardamom instead. The pork knuckle is candied in honey—the glazing giving it a sweetish barbecue flavor. The exposed brick interior is stunning, with

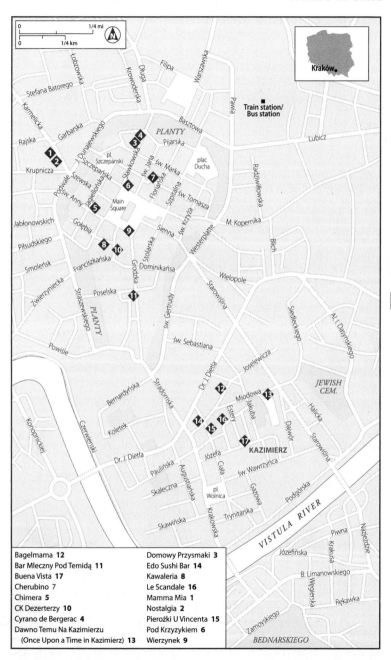

Bagelmama **12**
Bar Mleczny Pod Temidą **11**
Buena Vista **17**
Cherubino **7**
Chimera **5**
CK Dezerterzy **10**
Cyrano de Bergerac **4**
Dawno Temu Na Kazimierzu
  (Once Upon a Time in Kazimierz) **13**
Domowy Przysmaki **3**
Edo Sushi Bar **14**
Kawaleria **8**
Le Scandale **16**
Mamma Mia **1**
Nostalgia **2**
Pierożki U Vincenta **15**
Pod Krzyzykiem **6**
Wierzynek **9**

candlelight and white linens on the tables. The service is polished but can be slow on busy nights. Beware the prices on wines. Dress for this one and reserve in advance.

Sławkowska 26. ✆ **012/411-72-88.** Lunch and dinner items 40 zł–90 zł ($16–$36/£9–£20). Reservations recommended. AE, DC, MC, V. Mon–Sat noon–midnight.

Edo Sushi Bar ★★ JAPANESE   One of the best sushi restaurants in central Europe is on a quiet corner in Kazimierz. The hushed, spare, modern decor puts the emphasis firmly on the food. Very fresh nigiri sushi and some creative maki rolls keep the crowds happy. Ask the guys behind the sushi bar what looks good and settle in for a great meal.

Bożego Ciała 3. ✆ **012/422-24-24.** Lunch and dinner items 40 zł–60 zł ($16–$24/£9–£14). AE, DC, MC, V. Daily noon–11pm.

Pod Krzyżykiem ★★ POLISH   The chefs at this award-winning restaurant take traditional Polish cooking and give it a little tweak to good effect. The three-course lunch menu at 40 zł is particularly good value. The schnitzel, served with potato salad and berries, comes highly recommended from none other than the Polish version of *Newsweek* magazine, which also rated it one of the city's best places for a business lunch. The funky interior is literally "surreal"—you'll have to see for yourself.

Rynek Główny 39. ✆ **012/433-70-10.** Lunch and dinner items 40 zł–60 zł ($16–$24/£9–£14). AE, DC, MC, V. Daily noon–11pm.

Wierzynek ★★ POLISH   Less a restaurant and more a revered institution on par with Wawel Castle and the Old Town Tower. This esteemed eatery has played host to visiting dignitaries, celebs, and heads of state since way back in 1364, when owner Mikołaj Wierzynek threw a banquet in honor of the marriage between Holy Roman Emperor Charles IV and the granddaughter of Polish King Kazimierz the Great. The cuisine is an imaginative take on traditional Polish cooking, with the emphasis on treats such as wild boar, quail, and venison. This one is worth reserving in advance and dressing up for.

Rynek Główny 15. ✆ **012/424-96-00.** Lunch and dinner items 40 zł–90 zł ($16–$36/£9–£20). AE, DC, MC, V. Daily noon–11pm.

Expensive

Cherubino ★ (Kids) POLISH/ITALIAN   Eclectic Polish-Italian restaurant popular with both students and parents with small children (lots of wooden rocking chairs and crayons are on hand to keep the kids busy). Expect indifferent service but very good grilled pork and beef dishes, and more than passable Italian fare.

Św. Tomasza 15. ✆ **012/429-40-07.** Lunch and dinner items 25 zł–45 zł ($10–$17/£5.60–£10). No credit cards. Daily 9am–8pm.

Chimera ★★ POLISH   Really two restaurants in one: first, an expensive but delicious Polish restaurant, featuring old-style recipes centered on lamb, goose, and game. Then there's also a cheaper salad bar that's better value and extremely popular around lunchtime, with about 40 different salads and lots of vegetarian offerings.

Św. Anny 3. ✆ **012/292-12-12.** Reservations recommended. Lunch and dinner items 40 zł–60 zł ($16–$24/£9–£14), salad bar (large plate) 16 zł ($6/£3.60). AE, DC, MC, V. Daily noon–11pm.

Dawno Temu Na Kazimierzu (Once Upon a Time in Kazimierz) ★★★ JEWISH   Finally, the kind of toned-down, less kitschy Jewish restaurant that Kazimierz has long been waiting for. It's relaxed and intimate, with the inevitable knick-knacks and "homespun" interior, but this time creating a warming—not distracting—effect (as with the other restaurants in the area). The food is great: especially recommended is the roast duck with cherries.

Szeroka 1. ℂ **012/421-21-17.** Lunch and dinner items 24 zł–40 zł ($10–$16/£5.40–£9). AE, DC, MC, V. Daily 11am–10pm.

Kawaleria ★ POLISH   Similar to Chimera (see above) in terms of the menu and presentation. The wild boar gammon is the highlight, served in a cranberry sauce with cabbage and chickpeas. The surroundings are impeccable and the location is just a short walk from the Rynek.

Gołębia 4. ℂ **012/430-24-32.** Reservations recommended. Lunch and dinner items 40 zł–60 zł ($16–$24/£9–£14). AE, DC, MC, V. Daily noon–11pm.

Nostalgia ★★ POLISH   A meal here is like dining in the country home of a well-to-do friend—warm and inviting yet still refined and special. The atmosphere extends to the cooking as well: Polish staples such as *pierogi*, pork, and game, but well turned out and served on fine china. This is a perfect balance between something like Cyrano de Bergerac (see above) and CK Dezerterzy (see below): the attention to detail of the former, but with the more relaxed feel and prices of the latter. Reserve in advance to be on the safe side.

Karmelicka 10. ℂ **012/425-42-60.** Reservations recommended. Lunch and dinner items 25 zł–45 zł ($10–$17/£5.60–£10). AE, DC, MC, V. Daily noon–11pm.

Moderate

Buena Vista ★★ LATIN AMERICAN   This highly recommended casual tapas restaurant in Kazimierz serves excellent Spanish- and Latin American–style food such as paella with chicken and spicy sausage. There's a full range of mojito drinks and tequila-based cocktails. In the evening, the bar area makes way for spirited salsa dancing.

Józefa 26. ℂ **0668/035-000.** Lunch and dinner items 25 zł–35 zł ($10–$14/£5.6–£7.80). AE, DC, MC, V. Daily noon–11pm.

CK Dezerterzy ★ POLISH   A cozy, family-style tavern serving well-prepared traditional Polish cooking in a warm setting down a side street off the Rynek Główny. It's perfect if you've just arrived and want a hassle-free, decent meal and don't want to stray too far from the hotel. The only possible drawback is that it's popular with guidebooks (like this one), so while you'll probably find many Poles on the night you're here, you may also wind up next to a table of guests from your own hometown.

Bracka 6. ℂ **012/422-79-31.** Lunch and dinner items 15 zł–30 zł ($6–$12/£3.40–£7). AE, DC, MC, V. Daily 10am–10pm.

Le Scandale ★ INTERNATIONAL   Great breakfast or light lunch spot right on Plac Nowy in Kazimierz. Decent bagels, eggs, and coffee are served starting at 8am. On weekends, arrive early to snag one of the highly coveted square-side tables, perfect for people watching while sipping your espresso. The lunch and dinner menu is heavy on international munchies, like quesadillas, simple pastas, and sandwiches, but also does well with steaks and seafood.

Plac Nowy 9. ℂ **012/430-68-55.** Lunch and dinner items 15 zł–30 zł ($6–$12/£3.40–£7). AE, DC, MC, V. Daily 9am–11pm.

Mamma Mia ★★ ITALIAN   Truly excellent wood-fired pizzas and a full range of pasta dishes, featuring the freshest ingredients. The refined space, not far from the main square, is perfect for business or pleasure, dressy or casual. Excellent wine selection, too.

Karmelicka 14. 𝄢 **012/430-04-92.** Lunch and dinner items 15 zł–30 zł ($6–$12/£3.40–£7). AE, DC, MC, V. Daily noon–11pm.

Inexpensive

Bagelmama ★★ JEWISH/MEXICAN   Great bagels, as well as very good lentil soup, and even decent burritos, in a tiny shop just near to where Kazimierz starts if you're walking from Wawel and the Old Town. This is *the* place to go for that classic bagel breakfast with smoked lox, onions, and capers. *Hint:* There are only three small tables, so be prepared to wait or get takeout.

Podbrzezie 2. 𝄢 **012/431-19-42.** Lunch and dinner items 12 zł–18 zł ($4.80–$7.20/£2.70–£4). No credit cards. Tues–Sat 10am–9pm, Sun 10am–7pm.

Bar Mleczny Pod Temidą ★ POLISH   Every visitor to Poland eventually has to have a "milk bar" experience and this is one of Kraków's best—and certainly its most tourist-friendly. A milk bar—the milk refers to the fact that no alcohol is served—has no direct American or Western European equivalent. *Cafeteria* sounds too sterile and *greasy spoon*, well, too greasy. But that's the idea: heaping steam tables of mostly meatless Polish specialties you line up for and point to. Not bad tasting and great value.

Grodzka 43. 𝄢 **012/422-08-74.** Lunch and dinner items 12 zł–18 zł ($5.20–$7.80/£3–£4.25). No credit cards. Daily 9am–8pm.

Domowy Przysmaki ★ POLISH   Informal self-service lunch counter, with excellent *pierogi* and other lighter Polish fare, including very good soups. The perfect spot for a filling, cheap lunch or early dinner in the Old Town.

Sławkowska 24a. 𝄢 **012/422-57-51.** Lunch and dinner items 6 zł–12 zł ($2.40–$5/£1.30–£2.60). No credit cards. Open 10am–9pm.

Pierożki U Vincenta ★★ POLISH   This tiny and inviting *pierogi* joint in Kazimierz serves every style of *pierogi* imaginable. The house version "Vincent" is stuffed with minced meat and spicy lentils and served with fried onions and bits of bacon. Other concoctions include couscous *pierogi* and "Górale" (highlander) *pierogi* stuffed with sheep's cheese. Try them with a cup of homemade beet broth.

Bożego Ciała 12. 𝄢 **0501/747-407.** Lunch and dinner items 9 zł–12 zł ($3.60–$5/£2–£2.60). No credit cards. Sun–Thurs noon–9pm; Fri–Sat noon–10pm.

CAFES

There is no shortage of cafes in Kraków catering to all tastes and budgets. You'll find the greatest concentration along the streets that radiate off the main square and around Plac Nowy in Kazimierz. In nice weather the entire Rynek Główny is transformed into a giant cafe.

Camera Café ★★ CAFE   A laid-back, student-y cafe just off the Rynek Główny, with silent movies projected on the walls (hence the name). The specialty here is chocolate-based drinks, but they also serve excellent coffee and the standard offering of soft drinks, as well as salads and light meals.

Wiślna 5. 𝄢 **012/429-37-40.** Coffee drinks 7 zł–10 zł ($2.80–$4/£1.60–£2.25). No credit cards. Daily 9am–midnight.

Jama Michalika ★ CAFE   In the early 20th century, this cafe used to be the epicenter of all things cool in Krakow and a major meeting point for the Młoda Polska crowd. Alas, those days are long gone, and now it's largely given over to tourists. The incredible

Art Nouveau interior and the evocative period paintings are definitely worth a look.
Beware, though, the unfriendly cloakroom attendants (coat and hat check mandatory).
The service is legendarily unfriendly and you may have to wrestle a waiter to the ground
to take your order.

Floriańska 45. © **012/422-15-61.** Lunch and dinner items 12 zł–27 zł ($4.80–$11/£2.70–£6). AE, DC, MC,
V. Daily 9am–midnight.

Les Couleurs/Kolory CAFE   During the day, this Kazimierz locale is an innocent
French-themed cafe, complete with good espresso drinks and arty French posters on the
wall. In the evening, it morphs into a crowded bar for an after-dinner beer or cocktail.
Just boisterous enough to feel lively, but quiet enough to hear yourself talk.

Estery 10. © **012/429-42-70.** Coffee 5 zł ($2.20/£1.40). (Mon–Fri 7am–2am; Sat–Sun 9am–2am.

Mleczarnia CAFE   Quiet, intimate, candlelit bar/cafe that's perfect for deep conversation or a low-key group outing. Highly recommended.

Meiselsa 20. © **012/421-85-32.** Sun–Thurs 9am–2am; Fri–Sat 9am–3am.

Noworolski ★★ CAFE   Lovingly restored Art Nouveau interior recalls Kraków's
elegant past. The perfect spot for a leisurely coffee and cake.

Rynek Główny 1. © **012/422-47-71.** Lunch and dinner items 12 zł–27 zł ($5.20–$12/£2.80–£6.50). AE,
DC, MC, V. Daily 9am–midnight.

AFTER DARK
The Performing Arts

Kraków is the cultural hub of southern Poland, and as such supports an active program
of live theater, dance, classical music, and opera. The **Cultural Information Center** (Św.
Jana 2; © **012/421-77-87**) is the first stop to find out what's on and to see if tickets are
available. The friendly staff can help guide you to the best events. The center for classical
music is the **Philharmonic Hall** (Zwierzyniecka 1; © **012/422-94-77**; www.filharmonia.
krakow.pl; box office Tues–Sat noon–7pm). The city supports several opera companies,
including the very good **Opera in Słowacki Theater** (Pl. Św. Ducha 1; © **012/421-16-
30;** www.opera.krakow.pl).

Bars, Pubs & Clubs

For drinking, dancing, and clubbing, both the Old Town and Kazimierz are natural areas
to start a night crawl. The Old Town caters more to tourists and students from nearby
Jagiellonian University; in Kazimierz, the scene is more diverse and a little older, with
young professionals, artists, and hipsters of all sorts attracted to some of the best clubs in
central Europe.

Alchemia   One of the original bars/clubs to lead the Kazimierz renaissance in the late
1990s when the former Jewish quarter morphed from a forgotten corner of Kraków to
its current "party amid the past" feel. The old furniture, faded photos, and frayed carpets
set a design trend that's still going strong. It's no longer the bar of the moment, but still
a great place to get a feel for what Kazimierz is all about. Estery 5. © **012/421-22-00.** Daily
10am–4am.

Dym ★   Dark, relaxing space given over to arty and intellectual types. The name
means "smoke"; indeed, this is the place to come if you like to have a cigarette with your
coffee or beer (and possibly a place to avoid if you don't). Św Tomasza 13. © **012/429-66-61.**
No credit cards. Daily 10am–midnight.

Ministerstwo   One of Kraków's best venues for DJs and house music (not to mention the essential lava lamp decor!). The action starts late and runs until dawn. Good location, just off the Main Square. Szpitalna 1. ☎ **012/429-67-90.** www.klubministerstwo.pl. Tues–Sat 11pm–5am.

Moment   Popular bar that always seems to have a seat when the rest of Kazimierz is full to bursting. The theme here is the passage of time, and the walls are filled with clocks, maybe encouraging you to make this your moment. Józefa 34. ☎ **0668/421-85-32.** Daily 9am–1am.

Nic Nowego   We hesitated before including this modern Irish-themed bar since it's so popular with tourists and is in every other guidebook. But if you're looking for a visitor-friendly place where English is spoken and the menu looks comforting and familiar, you could do far worse. In addition to decent cocktails and conversation, you'll find a nice array of burgers and sandwiches on the munchie menu. Breakfast is served daily, and the scrambled eggs and coffee here are probably a lot better than what your hotel or pension has planned for you. Św. Krzyża 15. ☎ **012/421-61-88.** Mon–Fri 7am–3am; Sat–Sun 10am–3am.

Pauza   You'll have to look around a bit for this moody little cocktail bar, which now numbers among the coolest drinking spots in the city despite few clues that it's even there. Order at the bar and head for the chill-out lounge in the back. Floriańska 18/3. ☎ **0602/63-78-33.** Daily noon–midnight.

Rdza   Another contender for best dance club in the Old Town. Choose something fashionable to wear in order to make it past the guys at the door, and then enjoy the trance, dance, and mood tunes served up by some of the best Polish and imported DJs on offer. Attracts an early-20s to 30s crowd. Bracka 3–5. ☎ **0600/39-55-41.** Daily 9pm–4am.

2 AROUND KRAKÓW: THE WIELICZKA SALT MINE

Believe it or not, a visit to an abandoned salt mine is far and away the most popular daytrip from Kraków. Of course, the Wieliczka Salt Mine (Kopalnia Soli Wieliczka), located in the suburb of Wieliczka about 16km (10 miles) from Kraków, is no ordinary mine. It's listed as a UNESCO cultural heritage site and draws something like a million people a year. The main attraction is not the salt itself, but rather what a number of talented miners and artisans through the ages have managed to do with it, carving out amazingly ornate chambers, cathedrals, and statues. A visit here takes about 3 hours and you'll want to leave a good half-day for it. Many travel agencies offer Wieliczka tour packages, complete with transportation and a guide. This is a good hassle-free way to do it; alternatively Wieliczka is an easy 20-minute drive from Kraków and also easily reachable by mini-bus or train. Several tour operators also offer combined Wieliczka–Auschwitz tours, presumably for people who have only one day and want to do it all. Resist the temptation to do this. It's far too physically and psychologically ambitious. If you've got only a day for the environs of Kraków, you're better off choosing one or the other.

ESSENTIALS
Getting There

BY TRAIN   Wieliczka is easily reached by regular train service from Kraków's main station, the Dworzec Główny (pl. Kolejowy 1; ☎ **012/393-11-11;** www.pkp.krakow.pl).

Departures average around one an hour. The journey from Kraków to the station Wieliczka Rynek takes about 25 minutes.

BY BUS/MINI-BUS The quickest way by bus is to grab one of the mini-buses that depart for Wieliczka every few minutes from bus stops near the main train station and at stops on Pawia and Dietla streets (at the corner of Dietla and Starowiślna). Tell the driver where you want to go and purchase tickets from him. In Wieliczka, leave the bus at the corner of Dembowskiego and Daniłowicza streets. Alternatively, take bus no. 304 that leaves from the Krakowska Galeria shopping center close to the train station.

BY CAR It takes about 20 minutes to drive to the suburb of Wieliczka from the center of Kraków in light traffic. Follow route E40 in the direction of Tarnów and turn right following signs to Wieliczka. Direction signs will guide you to parking lots around the mine.

TOP ATTRACTION
Wieliczka Salt Mine (Kopalnia Soli Wieliczka) ★★★ (Kids)
Salt has been mined here for around 1,000 years, and the oldest shafts date from the 13th century. In the Middle Ages, salt was a highly sought-after commodity, and much of the splendor of Kraków was financed by the white powder mined here. Commercial mining has since been abandoned and the only salt extracted here now is sold to visitors. The tour takes about two hours and begins with a long descent into the mine on foot. The tour takes you down about 130m (400 ft.), but the mine itself is much deeper, going to a depth of some 300m (nearly 1,000 ft.). The highlights of the tour include hundreds of statues sculpted by the miners over the years as well as underground lakes and incredibly ornate chambers and chapels, the most impressive of these being the Chapel of St. Kinga. Visits are by guided tour only. Polish-language tours run throughout the day; English-language tours are less frequent but still often enough (at least in summer) that you won't have to wait long (last English tour at 5pm). In winter, it's best to time your arrival to the tour schedule (10am, 12:30pm, 3pm, and 5pm). Be sure to pack a sweater since it's cool down there, and wear comfortable shoes for climbing stairs. Claustrophobics should obviously think twice, but mild cases shouldn't have any problem, since the chapels and tunnels are large and well ventilated.

Daniłowicza 10 (Wieliczka). ℭ 012/278-73-02. www.kopalnia.pl. Admission 64 zł ($25/£14) (includes foreign-language guided tour); 177 zł ($70/£40) family ticket for 2 adults and 2 children aged 4–16. Mid-Apr to mid-Oct daily 7:30am–7:30pm; mid-Oct to mid-Apr Tues–Sun 8am–5pm.

OUTDOOR ACTIVITIES
In & Around Kraków
WALKING/HIKING A great walk in the green that will take a good hour at a leisurely pace is simply to stroll the length of the Planty, making a full circle around Kraków's Old Town. There are plenty of benches to take a break and people-watch. For more adventurous outings in the wild, try **Las Wolski (Wolski Woods),** a forested area west of the city center between the street Królowej Jadwigi and the Vistula River. There are around half a dozen walking trails here as well as cycling paths. Here you'll find the **Kraków Zoo** (Kids) (Kasa Oszczędności Miasta Krakowa 14; ℭ 012/425-35-51; www.zoo-krakow.pl; admission 14 zł ($5.60/£3.15) adults, 7 zł ($2.80/£1.60) children; daily 9am–4pm), with its impressive collection of exotic animals, including a rare herd of pygmy hippos. It's also home to the **Piłsudski Mound,** an artificial hill built to commemorate Poland's interwar leader Józef Piłsudski. If memorial mounds are your thing, Kraków's most interesting mound stands about 4km (2.5 miles) from the city center and makes for a restorative jaunt

out of the center. The **Kościuszko Mound (Kopiec Kościuszki),** honoring Polish war hero (and American Revolutionary War hero) Tadeusz Kościuszko, was built in the 1820s and has recently been restored. You can walk to the top of the mound for good views over the city and countryside.

CYCLING   Biking is becoming increasingly popular, and the Tourist Information Office has free bike maps (*Mapa Szlakow Rowerowych Krakowa;* in Polish only) showing the best runs, including several bike trails along the Vistula River and through the park, the Planty, that rings the main square. One of the most popular daytrips follows the Vistula to the west about 8km (5 miles) to the village of Tyniec. That said, given the city's heavy traffic, for novices biking is a better bet for an hour or two of sightseeing rather than as a practical means for getting around. **"Cruising Kraków"** bike tours (ul. Basztowa 17; ✆ **0514/556-017;** www.cruisingkrakow.com) offers fun and instructional 2-hour city bike tours in summer in the afternoons and evenings. They also rent bikes and conduct longer trips, including a trip to Tyniec.

GOLF   The Royal Kraków Golf & Country Club (Ochmanów 124; ✆ **012/281-91-70;** www.krakowgolf.pl), in the village of Ochmanów between Wieliczka and Niepołomice, is 18km (11 miles) from Kraków's city center and advertises itself as the city's nearest golf course. It currently has a 9-hole course, and is planning to add an additional 9 holes in 2009. Greens fees for 9 holes start at 85 zł ($34/£19) on weekdays and 95 zł ($38/£21) on weekends.

SWIMMING   The Kraków Aqua Park (Park Wodny) ⓚ𝒾𝒹𝓈 (Dobrego Pasterza 126; ✆ **012/616-31-90;** www.parkwodny.pl; admission 40 zł ($16/£9) adult, 32 zł ($12.80/£7) children; family discounts available; open daily 8am–10pm) is Poland's biggest water park, with a giant indoor pool and huge water slides, as well as a sauna and spa. It's a great outing for kids in hot or cold weather, especially when the thought of yet another crowded museum brings howls of protest.

TENNIS   The best place for tennis relatively close to town is the **Eskada Sports and Recreational Center** (Szuwarowa 1; ✆ **012/262-76-47**). Phone ahead to reserve courts a day in advance.

SPECTATOR SPORTS   Football (soccer) is far and away Poland's biggest spectator sport, and Kraków is home to one of the country's biggest clubs: **Wisła Kraków** (stadium: ul. Reymonta 22; www.wisla.krakow.pl). Wisła traditionally challenges for the top of the first division, and taking in a match can be a real treat—especially if the opponent is archrival Legia Warszawa from Warsaw. Consult the website for game times. Buy tickets at the stadium at the sector B ticket window or at all ticket offices on game days 2 hours before game times. You'll need to show a photo ID to buy a ticket. You can get to the stadium on public transportation (trams 15 or 18; stop: "Reymana.")

3 AUSCHWITZ-BIRKENAU (OŚWIĘCIM)

A trip to Kraków provides an excellent opportunity to visit the former Nazi concentration and extermination camps at Auschwitz (*Oświęcim* in Polish) and Birkenau. The camps lie about 80km (50 miles) to the west of the city and can be visited in an easy daytrip. Getting there is relatively straightforward. There's regular train and mini-bus service that make the journey in about 90 minutes. Additionally, several tourist agencies run guided coach tours; these usually include transportation from Kraków's main square

Getting there may be easy, but taking in the experience is anything but. Auschwitz-Birkenau was Nazi Germany's most notorious death camp and has come to be seen as a symbol of the Holocaust itself. The exhibits are in turn shocking and depressing. At the end of the day, as you're slogging through the immense open fields at Birkenau, where hundreds of thousands of Jews as well as POWs and political prisoners were held before meeting their ends in gas chambers just yards away, you'll find yourself wallowing in a mix of despair and disgust. Kraków's colorful square, filled with people laughing over their coffees, seems a million miles away.

At the same time, there are powerful reasons for coming here, including bearing witness to the epic human tragedy. Alongside the exhibits of yards of human hair of the victims or empty canisters of Zyklon-B gas that was used as the killing agent, you'll also see rows and rows of photographs of those who died here, and learn the story of where they came from, how they got here, and what they went through. It's no exaggeration to say this will probably be the most moving experience you'll have in Poland and the impressions you form here will last a lifetime. That said, Auschwitz is no place for children. If you're traveling with younger children (under 14 or so), it's best to skip the camps altogether.

ESSENTIALS
Getting There
Getting to Auschwitz from Kraków is easy. Several operators run guided tours to the camps (see "Customized Tours"), and trains and mini-buses make the 90-minute trip several times a day. The tourist information office can supply complete information.

BY TRAIN Trains to Oświęcim (Auschwitz) leave from Kraków's main station and deposit you at Oświęcim station, which lies about 15 minutes by foot to the Auschwitz museum entrance.

BY BUS Mini-buses leave from and return to Kraków's main bus terminal, situated just behind the train station. The buses have the advantage of dropping you off at the front entrance to the Auschwitz museum. Buses cost about 18 zł ($7.20/£4) per person round-trip.

BY CAR By car it's an easy 70- to 90-minute drive. From Kraków, find the main A4 highway in the direction of Katowice. Turn south at the Czarnów exit and follow the signs first to Oświęcim and, once in town, to "Auschwitz Museum." There's plenty of paid parking near the museum. At the entrance, parking attendants will guide you to a free spot.

Visitor Information
There's a small book kiosk inside the main entrance to the Auschwitz museum where you can buy booklets and maps to self-guide your way through the camps. Otherwise, there's not much on-site provision for visitors. It's best to stock up on info at one of Kraków's tourist information centers. The **Austeria** bookstore in Kazimierz, next to the High Synagogue (Józefa 38; ✆ **012/430-68-89**), is an excellent source of information and books on Auschwitz and the Holocaust.

Getting Around
The two camps, Auschwitz and Birkenau, are about 2.5km (1.5 miles) apart. It takes about 30 minutes to walk from one to the other. Alternatively, the museum runs free

shuttle buses between the two camps. The timetable is posted at the stop outside the main entrance; the buses run about once an hour in both directions (less frequently in winter). A cab ride between the two camps will cost you about 15 zł ($6/£3.40).

TOP ATTRACTION

Auschwitz-Birkenau State Museum (Auschwitz-Birkenau Concentration Camp) ★★★

Whatever you've read or heard about the Nazi death camps, nothing is likely to prepare you for the shock of seeing them in person. Auschwitz is the best known of the two, though it's at Birkenau, south of Auschwitz, where you really see and feel the sheer scale of the atrocities. The precise number of deaths at the camps is unclear, but well over a million people were systematically killed in the gas chambers, or were hanged or shot or died of disease or exhaustion. Most of the victims were Jews, brought here from 1941 to 1944 from all around Europe, stuffed into rail cattle cars. In addition to Jews, thousands of POWs, including many Poles, Russians, and Gypsies *(Roma),* were exterminated here, too.

Most visitors start their exploration of the camps at Auschwitz, the first of three concentration/extermination camps built in the area. (The third, Monowitz, is in a suburb of Oświęcim and not included on most itineraries. This is the camp where acclaimed writer Primo Levi, author of *Survival in Auschwitz,* was held.)

Auschwitz got its start in 1940, when the Germans requisitioned a former Polish garrison town, Oświęcim, for the purpose of establishing a prisoner-of-war camp. The first groups of detainees included Polish political prisoners and Russian POWs. Conditions were appalling, and in the first year alone nearly all of the several thousand Russian POWs died of exhaustion and malnutrition. It was only later—in 1942, after the Germans adopted a formal policy of exterminating Europe's Jewish population—that Auschwitz became primarily a death camp for Europe's Jewry.

Admission to the Auschwitz museum is free, and you're allowed to roam the camp grounds at will, taking in the atrocities at your own pace. (If you're not employing a guide, pick up a copy of the *Auschwitz-Birkenau Guidebook* available from the small kiosk at the museum entrance.) On entering the museum, you'll first have the chance to see a horrific 15-minute film of the liberation of the camp by the Soviet soldiers in early 1945. The film is offered in several languages, with English showings once every 90 minutes or so (if you miss a showing, you can always come back to see it later). After that, you walk through the camp gates—passing below Auschwitz's infamous motto *Arbeit Macht Frei* (Through Work, Freedom). Once inside, the buildings and barracks are given over to various exhibitions and displays.

Don't miss the exhibition at Block No. 4, "On Extermination." It's here where you'll see the whole system of rail transports, the brutal "selection" process to see which of the new arrivals would go straight to the gas chambers and which would get a temporary reprieve to work, as well as the mechanics of the gas chambers, the canisters of the Zyklon-B gas used, and, in one particularly gruesome window display, yards and yards of human hair used to make rugs and textiles. Block No. 11 is called the "Death Block"; it's where prisoners were flogged and executed.

Birkenau, also known as Auschwitz II, lies about 2.5km (1¹/₂ miles) to the south. It's larger, more open, and even (if possible) more ghastly than Auschwitz. It's here where most of the mass gas-chamber exterminations took place at one of the four gas chambers located at the back of the camp.

Birkenau appears almost untouched from how it looked in 1945. Your first sight of the camp will be of the main gate, the "Gate of Death." The trains ran through this

entryway. The passengers were unloaded onto the platforms, where they were examined **149**
by Nazi SS doctors and their belongings confiscated. About 30 percent were chosen to work
in the camp and the rest—mainly women and children—were sent directly to the gas
chambers, just a short walk away. The scale is overwhelming—prisoner blocks laid out as
far as the eye can see. There are no films here and few resources for visitors. Instead, set aside
an hour or so to walk around the camp to take it in. Don't miss the remains of the gas
chambers situated toward the back, not far from the memorial to the Holocaust victims.
The Germans themselves attempted to destroy the gas chambers at the end of 1944 and
early 1945 to cover up their crimes once it was apparent the war could not be won. Now,
little remains of them. You can return to the main Auschwitz museum by foot, shuttle bus,
or taxi, and from Auschwitz back to Kraków by bus or train.

Panstwowe Muzeum Auschwitz-Birkenau. (© **033/843-20-22.** www.auschwitz.org.pl. Free admission,
groups of 10 or more required to rent an audio headphone (4 zł). Guided tours in English at 10am, 11am,
1pm, and 3pm (39 zł per person). Open Jun–Aug 8am–7pm; May, Sept 8am–6pm; Apr, Oct 8am–5pm;
Mar, Nov 8am–4pm; Dec–Feb 8am–3pm.

WHERE TO STAY & DINE

In deference to the victims of the camp and because of efforts to limit the commercializa-
tion of Auschwitz, there are few places to eat or stay within easy walking distance of the
main museum. There's a small, substandard canteen just to the right of the main entrance
where you can get soup and sausages. Across the street, near one of the main parking
areas, is a small strip of generic fast-food outlets that serve hamburgers, sandwiches, salads, and pizza that will do in a pinch. For something better, you'll have to drive, walk, or
take a taxi.

Hotel Galicja ★★   Only a small percentage of visitors to Auschwitz choose to stay
the night. This reconverted 3-star villa, about 3km (2 miles) from the Auschwitz state
museum, is probably the best option in town. The rooms are plain, but the facilities are
spotless and the reception desk helpful and friendly. There's secure parking (fee) in front
of the building. The Galicja is also arguably the best place to eat in town. Two in-house
restaurants, one serving traditional Polish food and the other pizza and pastas, are much
better than anything near the museum.

Dąbrowskiego 119. (© **033/843-61-15.** Fax 033/843-61-16. www.hotelgalicja.com. 32 units. 220 zł
($88/£50) double. AE, DC, MC, V. **Amenities:** Restaurant; room service; nonsmoking rooms. *In room:* A/C,
TV, dataport.

4 ZAKOPANE & TATRA NATIONAL PARK

Zakopane, in the foothills of the High Tatra Mountains, is Poland's leading mountain
resort. It's absolutely mobbed during the winter ski season, so advance preparations are
in order if you're coming from late December through March. The summer hiking season
is also busy, especially in August when the town hosts an annual folklore festival, though
it's not quite as overrun as in winter. During the rest of the year, it's possible to sense some
of the beauty and rustic charm that first began drawing artists and holidaymakers here in
the 19th century.

Zakopane plays a role in Poland's literary and cultural history that may be unprece-
dented as far as mountain resorts go. In the late 19th and early 20th centuries, members
of Poland's intellectual elite decamped here in a bid no less ambitious than to reinvent,

or at least reinterpret, Polish culture. Many of the country's leading young writers, poets, painters, and architects gathered here and found something uniquely Polish in the unspoiled nature and solid mountain cottages of simple people.

The two World Wars and the decades of Communism that followed put an end to the Zakopane art colony, but some of that special, funky feeling remains. Certainly the huge wooden 19th-century houses here—known throughout Poland as the "Zakopane style"—are some of the most beautiful you'll see anywhere, and in and among the trees and the gardens—and away from the crowds—you can still find traces of a uniquely Polish resort that feels very much of a different age.

Zakopane has three main "seasons." The most important is over Christmas and New Year's, when it can feel like half of Poland has descended for a week-long after-Christmas party. Hotel reservations are nearly impossible to get and rates are jacked up to the stratosphere. If you feel like this might be for you, be sure to reserve months in advance. Ski season runs from January through March and can be almost as crowded as Christmas. Summer walking season starts in June and runs through mid-September. Hotel rates are still high, but the crowds are less oppressive. The best time to come to have the mountains to yourself is in May or October. The air can be chilly, but the paths are blissfully free of tour groups. Bear in mind, though, that the trails on the highest elevations, including the trails that run across the mountain to Slovakia, are closed from November to mid-June.

ESSENTIALS

Getting There

BY TRAIN   Zakopane's tiny train station **Zakopane PKP** (Chramcówki 35; ℂ 018/201-50-31) is centrally located but practically useless. Most visitors come here from Kraków, and the bus is simply much quicker.

BY BUS   Several bus companies make the two-hour trip from Kraków's main bus station to Zakopane's main station, **Zakopane PKS** (Nowotarska 24; ℂ 201-46-03, information), at near-hourly intervals throughout the day. One of the leading bus companies for trips to Zakopane is **Szwagropol** (ul. Kościuszki 19a, ℂ **018/20–17–123;** www.szwagropol.pl). It offers 16 departures daily to and from Kraków. Tickets are 18 zł ($7.20/£4) each way. You can buy tickets at the station window or directly from the driver.

BY CAR   It takes about 2 hours to drive the 100km (60 miles) from Kraków. It's mostly a straight shot south, following signs first to Nowy Targ and then Zakopane. Be sure to watch weather conditions. It can be sunny and warm in Kraków but completely snow-covered in Zakopane, so be sure to have winter tires and antifreeze.

Getting Around

Central Zakopane is fairly compact and partly closed to car traffic, so walking is the only option for getting around. The town itself, though, spreads out a couple miles in both directions, so if you're staying outside the center (and don't have a car) you'll have to rely on taxis or local buses to get around. The main taxi stand is conveniently located just outside the main bus and train terminals. Bikes are another option in summer, but ask at the Tourist Information Office, since rental agencies change from season to season.

Tourist Information

You will be surprised by the sheer number of private tourist agencies offering everything from information to accommodation, lift tickets, and day trips. Zakopane's small **Tourist** can help with general orientation questions and provide maps, but that's about it. For more hands-on service, including booking hotel rooms, walk across the street to Tourist Punkt (Kościuszki 20; 🕿 018/200-01-77; www.tourist-punkt.pl). The helpful staff maintains lists of dozens of private rooms, pensions, and hotels at every price point. Simply describe what you're looking for and they will fix you up. Another private agency, **Zwyrtozłka,** two doors down toward town (Kościuszki 15; 🕿 018/201–52–12), maintains a list of rooms. Both agencies can help arrange day trips, including excursions to Slovakia, as well as sell lift passes and advise on things like ski and bike rental.

TOP ATTRACTIONS

Krupówki merits about an hour's stroll end to end. Toward the northern end of Krupówki (downhill), follow Kościeliska to the left for a couple of blocks to see two of the town's most interesting sites. One is a tiny wooden church, the **Church of St. Clement;** the other is the adjoining **cemetery,** with some of the most ornately carved wooden headstones you're likely ever to see. Look especially for the highly stylized totem pole that marks the grave of Stanisław Witkiewicz (see below), the architect who first set off the local craze for all things wooden.

Museum of Zakopane Style (Muzeum Stylu Zakopańskiego) ★★ Just beyond the wooden church and cemetery is the Villa Koliba, home to a small museum dedicated to the Zakopane style of wooden homes and a tribute to the work of Polish architect Stanisław Witkiewicz. The villa dates from 1894, and was the first to be built in this style, roughly Poland's equivalent of the "Arts and Crafts" movement in the U.S. and Britain. One of the draws here is simply the chance to walk around one of these big old houses, but there are also plenty of interesting examples of ornately carved furniture and accessories. Upstairs, there's a small gallery of the freaky and fascinating 1920s society portraits by Witkiewicz's son, Witkacy. He was portraitist of choice for Poland's Lost Generation.

Kościeliska 18. Wed–Sat 9:30am–4:30pm; Sun 9am–3pm.

Tatra Museum (Muzeum Tatrzańskie) This museum is a bit of a disappointment. There's not much information in English, so you're not likely to get much out of this exhibition of the personalities and events that have shaped Zakopane and the Tatras down through the ages. Still, there are some interesting displays of folk architecture and costumes on the ground floor. Children will like the stuffed animals on the second floor.

Krupówki 10. www.muzeumtatrzanskie.com.pl. Tues–Fri 9am–4:30pm; Sun 9am–3pm.

OUTDOOR ACTIVITIES

HIKING Zakopane has plenty of hikes for walkers of all abilities and fitness levels. Many of the trails lead off just a short distance from the center of town. The trails are clearly marked and good hiking maps are available from the tourist information office or shops around town that specialize in hiking equipment. Keep in mind that these are mountains and treat them accordingly: get an early start, pack plenty of water and sunscreen, and start heading down the mountain at the first sign of an afternoon thunderstorm. For more ambitious climbs, guides are available from the **Polish Association of Mountain Guides** (Polskie Stowarzyszenie Przewodników Wysokogórskich; Droga na

(Moments) **Exploring the High Tatras**

The real joy of any fair-weather visit to the Tatras is the chance to get out into the mountains. Even though Zakopane can get pretty crowded, it doesn't take long to put the throng behind you. One good out-and-back hike of about 4 hours of moderate to heavy exertion and some awesome views begins from just behind the Hotel Belvedere, about 2km (1.2 miles) from the center. Begin by following the yellow-marked path that cuts through the Biała Valley (Dolina Białego). After about a 90-minute ascent, turn onto the black trail, following the signs for Stążyska Polana, and returning to Zakopane via the red trail along the Stążyska Valley. The walk will leave you about 3km (1.8 miles) from the center. Be sure to take along plenty of water, some snacks, sunscreen, and rain gear (you never know what kind of weather you're going to get). Though the walk doesn't require any technical skill, wear decent boots or walking shoes to avoid slipping or turning an ankle. A less-demanding walk, and one that is very popular with the masses, follows the red-marked trail to Morskie Oko, the largest of the Alpine lakes, in the far southern corner of Poland's share of the High Tatras. Many travel agencies in town offer packages that include transportation to the trail head to the east of Zakopane, but once you get off the bus you'll have to walk or take a horse cart (40 zł/$16/£9) the 9km (5 1/2 miles) uphill to the lake.

Wierch 4; www.pspw.pl: Polish only). On the website you'll find a list of guides, with a photo and a telephone number for each. Individual guides start at daily rates of around 800 zł ($320/£180) for one person and 900 zł ($360/£200) for two. You can also sign up for one of the guided walking tours or extreme hiking tours offered by **Zakopane Tours** (www.zakopane-tours.com).

CYCLING Not surprisingly, in recent years Zakopane has become increasingly popular with mountain bikers, and a network of cycling trails now complements the hiking trails. Biking is also a good way to get around in nice weather, since the resort is spread out and walking from place to place can take a lot of time. Check in with one of the tourist information offices for rental information and to buy a cycling map.

SKIING In winter, the most popular hill for skiing is Kasprowy Wierch (1,987m/6,500 ft.); several slopes of all difficulty levels start here. The cable-car operator **Polskie Koleje Linowe** has an excellent website (© 018/201-45-10; www.pkl.pl) listing prices and timetables for lifts and cable cars, and also for the funicular to another popular destination, Gubałkowa. To reach it, take a bus from Zakopane to Kuźnice, and then by cable car to the peak. The **Harenda** ski area (Harenda 63; © 018/202-56-86; www.harenda zakopane.pl) is small but has several lifts and a snow park for boarding. **Nosal** (Balzera 30; © 018/206-27-00; www.nosal.pl) is another popular ski area, with ski rentals and a highly recommended ski school for beginners.

RAFTING (Kids) Zakopane is a good base for rafting the Dunajec River, which runs through a gorge in the Pieniny mountains east of the Tatras along the border with Slovakia. Rafting season runs from April through October, and on a sunny afternoon this can be a fabulous day out, especially for kids. It's less white-water rafting and more of a slow, gentle float down the river on group rafts manned by Górale mountain men kitted

out in their traditional folk garb. The boating center on the Polish side is at Sromowce
Kąty. For information, contact the main organizer, the unpronounceable **Polskie Stowarzyszenie Flisaków Pienińskich-Biuro Spływu** (© **018/262-97-21;** www.flisacy. com.pl). Prices start around 40 zł ($16/£9) per person. Alternatively, the **Info-Tour** travel agency (Kościeliska 11b; © **018/206-42-64**) is one of several agencies in Zako- pane that can arrange rafting trips, including transportation, for about 100 zł ($40/£22) a person.

WHERE TO STAY

Hotel rates in Zakopane are high, and this is one town in Poland where you may want seriously to consider staying in a pension or private room. These abound. If you arrive in town early, simply walk around and inquire where you see signs saying WOLNY POKOJE or NOCLEGI. Or to save time, try Tourist Punkt (see "Visitor Information," above). They maintain an extensive database of private accommodations (with photos) and will hap- pily book you a room. Make sure to specify that you want to be in the center; otherwise they may try to place you in a far-flung corner of town. Expect to pay about 60 zł ($24/£14) a person for a private room. Hotel and room rates rise considerably in the week between Christmas and New Year's. Aside from that, January, February, and August are the busiest times of the year, and pre-booking is essential. The rates below are for summer and winter season, outside of the Christmas and New Year period.

Very Expensive

Hotel Belvedere ★★   This 1920s-era mountain resort is one of the classiest places to stay in Zakopane. The "Jazz Age" ambience is updated with extras like a Roman spa and a game room, as well as a bowling alley and other more-modern pursuits. The in- house restaurant is top notch. The real advantage is the hotel's location, just where the mountains start, about 2km (1.2 miles) outside the center. That makes it a 10- to 15-minute walk down to Krupówki, but means you can also escape the masses and enjoy the mountains if you want. One of the nicest hiking trails along the Biała river valley starts just above the hotel's doors.

Droga do Białego 3. © **018/202-12-00.** Fax 018/202-12-50. www.belvederehotel.pl. 160 units. 690 zł ($276/£155) double. AE, DC, MC, V. **Amenities:** Restaurant; indoor swimming pool; spa; bike and ski rental; concierge; business center; shopping arcade; salon; room service; dry cleaning; nonsmoking rooms. *In room:* A/C, TV, dataport, minibar, hair dryer, safe.

Hotel Litwor ★   A luxury hotel occupying a handsome mountain chalet that admit- tedly looks a little out of place in the middle of busy Krupówki Street. When it opened in 1999, the hotel claimed to be the first 4-star hotel in this part of Poland. Certainly it's still one of the best in town, but the Belvedere offers more of a feeling of exclusivity, and the Grand Hotel Stamary is arguably smarter than both. The rooms are well-propor- tioned and furnished in contemporary browns and blues. Ask for one with a view to the mountains. Wi-Fi access is available throughout the hotel.

Krupówki 40. © **018/202-02-14.** Fax 018/202-02-50. www.litwor.pl. 63 units. 600 zł ($240/£140) double. AE, DC, MC, V. **Amenities:** Restaurant; indoor swimming pool; fitness room; spa; bike and ski rental; concierge; salon; limited room service; dry cleaning; nonsmoking rooms. *In room:* A/C, TV, minibar, hair dryer.

Expensive

Grand Hotel Stamary ★★★   Beautifully restored turn-of-the-century manor hotel that quickly whisks you away to the stylish 1920s and '30s with its elegant lobby and cocktail bar and wide corridors with dark-wood flooring. The period detailing extends to the rooms, furnished in browns and golds. The location is superb, just a short walk toward the center from the bus terminal. The main pedestrian street, Krupówki, is about 200 yards down the street—near enough to be convenient but far enough to be away from the commotion. The spa, with indoor pool and Jacuzzi, opened in 2007.

Kościuszki 19. ℂ 018/202-45-10. Fax 018/202-45-19. www.stamary.pl. 53 units. www.stamary.pl. 580 zł ($232/£130) double. AE, DC, MC, V. **Amenities:** Restaurant; indoor swimming pool; fitness center; spa; dry cleaning; nonsmoking rooms. *In room:* A/C, TV, dataport, minibar, hair dryer.

Hotel Villa Marilor ★★ Occupying a sprawling cream-colored villa just across the street from the Grand Hotel Stamary, it's another contender for "nicest place to stay in Zakopane." Peace and quiet is what they're offering here, and once you step onto the beautiful grounds you won't hear a sound. Everything feels refined, from the chandeliers and marble-topped desks in the lobby to the nicely sized rooms, furnished in late–19th century style. The hotel offers special rooms for people with disabilities. Wi-Fi access is available throughout the hotel and in the garden.

Kościuszki 18. ℂ **018/200-06-70.** Fax 018/206-44-10. www.hotelemarilor.com. 20 units. 580 zł ($232/£130) double. AE, DC, MC, V. **Amenities:** Restaurant; outdoor tennis court; fitness center, spa; concierge; business center; room service; dry cleaning; nonsmoking rooms. *In room:* A/C, TV, dataport, minibar, hair dryer.

Moderate

Hotel Gromada ★ Utilitarian, 1960s-era high-rise that offers amenities like a spa and fitness room at rates about half those of the competition. The rooms are boxy, but clean and comfortable. Ask for a room away from the busy street. The location is central, just a couple steps off Krupówki. It tends to fill up fast, so book in advance. The reception says the hotel is due for a makeover, so some of the facilities may be updated by the time you arrive.

Zaruskiego 2. ℂ **018/201-50-11.** Fax 018/201-53-30. 55 units. 230 zł ($92/£50) double. AE, DC, MC, V. **Amenities:** Restaurant; fitness room; sauna (with salt grotto); nonsmoking rooms. *In room:* TV, hair dryer.

Sabala ★★ This traditional inn—dating from the end of the 19th century and built from hefty wooden logs—is a nice trade-off between the upper end (and practically unaffordable) luxury hotels in town and a pension. The wood-beamed rooms are plainly furnished, but have the solid feel of a mountain chalet. The beds are big and comfortable, covered with thick wool comforters. There's a decent restaurant downstairs, and the location is good both for accessing the slopes and hitting Krupówki's shops and bars.

Krupówki 11. ℂ **018/ 201-50-92.** Fax 018/201-50-93. www.sabala.zakopane.pl. 51 units. 400 zł ($160/£90) double (high season), 330 zł ($132/£75) double (other times). AE, DC, MC, V. **Amenities:** Restaurant; nonsmoking rooms. *In room:* TV, dataport, hair dryer.

Inexpensive

Pensjonat Szarotka ★★ (Finds) This smallish, eccentric 1930s villa feels more in harmony with Zakopane's artistic past. The pension is not far from the Belvedere, about two kilometers out of the center of town, and close to the Biała valley hiking trail. The squeaky stairways, the cozy little reading room with a fireplace, and the evocative black and white photos on the wall will remind you of your grandmother's house. The lovely 1930s breakfast nook is a real treat. On the downside, the rooms are tiny and crammed

together (how did they carve 17 rooms out of this house?). Still, for the money, the **155**
atmosphere, and the location, it can't be beat.

Male Żywczańskie 16a. ℂ **018/206-40-50.** Fax 018/201-48-02. www.szarotka.pl. 17 units. 180 zł ($72/
£40) double. No credit cards. **Amenities:** Restaurant; nonsmoking rooms. *In room:* TV.

WHERE TO DINE

Zakopane has no shortage of places to eat, but it could certainly use a few more *good* places
to eat. Most restaurants are kitted out in wood, with carved wooden tables and animal skins
and wrought iron everything-but-the-kitchen-sink affixed to the walls. The servers are
made up to look like mountain folk, and you might even get a folk band to accompany
your meal. This is all great, but in practice it often means that little attention is paid to the
food. Most of the restaurants are situated in the center, on or near Krupówki.

Mała Szwajcaria ★★ SWISS   The mountain setting goes surprisingly well with the
fondues, savory crepes, and other hearty Swiss dishes offered here at this high-end chalet
restaurant. Main courses like grilled lamb chops and roast veal with mushrooms provide
a welcome change of pace from the bland Polish cooking served at most Zakopane restaurants. And the tasteful interior—with flowers and white linens—is a world away from
the Disney World–esque kitsch of "traditional" taverns that have sprung up all over town
in the past couple of years.

Zamoyskiego 11. ℂ **018/210-20-76.** Lunch and dinner items around 35 zł ($14/£7.80). No credit cards.
Daily 11am–10pm.

Otwarcze ★ POLISH   The loudest and most popular of a number of similar faux-
folk-style grill restaurants along the main pedestrian street. Rack after rack of yard-long
shish kebabs on the grill, an ensemble of highlander musicians to set the mood, and wait
staff decked out like a Polish episode of *Little House on the Prairie.* Don't panic. It's just
as kitschy for Poles as it is for everyone else, and the mood is definitely fun. The menu
runs several pages long, but most people simply order the *szaszłyk* (shish kebab), a mix
of grilled pork, sausage, and onions served with grilled potatoes and a self-serve salad.

Krupówki 26–28 (just around the corner from the Kolorowe.) No phone. Lunch and dinner items around
35 zł ($14/£7.80). No credit cards. Daily 11am–10pm.

Expensive

Kolorowe ★ POLISH   Similar in attitude but perhaps slightly quieter and more
civilized than Otwarcze next door. There's a similar menu, with mostly pork shish kebabs
on the grill, and accompanying live music and waitresses in full peasant regalia. They also
offer pizza and other dishes, but that's more of an afterthought. Stick with the grilled
meats and enjoy.

Krupówki 26. ℂ **018/150-55.** Lunch and dinner items around 30 zł ($12/£7). No credit cards. Daily
11am–10pm.

Moderate

Kalina ★★ POLISH   The quietest and altogether most pleasant of the Polish-style
restaurants on Krupówki is certainly worth seeking out. Here the folklore element is
low-key. You won't always find live music, but as compensation you'll get a cook who
pays more attention to what's on the plate and some alternatives to grilled pork, like
decent *pierogi* and roast duck. The interior is done up in traditional cottage style, meaning intricately carved woodworking, wood-beamed ceilings, and a nice warm fire.

Krupówki 46. ℂ **018/201-26-50.** Lunch and dinner items 25 zł ($10/£6). No credit cards. Daily 11am–10pm.

Pstrąg Górski ★ SEAFOOD   Popular little spot just off the main drag that specializes in grilled river fish, especially—as the name suggests—trout *(pstrąg)*. It's a good choice for a nice lunch or a light early meal. In addition to fish dishes, they also have a full range of grilled meats. In summer, eat on the covered terrace overlooking the throngs on Krupówki.

Krupówki 6. ✆ **018/206-41-63.** Lunch and dinner items 25 zł ($10/£6). AE, DC, MC, V. Daily 11am–10pm.

Soprano ★★ ITALIAN   If you're not in the mood for grilled meats and traditional food, you can still find pretty decent pizza around. Arguably the best is served here at Soprano, which offers the standard combinations but also has healthier options, like broccoli and fresh spinach toppings. Sit out on the terrace and enjoy the view, or have a quieter, candlelit pizza in the back.

Krupówki 49. ✆ **018/201-54-43.** Lunch and dinner items 23 zł ($9/£5). No credit cards. Daily 11am–10pm.

Inexpensive

Pizza Dominium ITALIAN   Not as good as Soprano, but cheaper and quicker. Dominium is a popular and successful Polish pizza chain going head-to-head with titans like Pizza Hut. The locals may have the advantage with thick-crust pizzas and fresh ingredients. This branch is on Krupówki, but they also have a restaurant at 2,000m (6,560 ft.) on the peak at Kasprowy Wierch, if you happen there.

Krupówki 51. ✆ **018/206-42-11.** Lunch and dinner items 15 zł $6/£3.40). No credit cards. Daily 11am–10pm.

SHOPPING

Krupówki is jammed wall-to-wall with souvenir shops, gold and silver dealers, and outdoor outfitters, all competing for your attention with a jumble of cafes, restaurants, pizza joints, and refreshment stands. Just about everything you might need you'll find along this busy 5 or 6 blocks. Most of the gift and souvenir stores peddle in the same sorts of imported, mass-produced junk—wooden toys, T-shirts, hats and scarves, and mock traditional clothing—that sadly have little connection to Zakopane. For something more authentic, try looking in at **Cepelia,** with two locations on Krupówki (nos. 2 and 48; ✆ **018/201-50-48**). Here you'll find locally produced carved wooden boxes, animal pelts, leather goods, and the odd knickknack or two. **Art Gallery Yam** (Krupówki 63; ✆ **018/206-69-84**) is about as funky as it gets in Zakopane. Check out the rotating exhibitions of contemporary Polish painters. Some riveting modern Tatra landscapes, and other works that draw on the absurdist visual style of Polish art in the 1970s and '80s.

One souvenir you won't be able to miss are those little rounds of sheep's milk cheese, **Oscypek,** that you see everywhere around town. The recipe apparently goes back some 500 years. The salty cheese goes great with beer.

AFTER DARK

Paparazzi   The local version of a regional chain of cocktail bar/nightclubs occupies a beautiful creek-side location that is *the* after-hours spot in town for a cold beer or glass of wine. Also offers passable versions of international dishes like chicken burritos and Caesar salads. Ul. Gen. Galicy 8; ✆ **018/206-32-51.** Daily noon–1am.

Piano Bar   Just next to Art Gallery Yam and draws on its artistic funkiness for a laid-back, hipster feel. Though it's just down a small alley from the Krupówki throng, it's a world away in attitude. Krupówki 63 (in the little alleyway). Daily 4pm–midnight.

5 TARNÓW

If you're not planning on traveling onward to Zamość (see p. 174), the town of Tarnów, about 80km (50 miles) east of Kraków, is probably your best opportunity to see a well-preserved example of Renaissance town planning as practiced in the 16th century. Borrowing from the Classical period, the idea behind Renaissance town design was to achieve balance and harmony through symmetry. In Tarnów's case that resulted in oval-shaped Old Town, with the Rynek and Town Hall *(Ratusz)* at the center, and main arteries radiating from there. Each part of town was given over to a specific purpose, and the core surrounded by walls and fortifications.

Tarnów is not as well preserved as Zamość. Part of the town walls were pulled down over the years and insensitive new buildings intrude on the overall effect, but enough of the older structures, including the dominant Town Hall, remain to lend a strong impression to how life was lived in the late Middle Ages.

Tarnów is also a significant stop on Jewish heritage tours. In 1939, at the outbreak of World War II, the town's Jewish population was around 25,000, making it the fourth largest concentration of Jews in this part of Poland, after towns like Kraków and Lwów. Here, as nearly everywhere else, during the war the town's Jewish population was subjected to draconian and humiliating rules, mass killings, confinement in tightly guarded ghettoes, and finally deportations to the extermination camps. There are few, if any, Jews left today, but the streets to the immediate east of the Rynek, including *Żidowska* (Jewish street), appear little changed from the old times and still evoke something of Jewish life here.

Tarnów makes a convenient overnight stop, with good transport connections to both Kraków and Lublin. Hotel and restaurant facilities are not yet up to the highest Polish standards, but city fathers are looking to attract more visitors and the future is certain to bring further improvements. The countryside here is especially pretty, and if you have your own wheels it's worth heading out to the village of the Lipnica Murowana to see the UNESCO-listed St. Leonard's church.

ESSENTIALS
Getting There
BY TRAIN   Polish rail, PKP (© **014/94-36**), operates several trains daily between Kraków's Główny station and Tarnów. The journey takes about 90 minutes. Several trains from Tarnów to Kraków continue onward to Katowice (3 hrs) and to Wrocław (6 hrs). Tarnów's rail station is about a 15-minute walk from the center on Krakowska.

BY BUS   Tarnów's bus station (Krakowska; © **014/93-16**) is situated just next to the train station and is about a 10- to 15-minute walk into town. Service is good to Kraków and surrounding cities and towns.

BY CAR   Tarnów is located 80 kilometers to the east of Kraków along the E40 international route.

Getting Around
Tarnów is small, and much of the center of the city is closed to car traffic. This makes walking the only option; it also means it's almost impossible to get around in a car. If you're traveling in your own wheels, try to get as close to the center as you can and then park the car at the first free space you see.

Tarnów's **Tourist Information Office** (Rynek 7; ✆ 014/688-90-90; www.go-tarnow. com) routinely places near the top in the annual "Best Tourist Office in Poland" competition, and it's easy to see why. The staff is young, enthusiastic, and English-speaking. They have more free info on Tarnów, including a great walking map, than you'd likely need for a week's stay. What's more, they stay open until 8pm, rent bikes, and even offer cut-rate, decent accommodation in rooms located above the office (see "Where to Stay").

TOP ATTRACTIONS

Before setting off on a walking tour, pick up a handy map of the **Old Town** *(Plan Starego Miasto)* at the Tourist Information Office (see "Visitor Information," above). The map outlines several interesting walking tours, including the **Renaissance Trail** and **Tarnów's Jewish Trail.** A good place to begin your exploration is naturally the main square, the Rynek. The square was first laid out in the 14th century when Tarnów acquired its town rights, but was redesigned in the 16th century in Renaissance style as Tarnów reached the height of its economic and political power. The handsome **Town Hall** has been a symbol of the city for centuries since it was built at the start of the 15th century. It was closed to visitors for reconstruction at press time and it was uncertain whether it would be open in 2009. While you're here, check at the house at Rynek 20/21, now home to the **Tarnów Regional Museum** and considered the most attractive Renaissance town house on the square. The **Cathedral,** still in use, is a couple of minutes' walk northwest of the Rynek. It was originally built in Gothic style in the 14th century but was given a neo-Gothic makeover in the 19th century. Nearby is the highly recommended **Diocese Museum,** holding the original altar removed from the UNESCO-listed St. Leonard's church from nearby Lipnica Murowana.

The former Jewish part of the city is situated to the east of the Rynek, bounded by the present streets of Żydowska and Wekslarska. The area is still a ghetto of sorts, today housing part of the city's impoverished Roma community instead of Jews. The houses, with their narrow courtyards, still evoke the feel of the ancient Jewish quarter, and here and there you can still pick out Jewish inscriptions on the houses. Opposite Żydowska 11, look for the still-standing bimah, the podium from which the torah was read and the only surviving piece of the former **"Old Synagogue"** that was burned to the ground by the Nazis on Kristallnacht, November 9, 1939. The former Nazi Jewish ghetto, where Jews were forced to live during the war, is situated farther to the north and east of here. Little remains of this ghetto today, but the gray, depressed housing stock still imparts a lingering sadness. The **Jewish Cemetery** *(Cmentarz Żydowski)* is about 15 minutes by foot northeast of the Rynek along Szpitalna and is one of the best-preserved of its kind in Poland. The several thousand graves, in varying states of repair and disrepair, are sadly all that remain of Tarnów's once-thriving Jewish community.

Tarnów Regional Museum   This sleepy regional museum is worth a look inside chiefly because it occupies the most architecturally valuable building on the square, a Renaissance town house from the 16th century. The museum occasionally holds blockbuster exhibits such as 2008's "Memories Saved from Fire," the story in words, pictures, and original documentation of the destruction of Tarnów's Jewry during the World War II (see box below).

Rynek 20/21. ✆ 014/621-21-49. www.muzeum.tarnow.pl. Admission 5 zł ($2/£1.10) adults. Tues–Sun 9am–4pm.

7

(Moments) "Memories Saved from Fire"

Tarnów is relatively rare in being one of a handful of Polish cities, including Kraków and Łódź, to embrace its Jewish past and to begin to put the pieces together of what happened here. A big part of that effort was a European Union–sponsored exhibit at the Tarnów Regional Museum in 2008 entitled "Memories Saved from Fire." The exhibit attempted to tell the story in pictures and words, including original Nazi documentation, of the rounding up and eventual destruction of Tarnów's pre-war Jewish population of 25,000. The Memories Saved from Fire exhibition closed in 2008, but the text and photos are still available on the Web at www.msff.eu and well worth taking a look at before or after your walk around town.

Tarnów's story is a tragic but familiar one. Following the German invasion in September 1939, the Nazis implemented increasingly restrictive measures on the city's Jews, including not being able to work or go to school and the obligatory wearing of yellow armbands. The city's Jewish population gradually swelled to 40,000 as Jews from around southern Poland sought refuge here. The darkest moment came during the week of June 11–18, 1942, when the Nazis forcibly took several thousand Jews from their homes and publicly executed them on the Rynek. At the same time, around 6,000 children and older people were taken and murdered at the Buczyna forest near Tarnów. Later, in June 1942, a walled ghetto for the remaining Jews was established here to the east and north of the city's traditional Jewish neighborhood, bounded by the streets of Lwówska, Starodąbrowska, Mickiewicza, and Plac pod Dębem. This was similar to the ghettos in Warsaw, Łódź, and Kraków-Podgórze. The population within this confined area swelled to 16,000, and entering and leaving the ghetto was by special permit only. More of what the Germans called "displacement actions" followed that autumn, when around 8,000 Jews were arrested and sent to their deaths at Bełżec. The final liquidation of the Tarnów ghetto was carried out in September 1943, when the 8,000 remaining Jews were rounded up and sent to their deaths at Bełżec, Płaszów, and Auschwitz.

Ethnographic Museum (Muzeum Etnograficzne) ★★   This attractive museum houses a fascinating permanent exhibition of the history and culture of Europe's Roma (Gypsy) population. The exhibit traces the emergence of the Roma from parts of modern-day India some 1,000 years ago to their arrival in Europe and subsequent (mostly tragic) history, including the large-scale destruction of the Roma population by the Nazis during World War II. Outside is a colorful collection of Roma wagons.

Krakowska 10. ℂ **014/622-06-25.** www.muzeum.tarnow.pl. Admission 4 zł ($1.60/£90p). Tues–Fri 9am–4pm, Sun 10am–2pm.

Diocesan Museum ★   This museum is the oldest of its kind in Poland, dating from 1888, and with an impressive collection of Gothic religious paintings and sculpture from the Middle Ages. The museum's most impressive holding is the original altar from the UNESCO-listed 15th-century St. Leonard's church from the nearby village of Lipnica Murowana. The altar was brought here to protect it from damage. The building that houses the museum, the Mikołajowsky House, dates from 1524, and is considered one of Tarnów's most beautiful Renaissance town houses.

Pl. Katedralny 6. ✆ **014/626-45-54.** www.diecezja.tarnow.pl. Admission 4 zł ($1.60/£90p). Tues–Fri 9am–4pm, Sun 10am–2pm.

OUTDOOR ACTIVITIES

The tourist information office can offer advice on hiking and cycling options around town, and even rent bikes. Around 20 hiking and biking trails fan out through the pretty countryside in all directions. There are also more than a dozen horseback-riding centers in the vicinity. Several offer riding lessons and group outings, including sledding in winter. For a kind of throwback Wild West experience, try the **Roleski Ranch** (✆ **0602/753-148;** www.roleskiranch.com.pl) in Stare Żukowice, about 15km (10 miles) north of Tarnów. They even have modest guest rooms if you'd like to spend the night.

WHERE TO STAY

If Tarnów is ever hoping to break into big-time tourism, it could use a couple more nice hotels. For the moment, you'll have to content yourself with the properties below.

Hotel Bristol   Tarnów's only 4-star hotel is crying out for a makeover. The 19th-century neoclassical building, on a main artery leading to the city's central square, is handsome, but the interior is gaudy. The overstuffed rooms are decorated in a heavy 1970s style—pink leather sofas and giant beds—that feels unintentionally retro. And the price tag for all this is somewhat inflated, reflecting the lack of quality accommodation in town. That said, it's clean and well run and close to the action. All the rooms have Internet access and there's plenty of free parking around (a relative luxury in Tarnów's Old Town).

Krakowska 9. ✆ **014/621-22-79.** www.bristol.tarnow.com.pl. 19 units. 320 zł ($128/£72) double. AE, MC, V. **Amenities:** Restaurant; room service; nonsmoking rooms. *In room:* A/C, TV, dataport, minibar, hair dryer.

Hotel U Janu ★   This hotel has a great location, right on the Rynek, with a beautiful and ancient cafe-restaurant on the ground floor and it still sports some Renaissance detailing from the 16th century. Check out the intricate doorway that links the bar and cafe. Unfortunately, the rest of the hotel is a bit of a letdown, with only ordinary rooms and nothing special in the way of service or amenities. Still, the price is right for the location, and it's not that much of a step down, actually, from the much more expensive Bristol.

Rynek 14. ✆ **014/620-20-01.** 12 units. 200 zł ($80/£45) double. AE, MC, V. **Amenities:** Restaurant; non-smoking rooms. *In room:* TV, dataport.

Tourist Information Office ★ Ⓥalue   Unusual for a Polish city, the tourist information office runs an informal lodging outfit, renting out the rooms above the office for some of the cheapest rates you'll find in the whole country. Don't expect luxury: The rooms are only modestly furnished with a bed and desk, but all are clean and have attached baths. Given the lack of much better accommodation in town, this might be the place to hunker down for a night and take it easy on the wallet. Although they claim the rooms have Wi-Fi, the signal doesn't reach very far. If you want to use your computer, the whole of Tarnów's main square is covered by free Wi-Fi.

Rynek 7. ✆ **014/688-90-90.** www.go-tarnow.com. 10 units. 100 zł ($40/£30) double. AE, MC, V. **Amenities:** Nonsmoking rooms. *In room:* TV, dataport.

Willa Krzyska ★★ This well-maintained, refurbished former mansion is the city's most comfortable lodging option, catering to an equal mix of tourists and visiting businessmen. It's a short walk to the Old Town, yet on a quiet street away from traffic. Free on-site parking and a reliable Internet connection are two big selling points. The in-house restaurant offers very good Hungarian cooking for a change of pace.

Krzyska 52b. ✆ **014/620-11-34.** www.willakrzyska.pl. 12 units. 240 zł ($95/£50) double. AE, MC, V. **Amenities:** Restaurant, nonsmoking rooms. *In room:* A/C, TV, dataport, minibar, hair dryer.

WHERE TO DINE

The choices are better where restaurants are concerned, including Poland's first and only "Gypsy" restaurant. Additionally, in warm weather, Tarnów's central square, the Rynek, becomes in effect a giant restaurant/cafe, with dozens of places offering a similar mix of coffee drinks, beer, and light food.

Ke Moro Original Gypsy Restaurant ★ (Finds) EASTERN EUROPEAN Poland's first and only restaurant specializing in Gypsy (or Roma) cooking is worth seeking out. Don't expect anything too radical. It turns out Gypsy food is very similar to Central European or Continental cooking—just a bit spicier, with an emphasis on stews and oversized portions. Many nights, you'll get a live Gypsy folk band. Fun, and one of a kind.

Żydowska 13. ✆ **012/688-90-98.** Lunch and dinner items 20 zł–30 zł ($8–$12/£4.50–£6.75). No credit cards. Daily noon–11pm.

Tatrzańska ★★ POLISH Excellent traditional Polish cooking in a refined setting that works both for a group night out or a quiet dinner for two. Unusual for a Polish restaurant, the menu offers lots of creative salads, making Tatrzańska a good choice for a light meal. The salad with blue cheese and chicken comes with warm, roasted pieces of chicken sprinkled with cheese, with lettuce and tomato served on the side. Finish off with a fresh piece of apple strudel, served with ice cream and drizzled with chocolate.

Krakowska 1. ✆ **012/622-46-36.** Lunch and dinner items 20 zł–30 zł ($8–$12/£4.50–£6.75). AE, DC, MC, V. Daily 9am–10pm.

Lublin & Southeastern Poland

Southeastern Poland is an enigma to most visitors to Poland. Lacking any international "must-sees" on the order of a Kraków or a Gdańsk, most visitors from outside of Poland choose to give it a miss. And maybe that's the best reason of all to come. The region's hub, the city of Lublin, has a delightful Old Town on par with Kraków's, though on a much more manageable scale and without the crowds. Lublin has a fascinating history at the confluence of Polish, Jewish, and Russian civilizations, and maintains a lively cultural life, fueled by the presence of several universities and thousands of students. Away from the big city, the smaller tourist towns of Zamość and Kazimierz Dolny have always been popular with Poles and are only now beginning to attract outside visitors. The former is a nearly perfectly preserved example of Renaissance town planning. It's undergone a thorough face-lift in the past few years, and is a great spot to relax for a day or two. Kazimierz Dolny, astride the Vistula River, is one of those arty towns that draws legions of gallery owners and antique shoppers and wouldn't be out of place in upstate New York or Vermont. It's a laid-back weekend spot for stressed-out Varsovians and Lubliners to hike and bike, browse the galleries, and just hang out. In summer, the town maintains an active cultural calendar; don't be surprised if you run into a Klezmer music festival or something similar while you're here.

Travelers with a special interest in Jewish heritage will want to spend extra time in Lublin, once called the ìJerusalem of the Polish kingdom.î World War II put an effective end to Jewish life here, but the city authorities are making an effort to reclaim part of that heritage. In Poland, youíre never far from World War II, and eastern Poland was brutally affected. Just outside of Lublin stands the former Majdanek concentration camp that was once planned by the Nazis to be the biggest such camp in all of Europe. South of Lublin, the Bełżec camp was where the Nazis fine-tuned their "Final Solution." Both are now state museums.

1 LUBLIN

Poland's eastern metropolis of Lublin is a surprisingly likable big city. There aren't many traditional tourist sites here, and not many foreign tourists either, but that's part of the charm. After visiting tourism behemoths like Kraków or Gdańsk—or even after spending time in the hustle and bustle of Warsaw—Lublin feels much more relaxed and "real." It's a decent place to plan an overnight stop, with a number of excellent hotels and restaurants, and enough evening activities like concerts and clubs to keep you occupied. During the day, be sure to take in the city's lovely and partially restored historic core, with two of the original town gates still standing.

Lublin traces its history back about 800 years, when it was an eastern outpost for the Polish kingdom to guard against invasions from Tatar and Mongol hordes. The town

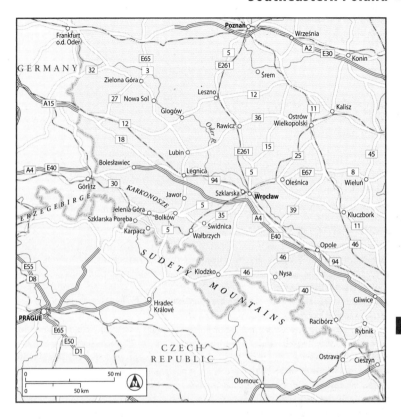

grew greatly in importance with the union between the Polish and Lithuanian kingdoms at the end of the 14th century and the formal union of 1569 (see box below). Before, Lublin had been a frontier town, but the union placed the city directly between the then-Polish capital, Kraków, and the Lithuanian capital, Vilnius. Lublin suddenly found itself at the center of a country stretching from the Baltic to the Black seas.

The city thrived into the 17th century as an important commercial and legal hub, and was the seat of Polandís royal tribunal; but, as elsewhere in Poland, the countless wars took their toll. Lublin was sacked at least half a dozen times, by Muscovites, Swedes, Cossacks, and others. The Polish partitions at the end of the 18th century brought more confusion to Lublin. The town first found itself on the Austrian side of the border, then a few years later it was attached to the Duchy of Warsaw, and then, ultimatelyófor most of the 19th centuryóit was ruled by tsarist Russia. The 19th century, however, brought industrialization and a measure of prosperity back to the city, and at the end of World War I, when Polish independence was fully restored, Lublin served for a short time as the countryís capital. World War II, though, brought renewed disaster. Lublin had tradition-ally been an important city for Jews and for Jewish scholarshipóits prewar population of 100,000 was more than one-third Jewishóbut the Nazis destroyed this civilization in a

It Happened Here: Poland & Lithuania Form Early European "Union"

When Poland joined the European Union in 2004, it was seen as a tremendous "first" in the country's history, but maybe it was a really a "second." In Lublin, all the way back in 1569, Poland and Lithuania agreed to fuse their considerable domains into a united entity that bears an uncanny resemblance to today's EU. From the original document: *"The Kingdom of Poland and the Grand Duchy of Lithuania are now one, inseparable and indistinguishable body, but also an indistinguishable, yet one, common republic which has coalesced into one people out of two states and nations."* As with the EU, the two agreed in principle to honor one authority, follow a single foreign policy, and adopt a common currency. At the same time, as with the EU, both retained separate treasuries, armies, and courts. The result portends both good and bad for today's EU. The union brought both kingdoms considerable prosperity and power—but only for a time. It eventually proved unworkable and left both at the mercy of more powerful neighbors.

few short years. Polish Jews here were first herded into a restricted ghetto just off of the Old Town, and then deported to nearby extermination camps at Majdanek (see below), Sobibór, and Bełżec (see below). The Nazis even made Lublin the wartime seat of "Operation Reinhard," their covert plan to exterminate the Jewish population of German-occupied Poland.

After the war and with the shifting of Poland's borders westward, Lublin again found itself on the frontier, but this time with the Soviet Union. Thousands of Poles fled here from the east and the city's population soared to its current 380,000. The Communist period was a mixed bag; Lublin acquired important industries, but the city suffered under insensitive planning and reconstruction. Even today, Lublin's many charms are arguably blighted by a sea of Communist-era housing blocks. During the post-Communist period, the city authorities have tried to restore something of the city's noble past. The Old Town is undergoing extensive long-term renovation, leaving elegantly restored Renaissance palaces standing next to fallen-down, abandoned ruins.

ESSENTIALS
Getting There

BY PLANE   Lublin does not have an international airport, but plans are afoot to build one at Świdnik, not far from the city. That facility, however, is expected to be finished only by 2011. For the time being, the best air route into Lublin is to fly into Warsaw's Fryderyk Chopin airport (see p. 62) and then take a train or bus to Lublin (about 3–4 hours).

BY TRAIN   Lublin is fully integrated into Poland's national rail network, and trains are a good option for travel to Warsaw and Kraków. The train station (PKP, Gazowa 4; © 081/94-36; www.pkp.com.pl) is a 15-minute walk to the city center, or reachable by public bus nos. 1 or 13 or trolleybus no. 150. Bus no. 28 is a direct connection from the station to the State Museum of Majdanek (see below).

BY BUS   Lublin's main bus station (PKS; Aleja Tysiąclecia 6; © 081/747-66-49; www.pks.lublin.pl) is situated about a 15–20 minute walk from the old center. You'll find regular connections here to Warsaw, Kraków, Katowice, Zakopane, Łódź, Zamość, and

other cities. The private carrier Polski Express runs buses to Warsaw from platform one.
Several other private companies operate between Lublin and smaller regional cities such
as Chełm, Puławy, and Kazimierz Dolny.

BY CAR   Lublin is easily reachable by car. The drive to Warsaw is about 170km (100
miles) and takes between two and three hours depending on traffic. Lublin itself can be
tricky to negotiate by car. Have a good map ready once you near the city and be careful
not to miss your exit on the highway.

Visitor Information

Lublin's helpful **Tourist Information Office** (Jezuicka 1/3; ✆ **081/532-44-12;** www.
um.lublin.eu or www.loit.lublin.pl) is located just inside the main gate to the Old Town.
In addition to providing city and regional maps and other information, there's also a
small gift shop for buying postcards, T-shirts, and souvenirs.

City Layout

Lublin is a sprawling city, ringed by major highways, but most of the main attractions
are located in a relatively compact area of the Old Town *(Stare Miasto)* and central city
(Śródmieście), connected by a long central boulevard called Krakowskie Przedmieście.
Part of Krakowskie Przedmieście is a pedestrian zone.

GETTING AROUND

Lublin has an excellent public transportation system consisting of buses and trolley buses,
but unless you're staying outside the center, you probably won't need them much. A car
will be useless for getting around, since the Old Town and a major portion of the main
street, Krakowskie Przedmieście, are off limits to autos.

ON FOOT   Once in the center, you'll find walking the easiest way of getting around.

BY BUS/TROLLEY BUS   Lublin's public transportation (Miejskie Przedsiębiorstwo
Komunikacji/MPK; ✆ 081/525-32-46; www.mpk.lublin.pl) is cheap and efficient.
Buses are a good way of getting to the train and bus stations, as well as out to the State
Museum of Majdanek (bus no. 23, trolleybuses no. 156 and 158) and the Open Air Vil-
lage Museum (bus nos. 5, 18, 20). Buy tickets (2.20 zł/$1/60p) from newsagents or
directly from drivers.

BY TAXI   Taxis are useful for reaching outlying hotels as well as for getting from the
center of Lublin out to Majdanek. You can hail them from the street, but watch out for
rogue drivers and always make sure the driver turns on the meter. There are several reliable cab companies, including Dwójki (✆ **0800/222-222**), Metro (✆ **0800/128-306**),
and Mercedes (✆ **0800/400-400**).

BY BIKE   Traffic is relatively heavy and bike-rental places are few and far between (ask
at the tourist information center), but there are a few designated bike lanes in Lublin.
The ride out to Majdanek (about 5km/3 miles) is fairly pleasant if you stick to the sidewalks, and once you're at the sprawling concentration camp, you'll be happy you brought
your own two wheels.

TOP ATTRACTIONS

Lublin's historic core is tiny and you can hit the major attractions in about two to three
hours of walking at a leisurely pace. Begin your exploration at the ancient entryway into
the city, the **Kraków Gate** *(Brama Krakowska),* a perfect Gothic-era photo op that's
welcomed visitors here since the middle of the 14th century. The gate houses a museum

It Happened Here: Jewish Lublin

It's no accident that Lublin bears two nicknames that attest to its once important status among Jews. The first is "Jewish Oxford," referring to a respected Yeshiva that was built here in 1515. The second is the "Jerusalem of the Polish Kingdom," a reference to the vitality of the city's Jewish community until the start of World War II. The history of Jews in Lublin goes back to at least 1316, when Jewish merchants settled in the city to take advantage of Lublin's trade position with Russia. Over the centuries, the community flourished. As hard as it is to imagine now, the vast area surrounding the Castle was filled with the warren of tiny streets of the former Jewish quarter. By the start of World War II, the Jewish community numbered nearly 40,000 out of a total city population of around 100,000. Sadly, little of this remains today. At the start of World War II, the Nazis forced the city's Jews into a tightly restricted ghetto area just down from the Kraków Gate along today's Lubartowska Street. The old Jewish quarter was razed. Eventually the residents were sent to concentration camps at Bełżec, Treblinka, Sobibór, and Lublin's own Majdanek. To add insult to injury, the Nazis made Lublin the headquarters of Operation Reinhard, the code name for its plan to murder the Jewish population of German-occupied Poland. After the war, many of the city's remaining Jews fled to newly formed Israel or the United States, and Lublin's Jewish community dropped to just a handful. Now city authorities are trying to reclaim some of this history and have created a **Heritage Trail of the Lublin Jews** (marked out in detail on the city's website: www.um.lublin.eu). To get the most out of the trail, first pick up a copy of the excellent pamphlet "Landmarks and Traces of Jewish Culture in Lublin" at the tourist information center. The trail begins in the Old Town and goes down through the Grodzka Gate into the former Jewish quarter and beyond. Don't miss the fascinating pre-war Lublin scale model of the Old Town and Jewish quarter at the **Grodzka Gate Theatre NN Centre** (Grodzka 21; ✆ 081/532-58-67; www.tnn.lublin.pl).

on the city's history. As you pass through the gate, you'll see the **Old Town Hall** *(Stary Ratusz)* in the center of the square, the Rynek. It's now used mainly for weddings and concerts, but the building has a grand tradition going back to the 16th century when it housed Poland's tribunal, the royal court of appeals. From here, it's best just to amble around and admire the mix of burghers' houses from the Gothic and Renaissance period. The Old Town is in the middle of a long-overdue renovation, and part of Lublin's charm is seeing virtual ruins standing side by side with sumptuously restored Renaissance palaces. Be sure to stop by the **Dominican Church and Monastery** to admire a famous painting, the 1719 *Fire of Lublin.* Exit the Old Town by way of a second preserved medieval gate, the **Grodzka Gate,** that leads to Zamkowa Street and the **Castle** *(Zamek).* This is sometimes referred to as the "Jewish Gate," because it once led to the city's enormous Jewish quarter that sprawled over a huge area from here to the castle. The Nazis razed the neighborhood and insensitive post-war planning has left the area feeling empty and barren. The castle is worth a peek inside. It was once a huge fortress built by King Kazimierz the Great to protect the kingdom's eastern flank from Tatar invasion. It was later partly destroyed and rebuilt in the 19th century as a prison. It houses the **Lublin Museum** and the **Chapel of the Holy Trinity.** At this point, you're free to follow your own interests, either exploring what little remains of the former Jewish Quarter or heading back to the Old Town for a meal or a drink.

Dominican Church and Monastery ★   The Dominican order came to Lublin in the 13th century, and this church is considered the city's finest example of sacral art. Much of the church was destroyed by fire in 1575, and the original Gothic architecture was lost. What you see today is the Renaissance church that was built in its place. The highlights include the first chapel to the right, which holds the famous painting of the *Fire of Lublin* (1719), and the Firlej Chapel, with its lavish dome and 17th-century wall ornaments.

Złota 9. ✆ **081/532-89-80.** www.dominikanie.lub.pl. Free admission. Daily 9am–4pm.

Lublin Castle & Chapel of the Holy Trinity ★★   The castle is home to a rather dry museum on Lublin and Polish history and a more interesting Gothic Chapel of the Holy Trinity. The chapel dates from the 14th century and the Byzantine frescoes are the work of a team of Ruthenian painters from 1418. The castle played an important role in Lublin's history. It was the second home of Polish kings during the union with Lithuania, when they would make their trek from Kraków to Vilnius. It was here, too, that the Polish-Lithuanian Union (see box) was signed in 1569. Look for the painting *The Union of Lublin* by the 19th-century master Jan Matejko that depicts the event. During World War II, the Nazis used the castle to hold political prisoners.

Zamkowa 9. ✆ **081/532-50-01.** www.zamek-lublin.pl. Admission (museum) 6.50 zł ($2.60/£1.50) adults, 4.50 zł ($1.80/£1) children. Wed–Sat 9am–4pm, Sun 9am–5pm. Castle Chapel of the Holy Trinity daily 9am–4pm.

Lublin Village Open Air Museum (Skansen) ★★   Poland's open-air museums are always a treat, and this one is one of the best in the region. This museum has some 50 historic buildings, ranging from a Greek-Catholic church removed from Tarnoszyn to an 18th-century manor house from Żyrzyn. It's fun just to stroll the gardens and take in the range of architectural styles in Poland over the years.

Warszawska 96. ✆ **081/533-85-13.** www.skansen.lublin.pl. Admission (museum) 8 zł ($3.20/£1.80) adults, 4 zł ($1.60/90p) children. English-speaking guide 90 zł ($36/£20). Apr–Oct daily 10am–5pm (in winter, phone ahead to book your visit).

Museum of Lublin History ★   A small museum dedicated to the history of the city. Non-Polish speakers are likely to find the photographs of how the city has changed from the late 19th century to the 1960s to be the most interesting part. You can also climb to the top of the gate for a beautiful panorama of the Old Town.

Łokietka 3 (at the Krakowska Gate); ✆ **081/532-60-01;** www.zamek-lublin.pl. Admission 3.50 zł ($1.40/ 80p) adults, 2.50 zł ($1/55p) children. Daily 9am–4pm.

CUSTOMIZED TOURS

Lublin Tours (✆ **081/445-71-84;** www.explorelublin.pl) is a husband and wife team who run a series of tours of Lublin and the surrounding region, including trips to Kazimierz Dolny and Zamość. The most popular Lublin trip is a 3- to 4-hour walking tour that includes the Old Town, the former Jewish ghetto, and the castle. They also offer a 2- to 3-hour walking tour tracing Lublin's Jewish past, called "Traces of Polish Jerusalem." Warsaw-based **Stay In Poland** (Miła 2; ✆ **022/351-22-22;** www.staypoland.com) offers a similar mix of historical Lublin city walks and other tours that highlight the city's Jewish heritage and the Holocaust.

Lublin is blessed with an enormous shopping center, the **Lublin Plaza** (Lipowa 13; *✆* **081-536-22-03;** www.lublinplaza.pl), just off of the main street Krakowskie Przedmieście, which is a real advantage if you've forgotten something at home. The mall houses dozens of shops, restaurants, and a multiplex cinema in case you get a rainy day.

WHERE TO STAY

Lublin has some excellent hotels, including a glamorous makeover of a former bank building, the **Grand Hotel Lublinianka** (see below), and a new boutique, the **Vanilla** (see below), that offers cutting-edge interiors and a location just off Krakowskie Przedmieście, a minute's walk from the Old Town.

Very Expensive

Grand Hotel Lublinianka ★★   The current top address in Lublin has hosted the princess of Thailand and the band Morcheeba among other notable guests. The handsome neoclassical building was once home to a bank and the property still exudes money and luxury. The lobby is the prettiest among Lublin's hotels, with a baby grand piano and a turn of the century cafe with gorgeous marble floors that's perfect to laze around in. The rooms are done in a classical style with high ceilings, chandeliers, and muted gold and beige interiors. There are a Turkish bath and Finnish sauna on the premises.

Krakowskie Przedmieście 56. *✆* **081/446-61-00.** Fax 081/446-62-00. www.lublinianka.com. 72 units. 620 zł ($248/£140) double. AE, DC, MC, V. **Amenities:** Restaurant; exercise room; sauna; concierge; business center; room service; nonsmoking rooms. *In room:* A/C, TV, dataport, minibar, hair dryer.

Hotel Europa ★   This beautiful hotel right on Krakowskie Przedmieście on the approach to the Old Town (a 5-minute walk away) dates from 1867, and a strong sense of history pervades the place even now. The lobby is small but tidy, with high ceilings and a kind of Colonial-era feel. The rooms are nicely proportioned; some of the more expensive ones come with period furnishings and antiques. Room 104 is a gorgeous double with a nice view over the adjoining park. The guest roll reads like a Who's Who of Polish society, including the noted Polish travel writer Ryszard Kapuściński and former President Aleksander Kwaśniewski.

Krakowskie Przedmieście 29. *✆* **081/535-03-03.** Fax 081/535-03-04. www.hoteleuropa.com.pl. 73 units. 420 zł ($168/£95) double. AE, DC, MC, V. **Amenities:** Restaurant; business center; salon; room service; nonsmoking rooms. *In room:* A/C, TV, dataport, minibar, hair dryer.

Expensive

Hotel Victoria   A modern high-rise that lacks character but is a solid choice for a business trip, with decent business amenities such as conference facilities and a large parking area. The rooms are small and plainly outfitted, but the bathrooms are modern and the facilities are generally of high quality. The near-central location is fine, but better suited to car travelers. The walk to the Old Town is about 10 to 15 minutes.

Narutowicza 58/60. *✆* **081/532-70-11.** Fax 081/532-90-26. www.hotel.victoria.lublin.pl. 120 units. 290 zł ($116/£65) double. AE, DC, MC, V. **Amenities:** Restaurant; exercise room; sauna; business center; room service; nonsmoking rooms. *In room:* A/C, TV, dataport, minibar, hair dryer.

Hotel Vanilla ★★★   Bold, contemporary boutique hotel a stone's throw from the Old Town on an inviting corner just off Krakowskie Przedmieście. The rooms are done up in jaw-dropping color schemes of bold reds, yellows, and oranges; the minimalist furnishings mesh perfectly with the strong colors. The bathrooms are a study in Japanese-style minimalism, while the corridors are plastered with bright orange faux brickwork. It sounds outrageous, and it is, but it works perfectly. This is one hotel you're not likely to forget. The English-speaking receptionist is more than happy to help guests. The cafe here is Lublin's favorite spot for an ice cream sundae.

Krakowskie Przedmieście 12. ✆ **081/536-67-20.** Fax 081/536-67-21. www.vanilla-hotel.pl. 18 units. 330 zł ($130/£75) double. AE, DC, MC, V. **Amenities:** Restaurant; exercise room; sauna; room service; non-smoking rooms. *In room:* A/C, TV, dataport, minibar, hair dryer.

Moderate

Hotel Campanile ★★ This local representative of the up-market French hotel chain strikes a good balance between comfort and price. Don't expect lots of character; these are basically business hotels, but the rooms are nicely appointed, clean, and have goodies like air conditioning and free in-room Internet. The buffet breakfast is the best in town. The location is less than ideal. The Old Town is a 15- to 20-minute walk, but the value for money more than makes up for it. Good choice if you're arriving by car, since the hotel entrance is just off one of the main access roads, and there are even a few free parking spots out front.

Lubomelska 14. ✆ **081/531-84-00.** Fax 081/531-84-01. www.campanile.com.pl. 81 units. 249 zł ($100/£56) double. AE, DC, MC, V. **Amenities:** Restaurant; exercise room; limited room service; nonsmoking rooms. *In room:* A/C, TV, dataport, minibar, hair dryer.

Waksman ★★ This small pension in the Old Town is a perfect choice for a romantic night. All the rooms are decorated with stylish, period-piece furniture, and have polished wood floors, big timber beds, and antique desks. Each room is accented in a different color, with red reserved for the honeymoon suite (which features a big waterbed). The suite, with a separate lounge area and a castle view, is a steal at this price.

Grodzka 19. ✆ **081/532-54-54.** Fax 081/534-75-53. www.waksman.pl. 7 units. 220 zł ($88/£50) double, 280 zł ($112/£63) suite. AE, DC, MC, V. **Amenities:** Limited room service; nonsmoking rooms. *In room:* TV, dataport, minibar, hair dryer.

Inexpensive

Lublin This is a standard Communist-era high-rise, situated about a 20-minute walk out of town, but good value for money with clean rooms and decent service. It's pretty bare bones, with the narrow twin beds that all hotels of this era seem to come with, but it's adequate for a night or two. It's particularly convenient if you're arriving by car or train, since it's on one of the main roads into town and is within walking distance of the train station. Ask for a room away from the road to cut down on noise.

Podzamcze 7. ✆ **081/747-44-07.** Fax 081/444-42-40. www.hotel-lublin.pl. 90 units. 175 zł ($70/£40) double. AE, DC, MC, V. **Amenities:** Restaurant; nonsmoking rooms. *In room:* TV, dataport.

WHERE TO DINE

Most of the restaurants are clustered along Krakowskie Przedmieście on the approach to the Old Town or in the Old Town itself, particularly on sloping Grodzka Street. Many of these places seem to specialize in the same mix of pizzas and sandwiches, and, with a few exceptions (see below), they are fairly ordinary. In summer, it's best to show up a little early on a nice evening (say, 6 to 7pm) to maximize your chances of snagging one of the highly coveted outdoor tables.

Very Expensive

Kobi ★★★ JAPANESE   One of the top sushi restaurants in Poland and certainly the best in this part of the country. The maki rolls are a specialty, with innovative fillings like avocado and salmon, and tuna, butterfish, and leek, standing alongside the usual offerings. The interior is warmer than the standard Japanese restaurant, but the service is still on the starchy side. Reserve in advance since this place fills up.

Kościuszki 10. ⓒ **081/443-36-66.** Lunch and dinner items 50 zł–70 zł ($20–$28/£11–£15). Reservations suggested. AE, DC, MC, V. Mon–Sat noon–11pm; Sun 1–10pm.

Expensive

Oregano Cafe ★★ ITALIAN/INTERNATIONAL   Charming cafe–restaurant specializing in Mediterranean cuisine from Italy, Greece, and other sunny locales. Appetizers include grilled calamari served in a hot-sweet chili sauce that may even merit a rave mention on your postcard home. Main courses include an inviting mix of pasta dishes and Greek specialties such as *moussaka.* The interior is intimate and candle-lit and ideal for a special night out.

Kościuszki 7. ⓒ **081/442-55-30.** Lunch and dinner items 30 zł–50 zł ($12–$20/£6.75–£11). AE, DC, MC, V. Mon–Sat noon–11pm; Sun 1–10pm.

Moderate

Złoty Osioł ★★ POLISH   Excellent, atmospheric Polish pub, serving homemade potato pancakes, *bigos* (hunter's stew), *pierogi,* and more refined dishes like duck, all washed down with very good Żywiec beer. Although it's a pub, on most nights the atmosphere is hushed enough to have a good conversation.

Grodzka 5a. ⓒ **081/532-90-42.** Lunch and dinner items 25 zł–40 zł ($10–$16/£5.60–£9). AE, DC, MC, V. Mon–Sat noon–11pm; Sun 1–10pm.

Inexpensive

Pub Samarta PIZZA   One of a number of generic pizza-pubs along Grodzka in the Old Town that draws crowds looking for cheap, filling food, lots of beer, and great open-air seating just off the main square. The thick-crust pizza actually isn't bad; one is more than enough to share between two people.

Grodzka 16/3. ⓒ **081/534-63-89.** Lunch and dinner items 15 zł–25 zł ($6–$10/£3.30–£5.60). No credit cards. Mon–Sat noon–1am; Sun 1–11pm.

U Szewca Irish Pub PIZZA/IRISH   Next to the Samarta. Despite its name, the "Irish Pub" serves pretty much the same style pizza as everywhere else—and seems to draw the same crowd of hedonists on a warm summer night. Most customers come for the fun and the wide selection of beer instead of the food. In addition to pizzas, you'll find lots of sandwiches and salads on the menu, but sadly nothing much authentically Irish.

Grodzka 18. ⓒ **081/532-82-84.** Lunch and dinner items 15 zł–25 zł ($6–$10/£3.30–£5.60). AE, DC, MC, V. Sun–Thu 11am–midnight; Fri–Sat 11am–2am.

AFTER DARK
The Performing Arts

Lublin is home to one of the country's finest orchestras, the **Lublin Philharmonic Orchestra** *(Filharmonia Lubelska im. H. Wieniawskiego)* (Marii Skłodowskiej-Curie 5; ⓒ **081/743-78-24** box office; www.filharmonia.lublin.pl). Consult the tourist information office to see what's playing while you're in town. The office or your hotel can help arrange tickets, or visit the theater box office (Mon 9am–4pm, Tues–Thurs 1–6pm, Fri 1–7pm).

Cafes, Pubs & Clubs

As the sun sets, do like everyone else in Lublin and head for the Old Town. The long pedestrian walkway Krakowskie Przedmieście is filled with clubs and late-night cafes. One of the most popular dance clubs is **Czekolada** (Krakowskie Przedmieście 19; ℭ **081/534-44-77**), complete with a glitzy crowd and pulsating electronic music. For more traditional pubs and beer drinking, most of the action is on Grodzka in the Old Town. In addition to Samarta, the U Szewca Irish Pub, and Złoty Osioł (mentioned above under "Where to Dine"), check out **Magma** (Grodzka 16; ℭ **081/534-42-65**), **Legenda** (Grodzka 1; ℭ **081/532-53-72**), and at least half a dozen other joints offering a similar mix of beer and conversation.

2 AROUND LUBLIN: MAJDANEK

The former Nazi concentration camp of Majdanek is not as well known as camps like Auschwitz-Birkenau, but Majdanek's sheer size and the fact that several crematoria here survived the war (those at Auschwitz were destroyed) are compelling reasons to visit even if you've already seen one or more Holocaust sites. Majdanek was originally conceived as a labor camp to hold up to 50,000 workers to help the Germans realize their resettlement aims for eastern Poland, but the plans were constantly revised upward. At one point, the Nazis planned to hold some 250,000 people here, which would have made it the biggest concentration camp in German-occupied Europe. Those ambitions were scaled down only once the Germans began to lose the war in the East. In the end, at least 150,000 people were eventually held here and 80,000 died, mostly Jews from across Europe, but there were also sizable numbers of Polish and Russian POWs and others. The single most horrific day at Majdanek came on November 3, 1943, when as many as 18,000 Jews were killed in one day. The camp was liberated by the Soviet Red Army on July 22–23, 1944. The Red Army assault came unexpectedly quickly and the Germans didn't have enough time to destroy the crematoria and other pieces of Holocaust evidence. In this respect, it's perhaps the best-preserved of the former concentration camps.

In addition to the fact that several crematoria survived the war, Majdanek is the only major Nazi concentration camp built close to a city. Most of the other camps were situated in isolated areas, well away from the eyes of the world.

Visiting the camp is not an easy experience. In addition to the emotional impact (children under 14 are not permitted), there's the sheer size of the camp. Be sure to take comfortable walking shoes and be prepared to use them. Allow at least three to four good hours to tour the camp.

The Majdanek museum continues to carry out historical research, and in late 2005 a group of Majdanek survivors returned to the camp to help archeologists find dozens of personal objects—such as watches and rings—that had been buried by the inmates so the Germans would not get them. Amazingly, after some 60 years, the returnees were able to locate the buried objects within a few minutes.

ESSENTIALS

Getting There

BY CAR Majdanek is located in a suburb of Lublin and is an easy 10-minute drive from the center of town following the main artery Droga Męczenników Majdanka for about 5km (3 miles). There is ample pay parking (5 zł/$2.20/£1.40).

BY BUS/TROLLEY BUS Majdanek can be reached via Lublin's public transportation (bus no. 23, or trolley bus no. 156 or 158). Buy tickets (2.20 zł/$1/60p) from newspaper kiosks or directly from the driver.

BY BIKE Majdanek is an easy 20-minute bike ride from the center of Lublin, but use the sidewalk since the main road, Droga Męczenników Majdanka, is busy.

Visitor Information

There's a small **Information and Education Center** (✆ **081/744-19-55**) near the entrance area that has a permanent photography exhibition as well as restrooms, vending machines, and a small shop.

TOP ATTRACTIONS

State Museum at Majdanek ★★★ Begin your exploration of the camp at the small museum and visitor information center, where you can pick up a map and get yourself oriented. The camp layout itself is confusing for first-time visitors. The highlights include two enormous stone monuments by Victor Tolkin built in 1969 to commemorate the 25th anniversary of the camp's liberation. One stands near the entrance to the camp and the other—in the shape of an enormous urn—is at the back. It's a mausoleum filled with the ashes of thousands of victims. Visitors are free to wander the camp, visiting the barracks, some filled with exhibitions. The overall impression remains one of bleakness and despair. The lights of Lublin can clearly be seen in the distance, something that would have been a constant reminder to the inmates of the relatively normal life that was going on just a few kilometers away. The surviving crematoria are at the back of the camp, not far from Tolkin's urn. Back at the museum you can see a small film about the camp and take in an occasional temporary exhibition.

Droga Męczenników Majdanka 67; ✆ **081/744-26-47**. www.majdanek.pl. Free admission (film 3 zł/ $1.30/80p). Tues–Sun 8am–4pm.

---

3 BEŁŻEC

Unless you have particular knowledge of the Holocaust, you may not know this obscure town and rail junction about 100km (60 miles) south of Lublin. Yet, it was here that the Nazis first launched their "Operation Reinhard," the code name of their plan for the mass extermination the Jewish population of the *Generalgouvernement,* the name of German-occupied Poland. Bełżec was chosen because it was small and little known, yet not far from major Jewish populations in the cities of Lublin and Lwów.

The Nazis used Bełżec to refine the techniques of mass killing that would later be applied at other death camps, including the use of poison gas in gas chambers and forcing the Jewish prisoners themselves to carry out much of the work, including burying and later burning the bodies.

Bełżec operated from March 1942 until the end of that year. In the relatively short period of eight months, some 450,000 people put were put to their deaths here. The process was horrific and sickening. Unlike other camps, there was no elaborate system of barracks and work routines. Instead, the victims would arrive on rail transports at one part of the camp and then quickly be forced through a small tunnel to the gas chambers at another part. Initially, the bodies were buried in mass graves, but by late 1942 the decomposition process became so bad that the bodies had to be dug up again and burned on enormous pyres.

Bełżec was dismantled by the Nazis in 1943 and much of the killing apparatus was destroyed to hide the evidence of what went on. Throughout much of the postwar period, Bełżec remained simply a fenced-off mass grave. With growing interest in the Holocaust in the post-Communist period, however, officials later built a monument with a small visitor center and permanent exhibition to tell the story of what happened here.

ESSENTIALS
Getting There
Bełżec is a small town and is not easy to get to without a car. If you're traveling from Lublin, the best bet is to take the bus. There are decent train connections to Bełżec from Zamość and Kraków, but you'll have to pre-plan since the number of trains is limited.

BY CAR   Bełżec lies about 100km (60 miles) south of Lublin and is an easy 90-minute drive. Once in Bełżec, follow the signs to the Bełżec Memorial. There are ample places to park.

BY TRAIN   Train connections between Lublin and Bełżec are poor, but there is a daily train between Bełżec and Zamość. The journey takes about 90 minutes. Trains also connect Bełżec with Kraków. The trip is about 6 hours. Once in Bełżec, the camp is about a five-minute walk.

BY BUS   A few buses run daily between Lublin's main bus station and Bełżec. Check the Lublin bus website (www.pks.lublin.pl) for an updated schedule. The trip takes around three hours and costs about 20 zł ($8.80/£5.50).

VISITOR INFORMATION
There's a small **visitor information center** (✆ 084/665-25-10) at the entrance area with a permanent photography exhibition as well as restrooms and a small bookshop.

TOP ATTRACTIONS
Museum and Memorial Site at Bełżec ★   A visit to Bełżec comprises two parts: the large monument that covers the entire former area of the camp and the small museum with a permanent photographic exhibition and explanatory materials. The monument itself is understated and deeply moving, simply a field of charred rocks to symbolize the scorched earth of the funeral pyres. A small tunnel runs through the middle, representing the "tube" the victims had to walk through from the trains directly to the gas chambers.

Zamojska 2; ✆ **084/665-25-10.** www.belzec.org.pl (Polish only). Free admission. Daily May–Oct 9am–6pm (shorter hours in winter).

4 ZAMOŚĆ

The UNESCO-protected city of Zamość is a fascinating curiosity: It's a totally planned community from the 16th century and, as such, an almost completely intact example of Renaissance town planning. Call it Poland's first-ever mixed-use real estate development, with shops, offices, and housing all positioned for maximum efficiency and aesthetic beauty. Zamość was the dream of Jan Zamoyski, a wealthy Polish nobleman who wanted to establish the family's seat and a regional center of culture and commerce. Zamoyski hired a noted Renaissance town designer, Italian architect Bernardo Morando, to design, in essence, a perfect town from scratch. Morando modeled the town on a hexagon, 600m (2,000 ft.) long and 400m (1,250 ft.) wide. The market square and town hall were situated at the center, with two lesser squares—Solny (Salt) and Wodny (Water)—positioned on the sides. Major axes were cut through the square at right angles and the side streets were laid out in a grid. The hexagon was surrounded on all sides by high walls with seven bastions and a moat, turning Zamość, effectively, into a fortress town. Much of this has survived to this day, including the impressive town hall, part of the walls and fortification system, and a good proportion of the houses. Indeed, it's a pleasure to stroll across the wide expanse of the Rynek and marvel at how well it all works today, more than 400 years later. Zamość was besieged time and again over the centuries—first by the Cossacks and then in turn by the Swedes, Saxons, and Russians—but the fortress managed to hold out. The Zamoyski family lasted until the 19th century, when under the Russian occupation the family was forced to exchange its town holdings for land. During World War II, Zamość was first occupied by Soviet soldiers and then by the Nazis, who rechristened it for a short time as "Himmlerstadt," after one of the architects of the Final Solution, SS Chief Heinrich Himmler. In the years before World War II, Zamość was a thriving center of Jewish culture and the town's synagogue still stands, even though most of Zamość's Jews perished in the Holocaust. Today, Zamość is a prosperous regional center of around 70,000 people. Because of its unique architecture and lively cultural calendar, including a festival of flowers in May and an international folk music festival in July, the town remains a popular weekend spot, with several good hotels and some excellent restaurants.

ESSENTIALS
Getting There
BY TRAIN Zamość's **train station** (Szczebrzeska 11; ✆ **084/94-36**) has infrequent connections to both Kraków and onward to Warsaw. Figure on about five hours' travel time to Kraków and longer to Warsaw. There's also a daily train connection from here to Bełżec (see above).

BY BUS Several buses and minibuses make the trip to and from Lublin daily; from there you can easily make onward train and bus connections. Contact **Dworzec PKS** (Hrubieszowska 1; ✆ **084/638-49-86**).

BY CAR Zamość is an easy drive from Lublin. Figure on about two hours behind the wheel at a leisurely pace.

Tourist Information
Zamość has an ambitious **Tourist Information Center** (Rynek 13; ✆ **084/639-22-92;** www.zamosc.pl), located on the ground floor of the Town Hall on the Rynek. It's a great source for town and regional hiking and biking maps as well as postcards, picture books,

Memories: Take That, Kraków!

Kraków's hourly bugle call from atop St. Mary's Church (p. 125) is well known across Poland. Less well known is the fact that Zamość, too, has a bugler. From May until September, a lone bugler sounds the noonday call from atop the Town Hall. It's not clear when the custom came into being, but it was probably introduced in Jan Zamoyski's day, when Zamość was first flexing its muscles as an important city. As per tradition, the bugler sounds his call in only three directions: north, south, and east, but never to the west toward Kraków. Legend has it that Zamoyski had a run-in with the nobles of Kraków and, as a result, the bugler has been snubbing Kraków ever since. It's not clear, however, if anyone in Kraków has ever noticed!

and souvenirs from Zamość. The staff can book rooms and will help sort out transportation options. It also offers guided tours of the city starting at 73 zł ($30/£16.40) for a standard 2¹/₂-hour tour. The Zamość tourist Web site (www.zamosc.pl) has an excellent list of the most architecturally significant houses on the square and an explanation of each.

Getting Around
Zamość is tiny; once you've arrived at the historic core, you can walk easily from place to place.

TOP ATTRACTIONS
Begin your exploration of Zamość at the center of Morando's 16th-century vision, the **Rynek Wielki (Great Square).** In keeping with the Renaissance ideal of perfect proportions, the square measures exactly 100m (300 ft.) across from top to bottom and side to side. Not surprisingly, this is the center of the action in Zamość and the site of numerous performances and cultural activities throughout the year, particularly in summer. The Rynek is dominated by the enormous **Town Hall (Ratusz),** which was purposefully placed off-center. The building still follows Morando's original design, though it was remodeled several times over the centuries. The sweeping fan-shaped double stairway was added later, in the 18th century. Many of the buildings that line the square have retained their original Renaissance arcades. The most noteworthy houses are the one at no. 25, where Morando himself once lived, and the colorful series of houses that start to the right of the town hall, known collectively as the Armenian houses both for their ornate appearance and the fact that a wealthy Armenian merchant built the house known as **"Under the Angel"** in 1632–34. The houses are now home to the **Zamojskie Museum.**

Follow Grodzka west across Akademicka to find the **Zamoyski Palace,** the family's former residence. While the palace was certainly fabulous in its time, it's a bit of a disappointment today. In 1809, the palace ceased to be the seat of Zamość's founders and was later sold to the state for use as an army hospital. Today it houses regional administrative offices (and is closed to the public). The **Cathedral** just across the street is more impressive and dates from the 16th century. You're free to walk around inside; the Zamoyski family are buried in the crypts below. You can also climb to the top of the balcony for a view of the Old Town and to see the old belfry. Also worth checking out are the two surviving town gates: The **Old Lubelska Gate,** which stands to the north of the Zamoyski Palace and which has been walled since 1604, and **Old Lwowska Gate,** toward the eastern end of Grodzka. This was once the town's main entryway from the east and was designed by Morando himself. The former Jewish quarter of Zamość ran north and east of the Rynek. There's little left today of this community that once numbered several thousand, though the city's grand **Synagogue** survived World War II and is now undergoing renovation.

Zamojskie Museum ★★   A visit to the museum is a nice way to sneak a peek inside the ornate Armenian houses, but it's also worth a stop for exhibits on the town's history, including a fascinating scale model of how Zamość looked around 1700, as well as exhibits on folk costumes and crafts.

Ormiańska 30. ✆ **084/638-64-94.** www.muzeum-zamojskie.one.pl. Admission 5 zł ($2/£1.10) adults. Tues–Sun 9am–4pm.

The Arsenal Museum of Weapons ★   A tribute to Zamość's role as a fortress town and of interest primarily to fans of military history. On the ground floor there is a permanent exhibition of 17th-century weaponry, firearms, and cannons, and an exhibition presenting the history of Zamość fortress, including a model of the town. The building itself was designed by Bernardo Morando in the 1580s.

Zamkowa 2. ✆ **084/638-64-94.** www.muzeum-zamojskie.one.pl. Admission 4 zł ($1.60/85p) adults. Tues–Sun 9am–4:30pm.

The Rotunda Museum of Martyrdom ★★   It's well worth the short walk south from the historic core to visit the Rotunda, a 19th-century military bastion once used to store gunpowder and ammo that earned a sinister reputation during World War II when the Nazis used it as a prison and interrogation center. Around 8,000 people were executed here and their bodies were burned. The graveyard surrounding the building contains the ashes of more than 45,000 people.

Męczenników Rotundy. ✆ **0600/353-392.** www.muzeum-zamojskie.one.pl. Admission 4 zł ($1.60/85p). Tues–Sun 9am–4pm.

Synagogue ★★   Zamość's impressive Renaissance synagogue dates from the early 17th century and must have been quite a palace in its heyday. Even now, while it's undergoing long-term renovation and is still derelict in parts, it's a beautiful space with an enduring spirit. The synagogue somehow managed to survive World War II (the Nazis turned it into a workshop) and later it was used as a public library. Visitors today can view two restored rooms and admire the elaborate, and still mostly intact, interior. There's a photo exhibition as well documenting the history of the town's Jewish community. The hopes are to transform it someday into a museum and cultural center.

Zamenhofa. ✆ **0608/409-055.** Admission 2 zł (80¢/45p). Tues–Sun 10am–3pm.

WHERE TO STAY

Artis ★★   Comfortable four-star hotel occupying a suburban villa in a green area about 4km (2.5 miles) north of the Zamość's historic center. The location is inconvenient if you're traveling by bus or train, but appealing if you have a car and are looking for something quieter away from the city. The beautiful gardens include a pond and children's playground set in a grove of old-growth trees. The rooms are furnished in contemporary style, but are on the plain side. Bathrooms have been updated, and everything is spotlessly clean.

Sitaniec 1. ✆ **084/616-62-62.** Fax 084/616-62-62. www.hotelartis.pl. 28 rooms. 278 zł ($111/£62) double weekdays, 250 zł ($100/£56) double weekends. **Amenities:** Restaurant; fitness club; room service; dry cleaning; nonsmoking rooms. *In room:* A/C, TV, dataport, minibar, hair dryer.

Orbis Hotel Zamojski ★ Widely considered the best address in town, both for its Rynek location, next to the Town Hall, and the highly regarded restaurant, though the Senator (see below) feels more cozy and exclusive. The reception desk is located under a handsome atrium created by linking three 16th-century townhouses. The rooms are on the plain side, but the amenities are the best around. Several rooms are outfitted for people with disabilities. The lobby is decorated with the portraits of the town's founding Zamoyski family—proof that money and good looks don't always go hand in hand!

Kołłątaja 2/4/6. (✆) **084/639-25-16.** Fax 084/639-25-16. www.orbis.pl. 45 rooms. 285 zł ($114/£64) double. **Amenities:** 2 restaurants; spa; fitness club; salon; room service; dry cleaning; nonsmoking rooms. *In room:* A/C, TV, dataport, minibar, hair dryer.

Renesans ★ The cheapest of Zamość's downtown hotels, the Renesans provides decent value for the money. You won't be bowled over by the 1960s-era building, which sticks out like a sore thumb amid Zamość's Renaissance architecture, or the 1970s chunky furniture in the rooms. You will, however, definitely appreciate the location, just a block from the main square, and niceties like a better than average buffet breakfast and free parking.

Grecka 6. (✆) **084/639-20-01.** Fax 084/638-51-74. www.polhotels.com. 25 rooms. 180 zł ($72/£40) double. **Amenities:** Restaurant; room service; nonsmoking rooms. *In room:* TV, dataport.

Senator ★★ A romantic, hideaway stuffed to the gills with antiques and period details that lend a homey rather than a cluttered feel. The rooms are well-proportioned and not nearly as festooned with mementos as the public areas. The reception desk staff is friendly and helpful, and the buffet-style breakfast is a cut above the normal fare with imaginative cheeses and smoked fish, among other relative rarities. Alas, there's no breakfast coffee aside from Nescafe instant. If you're coming by car, the hotel has a few free parking spaces.

Rynek Solny 4. (✆) **084/638-99-90.** Fax 084/638-76-13 www.senatorhotel.pl. 25 units. 268 zł ($107/£60) double. **Amenities:** Restaurant; room service; nonsmoking rooms. *In room:* A/C, TV, dataport, minibar, hair dryer.

WHERE TO DINE

For eating and drinking, your first port of call should be the Rynek, which is filled with cafes, pubs, and pizza joints that differ from each other chiefly in name. In nice weather, this is the place to be: Sit at an open-air table and sip a cappuccino—or, as the locals do, a beer sweetened with raspberry juice.

Muzealna ★★ POLISH A handsome and memorable restaurant set in three brick Renaissance cellars that look amazingly like the backdrop to a 16th-century royal banquet. The traditional Polish cooking is superb. Try the herring appetizer made with wonderfully fresh fish stacked with fresh cut onions.

Ormiańska 30. (✆) **084/638-73-00.** Lunch and dinner items 25 zł–40 zł ($10–$16/£5.60–£9). AE, DC, M, V. Daily 10am–10pm.

Arkadia ★ POLISH Informal Polish restaurant serving decent traditional dishes, including sweet and salty pancakes. In summer, the terrace on the Rynek here is one of the most popular spots in town for a dessert and coffee.

Rynek Wielki 9. (✆) **084/638-65-07.** Lunch and dinner items 25 zł–40 zł ($10–$16/£5.60–£9). AE, DC, M, V. Daily 11am–10pm.

Verona ★ ITALIAN   Part cafe, part stylish pizzeria, the Verona does a good job at both. The espresso drinks here are some of the best in town, and in summer you can sit on the terrace overlooking the Rynek. The pizza is very good and a nice alternative to the constant stream of *pierogi*.

Rynek Wielki 5. ℂ 084/638-90-31. Lunch and dinner items 20 zł–30 zł ($8–$12/£4.50–£6.70). AE, DC, M, V. Daily 11am–midnight.

5 KAZIMIERZ DOLNY

The charming riverside town of Kazimierz Dolny is Poland's version of any artsy week-end getaway, complete with a clutch of art and antique shops (some of possibly question-able artistic merit), the Polish version of aging hippies, and a lively festival calendar that features a lively folk festival in June and an increasingly popular Klezmer music festival in August. Most of the week it's relatively quiet, but come Friday afternoon, cars bearing license plates from as far away as Warsaw and Lublin stream into town for a relaxing weekend of hiking, gallery hopping, and even boating on the Vistula. It's a lovely spot and certainly worth a detour if you're traveling in this part of Poland and looking for a place to chill out before tackling another city. There are a couple of good hotels, includ-ing one of the most beautiful pensions in this part of the country, plus a smattering of good restaurants. There are enough traditional sights to keep you occupied for at least a day, and some great hikes if—just this one time—you're not up for seeing another castle.

ESSENTIALS
Getting There
Kazimierz Dolny is a little off the beaten track, but with some advance planning it's not that hard to get to. There's regular bus service that makes the two-hour trip from Lublin several times a day. There's no train station in Kazimierz Dolny, but the neighboring town of Puławy has decent train connections, and you can connect to Kazimierz Dolny via local bus (nos. 12, 14). By car, it's an easy two-hour drive from Lublin. Once in Kazimierz Dolny, follow the signs to the center. The immediate center of town is closed to motor vehicles, but there are plenty of paid parking lots where you can leave the car.

Getting Around
Walking is really the only option to see the town center, which is small and clustered around a compact town square, the Rynek. Walk or take a taxi to more far-flung destina-tions. In summer you can rent bikes, though the terrain is hilly and cycling can be chal-lenging. Check with the tourist information office (see below) for rental agencies.

Visitor Information
Kazimierz Dolny's small tourist information office, **PTTK Biuro Obsługi Ruchu Tury-stycznego** (Rynek 27; ℂ **081/881-00-46;** www.kazimierzdolny.pl; Mon–Fri 8am–4pm, Sat–Sun 10am–2:30pm), is situated in the center of town on a corner of the main square. The English-speaking staff will help you sort out hotel and restaurant choices as well as transportation options. They also stock lots of brochures and several good maps, includ-ing a free hiking and biking map of the area called "Kazimierz Dolny i okolice."

Part of the appeal of a resort like Kazimierz Dolny is that traditional tourist sites are definitely optional. It's perfectly fine just to stroll around the Rynek and go for a walk along one of the trails or out by the river.

Celej's House (Muzeum Kamienica Celejowska) ★   This is the town's general history museum, with everything you ever wanted to know about Kazimierz Dolny starting from the 8th century. It comprises exhibits on archaeology, history, and especially painting from the late 19th and early 20th centuries. Highlights include the town's important role in Polish visual arts.

Senatorska 11/13. ✆ **081/881-01-04.** www.muzeumnadwislanskie.pl. Admission 7 zł ($2.80/£1.60). May–Oct, Tues–Sun 9am–5pm; Nov–Apr, Tues–Sun 9am–4pm.

Janowiec Castle (Muzeum Zamek w Janowcu) ★★   It's worth the hike up here to see this partially restored 16th-century castle. The original building fell into ruins in the 19th century and a rehab is now slowly bringing the castle back to life. The controversial restoration involves leaving part of the castle as a ruin and using bright colors to enhance the architecture. The castle houses a Museum of Royal Interiors. The surrounding park is home to an open-air architecture museum.

Lubelska 20 (Janowiec). ✆ **081/881-52-28.** www.muzeumnadwislanskie.pl. Admission 7 zł ($2.80/£1.60). May–Oct, Tues–Sun 10am–5pm; Nov–Apr, Tues–Sun 10am–4pm.

Museum of Goldsmithery (Muzeum Sztuki Złotniczej) ★   A rich collection of decorative and religious objects crafted through the centuries from gold and other precious metals, including a valuable gold chalice from the 15th century.

Zamkowa 2. ✆ **081/881-00-80.** www.muzeumnadwislanskie.pl. Admission 6 zł ($2.40/£1.40). May–Oct, Tues–Sun 9am–5pm; Nov–Apr, Tues–Sun 9am–4pm.

OUTDOOR ACTIVITIES

HIKING   Kazimierz Dolny is a walker's paradise. The tourist information office has put together four comfortable day walks, suitable for families, that leave from the center. One of the most popular follows the Vistula south to the village of Józefów. Pick up the free map "Kazimierz Dolny i okolice" at the tourist information office.

CYCLING   The same tourist map used for hiking also shows some great cycling trails that start out from the center and head out into the surrounding hills. Since rental places change by the season, check with the tourist office for where to get bikes and which routes are suited to your fitness level and interests. The terrain away from the river gets hilly fast, but most of the cycling trails are only moderately difficult and follow little-used country roads.

BOATING   One of the most popular pastimes in this river town is a cruise up and down the Vistula on big party boats that hold up to 200 people. To find the port, follow Nadwiślańska out of town and take a right once you get to the river. Contact: Rejsy po Wiśle (✆ **081/881-01-35;** www.rejsystatkiem.com.pl) for details.

WHERE TO STAY

Kazimierz Dolny is a classic weekend getaway destination, so be sure to book ahead if you're arriving on a Friday or Saturday since rooms tend to book up. At other times, you're probably safe just showing up, but you still may not get the room you want. Hotels usually cut rates during the week to fill beds. There are several hotels within easy walking distance of the central square, but some of the nicer resort-type places are situated away from town and may require a cab or car ride.

Agharta Pensjonat ★   Pretty and comfortable pension built over an ethnic art gallery in a charming villa dating from the 1920s. The location is just a few minutes from the Rynek. The rooms reflect the good taste of the gallery below, with hardwood floors and eye-catching furnishings and fabrics from around the world. Don't expect much in the way of service, though.

Krakowska. ✆ **081/882-04-21.** www.agharta.kazimierzdolny.pl. 5 units. 200 zł ($80/£45) double. AE, DC, MC, V. **Amenities:** Restaurant; nonsmoking rooms. *In room:* TV.

Dom Architekta   The "House of Architects" occupies an attractive Renaissance townhouse right on the Rynek, making the location ideal. Unfortunately, the rooms are something of a letdown: plainly furnished in the kind of sterile style reminiscent of Communist-era hotels. The substandard breakfast completes the picture (so it's probably best to avoid the full-board pricing option), but still not a bad overall choice given the reasonable price and location.

Rynek 20. ✆ **081/883-55-44.** Fax 081/883-55-02. www.dom-architekta.pl. 37 units. 215 zł ($86/£48) double, 280 zł ($112/£63) double, including meals. AE, DC, MC, V. **Amenities:** Restaurant; nonsmoking rooms. *In room:* TV.

Hotel Król Kazimierz ★★   By far the most impressive big hotel in town and definitely the place to come if you're looking for a full-service hotel. Amenities include two bars, a big restaurant, and a beautiful indoor pool and spa. The rooms are bright and still have the brand-new feel of an upscale chain. The suites are built into a 17th-century granary behind the hotel and are fabulous (and priced accordingly), with oversized bathtubs and big canopy beds. The location is a little bit away from the action, on the left as you enter Kazimierz Dolny, about 2km (1.5 miles) from the Rynek.

Puławska 86. ✆ **081/880-99-99.** Fax 081/880-98-98. www.krolkazimierz.pl. 115 units. 670 zł ($268/£150) double, 1,000 zł ($400/£225) suite. AE, DC, MC, V. **Amenities:** Restaurant; spa; indoor pool; room service; dry cleaning; nonsmoking rooms. *In room:* A/C, TV, dataport, minibar, hair dryer.

Villa Bohema ★   Exclusive retreat in a hillside villa about a 10-minute walk from town. The tiled lobby is gorgeous, as is the formal dining room on the ground floor. The rooms have a country feel, with big beds and floral-print wallpaper. The property attracts a well-heeled, young-professional clientele who come for the good food, the indoor pool, and the pleasant, family friendly atmosphere.

Małachowskiego 12. ✆ **081/881-07-56.** www.villabohema.pl. 12 units. 360 zł ($144/£80) double. AE, DC, MC, V. **Amenities:** Restaurant; spa; indoor pool; room service; dry cleaning; nonsmoking rooms. *In room:* A/C, TV, dataport, minibar, hair dryer.

Vincent Pensjonat ★★★ (Finds)   An enchanting family-run pension, about 5 minutes from the center along Krakowska. Everything is done in white, from the walls, floors, and lobby furniture to the pebbles that line the walk to the front door. The rooms are traditional, with lovely period details such as ornately carved wooden wardrobes and old-fashioned bathtubs from the 1920s. The most inviting room is number 1, but all the rooms have personality. Relax in the adjoining garden on a sunny afternoon.

Krakowska 11. ✆ **081/881-08-76.** www.pensjonatvincent.pl. 11 units. 230 zł ($92/£50) double. AE, DC, MC, V. **Amenities:** Restaurant; nonsmoking rooms. *In room:* TV, dataport, minibar, hair dryer.

Knajpa U Fryzjera ★★ POLISH/JEWISH   Unique Jewish-themed tavern restaurant that serves old-fashioned cooking with a kosher twist. This is the place to come for chicken livers with onions, baked peppers stuffed with lamb, stuffed veal, brisket, and other home-style delights. In nice weather, plan to sit on the terrace in the back and relax over a very filling meal and several beers.

Witkiewicza 2. 🄫 **081/881-04-26.** Lunch and dinner items around 25 zł ($10/£5.60). AE, DC, MC, V. Daily 9am–midnight.

Staropolska ★★ POLISH   *The* place to come if you're looking for a traditional Polish meal including *kotlet schabowy* (breaded pork chops), or duck or game served in a refined but still relaxed atmosphere. This is a popular spot, so you may have to book in advance in high season.

Nadrzeczna 14. 🄫 **081/881-02-36.** Lunch and dinner items around 25 zł ($10/£5.60). AE, DC, MC, V. Daily noon–10pm.

Cafe Rynkowa CAFE   Not necessarily the best place for a substantial meal, but a great spot right on the Rynek for a light snack, cup of coffee, or glass of beer. Excellent espresso drinks are served in a kind of artsy space, with walls covered with paintings by local artists. There's a little Internet room next door, with computers for checking e-mail.

Rynek 7. 🄫 **081/881-00-12.** Snacks and coffee drinks around 10 zł ($4/£2.25). No credit cards. Daily 10am–10pm.

LUBLIN & SOUTHEASTERN POLAND

8

KAZIMIERZ DOLNY

Wrocław & Lower Silesia

The southwestern province of Lower Silesia (*Dolny Śląsk* in Polish) and its capital Wrocław are often overlooked by travelers to Poland who are focused on more traditional tourist destinations such as Kraków. That's a shame. Wrocław is an engaging, cosmopolitan city with one of the country's largest and liveliest central squares and a compelling story of destruction and rebirth that can rival even Warsaw or Gdańsk. The rolling Silesian countryside, filled with farms and forests, is picture-perfect. To the south, along the border with the Czech Republic, the highlands give way to actual mountains: the Karkonosze range. Here you'll find some of the country's best skiing and hiking facilities, as well as a burgeoning mountain-biking culture in the warmer months.

In many ways, Lower Silesia is the least traditionally "Polish" of the country's main regions. While Poles have been present here for more than 1,000 years, a complicated succession through the centuries saw Silesia go from Polish rule to Bohemian, and then Austrian, Prussian, and most recently German. This historical version of musical chairs has lent a fascinating architectural and cultural overlay to the region, with castles that date back to the traditional Polish and Bohemian dynasties overlooking villages that a scant generation or two ago were part of Germany. In addition to Wrocław and the Karkonosze range, don't miss the spectacular wooden churches of Jawor and Świdnica, both on UNESCO's World Cultural Heritage list, as well as the enormous Książ Castle at Wałbrzych near Wrocław. The charming district capital of Jelenia Góra makes a good base for exploring the Karkonosze and border lands with the Czech Republic. More adventurous travelers will want to spend time in Kłodzko, a largely forgotten Polish region that extends like a dagger deep into the territory of the modern-day Czech Republic and where the Polish, Bohemian, and German cultural mosaic is still keenly felt.

1 WROCŁAW

Wrocław, the capital of Lower Silesia, is a surprisingly likable big city. Although it was extensively damaged during World War II and stagnated under Communism, it's bounced back in a big way. Part of the reason has been its western location not far from the German border, which makes it easily accessible to the prosperous German daytrippers who pour over the border for a coffee and strudel. It's also drawn outside investment, particularly from the Japanese, who are eager to reach the rich markets of Western Europe while producing in still-low-wage Poland.

The heart of the city is a beautifully restored central square, the Rynek, and the playfully colorful baroque and Renaissance houses that line the square on all sides. On a warm summer's evening, the square comes to life as what seems like the entire city

descends for a glass of beer or a cup of coffee. Most of this area lay in ruins in 1945, when the Germans held out for months against an intense Russian barrage. But all that seems forgotten now. Only the presence of several battle-scarred red-brick Gothic churches evokes a sense of the scale of the destruction. Wrocław was founded some 1,000 years ago by Slavs, but its population had become increasingly Germanized through the centuries. Until the end of World War II, Wrocław was known as the German city of Breslau. The city came under Polish control with the defeat of Nazi Germany and the shifting of Poland's borders hundreds of kilometers to the West. The surviving Germans were driven out of the city and Wrocław was repopulated by Poles—many coming from the east of the country, particularly the city of Lwów, which came under Soviet domination. In spite of the border change and population shift, the city retains a Germanic feel, especially in the Rynek and the wonderfully atmospheric streets of the Old Town. Be sure to spend time as well along the Odra River, which passes just to the north of the Rynek, and the peaceful *Ostrów Tumski*, the "Cathedral Island," which is home to the city's leading religious sites.

The "Battle for Breslau"

There's a kind of macabre competition among cities in Poland as to which one suffered the most during World War II and the epic battles between the Russians and Germans fought largely on Polish soil. Certainly Warsaw—which was 85% destroyed in the war—could win the prize, and Gdańsk was flattened, too, but Wrocław, or more precisely "Breslau," could also make a strong case. In 1944, as the war was turning decisively against the Germans, Adolf Hitler declared Breslau to be a fortress city and ordered that it be defended at all costs. By February 1945, the advancing Red Army had reached the city's outskirts and began an assault that was to last nearly three months, until the end of the war in May. The Germans had leveled much of the center of the city to build an airstrip to fly in supplies, but Ukrainian and Russian units surrounding the city successively knocked down the buildings street by street through a mix of artillery and mortars and simply setting whole blocks on fire. The Nazis capitulated on May 6, just a day before Germany's total surrender. Casualty figures vary, but some German sources say more than 150,000 civilians died in the fighting. In the aftermath of the war, the surviving Germans were expelled to the German heartland, leaving just 3,000 Germans from a pre-war population of around 700,000. The city was eventually repopulated by Poles brought in from the east, from territories ceded to the Soviet Union after the war, including from the former Polish (now Ukrainian) city of Lwów. Don't be surprised by the many restaurants around town offering "Ukrainian" cooking and specialties from eastern Poland—it's the real deal. The post-war population resettlement created an irony that persists to this day: Poland's westernmost metropolis is still in many ways its most "eastern" city.

ESSENTIALS
Getting There

BY AIR **Nicolaus Copernicus Airport** (Skarżyńskiego 36; © 071/358-13-81; www.airport.wroclaw.pl) is a decent-sized airport with flights throughout Europe, including to London's Luton and Stansted airports. The airport is about 14km (9 miles) northwest of the city center. To get to town take bus 406, which will drop you just behind the train station (see below). The trip costs 2.40 zł ($1/55p). Leave about 40 minutes for the journey (more during rush hour). Taxis to and from the airport cost about 50 zł ($20/£12). The taxi company recommended by airport authorities is Ascotaxi (© 071/94-55).

BY TRAIN The main train station, **Główny** (Piłsudskiego 105; © 071/717-16-74; www.pkp.pl), is a tourist site in its own right: a spooky-looking multi-turreted castle dating from the 19th century. It's about a 15-minute walk to town from the station, or you can take a taxi. Wrocław is well served by rail and connections to major Polish cities are frequent, though the bus is usually a quicker bet for getting to Warsaw.

BY BUS The main bus station, **Dworzec Centralny PKS** (Sucha 1/11; © 0300/300-122), is located just behind the train station, making it convenient for connections. To get to the center, walk 15 minutes or take a taxi. The bus station lacks facilities, so use the train station for finding ATMs, lockers, and restaurants.

BY CAR Wrocław lies on the main four-lane highway (A4) linking the German border with Kraków, so getting here from Germany or Kraków is easy. The stretch from Kraków to Katowice will cost a toll of 6.50 zł ($2.60/£1.45), but is well worth the money because of the time you save. Once in town, finding a parking spot may prove a challenge. Public parking costs 3 zł ($1.20/67p) per hour in the immediate center and 2 zł (80¢/45p) per hour in other areas. Buy tickets from special machines scattered around town and display your ticket inside the car on the dashboard.

Visitor Information

Wrocław's helpful tourist information center is situated on the Rynek (Rynek 14; © 071/344-31-11; www.wroclaw-info.pl), open daily 9am to 9pm (8pm in winter). In addition to handing out maps and selling postcards, the staff can help arrange tours of the city, book hotel and restaurant reservations, sort out bus and train tickets, and even rent bikes. Another recommendable source of information, especially on cultural events, is **Wrocław-Info Coffee2Go** (Sukiennice 12; © 071/342-01-85; www.wroclaw-info. pl), open daily 9am to 8pm. A good source of general information is the free publication *The Visitor,* updated every 2 months, or the very helpful *Wrocław, In Your Pocket,* sometimes given out free at hotel reception desks.

City Layout

Wrocław is a sprawling city with roads and commerce spreading out in all directions. Most of the main sights, however, are located in the compact center around the enormous main square, the Rynek. Another clutch of main sights is situated on the Ostrów Tumski, across the Odra River and northwest of the city center, about a 10- to 15-minute walk from the Rynek.

Getting Around

Cars are prohibited from driving within the immediate city center, so you'll find yourself doing a lot of walking. For journeys outside the center, there's a huge network of trams and buses. Driving is pointless since traffic is usually heavy and you probably won't be able to park close to where you want to go anyway.

ON FOOT The center is compact and easy to manage on foot.

BY TRAM/BUS Outside of the Old Town, tram and bus lines are extensive. Tickets cost 2.40 zł ($1/55p) for regular service and 2.80 zł ($1.12/63p) for night buses, and are available from vending machines around town or newspaper kiosks. Validate your ticket on entering the vehicle and hold on to it for the duration of the ride.

BY TAXI Taxis are useful for getting to and from the airport, train station, and bus station but you probably won't need them for anything else. Dishonest drivers have sometimes been a problem. Never get into an unlicensed taxi, and use reputable firms when possible. **MPT Radio Taxi** (© 071/91-91) and **Lux** (© 071/96-23) are two of the best.

BY BIKE The city is relatively flat and bikes are generally exempt from basic traffic prohibitions like driving along pedestrian roads and on one-way streets, but the appeal of bike travel is limited by busy roads and a lack of dedicated bike trails. The main tourist information office on the Rynek (see above) rents bikes.

Wrocław's main attractions can be seen in a few hours of leisurely strolling. The natural place to start is the enormous central square, the **Rynek,** dominated (and that really is the right word in this case) by the Town Hall, the **Ratusz,** in the middle. The Rynek is lined with some of the most cheerful baroque and Renaissance facades to grace a Polish town square. On the northwest corner of the square is the foreboding Gothic red-brick St. **Elizabeth Church** (Kościół Św. Elżbiety), Wrocław's most impressive. You can climb the tower, but keep in mind that it's over 90m (280 ft.) high and is pretty strenuous. To the east of the Rynek is another evocative and beautiful church, the **Church of Mary Magdalene** (Kościół Św. Marii Magdaleny). Just next to the Rynek, past the Tourist Information Office, is the smaller **Plac Solny,** the former salt market that's now given over to an enormous flower market. The side streets that lead off the square in all directions merit at least a couple hours of ambling. North of the Rynek, and along the Odra River, is the university district, where you'll find some of the city's best nightspots. To the northwest of the Rynek, around Kiełbaśnicza, is Wrocław's arty district—formed amid some weathered but pretty blocks of buildings that survived the onslaught of World War II.

From the university district, follow the Odra River to the right over a series of small, picturesque islands to the peaceful, restorative **Ostrów Tumski,** home to the city's cathedral and the spiritual heart of Wrocław. It's perfect for a picnic and a few hours of contemplative strolling.

Town Hall (Ratusz) ★★

One of Poland's largest and most awe-inspiring town halls, it was originally built in the late 13th century, but has been added to and renovated time and again over the centuries. Surprisingly, it survived World War II and now lends an immense amount of character to the town square. It has lost its administrative function and now serves a mostly decorative role—a place to situate a huge tower and hang an astronomical clock. The city museum inside is worth a quick peek, but more to see the inside of the building than to peruse the exhibits at length. After you've toured the building, have a meal and a cold one at one of the city's best beer halls, conveniently located in the Town Hall basement.

Rynek. ☎ **071/347-16-93.** www.mmw.pl. Admission (museum) 10 zł ($4/£2.20) adults, 7 zł ($2.80/£1.50) children, free Wed. Wed–Sun 11am–5pm.

Panorama of the Battle of Racławice (Panorama Racławicka) ★

This enormous 140m-long (459-ft.) "panorama" painting dates from the late 19th century and depicts the battle of Racławice, when Polish forces led by national hero Tadeusz Kościuszko defeated the Russian army on April 4, 1794. The battle came at a time when Poland faced threats from the east, west, and south, and aroused hopes that Poland might survive as a nation. Those hopes proved short-lived. A few months later, in November 1794, the Polish uprising was crushed, and Poland was later divided among Prussia, Russia, and Austria in the infamous Polish partition. The painting itself, executed while Poland was still partitioned, was a bold national statement at the time, and still evokes strong national sentiment. In the years following World War II, the painting was hidden from view in case its anti-Russian sentiments offended Poland's Soviet overlords. With the rise of Solidarity in the 1980s, the painting was finally again made available to the general public in 1985.

Purkyniego 11. ☎ **071/344-23-44.** www.panoramaraclawicka.pl. Admission 20 zł ($8/£4.50) adults, 15 zł ($6/£3.40) children. Tues–Sun 9am–5pm.

(Moments) Picnic on "Cathedral Island"

If the sun is shining and you want to enjoy the fresh air, head across the Odra River to the acres of green grass and park benches on **Ostrów Tumski** (Cathedral Island). First, pick up some fresh bread, cheese, sausage, and fruit for a picnic lunch at Wrocław's central market hall, the **Hala Targowa** (Piaskowa 17; ✆ **071/ 344-27-31**), open Monday to Friday 8am to 6:30pm, and Saturday 9am to 3pm. The hall, which dates from the early years of the 20th century, is a tourist sight in its own right and there's even a great *pierogi* stand as you enter on the right. The market hall is conveniently located just across from the bridge to the island.

National Museum (Muzeum Narodowe)   A vast collection of Polish art through the ages, combining the holdings of both the cities of Wrocław and Lwów, is on display here. The museum is very strong on medieval and religious painting and sculpture from both eastern and western Poland. That said, unless you're particularly interested in Polish religious art or have some specific historical knowledge, you're unlikely to get much from the detailed holdings here. The National Museum is located near the Panorama Racławicka (see above), and you can use the same ticket for entry to both.

Pl. Powstańców Warszawy 5. ✆ 071/372-51-50. www.mnwr.art.pl. Admission 15 zł ($6/£3.40) adults, 10 zł ($4/£2.20) children, free Sat. Wed–Sun 10am–4pm.

Ostrów Tumski (Cathedral Island) ★★   The name is slightly misleading since it's not an island at all, but it does lie on the opposite side of the Odra River from the Rynek. This is the spiritual heart of the city and where Wrocław was founded around 1,000 years ago. Today, it's home to several churches, including the main Cathedral of St. John the Baptist, as well as the city's Botanical Gardens and a lovely clutch of timeless lanes and handsome buildings. Be sure to allow at least a couple hours to take it all in. The cathedral is worth a special look, with its 16th-century altarpiece, giant organ, and tower with gorgeous views over the city. The church dates from the middle of the 13th century but was nearly totally destroyed in World War II, and much of what you see today is a careful reconstruction of the original.

Katedra Św. Jana Chrzciciela (Cathedral of St. John the Baptist). Pl. Katedralny 18. ✆ 071/322-25-74. www. katedra.archidiecezja.wroc.pl. Free admission. Mon–Sat 10am–4pm, Sun 2–4pm (no visits during mass).

Customized Tours

Aga Tours (✆ **0508/212-412;** www.agatours.pl) offers fun guided tours in a modified golf cart that holds up to five people. The most popular tours include "Wrocław by Night" and a combined tour that takes in both the Old Town and Cathedral Island. Both take a little over an hour and prices start at around 100 zł ($40/£22) per person. **Eko-Tur** (✆ **0663/222-660;** www.ekotur.wroclaw.pl) offers a similar range of tours. Both companies can be booked directly by phone or through your hotel or the tourist information center.

SHOPPING

The Rynek and the streets that radiate from it are packed with little curio shops, antique dealers, and art galleries. For a pleasant ramble, try the little street **Stare Jatki,** which runs off of Kiełbaśnicza, just a couple of minutes' walk down from the Rynek. This strip used to house the city's butcher stalls, but today it's home to numerous art galleries, studios, and little cafes where the shop clerks idle away the quiet hours.

WHERE TO STAY

Hotel prices have been rising in recent years in step with the growing economy and rising standards for accommodation. You can beat the high costs by planning your visit on a weekend, when rates are cut by as much as 50%. There's a good cluster of hotels along Kiełbaśnicza, in the northern part of the Old Town near the university. Most hotels offer parking for a fee of 20 zł to 30 zł a night.

Very Expensive

Holiday Inn ★   Not long ago, this was arguably the best place to stay in Wrocław. It's still an exceptionally nice hotel, but there are now equally comfortable places closer to the Rynek. The location, however, is excellent if you are arriving by train or bus, since the hotel is just a short hop from both. For business, this is probably still the best address in town, given the extensive business center and conference facilities. And it's still one of the few places offering warmed bathroom tiles and bathtubs as standard.

Piłsudskiego 49/57. ✆ **071/787-00-00.** Fax 071/787-00-01. www.wroclaw.azurehotel.pl. 164 units. 520 zł ($208/£120). AE, DC, MC, V. **Amenities:** Restaurant; exercise room; sauna; concierge; car-rental desk; business center; salon; room service; massage; executive-level rooms; nonsmoking rooms. *In room:* A/C, TV, dataport, minibar, hair dryer, trouser press (executive rooms only).

Best Western Prima ★   To be sure, this is a clean and well-managed hotel, but it feels overpriced given some of the newer properties on the market. Everything you would expect from the Best Western chain. The staff training is evident from the first encounter with the helpful reception desk. The rooms are upscale middle-market, and feel like a well-furnished suburban home with carpeting and floral prints. The Sir William restaurant is an excellent choice if you don't feel like venturing far from the hotel, with a surprisingly adventurous menu featuring a halibut salad and main courses such as venison ragout and stewed duck leg with red currant sauce.

Kiełbaśnicza 16/19. ✆ **071/782-55-55.** Fax 071/342-67-32. www.bestwestern-prima.pl. 79 units. 400 zł ($160/£90) double. AE, DC, MC, V. **Amenities:** Restaurant; exercise room; sauna; limited room service; nonsmoking rooms. *In room:* A/C, TV, dataport, minibar, hair dryer.

Expensive

Art Hotel ★   Occupying two renovated burghers' houses in Wrocław's art (and hotel) quarter, this funky, bright-orange property is a welcome alternative to the chains. The reception area is sleek and cool and each guest room has been furnished individually in an eclectic mix of modern and traditional. The restaurant gets high marks from local critics. It's popular, so make sure to book in advance.

Kiełbaśnicza 20. ✆ **071/787-71-00.** Fax 071/342-39-29. www.arthotel.pl. 77 units. 500 zł ($200/£112) double on weekdays; 320 zł ($128/£72) double on weekends. AE, DC, MC, V. **Amenities:** Restaurant; exercise room; business center; salon; room service; massage; nonsmoking rooms. *In room:* A/C, TV, dataport, minibar, hair dryer.

Hotel Patio ★★   Another renovated burgher's house on Kiełbaśnicza, but slightly cheaper than its rivals. The Patio is every bit as inviting as the Art and Best Western Prima hotels, but what's absent here are a fitness room, sauna, and air conditioning. The rooms, done in fresh colors, light woods, and whites, are even a notch more inviting than the competition.

Kiełbaśnicza 24/25. ℂ **071/375-04-00.** Fax 071/343-91-49. www.hotelpatio.pl. 49 units. 360 zł ($144/£80)
double. AE, DC, MC, V. **Amenities:** Restaurant; limited room service; nonsmoking rooms. *In room:* TV,
dataport, minibar, hair dryer.

Qubus Hotel ★★   This smallish and smart hotel just a short walk from the Rynek
caters to business people. Qubus is a growing chain of high-quality hotels and this one
competes head-to-head with the Prima/Best Western, but gets an extra nod for the in-
house swimming pool and a more modern feel. Note that rooms are heavily discounted
if you book on the Internet and reserve at least seven days in advance. Rates fall another
25% on weekends.

Św. Marii Magdaleny 2. ℂ **071/797-98-00.** Fax 071/341–09–20. www.qubushotel.com. 87 units. 400 zł
($160/£90) double (weekdays booked in advance). AE, DC, MC, V. **Amenities:** Restaurant; indoor pool;
sauna; limited room service; nonsmoking rooms. *In room:* A/C, TV, dataport, minibar, hair dryer.

Moderate

Dom Jana Pawła II ★★   This excellent-value hotel was purpose-built to welcome Pope
John Paul II on his second visit to the city, and is near the Cathedral of St. John the Baptist
on tranquil Ostrów Tumski. A kind of hushed holiness surrounds the hotel and greets you
the moment you enter the quiet lobby. This is not a good choice if you're in town to drink
and carouse; on the other hand, you won't find a cleaner or better-maintained hotel around.
Ask for one of the rooms overlooking the cathedral or the botanical gardens.

Św. Idziego 2. ℂ **071/327-14-00.** Fax 071/327-14-00, www.pensjonat-jp2.pl. 60 units. 290 zł ($116/£65)
double. AE, DC, MC, V. **Amenities:** Restaurants; concierge; business center; salon; room service; nonsmoking rooms. *In room:* A/C, TV, dataport, minibar.

Hotel Zaułek ★   A decent in-town choice given the excellent location and low price,
the hotel is run by a foundation for the university of Wrocław and does double-duty host-
ing visiting professors and university guests. From the outside, the hotel looks like an aging
housing complex, but on the inside it's neat, clean, and quiet. The rooms are modestly
furnished but perfect for a short stay and there's free Wi-Fi throughout the hotel.

Garbary 11. ℂ **071/341-00-46.** Fax 071/375-29-47. www.hotel.uni.wroc.pl. 12 units. 290 zł ($116/£65)
double. AE, DC, MC, V. **Amenities:** Restaurant; nonsmoking rooms. *In room:* TV, minibar, hair dryer.

Inexpensive

Avantgarde (Value)   An acceptable budget alternative if the Centrum (see below) is
booked up. This is a classic hostel, with cast-metal bunk beds and shared bathrooms.
Nevertheless, it's secure, the service is friendly, and the rooms are clean. There are few
amenities, but there's a computer terminal on the ground floor to check email and complimentary Wi-Fi throughout. The walk to the Rynek is about 15 minutes. There's free
parking at the hostel door if you're traveling by car.

Kościuszki 55. ℂ **071/793-08-70.** www.avantgardehostel.pl. 15 units. 120 zł ($48/£27) private double.
AE, DC, MC, V.

Centrum ★ (Value)   This property is highly recommended if you're on a budget and
show up in town on a weekday without a reservation. Technically a hostel, the Centrum
also offers private singles and doubles of average to high quality at excellent prices. Not
much in the way of amenities here, but expect clean rooms and hardwood floors in a
bright, shiny space. The central location is a 5-minute walk from the Rynek.

Św. Mikołaja 16/17. ℂ **071/793-08-70.** Fax 071/793-08-70. www.centrumhostel.pl. 12 units. 120 zł ($48/
£27) private double. AE, DC, MC, V.

The Rynek is lined with restaurants, cafes, and bars from corner to corner. Most restaurants post their menus out front, so peruse the square and see what you're hungry for.

Very Expensive

Sakana Sushi Bar ★★ JAPANESE   A standout sushi bar where you sit on stools around a counter and little boats of delicacies float by. You select the ones that fit your appetite (or your wallet). Each plate has a different color and price; white is the cheapest (starting at around 15 zł), and prices head north from there. Three plates makes for a filling meal—if you choose carefully you can stay on a budget, but what's the fun of that when the food is this good?

Odrzańska 17/1a. ✆ **071/343-37-10.** Lunch and dinner items 50 zł–70 zł ($20–$28/£11–£15). AE, DC, MC, V. Mon–Sat noon–11pm; Sun 1–10pm.

Expensive

Karczma Lwówska ★ POLISH/UKRAINIAN   Named for the former Polish, now Ukrainian, city from where many current Wrocław residents originally hail, the menu here features many hard-to-find specialties from eastern Poland. Specialties include gołąbki kresówki, peppers stuffed with spiced minced meat and mushrooms. Dine on the terrace in summer, or in the evocative, tavern-style interior in winter. Book ahead, especially on a warm summer evening, when the terrace fills to brimming.

Rynek 4. ✆ **071/343-98-87.** Lunch and dinner items 23 zł–45 zł ($9–$18/£5–£10). AE, DC, MC, V. Daily 11am–midnight.

Piwnica Świdnicka ★★★ POLISH   Try to have at least one meal here, at the city's best-known Polish pub. Local specialties, such as beef roulade served with beet puree, are some of the best you'll taste, and the atmosphere—either on the terrace in summer or down in the cellar in winter—is festive and memorable. There's great beer here, too.

Rynek-Ratusz 1. ✆ **071/369-95-10.** Lunch and dinner items 23 zł–45 zł ($9–$18/£5–£10). AE, DC, MC, V. Daily 11am–11pm.

Moderate

Abrams' Tower ★★ MEXICAN/FUSION   A "Mexican-Fusion" restaurant with the city's best burritos and fajitas, this derelict tower of one of Wrocław's medieval defense bastions is worth a visit just to check out the unusual setting. Dining is on three levels: the top floor, with a mix of tables and trendy Moroccan-style floor pillows, is the most popular. Both the Mexican and Asian-inflected dishes like Thai curry are excellent and good value.

Kraińskiego 14. ✆ **071/725-66-52.** Dinner items 25 zł–40 zł ($10–16/£6–£9). AE, DC, MC, V. Daily 4pm–midnight.

Novocaina ★ ITALIAN   A trendy entry on the Rynek that promises only the freshest ingredients, and the Italian-influenced menu mostly delivers. The pizzas are cooked in a traditional cherry wood-fired oven and come out just right. The high points are the salads and sandwiches, making this a good lunchtime pick and popular with Wrocław's young professional crowd. Very good coffee and free Wi-Fi are two more reasons to visit.

Rynek 13. ✆ **071/343-69-15.** Lunch and dinner items 25 zł–40 zł ($10–$16/£6–£9). AE, DC, MC, V. Daily 9am–11pm.

Inexpensive

Aladdin's MIDDLE EASTERN   A relative rarity in Poland is a decent Middle Eastern restaurant, and this one fits the bill. Big salads and falafel are a welcome departure from heavier Polish food. Aladdin's is close to the university and attracts an informal student crowd for both lunch and dinner.

Odrzańska 23. ✆ **071/796-73-27.** Lunch and dinner items 18 zł–24 zł ($7.20–$10/£4–£5.40). No credit cards. Daily 11:30am–10pm.

Rodeo Drive TEX-MEX   One of the better chain restaurants to emerge in Poland in the last few years; this one features "Texas-style" steaks, ribs, and burgers. In a land of mediocre burgers, this place stands out if you're in the mood for something more like home. The portions are enormous, so even 6-foot-2 cowboys might be content with a "cowgirl" portion—even if the waitress does raise an eyebrow when you order it.

Rynek 28. ✆ **071/343-96-09.** Lunch and dinner items 20 zł–35 zł ($8–$14/£4.50–£8). AE, DC, MC, V. Daily 11am–10pm.

AFTER DARK
The Performing Arts

Wrocław is renowned for its theater, which has been long regarded as some of the most daring and experimental in the country. For non–Polish speakers, though, this is likely to be of little interest. The Tourist Information Office at the Rynek is a good source of information on more accessible performances of classical music and opera. The **Wrocław Philharmonic** (Piłsudskiego 19; ✆ **071/342-24-59** (box office); www.filharmonia. wroclaw.pl) is a good bet for an excellent concert during the cultural season from September to May. The **Wrocław Opera** (Świdnicka 35; ✆ **071/344-57-79** (box office); www.opera.wroclaw.pl) is one of the country's leading companies.

Cafes, Pubs & Clubs

For culture of the lower-brow sort, Wrocław is a great drinking and partying town. Its festive spirit, not surprisingly, is bolstered by the presence of thousands of college students. The university area has more than its fair share of beer gardens, cafes, and cocktail bars. For a good pub crawl, try the Ruska and Kuźnicza streets that lead off from the Rynek. The Plac Solny is also lined with drinking spots, and the Rynek itself is a major draw. What appear to be normal restaurants and cafes during the day transform into everything from rowdy beer halls to ultra-chill dance clubs after sunset.

Graciarnia ★   In spite of its unpromising location and doorway, this is a great spot if you're looking for a quiet beer or drink a little bit away from the action. A self-described "chill zone" features antique furniture, a laid-back clientele, and very friendly servers.

K. Wielkiego 39; ✆ **071/795-66-88;** Mon–Fri noon–2am, Sat 5pm–2am, Sun 5pm–midnight.

---

2 AROUND WROCŁAW: KSIĄŻ CASTLE, ŚWIDNICA & JAWOR

The most popular day trips from Wrocław include the massive **Książ (Fuerstenstein) Castle,** near Wałbrzych, about 75km (46 miles) southwest of Wrocław, and the two remarkable 17th-century wooden "Peace" churches at Świdnica (60km/37 miles from Wrocław) and Jawor (80km/49 miles from Wrocław). If you have your own wheels, it's easy to combine the three sites in one day, setting off first for Świdnica from Wrocław, then continuing on to Wałbrzych and Książ, and then heading north to Jawor before looping back to Wrocław. It's also possible, but slower, to go by public transportation, taking the bus or train to Świdnica and Wałbrzych, and then continuing by bus to Jawor. Alternatively, several Wrocław tour operators offer day bus trips with guides. If you've got a couple of days, Książ Castle has three beautiful hotels and makes a great overnight choice. Świdnica is also worth an extra day and has at least two decent hotels. Jawor is smaller, but it's possible to put in there for the night too.

ESSENTIALS

Getting There

BY CAR Książ Castle is easily accessible from Wrocław by car, following signs to Wałbrzych along Polish route 35, and once in Wałbrzych following signs to Książ Castle on the outskirts of town. Conveniently, the route takes you through Świdnica, meaning it's easy to plan a stopover at the Peace Church there. There's ample parking at Książ Castle, and if you've booked a room at one of the hotels there you're permitted to drive practically up to the castle gates. To reach more remote Jawor from Wrocław, follow the A4 highway to Legnica and turn south on E65 when you see signs to Jawor. From Wałbrzych, drive along route 35 in the direction of Świdnica, following signs first to Strzegom and from there to Jawor.

BY TRAIN Both Wałbrzych and Świdnica are easily reachable by train from Wrocław. Train connections to Jawor exist but are less frequent. From Wałbrzych train station, use local bus connections to get to Książ Castle. From Świdnica train station, walk or take a taxi to the Peace Church.

BY BUS Wałbrzych, Świdnica, and Jawor are all on regular bus routes. Książ Castle is serviced by local Wałbrzych buses, or take a taxi from the bus station.

Visitor Information

Książ Castle has a small tourist information office just as you enter the castle compound in the lobby of the Książ Castle Hotel (Piastów Śląskich 1; ✆ **074/664-38-90;** www.ksiaz.walbrzych.pl). Don't expect much in the way of service or English, but they do carry a few brochures and maps. In Świdnica, the main tourist information office is conveniently located on the central square (Wewnętrzna 2 (Rynek); ✆ 074/852-02-90; www.um.swidnica.pl). Look for the brochure *Świdnica, Tradition of the Market,* which has a small map and a good list of sights and accommodation options. Jawor also has a small but helpful tourist information office on the main square (Rynek 3; ✆ **076/870-33-71;** www.gci.dja.pl). The English-speaking staff are eager to recommend hotels and restaurants and help sort out transportation options.

TOP ATTRACTIONS

Książ Castle (Fuerstenstein Castle) ★★ Reputedly the largest castle in Lower Silesia, the 400-room Książ Castle was originally laid out in the 13th century by members of the early Polish nobility. It's been refurbished and rebuilt several times through the centuries, resulting in today's baroque-renaissance-rococo-neoclassical mishmash. From 1509 to 1940, the castle was owned by the Hochberg family and its most famous resident—at least to English-speaking readers—is Winston Churchill's aunt, Princess Daisy Hochberg, who lived here from 1891–1923 and then again in the tempestuous years at the start of World War II, from 1938–40. During the latter half of World War II the castle was seconded by the Nazis, who dug huge tunnels in the ground below. It's never been fully revealed what the Nazis were up to, but theories include preparing the castle as a residence for Adolf Hitler or simply clearing space to build an underground munitions factory.

After the war, the occupying Soviet Army requisitioned the castle and, according to the Poles, stayed a suspiciously long time; perhaps trying to figure out what the Germans wanted to do here. After the Russians left, the castle languished unoccupied. Now it's making a comeback as one of the most popular tourist sites in these parts and also as a conference and party venue. You can tour the castle, but only with a guide, and English-speaking guides are few and far between. That said, only a fraction of the rooms are open for visitors, and the rooms that are open are scarcely furnished. Three tours are available, with the most popular focusing on the baroque Maximilian room. History buffs will want to take the third, and newest, tour, Secrets of World War II, which leads you underground to see the enormous tunnels the Germans dug.

Zamek Książ (Książ Castle). Piastów Śląskich 1. ✆ 074/664-38-50. www.ksiaz.walbrzych.pl. Admission 12 zł ($5/£2.70) Maximilian's route, 16 zł ($6.40/£3.60) Mysteries of World War II. Apr–Sep Mon–Fri 10am–5pm, Sat–Sun 10am–6pm; Oct–Mar Tues–Fri 10am–3pm, Sat–Sun 10am–4pm.

"Peace" Churches of Świdnica and Jawor ★★ The spectacular 17th-century wooden "Peace" churches of Świdnica and Jawor are both listed as UNESCO World Heritage Sites and have provisions for English-speaking visitors (written information and an English audio tape they will play in the church on request) that are often frustratingly lacking at other tourist destinations in Poland. The "Peace" in the names refers to the 1648 Peace of Westphalia that ended the Europe-wide Thirty Years War. Though the war finished inconclusively, this part of Europe fell under the domination of the staunchly Catholic Habsburg Empire. Local Lutherans sought the protection of the King of Sweden for the right to build three Lutheran churches in the area (a third church at Głogów later burned to the ground). The Habsburgs relented but stipulated that the churches could be built only under very difficult circumstances: they had to be constructed completely from wood, located outside the town walls, and completed within a calendar year. That the churches were finished at all was a miracle; that they turned out so beautifully is fitting testimony to the faith of the believers. The Świdnica church, which can hold up to 7,000, is regarded as the largest wooden church in Europe, but both structures are amazing in terms of their size, the engineering skills that went into their construction, and their enduring beauty.

Świdnica Peace Church: Pl. Pokoju 6. ✆ 074/852-28-14. www.kosciolpokoju.pl. Admission 6 zł ($2.40/£1.30). Apr–Oct Mon–Sat 9am–5pm, Sun noon–5. Open winter by appointment only. Jawor Peace Church: Park Pokoju 2. ✆ 076/870-32-73. www.luteranie.pl. Admission 6 zł ($2.40/£1.30). Apr–Oct Mon–Sat 10am–1pm, 3–5pm, Sun 3–5pm. Open winter by appointment only.

WHERE TO STAY

The three castle hotels include two of the nicest properties in this part of Poland. The problem with staying here, though, is that the castle is a bit remote, and once you've toured the castle and walked the grounds, there's not much else to do. In nearby Świdnica, there are two good hotels and the city is big enough to offer some diversions in the evening. Jawor has one decent hotel and a small town center worth about an hour of exploration. If you're traveling by car, the Hotel Bolków, 15km (10 miles) south of Jawor, offers cheap rates and one of the best restaurants in southwestern Poland.

Hotel Ksiąź   Not as luxurious inside as the brochures might indicate. The rooms are a bit spare and, compared to the two other hotels here, slightly overpriced. Nevertheless, this is a comfortable night's stay, with a very good in-house restaurant and just a short walk away from the main castle entrance.

Piastów Śląskich 1. ✆ **074/664-38-90.** Fax 074/664-38-92. www.ksiaz.walbrzych.pl. 20 units. 260 zł ($105/£57) double. AE, MC, V. **Amenities:** Restaurant; business center; room service; nonsmoking rooms. *In room:* A/C, TV, dataport, minibar.

Hotel Przy Oślej Bramie ★★ (Finds)   The most romantic of the three hotels within the castle complex, the hotel occupies several remodeled guesthouses that have been hewn together. Ask to see several rooms, since they are all a little different. Some are done out in period furnishings, and a few have retained the original arched ceilings.

Piastów Śląskich 1. ✆ **074/664-92-70.** Fax 074/664-92-71. www.mirjan.pl. 27 units. 250 zł ($100/£55) double. AE, MC, V. **Amenities:** Restaurant; room service; nonsmoking rooms. *In room:* TV, dataport, minibar, hair dryer.

Hotel Zamkowy ★★ (Value)   Another beautifully renovated former castle outbuilding that's been given the royal touch with beautiful red carpeting and contemporary room decor that looks both restrained and luxurious at the same time. Everything is spotless and the hotel is one of the few wheelchair-accessible properties around. The Zamkowy offers special horseback riding weekends that take advantage of the former castle stables just up the street.

Piastów Śląskich 1. ✆ **074/665-41-44.** Fax 074/665-41-44. www.hotelzamkowy.pl. 25 units. 275 zł ($110/£60) double. AE, MC, V. **Amenities:** Restaurant; exercise room; business center; room service; nonsmoking rooms. *In room:* A/C, TV, dataport, minibar, hair dryer.

Świdnica

Park Hotel ★★ (Value)   A nicely reconstructed villa lining a park about a 10-minute walk from the town center and about 15 minutes by foot from the Świdnica Peace Church. The rooms are slightly worn in spots, but the beds are comfortable with thick mattresses and cotton linens. The bathrooms are spotless, and come complete with nice soaps and shampoos and a hair dryer. Ask to see a couple of the suites if you're in the mood for a splurge. Room no. 3 is a corner with a delightful canopy bed and a rack rate that's not much higher than a standard double. The friendly reception desk will sometimes cut deals on slow nights. The very good restaurant downstairs seals the deal.

Pionierów 20. ✆ **074/853-77-22.** Fax 074/853-70-98. www.park-hotel.com.pl. 23 units. 220 zł ($88/£50) double. AE, MC, V. **Amenities:** Restaurant; room service; nonsmoking rooms. *In room:* A/C, TV, dataport, minibar, hair dryer.

Piast-Roman Hotel   A comfortable in-town option. The location, on a side street off the main square, is closer to the action than the Park, but the rooms are colder and not as homey. Wi-Fi is available on some floors; if this is important to you, be sure to ask. The restaurant comes highly recommended by the locals for its decent Polish and international dishes in a town that has relatively few good places to eat. You can walk to the Peace Church from here in about 10 minutes.

Kotlarska 11. ✆ **074/852-13-93.** Fax 074/852-30-76. www.hotel-piast-roman.pl. 23 units. 220 zł ($88/£50) double. AE, MC, V. **Amenities:** Restaurant; room service; nonsmoking rooms. *In room:* TV, dataport, minibar.

Bolków Hotel ★ (**Value**)   This small, family-run hotel about 15km (10 miles) south of Jawor in the town of Bolków is a good value and perfectly fine for a night. The rooms are tiny and no-frills, but the reconstructed roadside villa, which uses old black-and-white photos to evoke a 1920s feel, is a nice change of pace from characterless modern hotels. The hotel offers free Wi-Fi, but be warned that the connection is often fickle. This hotel is really only an option if you are traveling by car.

Sienkiewicza 17. 𝄐 **075/741-39-95.** Fax 075/741-39-96. www.hotel-bolkow.pl. 23 units. 150 zł ($60/£33) double, breakfast 15 zł ($6/£4). AE, MC, V. **Amenities:** Restaurant; nonsmoking rooms. *In room:* TV.

Hotel Jawor ★   Head and shoulders above anything else in town, this modern hotel makes a perfect overnight stop and is popular with both tourists and traveling businessmen. The rooms are done up in a contemporary style and are clean and comfortable. The restaurant is probably the best dining option in town, and there's a little cafe off the lobby that serves the only drinkable coffee for miles. The central location is an easy 10-minute walk to the town square and the Jawor Peace Church.

Staszica 10. 𝄐 **076/871-06-24.** Fax 076/871-15-46. www.hoteljawor.com.pl. 23 units. 265 zł ($105/£55) double. AE, MC, V. **Amenities:** Restaurant; room service; nonsmoking rooms. *In room:* TV, dataport, minibar.

WHERE TO DINE

Decent dining options are few and far between in these parts. At Książ Castle try the restaurant at the Hotel Książ (see above) or the informal terrace grill that offers sausages and beer in the summer (walk into the main castle entrance and follow the signs for "Grill"). If you're stuck in Jawor without a car, the restaurant at the Hotel Jawor will do in a pinch.

Świdnica

Park Hotel Restaurant ★ POLISH/CONTINENTAL   The best restaurant in town, the menu here runs the gamut from traditional Polish specialties such as *żurek* and *pierogi* to international pasta dishes, grilled salmon, and lots of meat and chicken entrees. There are also excellent salads and friendly service. Most nights you can just show up at the door, but book ahead on weekends.

Pionierów 20. 𝄐 **074/853-77-22.** Lunch and dinner items 25 zł–45 zł ($10–$18/£6–£10). AE, DC, MC, V. Daily noon–11pm.

Jawor

Bolków Hotel Restaurant ★★★ POLISH/CONTINENTAL   For one of the best meals on offer in this part of Poland, head to the restaurant at the Bolków Hotel. Specializing in home cooking done well, the menu includes big plates of roast meats served with mounds of mashed potatoes, and local specialties such as fresh grilled trout. The desserts are homemade and the throwback atmosphere is fun and inviting.

Sienkiewicza 17. 𝄐 **075/741-39-95.** Lunch and dinner items 20 zł–40 zł ($8–$16/£4.50–£9). AE, DC, MC, V. Daily 10am–11pm.

3 JELENIA GÓRA & KARKONOSZE NATIONAL PARK

To the south, the rolling hills of Silesia give way to a chain of low-rise mountains that run southeast and define the border between Poland and the Czech Republic. Nearly the entire area, including the Czech side of the border, is a protected national park (Karkonosze National Park in Polish; Krkonoše National Park in Czech). The origin of the word "Karkonosze" is not known, but in German and English the range is often referred to as the "Giant" mountains. This rather overstates the case. The highest peaks are in the 1,600m (5,200-ft.) range. Nevertheless, the mountains and the national park make for a perfect low-stress stopover for hiking or biking in summer, and skiing in winter. The region's major city, Jelenia Góra, has a beautifully preserved town square and is worth at least a few hours of poking around. With good transportation connections as well as decent hotels and restaurants, it makes a fine base for exploring the national park. Alternatively, if you're coming specifically to ski or hike, you'll probably want to stay within the boundaries of the national park itself at one of the main resorts of Karpacz or Szklarska Poręba.

ESSENTIALS

Getting There

BY TRAIN   Jelenia Góra is the main transportation center for this part of Lower Silesia and has decent rail connections with Wrocław and neighboring towns.

BY BUS   Buses link Jelenia Góra to cities across southern Poland, and buses are generally a quicker option than trains for reaching regional cities. Buses link Jelenia Góra to the mountain resorts of Karpacz and Szklarska Poręba, as well as the two towns with each other.

BY CAR   Jelenia Góra lies on the E65 highway, linking this part of Poland with the Czech city of Liberec. It's an easy 90-minute drive from Wrocław, and about an hour from Liberec. Szklarska Poręba is on the same highway, just 10km (6 miles) from the Czech border. Karpacz is more remote. To find it follow Poland Rte. 367 south out of Jelenia Góra about 20km (12 miles). Figure on about 30 minutes for the journey.

Tourist Information

The **Jelenia Góra Tourist and Cultural Information Center** (Bankowa 27; ✆ 075/767-69-25; www.jeleniagora.pl) is exceptionally helpful and offers maps and good advice for exploring the nearby Karkonosze National Park. The English-speaking staff can help arrange transportation, find a room, or recommend a good place to eat. There are several tourist information offices within the Karkonosze National Park. Main branches are at **Szklarska Poręba** (Jedności Narodowej 1a; ✆ 075/754-77-40; www.szklarskaporeba.pl) and **Karpacz** (Konstytucji 3 Maja 25; ✆ 075/761-97-16; www.karpacz.pl). In Karpacz, in addition to the tourist information office, just down the street you'll find an outdoor electronic kiosk open 24/7 showing which hotels and pensions have free rooms. The Szklarska Poręba branch carries a free cycling map and doles out information on bike and ski rentals.

Getting Around

Regular bus service connects Jelenia Góra with the mountain resorts of Karpacz and Szklarska Poręba, as well as the two resorts with each other. Most visitors come by car. Figure on about 30 minutes of driving from Jelenia Góra to each of the resorts, and about 40 minutes to drive from Karpacz to Szklarska Poręba.

Stalin Comes to the Mountains

A little known (or perhaps conveniently forgotten) fact in these parts is that one of the most famous visitors to the tiny resort of Szklarska Poręba was none other than Soviet dictator Josef Stalin. It was 1947, shortly after the end of World War II. Stalin was trying to rally his newly won satellite states (and trying to convince them to resist aid money from the United States) when he called a conference here of heads of Communist states and parties from around Europe. It was here that Stalin set the tone of confrontation with the West that would last for the next four decades. You'll look in vain for any information about the conference. In fact, it's not even certain anymore where exactly it took place. Historians believe the venue was a now-abandoned glass factory on the main road toward the Czech border about a kilometer south of town. The factory is now being renovated to house a resort or conference center, though it's unlikely they'll focus much attention on their most famous "guest."

TOP ATTRACTIONS
Jelenia Góra

This is the largest town in the vicinity of the Karkonosze Mountains and is a good jumping-off spot for exploring the mountains and Karkonosze National Park because of its decent lodging and dining options. The town's history goes back some 900 years. The focal point is an impressive medieval square, the Plac Ratuszowy, surrounded by baroque- and Rococo-facaded burghers' houses and with the town hall, the Ratusz, in the middle. There's not much in the way of traditional sightseeing options, though the burghers' houses deserve closer inspection. In the town's heyday, these were occupied by the wealthiest citizens and many are still marked with the signs of the traditional guilds. Today, the intact baroque arcades serve mainly to shield the customers of the many cafes and pubs that line the square. If you get a rainy day or have a few hours to spend in town, walk about 500m (1,600 ft.) south of the square to the Karkonosze Regional Museum, a good primer on the park's history and natural bounty.

Muzeum Karkonoskie (Karkonosze Museum)   Pleasant if slightly dull presentation of the history of the Karkonosze region as well as this part of Lower Silesia. Examples of traditional folk architecture and crafts, as well some atmospheric old photos of what was once certainly a golden age in these parts. Display information is in Polish and German only.

Jana Matejki 28. © **075/752-34-65.** www.muzeumkarkonoskie.pbox.pl. Admission 6 zł ($2.40/£1.35) adults, 2 zł (80¢/45p) concession. Tues–Fri 9am–3:30pm, Sat–Sun 9am–4:30pm.

Karkonosze National Park/Karpacz/Szklarska Poręba

Most visitors to Karkonosze National Park choose to base themselves at one of the mountain resorts of Karpacz and Szklarska Poręba, where the best hotels, restaurants, and tourist information offices are located. In truth, there's not much difference between the two. Karpacz is a little smaller and more remote than Szklarska Poręba, lying farther from a main highway. On the down side, the ski facilities here are slightly inferior, and in summer the mountain biking infrastructure is not as built up as in Szklarska Poręba.

WROCLAW & LOWER SILESIA

9

JELENIA GORA & KARKONOSZE NATIONAL PARK

Either resort is fine if you're just passing through for a couple of days to go walking in the mountains. Aside from the beautiful nature, along with hiking, biking, and skiing, there's not much here in the way of traditional tourist sites. If you get a rainy day, both resort centers are suitably picturesque and filled with little souvenir shops and diversions. Karpacz has two modest tourist attractions: A sports museum and a transplanted Norwegian church that's certainly worth seeking out.

Muzeum Sportu i Turystyki w Karpaczu (Museum of Sports and Tourism in Karpacz) The main exhibitions here focus on the history of the Giant Mountains. Exhibits start from the early 12th century when the first Polish armies slogged through here paving new routes to Bohemia and also include a history of sports in the mountains, particularly sledding and skiing in the 19th century.

Kopernika 2. (✆ 075/761-96-52. www.muzeumsportu.dolnyslask.pl. Admission 4 zł ($1.60/£85p) adults, 2 zł (80¢/45p) seniors, students, and children. Tues–Sun 9am–5pm.

Wang Church ★★ Probably the last thing you'd expect to find in the Giant Mountains of Poland is a 12th-century Norwegian church. This wooden beauty was transplanted here from Norway's Vang valley in 1842 by Prussian King Frederick William IV to serve as a place of worship for the local Lutheran community. It's one of just a handful of old Viking churches to survive anywhere in the world and is an excellent example of Old Nordic sacral architecture.

Na Śnieżkę 8. (✆ 075/761-92-28. www.wang.com.pl. Admission 5 zł ($2/£1.10) adults, 4 zł ($1.60/£85p) seniors, students, and children. Mon–Sat 10am–6pm, Sun 11:30am–6pm.

OUTDOOR ACTIVITIES

Biking, hiking, and skiing are the three most popular sporting activities here, but there are lots of other more adventurous pursuits such as bouldering, mountain climbing, and gliding that have become more popular in recent years. As operators change by the year, the best advice is to ask at the tourist information office to see what's available during the time of your visit.

BIKING In the last decade or so, Szklarska Poręba has evolved into the mountain biking capital of southern Poland. More than a dozen trails of more than 300km (180 miles) in length, catering to all skill levels, fan out from the town in all directions. Some of the trails are all-day affairs running 40km to 60km (24–36 miles) in length, while others are shorter and oriented toward recreational cyclists or families with children. Pick up the free cycling map *Rowerowa Kraina* from the tourist information office. They can also advise on the best routes and bike rentals. In Szklarska Poręba you'll find a bike rental outfit at Wzg. Paderewskiego 5 (✆ 075/717-20-74). In Karpacz, try the Karpacz Motor Shop, at Konstytucji 3 Maja 50 (✆ 075/761-94-16). Bike rentals start at around 5 zł ($2/£1.10) per hour and around 25 zł ($10/£5.60) for all day.

HIKING Most visitors come here for the opportunity to walk in the mountains. Karkonosze National Park is crisscrossed by hundreds of miles of marked trails and that number is effectively doubled if you count the trails on the Czech side. Note that you can freely walk across the border without having to show a passport, but it's always a good idea to carry it with you in the rare event you are stopped. Trails on both sides of the border follow an informal color guide, with the most popular and rewarding walks marked in red, and the hierarchy moving down to blue, green, and yellow. Both Karpacz and Szklarska Poręba are excellent hiking bases. The first port of call should be the tourist information office for advice on routes and maps. A popular day-long slog in summer is to the peak at Śnieżka, the highest point in the range at 1,602m above sea level.

SKIING Both Szklarska Poręba and Karpacz have excellent facilities for downhill and cross-country skiing. In downhill skiing, Szklarska Poręba gets the nod both for the number and quality of its slopes, as well as having the country's longest continuous run at around 4.5km (2.7 miles). The Masyw Szrenicy and the Łabski Szczyt region form the largest ski center, with five separate slopes and a joint length of about 20km (12 miles). Contact Ski Arena Szrenica (Turystyczna 25a; *C* **075/717-21-18;** www.sudetylift.com. pl) for details. In Karpacz, the center of the action is the Śnieżka Ski Complex (Turystyczna 4; *C* **075/761-86-19;** www.kopa.com.pl).

WHERE TO STAY
Jelenia Góra
Hotel Jelonek ★ The most pleasant of several choices directly in the city center, this small family-run hotel occupies an 18th-century townhouse just a 5-minute walk to the main square and 15 minutes by foot from the bus station. The rooms are simply furnished, but are warm and inviting with traditional wooden furniture and hardwood floors. Only some rooms have an Internet connection.

1-go Maja 5. *C* **075/764-6541.** Fax 075/752-3794. www.hoteljelonek.pl. 12 rooms. 215 zł ($86/£47) double (not including breakfast). **Amenities:** Restaurant; nonsmoking rooms. *In room:* TV, dataport, minibar.

Hotel Mercure ★ This chain hotel about 2km (1.2 miles) outside of the center lacks charm but compensates with a complete set of hotel amenities plus comfortable rooms and upscale bedding and bathrooms. The large lobby has a cafe as well as several little souvenir shops. The rooms are boxy and a little sterile, but have everything you need for a couple days' stay. Take a taxi, since it's a long walk from town with luggage.

Sudecka 63. *C* **075/754-91-48.** Fax 075/752-62-66. www.mercure.com. 190 units. 359 zł ($144/£80) double. AE, DC, MC, V. **Amenities:** Restaurant; exercise room; concierge; business center; room service; massage; nonsmoking rooms. *In room:* A/C, TV, dataport, minibar, hair dryer.

Pałac Paulinum ★★ (Finds) This elegant 19th-century *palais* was originally home to a Silesian textile baron and is now a stunningly renovated luxury hotel—but without the luxury price tag. The refined public areas are done out in parquets with ornately carved wall panels and impressive chandeliers. Rooms feature period furnishings but differ greatly in size, from tiny to gargantuan. Ask for an upgrade on a slow night. There are several restaurants on the premises as well as a full-service spa with salt grotto, a winter garden, and a billiards room. You will have to take a taxi (about 10 zł) from the center.

Nowowiejska 62. *C* **075/649-44-00.** Fax 075/649-44-03. www.paulinum.pl. 29 units. 320 zł ($128/£70) double. **Amenities:** Restaurant; exercise room; sauna; concierge; business center; room service; massage; nonsmoking rooms. *In room:* A/C, TV, dataport, minibar, hair dryer.

Karpacz
Relaks ★ A superb modern mountain chalet that makes up what it lacks in traditional charm with big clean rooms, great service, and one of the best hotel-based spas in Karpacz. It's outside the center by a couple of kilometers, so you'll have to take a taxi from town.

Obrońców Pokoju 4. *C* **075/648-06-50.** Fax 075/648-06-53. www.hotel-relaks.pl. 101 units. 259 zł ($103/£58) double (price includes access to spa and sauna). **Amenities:** Restaurant; exercise room; sauna; room service; massage; nonsmoking rooms. *In room:* A/C, TV, dataport, minibar, hair dryer.

Rezydencja ★★ This delightfully restored 350-year-old villa, just a short walk from town, is one of the most charming hotels in Karpacz. Most of the rooms are generously sized apartments, with a bedroom and separate sitting room. The furnishings are modern, but the colors are warm and inviting. The in-house restaurant is arguably the best in town and a new small fitness room is a comfortable place to unwind after a long day of biking or skiing.

Parkowa 6. ℂ **075/761-80-20.** Fax 075/761-95-13. www.hotelrezydencja.com. 14 units. 250 zł ($100/£110) double. **Amenities:** Restaurant; exercise room; sauna; car-rental desk; room service; massage; nonsmoking rooms. *In room:* A/C, TV, dataport, minibar, hair dryer.

Szklarska Poręba

Hotel Kryształ ★ A comfortable in-town option that's close to the better bars and restaurants and handy to the ski slopes. It's booked solid on weekends with socials and wedding parties, so book in advance. The rooms are on the small side, but the beds are big and comfortable and the reception desk is the friendliest in town. There's a popular in-house bar and bowling alley here, and a small spa.

1 Maja 19. ℂ **075/717-44-30.** Fax 075/717-44-30. www.hotelkrysztal.pl. 22 rooms. 230 zł ($92/£52) double. **Amenities:** Restaurant; exercise room; sauna; business center; massage; nonsmoking rooms. *In room:* TV, dataport, minibar, hair dryer.

WHERE TO DINE
Jelenia Góra

Cztery Pory Roku ★★ POLISH This popular restaurant right across the square from the Town Hall entrance is a good choice if you're looking for something substantial and delicious—like roast duck with apple or wild boar goulash. The toned down, refined interior is a breath of fresh air from the current vogue in Polish restaurants for the overly rustic, faux-peasant look.

Pl. Ratuszowy 39. ℂ **075/752-21-40.** Lunch and dinner items 25 zł–40 zł ($10–$16/£5.60–£9). AE, DC, M, V. Daily 11am–10pm.

Kawiarnia Naleśnikarnia ★ POLISH Excellent Italian espressos and other coffee beverages are on offer here as well as their signature enormous sweet pancakes filled with nuts and chocolate, and small items like sandwiches. Early opening hours makes for a convenient breakfast stop of a coffee and pancake.

Pl. Ratuszowy 2. ℂ **075/647-54-44.** Lunch and dinner items 10 zł–20 zł ($4–$8/£2.20–£4.40). No credit cards. Daily 9am–7pm.

Sorrento ★ ITALIAN This upscale Italian eatery just behind the Town Hall serves big salads, good homemade soups, and pizza. Decent pasta offerings include tagliatelle with wild mushrooms and an unusual but delicious spaghetti with tuna and spinach.

Pl. Ratuszowy 15–17. ℂ **075/752-59-28.** Lunch and dinner items 20 zł–30 zł ($8–$12/£4.50–£6.70). AE, DC, M, V. Daily 11am–10pm.

Szklarska Poręba/Karpacz

Both towns are stuffed with little dining places and pizza joints. In Karpacz, there's a big open-air eatery in the center of town that serves heaping platefuls of *bigos* (hunter's stew) and grilled sausages. Most of the hotels have good restaurants, including the highly recommended Hotel Rezydencja in Karpacz.

Alfredo ★★ (Finds) POLISH   This little hole-in-the-wall serves excellent home-style cooking including *pierogi,* kiełbasa, a popular (and very filling) potato pancake and goulash combo, and fresh-caught fried trout served with garlic butter and fries. Finish up with an espresso and a slice of very light homemade apricot cheesecake. From the outside it doesn't look like much, but it's one of the best and easiest meals around.

1 Maja 15 (Szklarska Poręba). No phone. Lunch and dinner items 10 zł–20 zł ($4–$8/£2.20–£4.40). No credit cards. Daily 11am–10pm.

Metafora/Klub Jazgot ★★ POLISH/CONTINENTAL   Most restaurants in town cater to undemanding groups of skiers and day-trippers, and standards are not very high. This ambitious combination of ground-floor restaurant and basement jazz pub is different. It's clear from the slick service and beautiful presentation that they really care about the food. The traditional pork cutlet served with beets and mashed potatoes is superb. Be sure to book well in advance in ski season and on weekends. Klub Jazgot is a popular pub and a good place to head for an after-dinner drink.

Objazdowa 1 (Szklarska Poręba). ℰ **075/717-36-89.** www.jazgot.pl. Lunch and dinner items 20 zł–30 zł ($8–$12/£4.40–£6.70). AE, DC, M, V. Daily noon–11pm.

Oberża u Hochoła POLISH   Exactly what you'd expect at a mountain resort: A loud, fun, rustic tavern with plenty of traditional Polish food and lots of beer to wash it all down with. Eat outside in nice weather. Great for groups, but you'll have to book in advance.

1 Maja 11 (Szklarska Poręba). ℰ **075/717-34-30.** Lunch and dinner items 20 zł–30 zł ($8–$12/£4.40–£6.70). AE, DC, M, V. Daily noon–11pm.

4 KŁODZKO

South and east of the Karkonosze range lies a sparsely populated region of woods and hills that extends southward deep into the territory of the modern-day Czech Republic. The Kłodzko region (www.powiat.klodzko.pl) was one of the first parts of Silesia to be settled by Slavs in the years before 1000 AD. During the early centuries of its existence Kłodzko was part of the Bohemian crown lands and ruled from Prague. Even today, the statue-lined main pedestrian bridge in the capital city bears a noticeable resemblance to Charles Bridge in Prague. When the Habsburgs assumed control of Bohemia in the 16th century, they got the Kłodzko region as well, only to lose it to Prussia in the 18th century. Later Kłodzko became part of Germany, and then, after World War II, it fell back into Polish hands. Today, while Kłodzko is unmistakably Polish, here and there you'll still find traces of the Prussian and Czech presence. The Polish spoken here is laced with traces of Czech, and in the countryside much of the rural architecture has a Prussian or German feel. Kłodzko is best explored by car since trains are scarce and bus timetables can be tricky to negotiate. The main sights include the beautifully preserved Prussian fortress town of Kłodzko and the popular—and eerie—bone church in Kudowa-Zdrój, which merits a diversion. Nature is another draw here, unspoiled and wilder the farther south you go toward the Sudety mountains and the popular hiking base of Międzygórze.

ESSENTIALS
Getting There
Kłodzko city is served by both regular train and bus service from Wrocław and other large cities. By car, from Wrocław, Kłodzko is a straight shot south down the E67 highway

about 120km (75 miles). Leave about 2 hours for the drive. Kłodzko is about 40km (25 miles) from the Czech border and is an easy drive to the Czech city of Hradec Králové.

Getting Around

Make Kłodzko your base and use buses or your own car to get around Kłodzko region. Buses connect Kłodzko with the towns of Kudowa-Zdrój and Międzygórze. The Kłodzko tourist information office can advise on transportation. Within Kłodzko city, walking is the only option. The city is small and 10 minutes on foot will get you anywhere you want to go.

Tourist Information

Kłodzko's Tourist Information Office is situated on the main square (Plac Bolesława Chrobrego 1; ℂ **074/865-89-70**). Don't expect much in the way of help, but it's a useful stop to check on trains and buses and see what's going on in town. The Tourist Information Office in Międzygórze (Wojska Polskiego 2; ℂ **074/813-51-95**) is a good starting point for hiking maps and suggestions on trails.

TOP ATTRACTIONS

Begin your exploration of Kłodzko by crossing the city's miniature version of Prague's Charles Bridge, a small Gothic stone crossing topped with baroque statuary. The bridge leads into the town's outsized central square, Plac Bolesława Chrobrego, which houses the Town Hall, the Ratusz, and the tourist information office. Continue walking to the city's main attraction, the enormous Prussian fortress, with its high tower vantage point and fascinating warren of underground tunnels. Church lovers will also want to peek in to the Parish Church of Our Lady NMP, with its stern Gothic façade hiding an elaborate Baroque interior.

Kłodzko Fortress ★★   The Kłodzko hill has played an important strategic role for centuries, straddling the traditional borderland first between the Polish and Bohemian kingdoms, and then later Prussia and Austria. There's been a fortress of one kind or another here for around 1,000 years. The present massive structure dates from the middle of the 18th century when the Prussians defeated the Austrians and embarked on a massive rebuilding project using prisoners of war as laborers. Early on, Napoleon shattered the fortress's illusion of invincibility by capturing it in 1807. During World War II, the Nazis used the fortress to hold political prisoners. Today, it is the region's leading tourist attraction, both for its tower with commanding views over Kłodzko's hinterland and its labyrinth of underground tunnels once used for troop mustering, hiding, and escape if necessary. The tunnels are viewable by guided tour only. Be sure to bring a jacket, even in summer, as it can get quite cold down there.

Twierdza Kłodzka (Kłodzko Fortress), Grodzisko 1. ℂ **074/867-34-68.** Admission 7 zł ($2.80/£1.60) adults, 5 zł ($2/£1.10) children (fortress only); 14 zł ($5.60/£3.15) adults, 10 zł ($4/£2.25) (fortress and tunnels); Tues–Sun 9am–7pm (summer), Tues–Sun 9am–4pm (winter).

Chapel of Skulls ★   A "bone-chilling" spectacle awaits at the Church of St. Bartholomew (Kościół Św. Bartłomieja) near the border town of Kudowa-Zdrój (35km/22 miles west of Kłodzko) in the village of Czermna. If you've already been to the Czech Republic, chances are you've seen the well-known ossuary (bone church) in Kutná Hora. If not, you have a real treat here: an entire chapel decorated with the skeletal remains of some 3,000 victims of the Thirty Years' War and other conflicts and epidemics to have hit this area over the centuries. Ghoulish and fascinating in equal measure, it may not be suitable for children.

Moniuszki 8. ✆ **074/866-17-54.** Admission 3 zł ($1.30/80p). Tues–Sun 9:30am–5:30pm (closes earlier in winter).

WHERE TO STAY & DINE

Kłodzko city is not exactly bursting with five-star lodging opportunities. The city has two modestly priced hotels, both of which will do in a pinch for a night or two. Both luckily have excellent restaurants; this is one destination where there's no good reason not to eat at the hotel.

Casa D'Oro ★   Kłodzko's nicest hotel is this modest inn on a relatively quiet corner close to the central square and above a decent Italian restaurant of the same name. The rooms are nicely furnished with big beds and cherry-wood furniture. The location is excellent, practically next door to Kłodzko's famed mini "Charles Bridge." There's free parking nearby and free in-room Wi-Fi.

Grottgera 7. ✆ **074/867-02-16.** Fax 074/867-02-17. www.casadoro.pl. 11 units. 180 zł ($72/£40) double. AE, MC, V. **Amenities:** Restaurant; room service; nonsmoking rooms. *In room:* TV, dataport, hair dryer.

Hotel Korona ★ (**Value**)   This roadside "motel" tucked away behind a gas station about 180m (600 ft.) outside the center looks like something you might see on the side of an American highway. The hallways are a little scruffy, but the rooms are clean and fine for a night. There's free Wi-Fi on the premises, but the signal doesn't stretch far beyond the reception desk. The high point is the restaurant, done out in a faux rustic style with a nice terrace in summer and a wood-burning fireplace in winter. Worth a stop even if you are not staying here. The big salads are especially recommended.

Noworudzka 1. ✆ **074/867-37-37.** Fax 074/867-07-73. www.hotel-korona.pl (in Polish and German). 40 units. 130 zł ($52/£30) double. AE, MC, V. **Amenities:** Restaurant; nonsmoking rooms. *In room:* TV, dataport.

10

Central & Northwest Poland

The central and northwestern region is the new Poland, awaiting your discovery. "New" it is, but only in the sense of tourism exposure. It is, in fact, a very old historical hotspot. The Polish state was founded here in the Middle Ages. Within the region, Gniezno and Poznań's Cathedral Island are the main contenders vying for the title as the cradle of Catholic Poland. In this distinct landscape of historical rubble, churches, castles, and palaces, you'll also find the impressive Iron Age settlement of Biskupin.

Poznań is the place to start your exploration. The city is unfairly brushed off as a stopover to get your business done as you hurry off elsewhere. That would be a mistake. The charming Old Town Square pulses with life force. The historical buildings and esoteric museums reflect the locals' pride in their history and identity. Moving in the northeasterly direction, you'll come to Toruń, the birthplace of Copernicus and the Gothic hotspot of the country. Take the time to meander among the red-brick towers and churches that survived the ages, then pause to munch on the gingerbread culture.

Outside of Poznań and Toruń the attractions are more spread out. It's easiest to see the area by car. To manage with just public transportation, you'll need to plan carefully.

1 POZNAŃ

Poznań, the capital of *Wielkopolska* (Greater Poland) and a bustling city of 600,000 people, is known mostly for its numerous annual trade fairs. Its tourism potentials are (mistakenly) underrated, hence during weekends you don't have to jostle with crowds, reservations aren't required in most restaurants, and hotel rooms are available at reduced rates. The city works well as a base for exploring the Piast Route (see below) and is a vibrant business and academic hub.

Poznań has a history of prosperity that's directly attributable to its position along the main transportation routes and astride the Warta River. A fortified settlement has been located here as far back as the 9th century. It was a key settlement of the Piast Dynasty,

Worker's First Stand

In 1956, Poznań was the home of the anti-Communist riots, the first-ever show of resistance in Poland against the Communist authorities. Tens of thousands of workers took to the streets to demand better working conditions and higher pay. The strikes turned violent and the government responded by deploying soldiers and tanks. The unrest was a major embarrassment throughout Central and Eastern Europe and pierced the veil of Communist Poland as a workers' state.

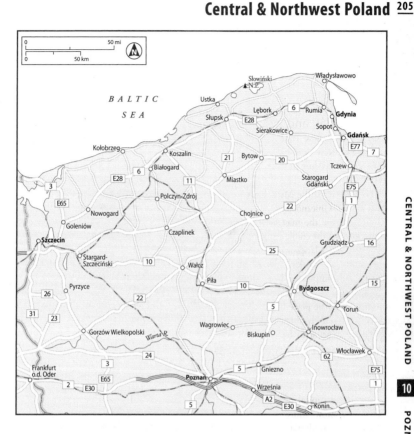

which ruled Poland from the 10th to the 14th centuries. During the Prussian occupation, when the town was known as Posen, it became one of the region's leading industrial centers, a position it retains to this day. Poznań's prosperity is evident in the sheer size of the square and in the many handsome buildings that stretch out along it in all directions. The Old Market Square has been the city's cultural and commercial center for centuries. Although much of it, and the city proper, were destroyed in World War II, many of the buildings you see today are faithful reconstructions of the originals.

ESSENTIALS

Getting There

BY PLANE Poznań's **Lawica International Airport** (Bukowska 285; ℂ **061/849-23-43;** www.airport-poznan.com.pl) is 5km (3 miles) west of the city center. It has grown in importance and has direct flights not only to Polish cities but also to a number of major European cities. Express bus line "L," regular bus no. 58, and night bus no. 242 take about 30 minutes to get to Poznań's central train station.

BY TRAIN Poznań lies on one of Europe's main east–west train lines, stretching from Paris and Berlin to Warsaw and Moscow. The **train station** (Dworcowa 1; ℂ **061/866-12-12)**

is 2km (1 mile) from the town center. It's a 15-minute walk, or a short tram or bus ride, to the center.

BY BUS   Poznań lies on major national and international bus routes. The **PKS bus station** (Dworzec Autobusowy, Towarowa 17/19; ✆ **061/664-25-25;** www.pks.poznan. pl) is near the train station.

BY CAR   Poznań is on the main Berlin–Warsaw Hwy. E30. The tolled highway is a dream to drive on, but make sure to set aside about 40 zł ($16/£9) for tolls. Unfortunately, the road is not yet upgraded all the way to Warsaw. On the stretch from Warsaw to Łódź (122km/73 miles) you'll still have to drive the old (but free) highway. From Warsaw (325km/195 miles), the journey takes about 4 hours.

Visitor Information

The city's main **Tourist Information Center** (Stary Rynek 59/60; ✆ **061/852-61-56;** www.city.poznan.pl) is open weekdays from 10am to 7pm and Saturday from 10am to 5pm. It's conveniently located on the Old Market Square and is a good place to pick up walking itineraries, maps, and advice on rooms. You can also get the printouts of thematic get-to-know-the-city games such as "Route of the Kings" and "Wielkopolska Uprising," created by **Gra Miejska** (www.gramiejska.pl). Pick up a copy of *Poznań, In Your Pocket* (5 zł/$2/£1.10), which has coverage of the city. The Polish *IKS* magazine (3.90 zł/$1.50/90p) has its cultural events listing in English. Another information point is the **City Information Center** (Ratajczaka 44; ✆ **061/851-96-45;** www.cim.poznan. pl), which is good on cultural activities and sells concert tickets. They are open weekdays 10am to 7pm and Saturday 10am to 5pm. If you hire a guide, it's best to incorporate the Parish Church, Cathedral Island, and Zamek in your tour. This will take 3 to 4 hours. Contact the Tourist Information Center on the Stary Rynek three days in advance to book a guide. The prices are 190 zł ($76/£42.75) for 2 hours; 260 zł ($104/£58.50) for 3 hours; and 320 zł ($128/£78) for 4 hours. *Note:* There's free Wi-Fi access, courtesy of the city, in the Old Town Square.

Getting Around

Poznań has an efficient public transportation system of buses and trams. Most of the attractions can be covered on foot. Tickets can be bought at Ruch kiosks (or nearly anywhere they sell newspapers and tobacco) and cost 3.60 zł ($1.40/80p) for rides of 30 minutes. There are also day and weekly passes priced at 13.20 zł ($5.30/£3) and 32 zł ($12.80/£7.20), respectively. You can also consider getting the **City Card** at the tourist information center. It includes access to buses and trams and free or discounted prices to the attractions. A day card is 30 zł ($12/£6.75). There are options for 2 and 3 days.

TOP ATTRACTIONS

Naturally, any exploration must start at the Old Town Square *(Stary Rynek),* a lively spot filled with color, people, and a range of performance art from early morning to late at night. Poznań's unofficial nickname could well be the "Museum City," for you trip on museums everywhere. Some notable ones are the **Poznań Model** (Franciszkańska 2; ✆ **061/855-14-35),** which has a meticulous miniature model of medieval Poznań and gives an audio narration of the city's history, and the **Musical Instruments Museum** (Stary Rynek 45–47; ✆ **061/852-08-57).** *Note:* Most museums have free admission on Saturdays.

is palpable on the peaceful and quiet Cathedral Island *(Ostrów Tumski)*. Excavations revealed the presence of a church on this site for more than a millennium. It is believed that Mieszko I (father of Poland's first crowned king, Bolesław the Brave) was baptized here in the 10th century. The crypt holds the rubble of the baptism bowl. Architectural tinkering and rebuilding through the years, and the 1945 fire in the cathedral, have greatly altered its appearance, giving it the current ensemble of everything from pre-Romanesque to Gothic, baroque, and Classicist. Eclecticism is also seen in the naves and chapels. The most eye-catching features are the frescos, dating from 1616, depicting the 12 apostles; the 19th-century Golden Chapel, with unabashedly brazen Byzantine designs; the crypt containing the remains of Mieszko and Bolesław the Brave; and the four Vischers bronze plaques that were looted by the Nazis, recovered by the Russians, and returned to the cathedral in 1990.

The cathedral has no guide service. If you want a guide, make arrangements at the city's tourist center. To cover the crypt and the major artifacts, it's about 1¹/₂ hours.

Mieszka I, Ostrów Tumski. ✆ **061/852-96-42.** www.katedra.archpoznan.org.pl. Mon–Sat 9am–6pm. Tram: 4, 8, and 17 to Ostrów Tumski stop. On foot, about 15 minutes from the Old Town; take Wielka Street east to Chwaliszewo Street. At the end of the street, turn right toward the Bolesława Chrobrego bridge. Use the underpass to get to the Cathedral Island.

Emperor's Castle (Zamek) ★ Built in the early 20th century, during the days when Poznań was a German outpost known as Posen, the castle once served as a residence of Kaiser Wilhelm II. In the late 1930s, the interior was refurbished as quarters for Adolf Hitler. Within the walls of this imposing neo-Romanesque building, Polish cryptologists worked to decode the Enigma Machine, the main secret-code generator used by the Germans. Their work contributed to the Allies' victory in War World II. In the clock tower, you can walk into the rooms done in the Third Reich style and look out of the balcony that was intended for the Fuhrer to inspect military parades. As the castle is still seen as a symbol of foreign domination (a fate shared by Warsaw's Palace of Culture), locals are ambivalent toward it. After World War II there were talks of demolishing it, but pragmatism for office space kept it standing. Today, it houses the **Castle Culture Center (Centrum Kultury Zamek),** which hosts exhibitions, theatre performances, and concerts and screens films. Use the exhibitions as an excuse to see the castle's interior, notably the golden mosaic ceiling on the clock tower's ground floor. A quick visit will take no more than 30 minutes. It's worth getting a guide (as part of a city tour) to show you the kaiser's marble throne, one of the few objects not accessible on a regular basis to visitors.

Św. Marcin 80/82. ✆ **061/646-52-00.** www.zamek.poznan.pl. Free admission for most exhibitions. Daily 9am–5pm. A 10-minute walk from the Old Market Square.

Lech Brewery Visitor Center Even bearing in mind this is a PR exercise for the brewery, it's still a fascinating insight into a plant that produces an average of 1.25 million bottles, 1 million cans, and 2,000 beer kegs daily. The bubbly guides walk you through the factory, filling your head with production ingredients, stages, and numbers. The bottling and canning process is the most interesting for kids and adults alike. The tour takes 2 hours, including a quiz, but you can squeeze out of the Q&A and head straight to the pub to fill up on complimentary beer. (See "Gniezno" to learn who Lech was.) Call a day ahead to book the tour.

Szwajcarska 11. ✆ **061/878-74-60.** Admission free. Mon, Wed 10am–8:30pm; Tues, Thurs–Fri 10am–2pm; Sat 10am–8pm. From Rondo Rataje, bus no. 81 in the direction of the M1 shopping mall. The brewery is opposite M1. Taxi from city center costs about 20 zł ($8/£4.50).

National Museum: Paintings and Sculpture Gallery ★★ This is one of Poland's top galleries and a great place to get acquainted with key Polish artists and their works. It's also notable for having had a Monet snatched from its premises in 2000. Start your visit in the Polish Baroque Room, which holds an extensive collection of "coffin portraits," hexagonal and octagonal-edged portraits that are the relics of funeral practices from the 17th to 18th centuries. Jan Matejko's sketch *Stańczyk* (the Court Jester) is one of the images Poles instantly recognize. From the *Młoda Polska* (Young Polish) movement of the late 19th to early 20th centuries, Jacek Malczewski's *Vicious Circle* is an enthralling study of brightness against darkness. Stanisław Wyspiański's pastels of his slumbering children, Mietek and Staś, are endearing. In the Interwar collection, see the portraits by Stanisław Ignacy Witkiewicz, who jotted on the corners of some canvases the drugs, nicotine, caffeine, and alcohol he ingested prior to unleashing his imagination on the fantasy works.

Marcinkowskiego 9. ✆ **061/852-59-69.** www.mnp.art.pl. Admission 10 zł ($4/£2.25) adult, 6 zł ($2.40/£1.35) seniors, children, and students; free Sat. Tues 10am–6pm; Wed 9am–5pm; Thurs, Sun 10am–6pm; Fri–Sat 10am–5pm. Call ahead for English-speaking guides (35 zł/$14/£7.90 per hour).

Old Town Hall (Ratusz) ★ Originally dating from the 14th century, the building was extensively renovated in the 16th century in Renaissance style by the Italian architect Giovanni Quadro. Much of the structure was destroyed in World War II, and little of the original walls remain. The best example of what survived is the early Gothic cellars, which today house the **Historical Museum of Poznań.** The museum is worth a visit if you're curious about Poznań's development from the 10th century on. Entry to the museum leads to the rich interior of the building itself. At noon, join the locals, schoolkids, and tourists in craning your neck at the clock outside the Town Hall to see two mechanical goats butt heads. There are several myths as to how and why these two animals locked horns; the most popular is that they were drawing the townspeople's attention to a fire and thus saved the town from burning down.

Stary Rynek 1. ✆ **061/856-81-91.** Admission 5.50 zł ($2.20/£1.20) adult, 3.50 zł ($1.40/£1) seniors, students, and children; free Sat. Museum Tues 9am–4pm; Wed 11am–6pm; Thurs–Fri 9am–4pm; Sat 11am–4pm; Sun 11am–3pm. Guided tours 25 zł ($10/£5.60); call ✆ **061/852-56-13** a day in advance.

Parish Church (Kościół Św. Stanisława) ★★ Built between 1651 and 1732, this beguiling baroque church used ingenious methods to create the illusion of grandeur at reduced cost. For example, even though the church seems to be adorned with a generous deployment of marble, all the fluted columns and pedestals are actually made from marble-toned stucco. The columns were also designed to make you think the nave is longer than its 40m. The façade uses larger statues on the first tier and significantly diminutive figures on the second tier to generate an illusion of imposing heights. Further intrigue can be found in the 19th-century piped organ, built by Friedrich Ladegast, one of the finest craftsmen of his time. Its construction was partially financed by an anonymous lady in black: Whenever the organ undergoes conservation work, her ghost is said to be sighted. (Her last visit was in 2002.) To fully appreciate the church, time your visit with a free organ concert. You can feel the chords reverberating on the pews as you take in both the unique architecture and the works depicting the lives of St. Stanisław and Mary Magdalene, the church's patron saints. At press time, plans were underway to open

up to the public the attic and the tunnels in the cellar, some of which reportedly lead to
the Town Hall.

Gołębia, at the Świętoławska crossing. Free admission. Concerts June–July Mon–Sat 12:15pm (about 45 min); off season, check the schedule and program at the Tourist Information Office.

Outside Poznań

Kórnik and **Rogalin,** both 20km (12 miles) south of Poznań and 12km (7 miles) apart from each other, visited together make for a good day out. The 14th-century neo-Gothic **Kórnik Castle** (Zamkowa 5, Kórnik; ✆ **061/817-00-81;** www.bkpan.poznan.pl) survived World War II and has many intriguing curios assembled by its former masters. The **Rogalin Palace ★** (Rogalin; ✆ **061/813-80-30**), an impressive late-baroque to early-Classicism palace, was the seat of the Raczyński clan, a politically influential noble family. Within the palace are works by the noted Polish painter Jan Matejko.

At press time, the palace was undergoing extensive renovation and was scheduled to reopen in late June 2009. It's business as usual, though, at the onsite restaurant, **Dwa Pokoje z Kuchnią ★** (✆ **061/898-17-47**), a homey spot that serves sweet and savory pancakes. At the nearby park are the **Oaks of Rogalin ★**, three great oak trees that are more than a thousand years old (and look very much like they're on their last legs). They are named Lech, Czech, and Rus, after the legendary brothers and founding fathers of Poland, the Czech Republic, and Russia. Public buses from Poznań serve both Kórnik and Rogalin.

Shopping

Antique Market at Stara Rzeźnia ★★   Located in the compound of a disused abattoir, this market has esoteric collector items ranging from old LPs to obsolete but still functioning amplifiers. The indoor stalls have a huge stockpile of tableware including pre-War samovars (with their original user manuals in German), silver cutlery, and ceramic sauceboats and tureens. It is open on weekends from 8am to 1pm. Garbary 101 (entrance from Północna Street). Tram: 4, 8, and 17.

WHERE TO STAY

Poznań's accommodation rates are reasonable—except when a trade fair comes to town and hotels unabashedly jack up their prices by 30% to 40%. The summer months are fairly safe, but the rest of the year sees a trade fair at least once a month (check www.mtp.pl for the trade fair schedule). Since business travelers fill the hotels, come on weekends—when many places offer reduced rates.

Huff and Puff

Michael Palin did it. In his 2006–07 jaunt through New Europe, the travel documentarian (and Monty Python comedian) veered west to Poznań to hop on a steam-engine train that chugs regularly from Poznań to Wolsztyn. The **Wolsztyn Experience** allows train enthusiasts to learn to drive a steam-engine train on a regular service line with commuters on board. Spring and summer programs are fully booked as early as a year in advance. For details, visit thewolsztyn experience.org.

IBB Andersia ★ Opened in early 2008, this is one of the newest hotels in town. Located in the first 9 floors of a glass-fronted office tower, IBB Andersia makes no bones that it targets business travelers. But it's situated next to the Stary Browar shopping mall and linked by a pedestrian street to the Old Town, so leisure travelers can very well enjoy the luxuries aimed at the expense-account set. The minimalistic but plush rooms in shades of brown are well designed for dependable comfort. The bathrooms are finished in granite and have heated floors. In some cases, only glass panels separate the bathroom from the bedroom, which might appeal to exhibitionists.

Plac Andersia 3. (C) 061/667-80-00. Fax 061/667-80-01. www.andersiahotel.pl. 171 units. Weekdays 460 zł ($184/£103.50) single; 525 zł ($210/£118) double. Weekends 365 zł ($146/£82) single; 430 zł ($172/£96.75) double. Rates include buffet breakfast. Extra person 170 zł ($68/£38). AE, DC, MC, V. Underground parking 50 zł ($20/£11). **Amenities:** Restaurant; bar; dry cleaning; laundry service; conference center; 24-hr. room service; concierge; nonsmoking rooms; health club; indoor pool w/water massage and access to outdoor rooftop terrace; Jacuzzi; dry and steam sauna; solarium; massage. *In room:* A/C, plasma TV, minibar, kettle, hair dryer, iron, safe, complimentary Wi-Fi.

Sheraton Poznań Hotel ★★ Everything in this hotel opposite the Trade Fair center still feels brand-spanking-new even though it's been open several years. Spacious rooms have dark wood furnishings and luxurious granite bathrooms. A modern gym has exercise bikes with built-in TVs, and the Qube Bar on the ground floor stirs up some of the best drinks in town. It's always lively at the Somewhere Else Restaurant, where guests gather for live music or sports on the widescreen. The top-notch staff here go beyond the perfunctory call of duty to make guests feel spoiled.

Bukowska 3/9. (C) 061-655-20-00. www.sheraton.pl. Weekdays 522 zł–774 zł ($209–$310/£117–£174) double; 612 zł–3,600 zł ($245–$1,220/£128–£810) suite. Weekends 396 zł–486 zł ($158–$195/£89–£109) double; 558 zł–2,880 zł ($223–$1,152/£126–£648) suite. Breakfast 79 zł ($32/£18). Extra person 108 zł ($43/£24). Children 10 and under stay free in parent's room. AE, DC, MC, V. Basement parking 80 zł ($32/£18). **Amenities:** 2 restaurants; pub; wine tower; nonsmoking room; lounge w/fireplace; concierge; 24-hr. room service; same-day dry cleaning; conference center; club floor; 24-hr. gym; sauna; indoor pool w/anti-current and city view; massage. *In room:* A/C, TV, minibar, kettle, paid movies, dataport, bathroom scale, hair dryer, iron, safe, Wi-Fi.

Expensive & Moderate

Hotel Brovaria ★★ (Value) For the money, it's probably the best bed (with a view) in town. Occupying three tastefully renovated town houses on the Stary Rynek, the hotel's location is ideal. Both single and double rooms are reasonably spacious. Furnishings, mostly brooding black-lacquered wood, fall somewhere between 1930s "modern" and contemporary. The carpet looks slightly worn, but the white ceramic bathrooms are fresh and recently renovated. Rooms facing the Market Square command a higher price; those on the third floor are quieter.

Stary Rynek 73/74. (C) 061/858-68-68. Fax 061/858-68-69. www.brovaria.pl. 21 units. 250 zł ($100/£56.25) single; 270 zł ($108/£60.75) single w/view; 290 zł ($116/£65.25) double; 310 zł ($124/£69.75) double w/view. Rates include buffet breakfast. Extra person 145 zł ($58/£33). AE, DC, MC, V. Public parking. **Amenities:** Restaurant (see p. 212); bar; limited room service; nonsmoking rooms; dry cleaning. *In room:* A/C, TV, hair dryer, complimentary Wi-Fi.

Hotel Royal ★ The location is excellent, situated between the railway station and the Old Town. The hotel is tucked in a little courtyard away from the street, making it very quiet. The Royal has a distinguished pedigree, dating from the turn of the 20th century, and was the first hotel in the city to open for business following World War II. The rooms are stylish, with floral-print spreads and high-quality woods throughout. The reception desk is more than happy to book restaurant reservations or advise on city tours.

Św. Marcin 71. ℂ **061/858-23-00.** Fax 061/858-23-06. www.hotel-royal.com.pl. 31 units. Weekdays 320 zł ($128/£72) single; 420 zł ($168/£95) double. Weekends 224 zł ($90/£50) single; 294 zł ($118/£66) double. Rates include breakfast. AE, M, V. Free parking. **Amenities:** Restaurant; concierge; business center; limited room service; dry cleaning; nonsmoking rooms. *In room:* TV, dataport, hair dryer.

Hotel Stare Miasto ★★ A relatively new hotel and a great choice for the price; rates are lower than you might expect for the quality because of the hotel's location in a slightly dodgy but still safe neighborhood, about a 10-minute walk from the Stary Rynek. The rooms are on the small side, but nicely furnished in a contemporary style. The doubles are not uniformly furnished, so ask to see a couple of different styles before choosing. The breakfast buffet is more inventive than most, and the cook will scramble eggs on request.

Rybaki 36. ℂ **061/663-62-42.** Fax 061/659-00-43. www.hotelstaremiasto.pl. 23 units. Weekdays 215 zł ($86/£48) single; 340 zł ($136/£76.50) double. Weekends 190 zł ($76/£43) single; 225 zł ($90/£51) double. Rates include breakfast. MC, V. Free parking. **Amenities:** Bar; tour booking; breakfast room; complimentary Wi-Fi. *In room:* A/C (some rooms), TV, dataport.

Hotel Rzymski ★ Despite this hotel's dated appearance the rooms here are in good condition, the staff is friendly and competent, and the location, just 500m from the Old Market Square, is great. This 150-year-old hotel has gone through several name and role changes during its long history, and during World War II, German solders even camped here. The high-ceilinged rooms are spacious and comfortable, but note that the many renovations have resulted in varying bathroom fixtures: some have showers, others baths of various lengths. Returning guests request their preferred room numbers when booking. Rooms looking out to Marcinkowskiego Street are drenched in morning sun but their occupants have to contend with the rumbles of passing trams and cars; rooms at the back have no views but are quiet.

Marcinkowskiego 22. ℂ **061/852-81-21.** Fax 061/852-89-83. www.hotelrzymski.pl. 87 units. Weekdays 245 zł ($98/£55) single; 300 zł ($120/£67) double. Weekends 195 zł ($78/£44) single; 240 zł ($96/£54) double. Rates include breakfast. Extra person 60 zł ($24/£13). AE, DC, MC, V. **Amenities:** 2 restaurants; bar; conference room; nonsmoking room; Internet terminal; tour booking; laundry room; safe; hair dryer. *In room:* TV, radio, complimentary Wi-Fi.

Inexpensive

Rezydencja Solei These rooms are near the Old Market Square but on a street lined with slightly jaded 19th-century townhouses. A flight of stairs leads up to the reception. The furnishing is best described as a fusion of country and baroque. The rooms are clean and big enough to swing two cats, but you'll have a bruised cat if you swing it in the en suite shower rooms. Another flight of steep stairs takes you up to the apartments on the attic level. Each apartment fits up to four guests and comes with a basic kitchenette. There's a rooftop terrace where you can spy on the restaurant downstairs. Friendly and accommodating staff will help you find the best meals in town. The sister hotel is on Wałecka 2 (ℂ **061/847-58-38**).

Szewska 2. ℂ **061/855-73-51.** www.hotel-solei.pl. 11 units. Weekdays 189 zł ($75/£42) single; 289 zł ($115.60/£65) double; 359 zł ($143/£80) apt. Weekend 160 zł ($64/£36) single; 239 zł ($95/£53) double; 299 zł ($199/£68) apt. Rates include breakfast. Extra person 60 zł ($24/£13). AE, DC, MC, V. Street parking. **Amenities:** Dry cleaning; complimentary Wi-Fi; breakfast room. *In room:* A/C (in apt), TV, hair dryer, kettle and coffee machine (in apt).

Hotel Lech The hotel is a high-rise building conveniently situated midway between the railway station and the Old Town. The rooms are plain but clean, and the high ceilings add to the sense of spaciousness. The front of the hotel looks out to a busy tram route, and you can hear them trundling by. It's not a bad deal, given the location and in-room amenities like free Internet access. It pulls in a lot of bus-tour packages, and even offers reduced rates for students. Avoid the restaurant downstairs; there's much better food just a short walk away.

Św. Marcin 74. ℭ **061/853-01-51.** Fax 061/853-08-80. www.hotel-lech.poznan.pl. 80 units. Weekdays 160 zł ($64/£36) single; 240 zł ($96/£54) double. Weekends 130 zł ($52/£29.25) single; 210 zł ($84/£47.25) double. Breakfast 14 zł ($5.60/£3). AE, DC, MC, V. Street parking. **Amenities:** Restaurant. *In room:* TV, dataport, hair dryer.

WHERE TO DINE

Food central is definitely around the Old Town Square. Away from the Old Town, **Zagroda Bamberska** (Kościelna 43; ℭ **061/843-41-14**) and **Młyńskie Koło** (Browarna 37; ℭ **061/878-99-35;** www.mlynskiekolo.pl) offer regional cuisine and are worthy of attention. Don't neglect **Stary Browar** (Półwiejska 32; ℭ **061/859-60-50;** www.starybrowar. pl), a shopping mall converted from an old brewery. It leases floor space to restaurants like the **Piano Bar** (ℭ **061/859-65-70**), where beautiful people come to be seen. If you want to try Poznań's version of *dans le noir* (eating in the dark), make a reservation at the **Dark Restaurant** (Garbary 48; ℭ **061/852-91-70;** www.darkrestaurant.pl).

Very Expensive

Bażanciarnia ★★ POLISH This is the northwestern outpost of Magda Gessler, one of Poland's top restaurateurs. Expect floral and candle-lit giddiness, and a menu replete with game and new Polish cuisine twists such as asparagus with lavender sauce. The competent staff makes this restaurant one of the brightest stars in the Gessler series. *Bażanciarnia* means an aviary for pheasants, but the house specialty is beef drizzled with a lip-smacking mushroom sauce. The *czernina* (duck blood soup) is both sour and mildly sweet from the addition of dried fruit, and very good. As for the desserts, pick any; you can't go wrong. The wine selection is an extensive coverage of Old and New World, some costing an arm and a leg. And before you leave, check out the fixtures in the washrooms.

Stary Rynek 64. ℭ **061/855-33-58.** www.bazanciarnia.pl. Main courses 56 zł–250 zł ($22.40–$100/£12.60–£56.25). AE, DC, MC, V. Reservations recommended. Daily noon–11pm.

Expensive & Moderate

Brovaria ★★★ EUROPEAN One of the hippest spots in town, where beer sloshing is the key activity of the evening. The house-brewed beer (you see the copper tanks at the far end), which is hoppier and tangier than the traditional Polish beer, comes in both a standard Pilsner or a recommendable honey-flavored lager. The menu is a balance of inventive international dishes and Polish standards with a view toward presentation and

---

Ⓕun Facts   Potato Heads!

Folks here are more potato-obsessed than the rest of the country. *Pyry* means potatoes in Poznań's dialect. It is also an affectionate nickname for the locals.

No Bloody Way

Don't miss the opportunity to try *czernina,* a soup made from duck's blood and bits of offal. Once upon a time (when kings ruled the land), if the parents in aristocratic households were to reject the proposal for their daughter's hand in marriage, they would dole out *czernina* to the unsuccessful suitor before sending him on his way. Such a scene was enacted in the epic poem "Pan Tadeusz," written by Polish poet Adam Mickiewicz (1798–1855). Apparently, saying no with *czernina* is still practiced in the countryside. The best place for *czernina* (and roast duck)—without having to propose to someone—is at **Hacjenda** ★ (Morasko 38; ✆ **061/812-52-78;** www.hacjenda.poznan.pl), located in the northern suburbs of Poznań. Reservations recommended on weekends.

use of fresh ingredients. The roast duck with apple comes nicely crisped with a side of beets and potatoes, and is absolutely delicious. The cheerful atmosphere, friendly staff, prime location on the Stary Rynek, and fair prices explain its popularity with trendy locals and visitors alike.

Stary Rynek 73/74. ✆ **061/858-68-68.** www.brovaria.pl. Lunch and dinner items 19 zł–56 zł ($7.60–$22.40/£4.30–£12.60). Sun–Thurs 7am–midnight, Fri–Sat 7am–1:30am.

Dom Vikingów ★ INTERNATIONAL The clients, mostly foreigners and all dressed to impress, can't seem to get enough of the tender steaks atop arty salads served by svelte waitresses. Danish ownership explains the "House of Vikings" moniker, and also the Danish herring on the menu. The interior is divided into several different themes, including a cafe and sports bar with an omnipresent scent of nicotine. In the evenings, muscular and tattooed staff watch over the proceedings. During summer, the outdoor terrace is the place to people-watch.

Stary Rynek 62. ✆ **061/852-71-53.** www.domvikingow.pl. Lunch and dinner items 35 zł–79 zł ($14–$31.60/£7.88–£17.78). AE, DC, MC, V. Daily 5–11pm.

Kresowa ★ POLISH Widely considered one of the top Polish restaurants in town, Kresowa has an impressive list of VIPs who have broken bread here. The place is a little hard to find, tucked away in the maze of buildings at the center of the Stary Rynek, but well worth the effort. The atmosphere is more formal than most, so dress smart to blend in with the businessmen, private parties, and Poles out for a special evening. The restaurant is named after a region in the eastern part of Poland known for its superb culinary traditions. Try the *bliny* and *kołduny,* the Lithuanian versions of pancakes and petite *pierogi.* The menu is padded with meat dishes, but the grilled salmon is also highly recommended.

Stary Rynek 3. ✆ **061/853-12-91.** Lunch and dinner items 24 zł–45 zł ($9.60–$45/£5.40–£10). AE, DC, MC, V. Reservation recommended. Mon–Sat 1pm–11pm, Sun noon–6pm.

Mykonos ★★ (Finds) GREEK On weekends, Mykonos has to turn away guests with no reservations. A plate of complimentary, fresh-made tapenade on toast kicks off the meal. Highlights of the menu include halumi with spinach and the seafood pilaf. To round things out there's Greek coffee, wine, and music to go with the deliciously caramelized walnut baklava. Service sometimes slips up slightly as waitresses strive to keep pace.

Saintly Buns

Rogale Święto Marcińskie is a croissant-shaped sweet bread with a poppyseed and dried fruit filling and a nut-encrusted glazed exterior. It's vying for the EU's Protected Designation of Origin label, which will launch the sweet bread into the rarefied company of other items made only in a particular geographic region, such as Parma ham and Champagne. The buns are for sale all year, but the most festive time to eat them is on Saint Martin's Day (November 11), when residents reportedly wolf down 300 tons' worth. Find them in the Old Town at **Cukiernia Gruszecki** (Stary Rynek 50; ⓒ **061/826-81-07**) or in an alleyway off Św Marcin at the no-frills "since 1958" **Pracownia Cukiernia Słodki Kącik** [S] (Św Marcin 26; ⓒ **061/852-06-34**).

Plac Wolności 14. ⓒ **061/853-34-36.** www.tawerna-mykonos.com.pl. Main courses 28 zł–45 zł ($11.20–$18/£6.30–£10). AE, DC, MC, V. Reservation recommended weekends. Mon–Fri 11am–11pm, Sat–Sun noon–11pm.

Pod Koziołkami ★★ ⓥalue POLISH   As you pass the grill station, note the trophies won by the chefs for their grilled meats and potato dishes in various regional and European culinary showdowns. The regional duck specialty is accompanied by a mushroom sauce that outshines the poultry, while the *pyzy* (steamed bun) is crisscrossed with a delectable cranberry sauce. The cellar walls are the original Gothic bricks, and during restoration the owner referred to old photos and paintings as authenticity aids. **Kredens,** run by the same folks, is on the ground floor. It serves inexpensive, homemade Polish classics, where 20 zł ($8/£4.50) will buy you more *pierogi* than you can handle in two weeks.

Stary Rynek 95. ⓒ **061/851-78-68.** www.podkoziolkami.pl. Main courses 20 zł–64 zł ($8–$25.60/£4.50–£14.40). DC, MC, V. Sun–Thurs noon–11pm, Fri–Sat noon–midnight.

Inexpensive

Avanti ★★ ITALIAN   Avanti shows that you can eat well and inexpensively on the Old Market Square. It looks like a McDonald's outlet doing pasta instead of burgers. Tidiness, cleanliness, and paper roses trailing the pastel-toned wall lend a homey atmosphere. Students, grandparents and their grandkids, and office workers queue for spaghetti, lasagna, and risotto in Styrofoam plates and bowls, and salads in plastic beakers. Spaghetti comes in size S, M, and L.

Stary Rynek 76. ⓒ **061/852-32-85.** www.avanti.poznan.pl. Main courses 4 zł–12 zł ($1.60–$4.80/90p–£2.70). No credit cards. Mon–Thurs 9am–11pm, Fri–Sat 9am–midnight, Sun 11am–11pm.

Mammamija INTERNATIONAL   Similar to Avanti in prices but with a menu extending to Mexican burritos, Polish staples, and snacks such as *zapiekanki*. It's a good place to try *pyry z grzikiem,* a simple dish of potatoes with cottage cheese. Like Avanti, it is popular with students and also has the self-service and seating at bar table concept. Its second outlet is on Św Marcin 12 (ⓒ 061/665-85-08).

Półwiejska 41. ⓒ **061/852-42-66.** www.mammamija.pl. No credit cards. Lunch and dinner items 4 zł–9 zł ($1.60–$3.60/90p–£2). Mon–Thurs 10am–9pm, Fri–Sat 10am–midnight, Sun 11am–10pm.

Cakes & Cafe Escapades

Żydowska Street in the Old Town is the cafe mile. In good weather, the loveliest clois-tered garden to escape to is **Cocorico Café ★★** (Świętosławska 9; ✆ 061/853-95-29). Sweets lovers vouch for the classic apple pies, cheesecakes, and cherry tarts. In winter, the indoor pub-like space can get smoky. Next door is **Weranda Caffe** (Świętosławska 10; ✆ 061/853-25-87). It also has a lovely patio out back. The delicious walnut meringue with a creamy mascarpone filling could feed two. The wait staff is young and sometimes inattentive and petulant. The sister outlet is **Zielona Weranda** (Paderewskiego 7; ✆ 061/851-32-90).

AFTER DARK
Performing Arts

The **Zamek Cultural Center,** Św. Marcin 80/82 (✆ 061/646-52-60; www.zamek.poznan.pl), is the first stop for information on happenings in Poznań. The ticket office is open daily 11am to 7pm. Event tickets can also be bought at the **City Information Center/CIM** (Ratajczaka 44; ✆ 061/851-96-45; www.cim.poznan.pl). **Teatr Wielki,** Fredry 9 (✆ 061/659-02-00; www.opera.poznan.pl) is the place for operas. The **Polski Teatr Tańca,** Kozia 4 (✆ 061/852-42-41; www.ptt-poznan.pl), hosts Polish and international troupes at various venues around town including Teatr Wielki. Tickets can be purchased at their website, the CIM, or Teatr Wielki. The **Poznań Philharmonic (Filharmonia Poznańska),** Św. Marcin 81 (✆ 061/852-47-08; www.filharmoniapoznanska.pl), hosts Polish and international musicians. The box office is open daily 1pm to 5pm.

Cafes, Pubs & Clubs

Near the Stary Rynek, **Żydowska Street** is crammed with cafes. One in four patrons is a student, which means beer is good business in this town. On the side streets of the Old Town Square the drinks get cheaper, so poke around **Woźna Street** for value deals. **Warta** (Świętosławska 12; ✆ 061/852-50-29), a cavernous bar, is where the eponymous beer company filmed its commercial. The basement fills with hundreds of revelers when they hold concerts. Dancing feet should make their way to **Cute** (Stary Rynek 37; ✆ 061/851-91-37; www.cute.poznan.pl), one of the city's best-known venues for house, techno, trance, and just plain dance music. **Blue Note Jazz Club ★★** (Kościuszki 76–78; ✆ 061/657-07-77; www.bluenote.poznan.pl) is a reputable venue with top-notch live jazz by leading Polish and international musicians. However, it also plays teenybopper tunes.

---

2 GNIEZNO

Gniezno is generally regarded as the first capital of Poland, though there are contentions from other places. Gniezno's story dates back to the legend of Lech, the founder of Poland. It's said that he came across a white eagle guarding her nest (*gniazdo*) and decided to settle there, naming it Gniezno (the Polish adjective for nest) and adopting the white eagle as his emblem (which today is still the symbol of Poland). From recorded history, Gniezno's importance came about as the coronation site of Poland's first king, Bolesław the Brave. The capital has moved on, but Gniezno has not turned into a sleepy town propped up by school excursions. The cobblestoned Old Town has brightly painted early 19th-century tenement houses, sunshine-filled beer gardens, and side streets filled with quaint, time-warped shops. It is an easy day trip from Poznań.

ESSENTIALS

Getting There

Gniezno is 286km (171 miles) to the east of Warsaw, and 50km (34 miles) to the northeast of Poznań.

BY CAR　From Poznań take Rd. 5. If you're coming from Warsaw, take E30, exit at Września, then turn north on Rd. 15. Figure on 4 hours' driving time from Warsaw and 1 hour from Poznań.

BY TRAIN　Trains run regularly from Poznań to Gniezno's train station. Tickets cost 16 zł ($6.40/£3.60) and the journey time is 45 minutes. The Town Square is a 10-minute walk in the northwest direction.

BY BUS　Frequent bus service is available from Poznań's PKS bus station.

VISITOR INFORMATION

Gniezno Tourist Information Center (Tumska 12; ✆ 061/428-41-00; www.szlak piastowski.com.pl) is open from April to October, weekdays from 8am to 6pm, Saturdays from 9am to 3pm, and Sundays from 10am to 2pm. Off-season, it's open weekdays only from 8am to 4pm. It is an excellent place for maps, English-language resources, and hotel and restaurant listings. They can advise on the Piast Route beyond Gniezno. The Piast Route map by Bik (6 zł/$2.40/£1.35) has blown-up maps of Gniezno, Biskupin, and Lake Lednica. To book English-speaking tour guides, call two days in advance. It's 210 zł ($84/£47.25) for 3 hours; that covers the cathedral and the two museums. A 1-hour guide for the cathedral alone is 90 zł ($36/£20.25). Another tourist information point is the **PTTK** office (Łaskiego 10; ✆ 061/426-36-60). The *Poznań, In Your Pocket* guide, available in Poznań, has a section on the other minor attractions in Gniezno.

TOP ATTRACTIONS

Gniezno Cathedral ★　The original cathedral was built by Mieszko I before 977. If the present cathedral looks newer than that to you, it's because centuries of fires and invasions took their toll and the building was reconstructed in the 14th century. Baroque chapels and steeples were added over the years. Most visitors make a beeline to see the 12th-century Romanesque bronze doors, regarded as the finest example of their kind in Poland. The 18-panel doors are diminutive in stature but glorious in bas-relief, depicting the life of St. Adalbert. You could easily spend 30 minutes studying the key moments leading to his death in the hands of pagans during his mission to evangelize Northern

---

Journey into the Piast

The **Piast Route (Szlak Piastowski)**, meandering from Poznań to Kruszwica, strings together the major and minor sites related to the beginnings of Poland. Poznań, Gniezno, Biskupin, and Lake Lednica *(Ostrów Lednicki)* are the key stopovers. The trail is strewn with churches; legends, saints, and royalty; pottery, tools, and bones dug up or recovered from lakes; and esoteric anthropological and ethnographical museums. The route is strictly for those keen on historic interests and folk culture. A good place to dig for information and guides is Gniezno's tourist information office (see below).

Model Behavior

If you're into folk culture, head to the **Wielkopolska Ethnographic Park** [S] (Dziekanowice 32, Lednogóra; ℂ **061/427-50-40;** www.lednicamuzeum.pl), an open-air park 18km (11 miles) to the west of Gniezno. It has 50 life-sized models of historical folk architecture from the last 250 years. The pieces, from all over the country, include farmsteads of rich peasants, a potter, windmills, a chapel, a cemetery, and a manor house. It's a fair bit of walking, so wear comfortable shoes. It's closed on Mondays. To get there by bus, take any of the buses to Poznań or Pobiedziska and alight at Komorowo. The park is a 5-minute walk away. By car, take Road no. 5 toward Poznań.

CENTRAL & NORTHWEST POLAND

Poland. His remains lie in the sliver sarcophagus in the cathedral's nave. Outside the cathedral is the statue of Bolesław the Brave, the first Polish king crowned here, in 1025. Four subsequent kings had their coronations here before the capital moved to Kraków. The rather kitschy portraits of these royals are hung above the portal opposite the bronze doors.

Łaskiego 9. ℂ **061/426-19-09.** Doors of Gniezno admission 2 zł (80¢/45p). Mon–Sat 9–11:50am and 1–5pm, Sun 1–3pm and 4–6pm. Viewing tower Mon–Sat 9:30am–5:30pm, Sun 1–6pm. Underground crypts accessible only with a guide ℂ **0602-708-231.**

WHERE TO STAY & DINE

Hotel Adalbertus ★ (Value) You can't get nearer to the cathedral than this. This hotel is part of the Pietrak Hotel (see below) chain, but it feels cozier here than at its big brother's on Chrobrego Street. The exterior retains the charm of the monastery the property used to be, but the interior has had all its monastic character renovated out of it. Nevertheless, the pokey rooms are nicely furnished and the cramped bathrooms are clean. **Restauracja Tumska** does Polish cuisine, while **Ristorante Italiano Vicino Alla Cattedrale** has pizza and pasta. The set lunches, priced at 11 zł ($4.40/£2.50), are delicious as well as a good value.

Tumska 7A. ℂ **061/426-13-60.** www.pietrak.pl. 24 units. 160 zł ($64/£36) single; 190 zł ($76/£42.75) double; 300 zł ($120/£67.50) apt. 20% discount on weekends. Rates include breakfast. Extra person 90 zł ($36/£20.25). Children 8 and under stay free in parent's room. DC, MC, V. Parking 15 zł ($6/£3.30). **Amenities:** 2 restaurants; dry cleaning; tour booking; complimentary Wi-Fi. *In room:* TV; radio; hair dryer (in apt).

Hotel Pietrak The location is ideal, along the main street of the Old Town lined with lively pubs and restaurants. Roman fountains and plastic plants in the lobby make it no surprise to find green carpets and brown lacquered furniture in the neo-classical rooms. The single and double rooms are similar in size. The hotel has hosted many key political figures, so the staff is fine-tuned to the art of hospitality. The restaurant has seen diners such as the former German Chancellor Helmut Kohl, and serves European fare with a selection of vegetarian options.

Chrobrego 3. ℂ **061/426-14-97.** www.pietrak.pl. 54 units. 180 zł ($72/£40.50) single; 210 zł ($84/£47.25) double; 320 zł ($128/£72) suite. Rates include breakfast. Weekend 20% discount. Extra person 100 zł ($40/£22.50). Breakfast for extra person 30 zł ($12/£6.75). DC, MC, V. Parking 15 zł ($6/£3.38). **Amenities:** 3 restaurants; bar; conference room; dry cleaning; 24-hr. room service; tour booking; gym; Jacuzzi. *In room:* A/C (in suite); TV, complimentary Wi-Fi, minibar, hair dryer.

10

GNIEZNO

Kresowianka ★ (Finds) EASTERN EUROPEAN   It's a bit out of the way, but worth it if you want to escape the spate of grilled meat and pizzas in town. The restaurant resembles the living room of a socialite aunt who has lost the steam to keep up with the trends in *Country Living*. The ominously dim lighting doesn't seem to bother the diners who come here for Lithuanian dishes such as buckwheat *bliny, chłodnik* (a cold beetroot soup), and Estonian herring. The *czernina* (duck's blood soup) is less sour than elsewhere. For dessert, try the Lithuanian sweets.

Roosevelta 123. © 061/428-23-93. www.kresowianka.pl. Mains 18 zł–48 zł ($7.20–$19.20/£4–£10.80). AE, DC, MC, V. Daily 11am–11pm. Taxi from town 15 zł ($6/£3.40).

Bistro Pod Piątka EUROPEAN   "Bistro at No. 5" is a charming space opposite the alleyway where the tourist information center is located. Salvaged and restored antique tables, chairs, and benches dress up the place. In terms of range, the food is similar to Hotel Pietrak's; that is, the local favorites of Polish and Italian. The fragrant grilled steaks stand out. In summer, the patio, with a view of the cathedral's spires, is very inviting.

Tumska 5. © 061/426-18-00. www.5.gniezno.pl. Mains 12 zł–25 zł ($4.80–$10/£2.70–£5.60). DC, MC, V. Daily 11am–10pm.

3 BISKUPIN

Dubbed the "Polish Pompeii," Biskupin is the only known Iron Age settlement in Poland. It is also one of the most engaging attractions on the Piast Route. Though it is not connected to the Piast Dynasty, it is regarded as a key fragment in piecing together the origins of the country. The site was discovered by accident in 1933 by a teacher on a school excursion to Lake Biskupieńskie. Wooden stakes sticking out of the lake caught his eye. Excavations revealed a network of well-preserved wooden foundations and defensive ramparts, and evidence indicates it was a fortified settlement of the Lusatian clan dating from around 550 BC.

The present-day settlement you see is an impressive mockup of an Iron Age village. As the site is in the middle of nowhere, careful consideration has been given to make this a satisfying and complete afternoon out. There is a museum to give context to the place, and, in season, daily demonstrations of pottery, archery, fire working with flint stone, and pony and leisure-boat rides. The archeological festivals in September showcase earlier civilizations—from not just Europe but also around the world, so don't be surprised to see a samurai gaiting by.

Biskupin can be stringed along with Gniezno as a day trip from Poznań.

ESSENTIALS
Getting There

BY BUS   From Gniezno, regular buses run to Żnin (10km/6 miles to the north of Biskupin) and Gąsawa (2 km/1.2 miles to the south of Biskupin). The journey is about an hour. From either Żnin or Gąsawa, you catch a bus or the train to Biskupin. The bus service runs regularly on weekdays. Should you miss your bus at Gąsawa, the 2km (1.2 miles) to Biskupin is manageable on foot.

BY TRAIN   The narrow-gauge railway (© 052/302-04-92) runs from Żnin to Gąsawa and stops right in front of the reserve. From mid-April to August, the trains run from 9am to 3pm every 1½ hours. There is an additional run at 4pm during the archaeological festival in September. The journey takes 40 minutes from Żnin and 25 minutes from Gąsawa. Tickets, bought from the train driver, are 10 zł ($4/£2.25) for one way and 18 zł ($7.20/£4.05) round-trip.

BY CAR From Poznań, it takes 1¹/₂ hours. Leave the city on Rd. 5, turning north at Gniezno. As you approach Gąsawa, you will see signs for the reserve.

Visitor Information

The guides, demonstrations of pottery, and flint stone fire working have to be booked in advance by calling ℂ **052/302-50-55.** The ticket office sells a good map of the Piast Route by Bik (6 zł/$2.40/£1.35).

TOP ATTRACTION

Archaeological Reserve (Rezerwat Archeologiczny) ★ (Kids) On the way to the centerpiece Iron Age Village you'll pass the museum, which has a small but well-designed exhibition of artifacts and models depicting life in the area some 2,700 years ago. Press on to the village at the northern edge of the park by the lake, and follow the "tour direction" *(Kierunek Zwiedzania)* boards to see the palisades and rampart fortifications, thatched roofs, wood-beam floors, and wicket doors of the settlement. In this compound you'll find demos of pottery and other aspects of Iron Age life, all enacted by enthusiastic and educated staff sporting coarse robes. If you haven't made reservations for the demos, keep an eye out for school groups and just piggyback on their demo sessions (they will be in Polish, but you don't need to understand the talk to appreciate the crafts). It takes no more than an hour to cover the grounds. The kids might want to have a go at the pony rides or a trip on the leisure boat to nowhere. Although it opens at 8am the settlement is only in full swing at about 10am. It's an outdoor museum, so April through September is the best time to visit.

Biskupin. ℂ **052/302-54-20.** www.biskupin.pl. Admission 8 zł ($3.20/£1.80) adult, 6 zł ($2.40/£1.35) concession seniors, students, and children. Summer daily 8am–6pm; winter daily 8am–dusk. Parking 5 zł ($2/£1.10).

WHERE TO STAY & DINE

At the reserve's parking lot, several outdoor stalls serve snacks and meals. Across the road, **Karczma Biskupińska** (Biskupin 6; ℂ **052/302-50-14;** www.karczma-biskupinska.pl) offers a similar spread but with indoor seating. They also have basic accommodations, priced at 60 zł ($24/£13.50) for a single and 70 zł ($28/£16) for a double.

Restauracja-Hotel Pałacowa ★ (Finds) Smack dab in the middle of wheat fields and farmstead terrain is this palatial, white-washed Polish manor house with a garden the size of a small park. The building, dating from the late 1800s, has been restored to emulate the country getaway of a well-to-do nobleman with a penchant for antiques, wine, and hunting. All rooms are spacious doubles and are decked out differently, but all have European antiques and the occasional Oriental knick-knacks. Most guests are on their way to and from the Mazurian Lakes or doing the Piast Route. The restaurant, open 10 to 10, features starched linens and fine glass and has a Polish menu with a strong presence of game.

Grochowiska Szlacheckie 2, Rogowo. ℂ **052/304-70-01.** www.palac-grochowiska.com.pl. 8 units. 250 zł ($100/£56.25) double; 350 zł ($140/£78.75) room w/Jacuzzi. Extra person 120 zł ($48/£27). Children 12 and under 70 zł ($28/£15.75). Rates include breakfast. DC, MC, V. Free parking. The hotel is at the edge of Gąsawa. Road no. 5 from Gniezno to Biskupin, turn right in the direction of Gąsawa. The building is on the left side of road in the village of Grochowiska Szlacheckie. **Amenities:** Restaurant; bar; billiard room; lounge; sauna; laundry service; complimentary Wi-Fi. *In room:* TV, hair dryer.

4 TORUŃ

Toruń is a picturesque university town with at least three things in its favor. First, it has an unrivaled stock of Gothic buildings. Unlike many Polish towns its size, Toruń escaped major damage in World War II. The Old Town joined UNESCO's World Heritage List in 1997. Now, gearing up as the European City of Culture in 2016, Toruń's theme is *Gotyk na Dotyk* (literally, "Touch Gothic"). Beneath the baroque, renaissance, and classical façades are the medieval Gothic red bricks. Second, this is the birthplace of "the man who stopped the earth and moved the sun," Nicolaus Copernicus. Third, it had knights. Not the Templar, but the no less formidable Teutonic Order (see "Malbork," p. 253), a German religious order that was originally invited by Polish kings to secure the area but later turned on its hosts and amassed its own empire.

You can make a whirlwind tour of the town in a couple of hours, but that would be a shame. Toruń is ideal for a slow and easy weekend. Be sure to stroll along the river *(Bulwar Filadelfijski)* for a spectacular view of the town walls that is especially pretty at night. And stop by the ruins of the former castle of the Teutonic knights (at the crossing of Przedzamcze and Bulwar Filadelfijski).

ESSENTIALS
Getting There

Toruń lies on major bus and rail links, with frequent daily service to major cities.

BY CAR   From Warsaw (200km/120 miles) take Rd. E77 and switch to A10 in Płońsk. From Gdańsk (207km/124 miles), take E75. From Poznań (150 km/90 miles), it's E261 followed by A10 at Bydgoszcz. Figure on 2 to 3 hours' driving time from any of these starting points. You'll find parking along the river on Bulwar Filadelfijski.

BY TRAIN   Trains arrive at **Toruń Główny** (Kujawska 1; ✆ **056/ 621-30-44;** www.intercity.pkp.pl) in the south of the city, across the Vistula river. Take bus nos. 22 or 27 to get to town.

BY BUS   The **PKS bus station** (Dąbrowskiego 8–24; ✆ **056/655-53-33;** www.pks.torun.com) is about 5 minutes to the east of the Old Town.

You Made the Earth Move Under My Feet?

Nicolaus Copernicus (1473–1543), or Mikołaj Kopernik in Polish, is Toruń's most famous son and an archetype Renaissance man. During his lifetime he served not only as a priest, but also as a physician, classical scholar, jurist (church law), governor, military leader, diplomat, and economist. However, he is first and foremost remembered for *De Revolutionibus Orbium Coelestium (On the Revolutions of the Heavenly Spheres)*, where he presented his theories of the earth revolving around the sun. The Church initially viewed it as blasphemy. Copernicus died shortly after *De Revolutionibus* was published, though he probably never saw it in print. His work paved the way for a series of astronomical breakthroughs in the 16th and 17th centuries, including the work of Galileo, Tycho Brahe, and Sir Isaac Newton. Learn more at the **House of Nicolaus Copernicus (Dom Mikołaja Kopernika)** (Kopernika 15/17; ✆ **056/622-70-38**), which has some of the oldest editions of *De Revolutionibus*.

Make your own decorative gingerbread at the **Gingerbread Museum (Muzeum Piernika)** (Rabiańska 9; ✆ **056/663-66-17;** www.muzeumpiernika.pl). In a hall emulating a 16th-century abode, the cheerful English-speaking crew here gets you to chant an oath to keep the secrets of gingerbread crafts before allowing you to play dough. Sessions start every hour on the hour with a minimum group size of 5. Be sure to book in advance.

Visitor Information

The Toruń Tourist Information Center (Rynek Staromiejski 25; ✆ **056/621-09-31**) is centrally located in the Old Town Square and staffed by friendly English speakers who will bring you up to date on events in town. There is a free Internet terminal here as well. Guide tours cost about 170 zł ($68/£38.25) for 2 hours. The center is open on Monday from 9am to 4pm, Tuesday through Friday from 9am to 6pm, and Saturday from 9am to 4pm. From May to August, it's also open on Sundays from 9am to 1pm. For quirky holiday photos, hire the guides from **Centrum Przewodnickie** (Żeglarska 10/14; ✆ **056/622-30-02;** www.visittorun.eu), who are dressed up as medieval townsmen and women and Copernicus and Teutonic knights. The rates are 245 zł ($98/£55.10) for 2 hours and 341 zł ($136.40/£76.70) for 3 hours. Call a day in advance to book. *Note:* From May to December, there's free Wi-Fi access in the Old Town Square.

TOP ATTRACTIONS

Cathedral of St. John the Baptist & St. John the Evangelist (Katedra Świętego Janów) ★★

The construction of the cathedral that dominates Toruń's skyline started in the 1260s and took 200 years to complete. The star attraction is the Tuba Dei, the oldest medieval bell in Poland, cast in 1530. It's also one of the 11 historic bells in Toruń that survived looting and recasting into weaponry. In the past, Tuba Dei's peal heralded the arrival of popes and Polish kings. A twirl up the claustrophobic spiral stairway gets you a view of the bell and the added bonus of postcard views of the Old Town Square and the river. The cathedral's 15th-century clock has a single hand, referred to as *Digitus Dei* (God's finger).

Żeglarska, admission 3 zł ($1.30) adult, 2 zł (80¢/45p) concession students, seniors, and children. Tower admission 6 zł ($2.40/£1.35) adult, 4 zł ($1.60/90p) concession; May–Sept Mon–Sat 9am–5pm, Sun 1–5pm; Nov–Mar daily 10am–1pm.

Old Town Hall (Ratusz Staromiejski) ★

This 14th-century red-brick Gothic building dotted with 365 windows and crowned with four pinnacles is one of the most captivating Town Halls in the country. It started life as a site for trading stalls. The Renaissance turrets were added later. Inside, there's the town museum where you'll find an impressive collection of stained glass, gingerbread molds and other crafts through the ages, and paintings of former prominent residents. It's worth panting up the 42m (13-ft.) tower for a view of the city and across the river.

Rynek Staromiejski 1. ✆ **056/622-70-38.** www.muzeum.torun.pl. Museum admission 10 zł ($4/£2.25) adult, 6 zł ($2.40/£1.35) concession, free Wed. May–Sept Tues–Sun 10am–6pm; Oct–Apr Tues–Sun 10am–4pm. Tower admission 10 zł ($4/£2.25) adult, 6 zł ($2.40/£1.35) seniors, students, and children. Tower hours: May–Sept daily 10am–8pm, Oct–Apr daily 10am–5pm.

Synonymous with Toruń is *piernik* (gingerbread). The decorative ones with motifs such as *kareta* (horse-carriage), *katarzyna* (indented rectangles), and burgher houses are toothbreakers. They are meant as keepsakes. The edible ones are soft and filled with preserves, such as plum, and icing-glazed or chocolate-coated. One supplier, **Kopernik** (Stary Rynek 6; © **056/628-88-32**), overruns the town. At **Pierniczek** (Żeglarska 25; © **056/621-05-61**), you can buy the goods by weight. **Emporium ★★** (Piekary 28; © **056/657-61-08**) is best for a variety of souvenirs. The presents are bundled up with a wax seal imprinted with the emblem of Toruń. They also do bike rentals at 5 zł ($2/£1.10) an hour. Just leave your ID as a deposit.

WHERE TO STAY

Expensive

Mercure Helios Toruń   Part of the Orbis hotel chain, it has all the reliable comforts of a mid-sized hotel such as ample parking, which some of the boutique hotels in the Old Town lack. Located 700m from the Old Town, it's an easy walk to the sights. The rooms are not soulful, but clean and cheerful with pictures of Copernicus's Helios system. The TV comes with a Japanese channel to cater for the business travelers linked to the Japanese investments near Toruń.

Kraszewskiego 1/3. © **056/619-65-50**. Fax 056/622-19-54. www.mercure.pl. 110 units. 354 zł ($138/£78) single; 423 zł ($169/£95) double; 600 zł ($240/£135) apt. Rates include breakfast. Option to book without breakfast. Extra breakfast 29 zł ($11.60/£6.50). AE, DC, MC, V. Parking 36 zł ($14.40/£8.10). **Amenities:** Restaurant; bar; business center; conference room; gym; dry cleaning; tour booking; concierge. *In room:* A/C, paid TV, hair dryer, minibar, kettle (in apt), dataport.

Moderate

Hotel Gotyk   This hotel's location opposite the Hotel Petite Fleur is superb. Rooms are fashioned in dark tones of the new classical look. Compared to Petite Fleur, the rooms are much bigger, but the quality of the furnishings is lower and the atmosphere is more casual; they do, however, have parking and elevators here, which the Fleur doesn't.

Piekary 20. © **056/658-40-00**. Fax 056/658-40-01. www.hotel-gotyk.com.pl. 38 units. 190 zł ($76/£42.75) single; 270 zł–320 zł ($108–$128/£60.75–£72) double. Rates include breakfast. Weekend 10% discount. Extra person 70 zł ($28/£15.75). AE, DC, MC, V. Limited street parking 20 zł ($8/£4.50). **Amenities:** 2 restaurants; bar; billiard table; conference room; safe; hair dryer. *In room:* A/C (some rooms), Wi-Fi.

Hotel Heban   The hotel occupies two renovated townhouses in the section between the Old and New Towns. One building, much more atmospheric, dates from the 17th century, and the other, across the street, from the 19th century. The latter is pitched at business clients. Ask for room number 3 in the older building: it's a picture-perfect double with hardwood floors and wood-beamed ceilings, just waiting for a vase of beautiful flowers to complete the picture. *Note:* There are no elevators in the older building.

Małe Garbary 7. © **056/652-15-55**. Fax 056/652-16-65. www.hotel-heban.com.pl. 22 units. 190 zł ($76/£42.75) single; 300 zł ($120/£68) double; 350 zł ($140/£79) apt. Rates include breakfast. Extra person 100 zł ($40/£22.50). AE, DC, MC, V. **Amenities:** Restaurant; bar; conference room; billiard room; tour booking. *In room:* TV, radio, fridge, dataport, Wi-Fi, hair dryer.

Hotel Petite Fleur   Located in the Old Town, this boutique hotel occupies two stunningly renovated Renaissance burghers' houses. The rooms, some with wood-beamed ceilings and exposed red-brick alcoves, are cozy and tastefully adorned with floral paintings. Steep stairs lead to the rooms. (*Note:* There are no elevators.) Mind where the corridor light switches are; otherwise, you'll be groping in the dark. The so-called "guesthouse rooms" are in another building on the same street (no. 28). If you stay at the guesthouse, you must walk to the hotel for your breakfast.

Piekary 25. ℂ **056/663-44-00**. Fax 056/663-54-54. www.petitefleur.pl. 16 units. Guest room 150 zł ($60/£33.75) single; 190 zł ($76/£42.75) double. Hotel room 165 zł ($66/£37) single; 210 zł–270 zł ($84–$108/£47–£61) double. Rates include breakfast. AE, DC, MC, V. **Amenities:** Restaurant; safe; hair dryer. In room: A/C (some rooms), TV, radio, dataport, complimentary Wi-Fi.

Hotel Retman   Also in the Old Town, this is a clean, quiet, family-run inn. Rooms are on the small side, but scrubbed clean and have agreeable dark wood finishings. Skip the mediocre breakfast unless you wake up starving.

Rabiańska 15. ℂ **056/657-44-60**. Fax 056/657-44-61. www.hotelretman.pl. 29 units. Weekdays 190 zł ($76/£43) single; 250 zł ($100/£56) double. Weekends 160 zł ($64/£36) single; 200 zł ($80/£45) double. Rates include breakfast. AE, DC, MC, V. **Amenities:** Restaurant, pub. In room: TV, dataport, Wi-Fi.

Hotel Spichrz ★★   Located by the Bridge Gate in the Old Town, the hotel occupies a restored Swedish granary built in 1719. Don't be put off by the modern lobby, for the rooms retain the original building details including wooden columns, ceiling beams, and granary windows. Rooms are small to medium in size, with modern bathrooms. Some look out to the Vistula River. The restaurant's forte is meat and more meat, but also sample the hard-to-find sauerkraut and beetroot juices.

Mostowa 1. ℂ **056/657-11-40**. Fax 056/657-11-44. www.spichrz.pl. 19 units. 210 zł ($84/£47.25) single; 270 zł ($108/£61) double; 370 zł ($148/£83) apt. Sept to March 20% discount on weekends. Rates include breakfast. Children 5 and under stay free in parent's room. Children 6 and over 50 zł ($20/£11). AE, DC, MC, V. **Amenities:** Restaurant; conference room; billiards room; Wi-Fi. In room: A/C (in apt), TV, minibar, hair dryer, safe.

WHERE TO DINE

Toruń is a great place to escape from hotel dining and slip into places with great ambience and reasonable prices.

Bar Miś ⓥalue POLISH   This is a milk bar, delicatessen, and butcher thrown into one. It fashioned itself after a Polish cult movie of the same name, which parodied life during the Communist era. The hay "bear" at the window is an icon from the movie. So are the aluminum bowl screwed to the bar counter and the two spoons chained together. A whack of chunky, sausage-laden *bigos* (hunter's stew) is only 3.50 zł ($1.40/79p); *pierogi* and pork chops are also popular. Return your plate to the service hatch when you're done.

Stary Rynek 8. No phone. Main courses 9 zł–15.50 zł ($3.60–$6.20/£2.03–£3.49). No credit cards. Mon–Fri 9am–6pm, Sat 8am–3pm.

Leniwa ★★ ⓥalue ⒻFinds POLISH   Delicious scents reel you in to this IKEA country-style space. *Leniwa* is a typical Polish starchy staple and it also means "lazy." But the genial folks here are anything but lazy in making some of the best *pierogi* ever. Sample the various types of sweet and savory dumplings at bargain basement prices. Locals tuck in here, so be prepared to wait for your freshly made orders.

Ślusarska 5. ℂ **056/477-54-03**. www.leniwa.pl. Pierogi 7 zł–10.50 zł ($2.80–$4.20/£1.60–£2.40). No credit cards. Daily 11am–9pm.

Manekin ★ PANCAKE   Manekin gets rave reviews from pancake fans. The square packages, made from wheat or buckwheat flour, are padded with sweet or savory fillings. Those with chicken, beans, and onions, topped with spicy tomato sauce, are filling without going overboard. For the sweet tooth, the simple apple with cinnamon is an all-time winner. In summer, you can eat on the terrace overlooking the Old Town Square.

Rynek Staromiejski 16. ⓒ **056/621-05-04.** Pancakes 7 zł–12.50 zł ($2.80–$5/£1.60–£2.80). AE, MC, V. Sun–Thurs 10am–11pm, Fri–Sat 10am–midnight.

Róże i Zen ★★ (Finds POLISH From the street, you wouldn't know that this cafe and restaurant hides a secret garden sheltered by trees and cloistered by old walls. The homey-feeling inside showcases an eclectic array of antiques. There's sophisticated home cooking featuring chanterelle quiche and buckwheat *bliny* with caviar (58 zł/$23/£13). Many come especially for the house-made cheesecake and tarts. On weekends a guitarist strums away, enticing you to linger.

Podmurna 18. ⓒ **056/621-05-21.** No credit cards. Mains 19 zł–27 zł ($7.60–$10.80/£4.30–£6). Sun–Thurs 11am–10pm, Fri–Sat 11am–11pm.

AFTER DARK

New life surfaces in the Old and New Towns after sunset. **Piwnica Pod Aniołem** (Rynek Staromiejski 1; ⓒ **056/622-70-39;** www.podaniolem.art.pl), one of the most famous clubs in Toruń, hosts concerts as well as photography and art exhibits. Located in the Town Hall's cellar, its vaulted ceilings contain pungent clouds of nicotine. **Tantra** (Ślusarska 5; ⓒ **0697-133-569**) breaks from the Gothic spirit to ply you with Tibetan and Nepalese vibes. If you miss hearing English, go to **Złote Jajo** (Przedzamcze 6B; ⓒ **0508/940-017**), a casual pub converted from an old mill and run by an American professor.

Gdańsk &
the Baltic Coast

Gdańsk and the Baltic Coast don't have to do much to attract visitors; they come without bidding. The region is a treasure trove of historical gems, and the backdrop of sandy beaches is never far away. As an affluent Baltic port for centuries, Gdańsk has an enchantingly rich architectural heritage that lends itself to endless discoveries. Then there's the jolting experience of walking on Westerplatte, the spot where the first shots of World War II were fired. As the birthplace of the Solidarity movement, the city also makes you aware how far Poland has come since the anti-Communist struggle in the 1980s. But it's not all about reflecting on the past. Gdańsk, Sopot, and Gdynia form the Tri-City *(Trójmiasto)*. As a team, the coastal trio gives you beach life, value-for-money restaurants, first-rate accommodation, and sophisticated cosmopolitan nightlife.

Don't leave the region without making a stop at Malbork Castle, the largest brick fortress in the world and the medieval stronghold of the Teutonic knights. If your appetite for brickwork is still unsated after your visit, there's the equally imposing Kwidzyn Castle, 40km (24 miles) from Malbork.

For winding down, options abound. Within the Tri-City, you can ramble on the white-sand beaches of Sopot. A quick boat cruise lands you on endless stretches of pristine shores and the sleepy fishing villages of the Hel Peninsula, the nation's summertime playground by the Baltic Sea. Mingle with the locals on the slow, sandy lanes or get an adrenaline rush kite surfing or deep-sea fishing. Idyllic seashore living can be also found in Łeba. From Łeba, you're a just a hop away from the famous "moving dunes" of Słowiński National Park. Another form of slowing down is on the Elbląg-Ostróda Canal. The canal, singled out by Poles as one of the nation's Seven Wonders, is the only one of its kind in Europe, where waterways are linked with rail tracks giving you the sensation of a boat cruise and a San Francisco cable-car ride packaged into one.

Though the region is most popular in summer, the autumn hues are spectacular and in winter snow-white beaches reward hardy souls with breathtaking sights. Speaking of hardy, a note on keeping warm: Even in summer, sea gusts dip the mercury, especially after sunset. So be sure to pack some warm layers with you.

1 GDAŃSK

Gdańsk is a sensory blast. If you were expecting a dingy Baltic seaport, perhaps reinforced by that foggy, black-and-white TV footage of Lech Wałęsa and the embattled Solidarity dockworkers, you are in for a pleasant surprise. Modern-day Gdańsk is a beautiful seaside town, with a lovingly restored Old City. The city was severely damaged in World War II, with the Russians and Allied bombers effectively finishing up where the Germans left off. But Gdańsk is luckier than many Polish cities in that the reconstruction after the war was commendably sensitive. And, unlike the reconstruction of Warsaw's Old Town (which mostly benefits tourists), Gdańsk's newly built Old City feels thoroughly authentic and lived-in by the locals. In this vibrant atmosphere, it's easy to forget that the first shots of World War II were fired here—and that this is also where history took another sharp turn when the shipyard's dockworkers, led by Lech Wałęsa, brought down the Communist government. You can still see the shipyards, about a 15-minute walk north of the Old Town, and visit an inspirational museum, the **Roads to Freedom,** that details the tense moments of the 1980s. On arrival you'll immediately want to extend your stay, so make room for squeezing in another day or three.

ESSENTIALS
Getting There

BY PLANE   Lech Wałęsa International Airport (Słowackiego 200, Gdańsk-Rębiechowo; ℂ 058/348-11-63; www.airport.gdansk.pl) is the main airport in northeastern Poland, and it has good direct domestic and international routes. Flights take off from here to major European cities including London (Gatwick, Luton, and Stansted) and Frankfurt, and several Scandinavian cities. It's served by, among others, LOT, SAS, and WizzAir. The airport is about 10km (6 miles) west of the city. To get to town from the airport take bus B, which runs twice hourly during daylight hours, to Gdańsk Główny (the central train station). Bus N3 is the night bus to the main railway station and the Wrzeszcz railway station. The trip costs 3 zł ($1.20/70p). Leave about 40 minutes for the journey (more during rush hour). A taxi from the airport to Gdańsk costs about 50 zł ($20/£11.25), to Sopot about 60 zł ($24/£13.5), and to Gdynia 90 zł ($36/£20.25). The taxi company recommended by the airport authorities is **City Plus Taxi** (ℂ **9686**).

BY TRAIN   For most arrivals, **Gdańsk Główny** train station (Podwale Grodzkie 1; ℂ **058/721-94-36;** www.pks.pl), to the southwest of the Old City, is the first port of call. The Old Town is a 5-minute walk away; use the underpass to cross the highway. Gdańsk is well served by railroad, and departures to Warsaw and other major cities are frequent. Local trains to Sopot and Gdynia also depart from here.

BY BUS   The main bus station, **Dworzec PKS** (3 Maja 12; ℂ **058/302-15-32;** www. pks.gdansk.pl), is located just next to the train station. As Poland's Baltic hub, the city is a primary destination for domestic and international bus lines.

BY CAR   The roads to Gdańsk are improving, but traffic nightmares are frequent. The major and seemingly permanent road works have badly tied up routes coming from all directions, so leave plenty of time to get there. The main roads running south are the E75 to Toruń and E77 to Warsaw. The E28 is the main route to the west toward Germany. Coming from the west, it skirts Gdańsk as it heads south. The E28 is planned to be a major four-lane north–south artery. Once you arrive in the city, brace yourself for hour-long jams during the morning and evening rush hours. The drive from Warsaw may take anything from 4 to 5 hours.

BY BOAT   It is possible to arrive in Gdańsk by ferry from Sweden. **Polferries** (www. polferries.pl) offers regular service between the Swedish port of Nynäshamm (60km/36 miles south of Stockholm) and **Gdańsk's Nowy Port** (Przemysłowa 1; ℂ **058/343-00-78**), which is 7km (4 miles) south of the city. Bus no. 150 from the train station gets you to the ferry terminal in about 15 minutes. The ferries depart from Sweden every second or third day at 6pm and arrive at noon. Returns from Gdańsk follow the same schedule. Tickets cost about 198 zł ($79.20/£44.60) each way. In peak season, from May to September, it's 237 zł ($94.80/£53.30). There are also options for basic sleeping berths and

Changes of the Guard in a Nutshell

Even for Poland, Gdańsk has a particularly twisted past, with convoluted shifts of power. The city rose to prominence in the 16th and 17th centuries as one of the most vital towns of the Hanseatic League, a grouping of prosperous river- and seaport cities that controlled much of the trade in the North and Baltic seas. Due to its wealth, Gdańsk was hotly contested between German and Polish interests, though it managed to retain its status as a semi-autonomous city-state. After the Polish partition at the end of the 18th century, the city fell under Prussian rule and became firmly identified as "Danzig," its German moniker. Following Germany's defeat in World War I, the city's status became one of the thorniest issues facing the drafters of the Treaty of Versailles. They opted to create what they called the "Free City of Danzig"—neither German nor Polish—alongside a Polish-ruled strip of land that would effectively cut off mainland Germany from its East Prussian hinterland. Hitler was able to exploit very effectively the existence of this Polish "corridor" as part of his argument that the Treaty of Versailles was highly unfair to Germany. He even chose the port of Gdańsk to launch his war on Poland on September 1, 1939, when German gunboats fired on the Polish garrison at Westerplatte.

During the communist period, Gdańsk was in the public's eye as the home of the Lenin Shipyards and the Solidarity Trade Union. It was here, now known as the Gdańsk shipyards, where intense negotiations in August 1980 between Solidarity, led by a youngish Lech Wałęsa, and the government resulted in the August Treaty, an official recognition of the first independent trade union in Communist Central and Eastern Europe. The government later reneged on the agreement and imposed martial law, but Gdańsk continued as a hotbed of labor unrest and strikes. Roundtable talks in the late 1980s saw the government agreeing to a power-sharing arrangement that in 1989 led to the first semi-free election and a nationwide political triumph for Solidarity. The events here eventually triggered the toppling of Communist regimes in Poland and throughout Eastern Europe.

luxurious cabins for two. Due to rising fuel costs, prices are subject to an additional 20% fuel surcharge. **Stena Line** (www.stenaline.pl) runs a similar service from the southern Swedish city of Karlskrona (500km/300 miles south of Stockholm) to Gdynia's passenger ferry port. In summer, the ferries make the 10-hour journey twice daily at 9am and 9pm. One-way tickets (without car) are 185 zł ($74/£41.60) from June to August; and 155 zł ($62/£34.90) during the rest of the year.

Visitor Information

The city's main tourist information office, **PTTK office** (Długa 45; © **058/301-91-51;** www.pttk-gdansk.pl) is conveniently located in the heart of the Główne Miasto, opposite the Neptune Fountain. This office is overstretched in the summer. They can book hotel rooms as well as sell you a ticket for the philharmonic and opera for a 5 zł ($2/£1.10) fee. To hire a city guide, you need to call in advance. The price is 80 zł ($32/£18) per person for a 2- to 3-hour walking tour. Pick up a copy of the *Gdańsk, Stare Miasto* map, a large-format, easy-to-read guide to all the major sights in the center of town. Also look for the free brochure *The Best of Gdańsk*, a comprehensive, self-guided walking tour in English. The office sells copies of *Gdańsk, In Your Pocket* (5 zł/$2/[b]1.10), which has an excellent overview of the city, including sections on Sopot, Gdynia, and Malbork. For more extensive exploration, the **Copernicus** Tri-City map with public transport routes is a good buy. There are also seasonal tourist information branches open only in summer and shoulder months. **GTO Information Center** (Targ Rybny 6A; © 058/320-85-12) is open in May on weekdays from 8am to 4pm, and June to September Monday through Saturday from 10am to 6pm, and Sunday from 10am to 2pm. The other seasonal office is **ROP PTTK Tourist Information Center** (Powroźnicza 19/20; © 058/301-48-18). It is open weekdays in July and August from 9am to 5pm. There are also **mobile tourist information officers** on bikes deployed at various locations in Główne Miasto and Długie Pobrzeże.

City Layout

Unlike other Polish cities, the heart of Gdańsk is technically not called the "Old Town" *(Stare Miasto)*. There is a **Stare Miasto,** but it lies just to the north of the main center, the **Główne Miasto** (Main Town). The Główne Miasto is where you'll find the main pedestrian walks, **ul. Długa** (Long Street), **Długi Targ** (the Long Market), and interesting side streets. Then comes **Długie Pobrzeże,** a major pedestrian walkway along the **Motława Canal.** Stare Miasto is about a 15-minute walk north, and it is here you'll find the **Gdańsk shipyards** and the **Solidarity memorial,** and the **Roads to Freedom** exhibit. To the south of Główne Miasto is **Stare Przedmieście** (Old Suburbs). Farther to the north, in the direction of Sopot, lies the unlovely **Nowy Port,** as well as the serene suburbs of **Wrzeszcz** and **Oliwa.** The former is home to many of the city's more affordable hotels and pensions. The **Tri-City** *(Trójmiasto)* refers to the trio of Gdańsk, Sopot, and Gdynia. The heart of **Sopot** is about 6km (4 miles) to the north of Gdańsk city center. **Gdynia** is about 15km (10 miles) to the north.

Getting Around

Walking is the most enjoyable mode to see the city's historical sites. To get to Sopot, Gdynia, or farther afield, use the city's good network of public transportation or ferry services targeted at tourists. If you plan to use the trams and buses (run by ZKM) and the SKM commuter trains throughout the Tri-City, you can get a day ticket for 18 zł ($7.20/£4.10).

ON FOOT   Much of central Gdańsk, including ul. Długa and the walkway along the Motława Canal, is closed to motor vehicles. The center is compact and easy to manage on foot.

BY TRAM   Gdańsk has an efficient network of **trams** (© 058/341-00-21; www.zkm. pl) that whisk you from the center of the city to the suburbs of Wrzeszcz and Oliwa in a few minutes. Note that trams do not run to Sopot and Gdynia. Tickets cost 2 zł (80¢/ 45p) for a 15-minute ride; a day ticket costs 9.10 zł ($3.60/£2). Buy tickets at Ruch kiosks, newspapers counters, and from the ticket machines.

BY BUS   City **buses** (www.zkm.pl) are useful for getting to some of the suburbs. Bus nos. 117, 122, and 143 go to Sopot, while bus no. 171 gets you to Gdynia. Ticketing is the same as for the trams.

BY SKM COMMUTER TRAIN   The **SKM** *(Szybka Kolej Miejska),* nicknamed **Kolejka,** is a quick and reliable local "urban train" service, linking the main stopovers of the Tri-City. The SKM runs at about 10-minute intervals from 5am to 7pm through the Tri-City. Get tickets in any of the main stations or from the ticket vending machines located on the platforms. (*Note:* Ticket machines are prone to breaking down. You can also buy the tickets from the conductor at the front of the train.) Validate your tickets before boarding. From Gdańsk, it takes about 20 minutes and a 4 zł ($1.60/90p) ticket to reach Sopot, and 30 minutes and a 4.50 zł ($1.80/£1) ticket to reach Gdynia.

BY TAXI   Taxis are a good way to get to your hotel from the bus or train stations, but you won't need taxis much once you've sorted out the public transportation system. Figure on about 25 zł ($10/£5.60) for rides in town.

BY BOAT   It's fun and relaxing to hitch a boat from Gdańsk to several local and regional destinations. The service is run by **Żegluga Gdańska** (Długie Pobrzeże; ✆ 058/ 301-49-26; www.zegluga.gda.pl). The main ferry landing and ticket office is near the intersection of the Długi Targ and the Motława Canal. In the summer months, the **water trams** *(tramwaj wodny)* (Nabrzeże Motławy; ✆ 058/309-13-23; www.ztm.gda.pl) go to Nowy Port, Sopot, and the Hel Peninsula. Note that it's only from late June that the trams operate daily. Tickets, sold at Targ Rybny 6, cost 8 zł ($3.20/£1.80) to Nowy Port, 10 zł ($4£2.30) to Sopot, and 18 zł ($7.20/£4.10) to Hel.

BY BIKE   Gdańsk is navigable by bicycle, and several new bike lanes now connect the center with the suburbs of Wrzeszcz and beyond, toward Sopot. That said, the network is spotty and there are plenty of places where you'll still have to contend with stairways, sidewalks, heavy traffic, and Polish drivers unaccustomed to cyclists. The rental of choice is **Rowerownia** (Fieldorfa 11/3; ✆ **058/320-61-69;** www.rowerownia.gda.pl), which also issues sturdy locks.

TOP ATTRACTIONS

Amber Museum ★   A must for all fans of the ossified pine resin that continues to make Gdańsk prosper. On six floors of exhibits, located inside the medieval Torture Tower, you'll learn everything you'll ever need to know about amber, including how it's mined and processed, what it looks like under a microscope, and how it was used through the ages, not just as jewelry but in art and medicine. If you're thinking of buying some amber while in Gdańsk, stop here first for an educational primer. One part of the exhibition is given over to fake amber and how to identify the genuine stuff.

Targ Węglowy. ✆ **058/301-47-33**. www.mhmg.gda.pl. Admission 10 zł ($4/£2.30) adults, 5 zł ($2/£1.10) children and seniors, free Tues. Tues 10am–3pm, Wed–Sat 10am–6pm, Sun 11am–6pm.

Artus Court (Dwór Artusa) ★   One of the most impressive houses in the city was reopened to the public after extensive renovation. The Court, so named after King Arthur (though he had nothing to do with this place), was founded as a meeting place for the town's wealthiest traders and leading dignitaries. The house dates from the 14th century, but was remodeled several times, including once in the 19th century when it was given its neo-Gothic look to be in vogue with the prevailing trends. The exterior was demolished in World War II, but many of the interior pieces had been removed beforehand and survived the fighting.

Długi Targ 43/44. ✆ **058/346-33-58**. Admission 8 zł ($3.20/£1.80) adults, 5 zł ($2/£1.10) children and seniors, free Tues. Tues–Sat 10am–4pm, Sun 11am–4pm.

Central Maritime Museum   The best of four separate museums that highlight Gdańsk's history as a port city. Here, you'll find an excellent A-to-Z compendium on Polish maritime history, from the turn of the first millennium to modern times. Some of the finest exhibits are the detailed models of ships, lots of old weaponry, and the oil paintings of old boats. The museum is housed in three Renaissance-era granaries.

Ołowianka 9/13. © **058/310-86-11.** www.cmm.pl. Admission 6 zł ($2.40/£1.35) adults, 4 zł ($1.60/90p) children and seniors. Tues–Sun 10am–4pm; July Tues–Sun 10am–6pm.

Long Waterfront (Długie Pobrzeże) ★   As you turn off Długi Targ Street, you come to the Motława Canal waterfront, a touristy but nevertheless delightful promenade of restaurants, cafes, amber boutiques, and souvenir shops. Street buskers add to the outdoor merriment. Just beyond the **Gate of the Holy Spirit (Brama Św. Ducha)** is another Gdańsk landmark, the **Crane (Żuraw)** (Szeroka 67/68; © **058/301-53-11;** www.cmm.pl). Built mid-15th century, it was the biggest crane in medieval Europe. It is no longer operational, but up until the mid-19th century it was used to unload cargo as heavy as 4 tons.

Długie Pobrzeże

Monument to the Fallen Shipyard Workers   This gigantic steel monument, some 40m (125 ft.) high, was built in 1980 to commemorate the 44 people who died during the bloody anti-Communist riots of 1970. Its construction was one of the demands put forward by the striking workers in August 1980. The design is replete with symbolism. The crosses depict resurrection and victory, while the anchors nailed on the crosses represent the "crucifixion" of hope. The structure emerges from broken concrete to denote the idea of defeating Communism. From the monument's center, "roads" spiral outward—showing that the idea would spread around the world.

Plac Solidarności.

Roads to Freedom Exhibition (Drogi do Wolnośći) ★★   An inspiring, sobering, and thorough history lesson of the anti-Communist struggle in Poland. By the entrance to the underground exhibition, you see an example of a military tank that was a common and menacing sight during the riots on Gdańsk's streets. The mock-up of a typical empty grocery store in the late 1970s, grainy news reels, interactive displays, and documentary films keenly capture the atmosphere of the times. The multilingual exhibition walks you through the riots in 1970 that tore the country apart to the rise of the Solidarity trade union later that decade and finally to the historic agreement, the August Accords. The Solidarity movement was the first independent trade union to be recognized in the Eastern bloc. It eventually paved the way for the first semi-free election in 1989, and finally the toppling of Communist regimes in Poland and throughout Eastern Europe. The exhibition also acquaints you with Lech Wałęsa, the key figure behind Solidarity who went on to be the President of Poland and winner of the Nobel Peace Prize in 1983.

Wały Piastowskie 24. © **058/308-47-12.** www.fcs.org.pl. Admission 6 zł ($2.40/£1.35) adults, 4 zł ($1.60/90p) children and seniors, 2 zł (80¢/45p) May–Sept Tues–Sun 10am–5pm; Oct–Apr Tues–Sun 10am–4pm.

ⓂMoments   Chew the Lard

In summer, you'll find makeshift food shacks along the **Motława Canal** waterfront. Join the queues for the torso-padding "open sandwich": A thick slab of country bread the size of two palms, slathered with lard, studded with bits of bacon, and layered with pickled cucumber.

The Royal Route: The Long Street and Long Market (Długa and Długi Targ) ★★ You couldn't ask for a more strikingly beautiful and colorful main street than Długa and Długi Targ, the thoroughfare of the Main Town *(Główne Miasto)*. As you walk its length, from the **Golden Gate** at the western end to the magnificent **Green Gate** at the eastern end, bear in mind that nearly everything you see was rebuilt after World War II. The bas-reliefs and colorful frescos on the burgher houses and gabled town houses will keep your eye darting about. Musicians and street performers are out in force; no sooner is one violinist out of earshot than another string quartet fills the air with Vivaldi's *Four Seasons.* An iconic landmark is the **Neptune Fountain,** for the god of the sea, which dates from 1549. Legend has it that this was the source of Goldwasser, vodka with gold flakes. At the corner is the **Town Hall** (see below). The **Green Gate,** erected in the 1560s, was originally meant to house visiting royalty. Now, it functions as an exhibition space and the office of the former President of Poland and Solidarity leader Lech Wałęsa. Just before the Green Gate is **Artus Court** (see above).

Długa and Długi Targ.

Vantage Points

Gdańsk has stunning bird's-eye views. Aside from the towers in St. Mary's Church and the Town Hall, the **Archaeological Museum** (Mariacka 25/26; ℭ **058/301-50-31**) also has a viewing tower.

St. Mary's Church (Bazylika Mariacka) ★★   This enormous red-brick church is the largest of its kind in the world. Its nave and 31 chapels can hold more than 20,000 people. The church endeared itself to the people of Gdańsk in the years after the imposition of martial law in 1981, when members of the Solidarity trade union took shelter here. The sheer size of the church is just as impressive from the inside as it is from the outside. During World War II, it was severely damaged. Most of the walls were painted over in white, but some frescoes can be found behind the altar. Note the 500-year-old astronomical clock, dating from 1464, an oddity for a medieval Catholic establishment: It not only tells time, but also gives the phases of moon and shows the position of the sun and the moon in relation to the zodiac signs. There is a theatre of figures at the top tier, which rotates at the hour. Also note the series of Ten Commandments paintings: The left sides depict the lives of commandment-abiding believers; the right sides depict the waywards. Climb the 402 steps to the top of the tower for an unparalleled view of Gdańsk.

Podkramarska 5. ℭ **058/301-39-82.** www.bazylikamariacka.pl. Admission 2 zł (80¢/45p) adult, 1 zł (40¢/20p) children and seniors. Viewing tower 4 zł ($1.60/90p) adults, 2 zł (80¢/45p) children and seniors. Mon–Sat 9am–5:30pm, Sun 1–5:30pm.

St. Mary's Street (ul. Mariacka) ★★★   You can easily while away an afternoon on this cobblestone lane, drifting from one amber jewelry boutique to the next, stopping at arts and crafts stands (see "Shopping"), and, in between, resting your feet in any of the enticing cafes while you take in the masonry details of the 17th-century burgher houses. The street was severely damaged in World War II and beautifully reconstructed after the war.

Mariacka.

Town Hall ★★   This is easily one of the country's finest town halls. The original building dates from the 14th century, but it was badly damaged during World War II and what you see today is a meticulous reconstruction. Check out the Red Room (*Sala Czerwona*), which lives up to its name with a blushing color scheme and sumptuous furniture, ornate ceilings, and wall paintings. The centerpiece is a painting entitled *The Glorification of the Unity of Gdańsk with Poland*. For a contrasting experience, walk through the historical museum here, noting the black-and-white photographs of Gdańsk in 1945 and its near total destruction in the war.

Długa 47. ℭ **058/767-91-00.** Admission 8 zł ($3.20) adult, 20 zł ($8/£XX) family; free Tues. May–Sept Tues–Sat 10am–6pm, Sun 11am–6pm, Mon 10am–3pm; closed Mon Oct–Apr.

Westerplatte ★★   World War II began here. On September 1, 1939, the German gunboat *Schleswig-Holstein* first fired on a small garrison of about 180 Polish troops on the Westerplatte Peninsula. The Poles, though severely outnumbered, held out valiantly, repelling 3,000 German soldiers for seven days. The buildings have been left pretty much

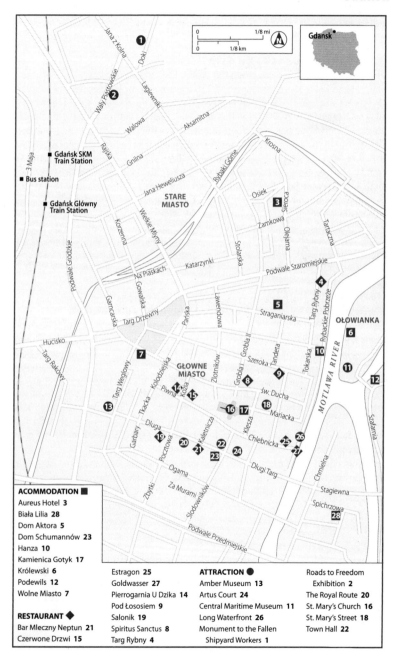

ACOMMODATION ■
Aureus Hotel **3**
Biała Lilia **28**
Dom Aktora **5**
Dom Schumannów **23**
Hanza **10**
Kamienica Gotyk **17**
Królewski **6**
Podewils **12**
Wolne Miasto **7**

RESTAURANT ◆
Bar Mleczny Neptun **21**
Czerwone Drzwi **15**

Estragon **25**
Goldwasser **27**
Pierrogarnia U Dzika **14**
Pod Łososiem **9**
Salonik **19**
Spiritus Sanctus **8**
Targ Rybny **4**

ATTRACTION ●
Amber Museum **13**
Artus Court **24**
Central Maritime Museum **11**
Long Waterfront **26**
Monument to the Fallen
  Shipyard Workers **1**

Roads to Freedom
  Exhibition **2**
The Royal Route **20**
St. Mary's Church **16**
St. Mary's Street **18**
Town Hall **22**

as they were after the battle, and you can walk past the badly damaged guardhouse and barracks. A small museum outlines the events of those first few days of the war.

Sucharskiego 1. ℂ **058/343-69-71**. Museum admission 5 zł ($2/£1.10). May–Oct Tues–Sun 9am–4pm. Bus: 106 or 158 from Okopowa Street by the Main Town wall.

Outside the Gdańsk Old City

Oliwa Cathedral (Katedra Oliwska) ★★ The cathedral's centerpiece is its organ, which has an impressive 7,896 pipes and 110 registers, allowing it the dynamic range to produce rousing renditions of Beethoven's masterpieces, the chirping of birds, the humming of human voices, or the rippling of water. Johann Wuff constructed the organ, which has an oval stained glass in the middle and is flanked by cherubs and trumpet-wielding angels, from 1755 to 1780. At the time, it was the largest instrument of its kind in Europe. The imposing three-nave vaulted basilica started life as a wooden structure in the 12th century. Since its expansion in 1224, it has had its share of fires and plunders through the ages by Prussians, Teutonic knights, the Swedish invasion, and World War II. Time your visit with the free organ concerts. During the 20-minute concerts, the main entrance is closed but you can gain access via the side entrance.

Biskupa Edmunda Nowickiego 5. ℂ **058/552-47-65**. Free admission (donations welcomed). Concerts start on the hour but the timetable changes monthly. In summer 6 performances on weekdays starting at 10am; 4 performances on Saturdays starting at 10am; 3 performances on Sundays starting at 3pm. Mon–Fri 9am–7pm, Sat 9am–3pm, Sun 2–7pm. SKM: Exit at Gdańsk-Oliwa. Tram: 6, 8, and 12.

Outside the Tri-City

Stutthof (Sztutowo) Death Camp ★ Often labeled as the "forgotten camp," Stutthof was the first concentration camp built outside of Germany by the Nazis. Constructed in September 1939, it was also the last camp to be liberated by the Allies in May 1945. Out of the 110,000 Jews and others held here, an estimated 70% were killed by lethal injections, firing squads, hanging, or gas chamber. The barracks and crematoria, the "hospital," the "holocaust stake" (a memorial on the site of an excavated mass grave), and the exhibits in the museum give you an unnervingly vivid and harrowing picture of the atrocious and inhumane conditions the inmates here endured. *Note:* Children aged 13 and under are not admitted. On site, there is a shortage of English information. Guided tours in English cost 140 zł ($56/£31.50) per group (up to 40 people) and must be booked in advance. The tour lasts 1¹/₂ to 2 hours.

Muzealna 6, Sztutowo. ℂ **055/247-83-53**. www.stutthof.pl. Free admission (donations welcomed). May–Sept daily 8am–4pm; Oct–Apr daily 8am–3pm. Stutthof lies 55km (33 miles) to the east of Gdańsk. From the main bus station, buses to Sztutowo (in the direction of Krynica Morska) take 1¹/₂ hours. By car, journey time is an hour.

Customized Tours

Joytrip.pl ★★ (Fieldorfa 11/3; ℂ **058/320-61-69;** www.joytrip.pl) has energetic guides that will take you around the Tri-City on foot, bike, kayak, or any other means of transportation you're interested in. While you bounce on bikes along the cobblestone lanes of the Old City (or off the beaten tracks), the guides pump you full with facts on history, art, and culture. After a short break, they are ready to party with you in bars and clubs. They'll tailor the ride to your fancies, going to Malbork if that's what you have in mind. The cost, naturally, depends on the package. It's roughly 450 zł ($180/£101) for 4 hours and 650 zł ($260/£146) for 8 hours.

Where to Stay

Very Expensive

Hanza ★★   This luxurious, modern, privately owned hotel right along the river promenade boasts an impressive roster of actors and politicians on its list of distinguished guests. The understated, contemporary look in the lobby and the public areas extends to the comfortable rooms, finished in shades of brown. Be sure to ask for a room with a view over the canal and yacht harbor. Breakfast is in a sunny room overlooking the canal. One big perk: It's one of the few hotels in the center to offer a full-service spa and sauna, and their masseurs are well reputed in the city.

Tokarska 6. ⓒ **058/305-34-27.** Fax 058/305-33-86. www.hotelhanza.pl. 60 units. 445 zł–665 zł ($178–$226/£100–£150) single; 495 zł–695 zł ($198–$278/£111–£156) double; 685 zł–885 zł ($274–$354/£154–£199) junior suite. Rates include breakfast. Extra person 95 zł ($38/£21) in season; 75 zł ($30/£19) off season. AE, MC, V. Free parking. **Amenities:** Restaurant; bar; conference room; dry cleaning; limited room service; concierge; gym; Jacuzzi; sauna; beauty salon; massage and facial; nonsmoking rooms. *In room:* A/C, TV, dataport, complimentary Wi-Fi (in suites), hair dryer, bathroom scale.

Podewils ★★   This relatively small, old-fashioned villa across the river from the town center is widely billed as the city's finest hotel, though for less money you'll get more amenities at the Hanza and a better view of the Królewski. The Podewils's location will be much improved once the apartment buildings under construction next door are finished. Be sure to ask for a city view, not one that looks out onto the building site. That said, each room is meticulously decorated with fine antiques, and the professional staff will see to your every whim. Don't pass up the chance to have a meal or a glass of wine on the terrace overlooking the canal and the Old Town.

Szafarnia 2. ⓒ **058/300-95-60.** Fax 058/300-95-70. www.podewils.pl. 10 units. Apr–Oct 659 zł–720 zł ($264–$288/£148–£163) single; 806 zł–889 zł ($322–$355/£181–£200) double. Nov–Mar 529 zł–580 zł ($212–$232/£119–£131) single; 655 zł–709 zł ($262–$284/£147–£160) double. 1,771 zł–2,588 zł ($708–$1,035/£399–£582) suite. Rates include breakfast. AE, DC, MC, V. Free parking. **Amenities:** Restaurant; 24-hr room service; dry cleaning; laundry service; tour booking; currency exchange; umbrella; DVD movie library; Turkish and Finnish sauna. *In room:* A/C, TV, dataport, complimentary Wi-Fi, minibar, hair dryer, safe, showers w/hydro massage, twice-daily room cleaning.

Expensive

Aureus Hotel ★   Tucked away from the buzz in the Old Town but still a stone's throw from the attractions, this 5-story hotel is made up of two adjoining structures: an 18th-century town house and a newer building. The exposed brick walls show off the building's origins. The plush rooms are modern yet homey, employing a combination of light blonde and dark woods. You can hear St. Bridget's church bells tolling. That, plus its proximity to the old Gdańsk post office, adds to your sense of being right in the heart of history.

Sieroca 3. ⓒ **058/326-07-50.** Fax 058/326-07-51. www.hotelaureus.pl. 32 units. Apr–Sept 370 zł ($148/£83) single; 410 zł ($164/£92) double. Oct–Mar 310 zł ($124/£70) single; 340 zł ($136/£77) double. Rates include breakfast. AE, DC, MC, V. Free parking. **Amenities:** Restaurant; conference room; limited room service; tour booking; dry cleaning; babysitting. *In room:* TV, dataport, hair dryer, safe.

Królewski ★★★   This sleek, modern hotel is in a tastefully remodeled former granary just across the canal from Gdańsk's town center. If you can get it, ask for room no. 310, a corner double with drop-dead stunning views of the riverside and all of Gdańsk's spires and gables. All the rooms are tastefully modern, some with hardwood floors and bathtubs. The restaurant and breakfast room look out over the river through a round little window like you're on a cruise. It's a truly memorable place. If you're not staying here, pop by for the Sunday lunch (50 zł/$20/£11).

Ołowianka 1. ℂ **058/326-11-11.** Fax 058/326-11-10. www.hotelkrolewski.pl. 30 units. May–Oct 20 370 zł ($148/£84) single; 440 zł–480 zł ($176–$192/£99–£108) double; 600 zł–800 zł ($240–$320/£135–£180) suite; Jan–Apr 4 and Oct 21–Dec 300 zł ($120/£68) single; 360 zł–400 zł ($144–$160/£81–£90) double; 520 zł–660 zł ($208–$264/£117–£149) suite. Weekends off season 250 zł ($100/£56) single; 295 zł–355 zł ($118–$142/£66–£80) double; 460 zł–580 zł ($184–$232/£104–£131) suite. Rates include breakfast. Extra person 70 zł ($28/£16). Children 5–12 35 zł ($14/£8). AE, DC, MC, V. Free unguarded parking. Guarded parking 10 zł ($4/£2.30). **Amenities:** Restaurant; bar; dry cleaning; limited room service; tour booking. *In room:* TV, complimentary Wi-Fi, minibar, hair dryer.

Wolne Miasto ★   The beautiful antique reception desk sets the tone at this well-run, attractively appointed hotel, popular with business travelers. The decor has a restrained traditional look, and the rooms, named after Gdańsk's streets, are fitted out with maroon carpets, champagne-gold wallpaper, and antique wardrobes. Black and white pictures of the Old City decorate the walls, while quality fixtures complete the bathroom. The hotel's **Zeppelin** restaurant gets good reviews for its *cepeliny* (Lithuanian potato dish).

Św. Ducha 2. ℂ **058/322-24-42.** Fax 058/322-24-47. www.hotelwm.pl. 43 units. Mar–Oct 360 zł ($144/£81) single; 410 zł ($164/£92) double; 500 zł ($200/£113) deluxe double. Nov–Feb 300 zł ($120/£68) single; 350 zł ($140/£79) double; 400 zł ($160/£90) deluxe double. Rates include breakfast. Extra person 50 zł ($20/£11.30). Reduced weekend rates. Children under 3 stay free in parent's room. AE, DC, MC, V. Limited public parking. **Amenities:** Restaurant; bar; limited room service; dry cleaning; solarium; massage room; conference room; tour booking. *In room:* TV, dataport, minibar and kettle (in deluxe rooms), complimentary Wi-Fi, safe.

Moderate

Biała Lilia ★★   Somewhere between a small hotel and a pension, the property offers excellent value given the crisp modern furnishings and the in-town location, just across the bridge from the Green Gate and the delights of Długa Street. After so many sterile contemporary rooms, it's refreshing to see one that actually looks inviting. On the second floor, there is a unique garden terrace at the back.

Spichrzowa 16. ℂ **058/301-70-74.** Fax 058-320-14-73. www.bialalilia.pl. 16 units. May–Sept 260 zł–280 zł ($104–$112/£59–£63) single; 320 zł–340 zł ($128–$136/£72–£77) double; 420 zł ($168/£95) studio w/ kitchenette. Oct–Apr 220 zł–240 zł ($88–$96/£50–£54) single; 290 zł–310 zł ($116–$124/£65–£70) double; 380 zł ($152/£86) studio w/kitchenette. Rates include breakfast. Extra person 60 zł ($24/£13.50). AE, DC, MC, V. Parking 20 zł ($8/£4.50). **Amenities:** Restaurant. *In room:* TV, dataport, minibar.

Dom Aktora   Located in the Old Town and a short walk to the Motława Canal, this warm and homey setup has rooms and apartments in different shapes and sizes. The fixtures in the bedrooms, kitchens, and bathrooms are basic but clean and in a charming way are reminiscent of humble abodes during the Communist period. The rooms have fridges and the apartments, which can take 2 to 4 occupants, come with fully equipped kitchens. Proximity to a nearby farmers' market makes Dom Aktora a good self-catering option. A helpful English-speaking manager mans the front desk.

Straganiarska 55/56. ℂ **058/301-59-01.** www.domaktora.pl. 12 units. May–Sept 250 zł ($100/£56) single; 340 zł ($136/£77) double; 410 zł–540 zł ($164–$216/£92–£122) apt. Mar–Apr and Oct–Nov 200 zł ($80/£45) single; 260 zł ($104/£59) double; 345 zł–490 zł ($138–$196/£78–£110) apt. Dec to Feb 170 zł ($68/£38) single; 200 zł ($80/£45) double; 270 zł–380 zł ($108–$152/£61–£86) apt. Rates include breakfast. AE, MC, V. Free parking. **Amenities:** Lounge. *In room:* TV, radio, fan, kettle, fridge, kitchen (in apt), complimentary Wi-Fi.

Dom Schumannów ★ Perched above the main tourist information office on Długi Targ, the rooms here are right in the heart of the Royal Route. For a view of the thoroughfare, however, you've got to put up with the high decibels. The quarters facing the courtyard in the back are quiet and cozy. The small rooms provide just enough space to stretch, but are definitely atmospheric with period furniture, velvet cushions, and bright, puffy bed covers. The shower rooms are new and clean. *Note:* there are no elevators, and some rooms are without curtains.

Długa 45. 𝄯 **058/301-52-72.** Fax 058/301-91-51. www.domschumannow.pl. May–Sept 220 zł ($88/£50) single; 250 zł–280 zł ($100–$112/£56–£63) double; 310 zł–495 zł ($124–$198/£70–£111) suite. Oct–Apr 180 zł ($72/£41) single; 230 zł–250 zł ($92–$100/£52–£56) double; 290 zł–410 zł ($116–$164/£65–£92) suite. Rates include breakfast. AE, DC, MC, V. Guarded parking (5-minute walk) 30 zł ($12/£6.80). **Amenities:** Breakfast room. *In room:* TV, kettle, dataport.

Kamienica Gotyk ★★★ (Value) Ordinarily you'd part with a fortune for the location in Gdańsk's oldest house (1541) and on its loveliest street, so get organized and book early at this petite B&B. The facade is crenellated and the stone stairs are flanked by original Gothic portals. Gothic details continue indoors, where arched doorframes usher you into the small but brightly furnished rooms. The windows are thoughtfully equipped with blackout blinds. You'll like the stone-engraved mirror frames in the bathrooms. Breakfast on the petite patio in the shadows of St. Mary's church adds to the sense of history.

Mariacka 1. 𝄯 **058/301-85-67.** www.gotykhouse.eu. 5 units. May–Sept 280 zł ($112/£63) single; 310 zł ($124/£70) double. Oct–Dec 220 zł ($88/£50) single; 250 zł ($100/£56) double. Jan–Apr 190 zł ($76/£43) single; 220 zł ($88/£50) double. Rates include breakfast. Extra person 80 zł ($32/£18). Children 4 and under stay free in parent's room. Children 5 and above 50 zł ($20/£11). MC, V. Public parking 14 zł ($5.60/£3.20). **Amenities:** Breakfast room; laundry service; kettle. *In room:* TV, complimentary Wi-Fi.

Inexpensive

Angela ★★ It's quieter than it looks here, since the pension is perched with its back away from the busy suburban street. The back of the house is a lovely garden setting. Angela is a very clean and well-run pension; the rooms are basic, but a good value in Gdańsk's overpriced hotel market. Take a cab on arrival to find the place; once you've checked in and gotten situated the receptionist can help you with the buses in and out of the center.

Beethovena 12. 𝄯 **058/302-23-15.** Fax 058/326-07-78. www.villaangela.pl. 18 units. July 225 zł ($90/£51) single; 280 zł ($112/£63) double; 295 zł–350 zł ($118–$140/£66–£79) suite. Aug–mid-Sept 250 zł ($100/£56) single; 310 zł double ($124/£70); 295 zł–350 zł ($118–$140/£66–£79) suite. Mid-Sept–Apr 165 zł ($66/£37) single; 195 zł ($78/£44) double; 240 zł–280 zł ($96–$112/£54–£63) suite. Rates include breakfast. Extra person 50 zł ($20/£11). Children 5 and under stay free in parent's room. AE, DC, MC, V. Free parking. *In room:* TV.

Where to Dine

Most of the places in the Główne Miasto, though in a touristy zone, offer good value and quality food; you don't have to stray far from Długa Street for a satisfying meal. But if you prefer to wander from the Główne Miasto, there are great finds there, too.

Very Expensive

Pod Łososiem EUROPEAN Every city in Poland has an establishment with a track record of feeding and watering visiting royalties and dignitaries: Pod Łososiem is Gdańsk's. It boasts an impressive string of VIPs on the "Been Here and Dined Here" list.

Expect renditions of high-end European fare served in a grandiose baroque-style dining room. It is reportedly the original source of the Goldwasser Vodka, so round out your meal with a shot of the gold flakes–imbued liquor. There are also reports that the food is overrated, but you get the satisfaction of dining in the same place where a pope, prime minister, president, and princess once broke bread.

Szeroka 52–54. ✆ 058/301-76-52. www.podlososiem.com.pl. Main courses 55 zł–95 zł ($22–$38/£12.40–£21.40). AE, DC, MC, V. Daily noon–11pm.

Restauracja Villa Uphagena ★★ POLISH   Located in the suburbs of Wrzeszcz, this grand manor house is for special occasions. The high-ceilinged, opulent rooms drip with chandeliers and are lavished with period furniture and tables decked out with whiter-than-white linen. There are five dining rooms; for a party of two the Crystal Room and the Orangery are the coziest. Start off with steak tartare—or, if you've had *barszcz* (beet soup) elsewhere and wondered what the fuss is about, try it here. The wild boar roulade is tender and flavorful. Top it off with the walnut meringue.

Jana Uphagena 23, Gdańsk Wrzeszcz. ✆ 058/345-83-72. www.villauphagena.pl. Main courses 36 zł–73 zł ($14.40–$29.20/£8.10–£16.40). AE, DC, MC, V. Daily noon–11pm.

Salonik ★ POLISH   This elegant upmarket "salon" is just down the street from the Neptune Fountain on ul. Długa. The sign out front labels this a "Polish" restaurant, but we're not talking about *pierogi* and potato pancakes here. Instead, think more along the lines of pork with porcine mushrooms, or pike fillet with spinach and leeks. The mood at lunch is less formal and the street-side terrace makes for a very memorable midday meal. In the evenings, you'll want to dress up to blend in with the posh surroundings. The bow-tied waiters are a cheerful and competent lot.

Długa 18/21. ✆ **058/322-00-44.** www.restauracjasalonik.pl. Main courses 52 zł–77 zł ($20.80–$30.80/£11.70–£17.30). AE, MC, V. Daily noon–midnight.

Expensive

Goldwasser ★★ INTERNATIONAL   A local institution and well worth a splurge as much for the food as for the unbeatable riverside location. Slip into one of the dining booths, either sunken below or elevated above the floor level in this brazenly embellished scarlet space. Get the bow-tied, black-aproned waiters to bring you an aperitif of Goldwasser (10 zł/$4/£2.30), a slightly sweet vodka imbued with, among other things, flakes of real gold. Everything gets the thumbs up, but the fresh fish dishes come highly recommended, as do the house-made *pierogi*. The excellent service leaves the guests in high spirits. In summer, sit out on the terrace. In winter, warm yourself up in the cozy tavern-like surroundings.

Długie Pobrzeże 6. ✆ **058/301-88-78.** www.goldwasser.pl. Main courses 24 zł–68 zł ($9.60–$27.20/£5.40–£15.30). MC, V. Daily 10am–10pm.

Spiritus Sanctus ★★ CENTRAL EUROPEAN   An outstanding wine bar showing that less on the menu is more. Reflecting the practices of organic and slow food ideology, items on the one-page menu are subject to change based on seasonal produce and the kitchen's whims. So today it could be Bulgarian cold soup made from natural yoghurt, cream, and nuts; and then braised lamb a few days later. What are perennial are the excellent cheeses, including *ser bursztynowy* (amber cheese), cold meat platters, and house-made country bread. These are great for communal eating, since you'll want to try a bit of everything. Leave it to the staff to choose your wine from the stash of Bulgarian, Moldavian, and Georgian bottles. However, if you order by the glass, you might end up with only Spanish to choose from. The dining room resembles the classy den of a compulsive art collector, so you'll have plenty of arty fodder for discussion.

Grobla I/13 (at the crossing with Św Ducha). ℭ **058/320-70-19.** www.spiritus-sanctus.pl. Cheese and cold cuts platter 40 zł ($16/£9). Main courses 60 zł($24/£13.50). Wine from 12 zł ($4.80/£2.70) per glass. AE, DC, MC, V. Reservations recommended. Daily 3–10pm.

Moderate
Restauracja Targ Rybny ★ SEAFOOD   The name means fish market, and it's one of the best places for fish in town, both grilled and fried. It's located in the northern end of Motława Canal walkway with a good view of the granary building that houses Hotel Królewski. Inside, it's homey lightwood furniture and tables covered with blue checkered cloths. Many of the dishes have an Italian touch; recommended dishes include the grilled salmon and the whitefish *pierogi*. In summer, sit on the terrace overlooking the square called—appropriately enough—Fish Market. In winter, enjoy the cozy fireplace and jazzy tunes.

Targ Rybny 6C. ℭ **059/320-90-11.** www.targrybny.pl. Main courses 20 zł–90 zł ($8–$36/£4.50–£20.30). MC, V. Daily 11am–11pm.

Czerwone Drzwi ★ INTERNATIONAL   Its concise menu consistently wins praise from the locals. Behind the red door (as the name translates), you'll find an inviting compact, chimney-like space filled with eclectic antiques. The orange walls are plastered with an equally mishmash selection of paintings. There's the traditional pasta and *pierogi*, but the excellent veal with Gorgonzola sauce and mini dumplings best represents the strong suits of the house. End your meal with *pascha,* a supremely sweet dessert made from farmer's cheese and lots of raisins.

Piwna 52/53. ℭ **058/301-57-63.** www.reddoor.gd.pl. Main courses 18 zł–65 zł ($7.20–$26/£4.10–£14.60). AE, MC, V. Daily noon–midnight.

Estragon ★ (Kids) INTERNATIONAL   Located in an old town house off Długa, this eatery combines high-quality international dishes with a stylish yet unpretentious atmosphere. It's also child-friendly, offering kiddy specials such as fish fingers, chicken cutlets, and pancakes with cheese filling. The grown-ups' menu is strong on "new Continental" cuisine of steaks, pork cutlets, and stuffed chicken breast. The chicken stuffed with spinach is delicious and a lighter alternative to heavy Polish cooking. Vegetarians will welcome the soy burger. The down-to-earth presentation is reminiscent of something you might see in downtown New York, and the cook serves up a reasonable and recommendable facsimile of a New York–style cheesecake.

Chlebnicka 26. ℭ **058/309-17-00.** www.estragon.pl. Main courses 19 zł–49 zł ($7.60–$19.60/£4.30–£11). MC, V. Daily 11am–10pm.

Pierogarnia U Dzika ★★ POLISH   *Pierogarnia* are restaurants specializing in *pierogi*. Once dismissed as dowdy, they're now all the rage as you no doubt have noticed. This one, centrally located, is better than most and a good place to sample the ubiquitous doughy dumplings and, naturally, a glass of beer to wash them down. The interior is 1980s–90s Polish chic, with taxidermy to justify the "Dzik" (wild boar) in the name. The menu includes both the usual fillings, like ground beef and cabbage, plus a few inventive variants including *pierogi* "Wileński"—a rarity these days—padded with buckwheat and bacon. Servings are 10 pieces per plate, enough for a full meal and then some.

Piwna 59/60. ℭ **058/305-26-76.** www.pierogarniaudzika.com. Main courses 18 zł–52 zł ($7.20–$20.80/£4.10–£11.70). AE, MC, V. Daily 11am–11pm.

GDAŃSK & THE BALTIC COAST

Bar Mleczny Neptun (Value POLISH If you haven't checked off the "milk bar" experience yet, here's a decent one to try out. There are few budget eateries that are as brightly lit by natural light as this one or located at as prestigious an address: the upstairs seating comes with a view of the Royal Route. Decide on what you want before you join the queue—it moves faster than you think. When it's your turn, choose your main course, sides, and sauces, collect the food, and then pay. When in doubt, go for *kotlet schabowy* (meat cutlet; but take care, some are embedded with splinters of bone), *pierogi,* or *bigos* (hunter's stew). Food is sold out pretty quickly to students and retirees, so get there around noon to have the best selection.

Długa 33/34. ✆ **058/301-49-88.** Meat dishes 5 zł–7 zł ($2–$2.80/£1.10–£1.60), sides 2 zł–5 zł (80¢–$2/45p–£1.10). No credit cards. Mon–Fri 7:30am–7pm; Sat 10am–6pm; June–Sept Sun 10am–6pm.

Shopping

For centuries, the center of the Baltic amber trade was Gdańsk, and it's still *the* place to get amber accessories and other amber crafts. You'll find no shortage of amber dealers in town. The biggest concentration is on the main street of **Długa,** and along the prettier but just as crowded **Mariacka.** While the majority of the dealers are reputable, amber fakes abound, so it's caveat emptor. The Amber Museum is a good place to learn how to detect the real McCoy. If you haven't time for the museum, the **Millennium Gallery** (Długi Targ 25/27; ✆ **058/307-59-59**) has several outlets along the Motława Canal where you can get a quick demo on recognizing the genuine article. (*Note:* Real amber floats in salt water, while the fakes simply sink.) **Galeria S&A** (Mariacka 36; ✆ **058/305-22-80;** www.s-a.pl) is one of three shops on Mariacka Street with a certification from *Societas Svccinorvm in Polonia* (the International Amber Association).

Another 100% Gdańsk take-away is **Goldwasser Vodka.** While the sweetish taste is not everyone's glass of tipple, who could pass up flakes of gold in their cocktail? You can buy a gift box at the Goldwasser restaurant (see "Where to Dine"). **Kashubian folk art** (Kashubian is an ethnic minority group) in the form of embroidered linen is also a unique regional gift. You'll find them on Mariacka Street. **Benedicte** (Garbary 5; no phone; www.benedicite.pl) is good for tea, honey, and fruit preserves made by Benedictine monks in Poland and other Central European countries. Head to **CiuCiu Cukier Artist** (Powroźnicza 19/20; ✆ **058/301-24-11**; www.ciuciu.pl) for cutesy boiled sugar

---

Get "Stoned"

After a tour of the Amber Museum you'll know amber is not just for dressing up, but did you know that you could drink it too? Steeping fruits, nuts, and spices in vodka to make *nalewka* is a very homey Polish pastime. But even for *nalewka*-savvy Poles, immersing amber granules in vodka comes as a novelty. Don't go dunking your funky pendants into alcohol; you need the unpolished pebbles. You can find them in stalls along the Motława Canal or Mariacka Street. **Brama Mariacka** (Mariacka 25/26; ✆ **0668/163-303**) sells them in packets or bottles at 7 zł ($2.80/£1.60). Add 50g of amber into 0.5 liter of pure vodka and leave in a dark place for 10 days for the resin to dissolve. It's reportedly good as a rub on temples to alleviate headaches. Or add to tea as a warmer on chilly days.

in all shapes, colors, and designs. It's a treat for both kids and adults to watch "sugar artists" wielding molten syrup into edible crafts.

After Dark
The Performing Arts
Most of the serious culture here revolves around two venues: the **Fryderyk Chopin Baltic Philharmonic** (Ołowianka 1; © **058/320-62-62;** www.filharmonia.gda.pl) and the **State Baltic Opera** (al. Zwycięstwa 15; © **058/763-49-12;** www.operabaltycka.pl). The Philharmonic's main home base is the stunningly restored site right across the Motława canal in the center of the Old City. You can buy tickets at the Motława box office (© **058/320-62-52)** or at the performance venue up to 4 hours before the show. The Opera maintains a lively program in season, with visiting and local companies. You can buy tickets online or at the box office during office hours, Tuesday to Friday from noon to 7pm and Saturday from 2 to 7pm. Gdańsk's **Miniatura Theater** (Grunwaldzka 16; © **058/341-12-09;** www.miniatura.prv.pl) maintains a lively and excellent repertoire of puppet shows and fairytales aimed at children, but shows are almost exclusively in Polish.

Cafes, Pubs & Clubs
Most night owls make a beeline for Sopot after sunset, but the nightlife in Gdańsk isn't lackluster, especially in the recent years. It's worked (and partied) hard in shedding its image as a venue suitable only for teens and students.

Café Absinthe Fun and highly recommended bar where the emphasis is definitely on drinking, though not necessarily absinthe. It's all DJs and dancing-on-tables from Thursday to Saturday. Św Ducha 2. © **058/320-37-84.** www.cafeabsinthe.pl.

La Dolce Vita Café Absinthe's crowds often migrate to its sibling, a club cum lounge bar, where live concerts and dancing can be found. Chlebnicka 2; © **058/304-78-87.**

Ksantypa One of the most popular clubs in town for techno, trance, drum and bass, or whatever happens to be on the DJ's mind that night. It attracts a young crowd who come mainly for the booze and the beat. Piastówska 210. © **058/553-14-59.**

---

2 SOPOT & GDYNIA

Sopot and Gdynia are the duo that make up the other two cities of the Tri-City area. Neither can outmatch Gdańsk's historical sites, but each has its own distinct appeal.

Sopot's blend of small-town charm and cosmopolitan chic give it a special spot in the hearts of Poles. The century-old villas embellished with turrets and crowned with cupolas contribute to a beguiling, fairytale-like atmosphere. In 1823, Jean Georges Haffner, a doctor in Napoleon's army, introduced the idea of reaping the health benefits of sea-bathing in the waters of Sopot, and subsequently elevated the town into a fashionable seaside resort of the moneyed classes. This was the kind of place where in order to properly summer you had to be somebody. During the Communist period the resort lost some of its sheen; the idea of decadent seaside frolicking didn't chime with the reigning ideological aesthetic. Since 1989, however, Sopot has mounted a comeback, cashing in on its former glamour while affirming its identity as Poland's top summer party town. During the day, its waterfront attracts sun, sea, and sand lovers. After dark, party animals flock to the most happening clubs in the Tri-City. In July and August, the visitor density surges up; late spring and early autumn are the best time to enjoy Sopot without jostling for hotel rooms or beach space.

While Sopot has obvious appeal, Gdynia, the most northerly of the Tri-City group, is often skipped by tourists. You, too, could do the same unless you have time to spare. It is a concrete mass that started life as a quiet fishing village. In the early 20th century, the Treaty of Versailles created the Free City of Gdańsk and thrust Gdynia into the newly reformed Polish State. It became Poland's access point to the sea and, in May 1921, the development started to convert it into a modern port. Today, it is a port city with all the trappings of a seaside town.

ESSENTIALS
Getting There
Sopot and Gdynia share the same transport network as Gdańsk. See "Gdańsk: Getting There and Getting Around," above.

Visitor Information
The **Sopot Tourist Office** (Dworcowa 4; ℂ 058/550-37-83; www.sopot.pl) is opposite the train station. From June to September, it's open daily from 9am to 8pm. The rest of the year, it's open daily from 10am to 6pm. The attentive staff can help you with booking rooms and hand out complimentary maps. As for Gdynia, from May to September the handiest place to go is the **Baltic Point of Tourist Information** (Molo Południowe, Gdynia; ℂ 058/620-77-11; www.gydnia.pl), located at the eastern tip of Skwer Kościuszki. It's open weekdays from 9am to 6pm, on Saturday from 10am to 5pm, and on Sunday from 10am to 4pm. If you're arriving by SKM, pop by the tourist information booth at the railway station for a map.

TOP ATTRACTIONS
Sopot
Life centers on the pedestrian **Bohaterów Monte Cassino Street** (nicknamed "Monciak"), the main axis of trendy cafes, clubs, and restaurants. You'll see the much-photographed **Crooked House** (Bohaterów Monte Cassino 53; ℂ 058/555-51-23), though it's not much to write home about. At the end of Monciak, you'll come to a 5km (3-mile) stretch of sandy beach and the **Pier (Molo)** ★★. Built in 1928, and stretching 515m (0.3 miles) into the Gulf of Gdańsk, it is the longest wooden pier along the Baltic coast. Strolling on the Pier is a Sopot *de rigueur*, and a certifiable must-do for the romantically inclined. In summer, you'll find opera singers crooning tunes from Sopot's heyday in the 1930s and old-timer sailors selling tickets for peeping into binoculars. To the north of

---

(Moments) **Catch of the Day**

Fish lovers, make your way to **Przystań Rybacka w Sopocie** (Wojska Polskiego 7, Sopot), next to Bar Przystań, on the beach. At about 8am, from Monday to Saturday, fishermen return from the sea with their freshly caught haul. Join the early birds to buy the best of the Baltic Sea and then cajole your hotel kitchen into cooking it up for your lunch. In the same building, throughout the day from 8am to 6pm, there's flavor-packed smoked fish from Hel Peninsula for take-aways.

the beach is another stunning landmark of Sopot: the **Grand Hotel** (see "Where to Stay"). Once you have had enough of the sun and sand, you can escape to the greens and shades of the hilly **Opera Park (Opera Leśna)** (Moniuszki 12). The annual **International Sopot Festival** (www.sopotfestival.onet.pl) has been held here every August for the last four decades.

Gdynia

Most of the tourist attractions are by the **Southern Pier (Molo Południowe)** waterfront. The destroyer *Błyskawica* ★ (☎ **058/626-36-58**) is moored here and a must-see for fans of maritime history. Upon news of imminent invasion by the Germans in 1939, the vessel was dispatched to join the Allied naval forces. Retired from active service, it became the only Polish ship to receive the Golden Cross of Military Virtue in 1987. Chirpy, uniformed mariners conduct you through the engine rooms and the on-board museum. The tour is in Polish, but English information booklets are available for sale at the ticket booth. A quick tour of the ship will take about 30 minutes, but you might spend more time queuing, as this is a popular attraction. On the opposite side of the Southern Pier is the **Oceanographic Museum & Aquarium (Muzeum Oceanograficzne i Akwarium)** (Kids) (Al. Zjednoczenia 1; ☎ **058/621-70-21**; www.akwarium.gdynia. pl). A state-of-the-art facility it is not, but it has some rare specimens such as Chinese water dragons and snapping turtles to make a less-than-an-hour visit enjoyable.

Outdoor Activities
In & Around the Tri-City

BEACHES   Come fair weather, and the beaches and waters of Sopot and Gdynia are inundated by throngs of sun worshippers. Both locations have changing rooms and shower facilities. **Gdańsk-Orłowo** has a beach and a pier that's smaller than Sopot's, but still quite charming. Volleyball courts are found here as well. But if you've got a day to spare and the sun is shining, why not go for something a little more remote? The sandy stretches of the **Hel Peninsula** (see p. 247) make a fun and relaxing change of pace.

BANANA BOATS   On the pier in Sopot, youth sporting the vests of the **Water Taxi Company** (☎ **502/334-534**) will entice you to strap on a lifejacket and get bounced about in a motor boat on the Gulf of Gdańsk. The rides are 15 to 20 minutes in duration and will set you back 20 zł ($8/£4.50).

CATAMARAN & WINDSURFING   The **Sopot Sailing Club** (Hestii 3; ☎ **058/555-72-00**; www.skz.sopot.pl) is about a 20-minute walk from the Pier. The club houses a few facilities. For windsurfing equipment rentals, the **Sopot Surf Centrum** (☎ **0692/074-827**; www.ssc.com.pl) hires out the complete set of equipment for 30 zł ($12/£6.80) per hour. They also offer individual and group lessons. **Navigo** (☎ **0503/114-384**; www. katamaran.sopot.pl), located in the third hangar on the left side of the entrance, is where the catamaran people are. Call ahead; the site can be deserted when the crew is out on the waters conducting the courses. If you're here for the watersports, the **guest rooms at the Sopot Sailing Club (Hotel-Pokoje Gościnne Sopocki Klub Żeglarski)** ★ (Value) (Bitwy Pod Płowcami 67; ☎ **058/555-72-03**; www.skz.sopot.pl) are clean and spacious and equipped with basic kitchenettes. Some rooms can take up to 8 people. Prices are 150 zł ($60/£33.80) for single rooms and 220 zł ($88/£50) for double rooms.

CYCLING   An easy and tranquil 10km (6-mile) bike lane skirts the beaches from Sopot to the northern Gdańsk suburbs. Bikes for hire can be found at **Rowerownia** (Bitwy Pod

11

Płowcami 39; ☎ **058/551-11-76**), and in summer outside Zhong Hua Restaurant on Al. Wojska Polskiego to the south of the Pier.

DEEP-SEA FISHING At the price of 500 zł ($200/£113) per hour, the **Water Taxi Company**—the same folks doing the banana boat tumbles—can take up to seven people angling in the Gdańsk Bay. Call two days in advance to book.

DIVING **Ticada Centrum Nurkowania** (Chwaszczyńska 70, Gdynia; ☎ **058/629-48-46;** www.ticada.pl) offers diving excursions to more than 10 shipwrecks in the Bay of Gdańsk. Excursions are from 50 zł ($20/£11.30).

GOLF There are several golfing facilities in and around the Tri-City. The handiest is **Golf Park Gdynia** (Spółdzielcza 1, Gdynia; ☎ **058/721-24-24;** www.golfparkgdynia. pl), an outdoor driving range that also has an indoor simulator. Robert (☎ **0606/366-000**), the golf instructor, speaks English. Farther afield, as you head north of the Tri-City and then turn west at Reda, you'll come to the **Sierra Golf Club** (Pętkowice, Wejherowo; ☎ **058/778-49-00;** www.sierragolf.pl). The greens fee for the 18-hole course is 175 zł ($70/£40) on weekdays, and 250 zł ($100£56) on weekends and holidays. The club is only 52km (31 miles) from Gdańsk, but should you wish to stay overnight accommodation can be found at the nearby **Hotel Wieniawa** (Lipowa 24, Rekowo Górne; ☎ **058/673-92-80;** www.hotelwieniawa.com). The **Postołowo Golf Club** (Postołowo, Ełganowo; ☎ **058/683-71-00;** www.golf.com.pl), 26km (16 miles) south of Gdańsk, is a spectacular 18-hole golf course. Expect to negotiate waters along the very challenging courses, nestled in the midst of the greenery of the Kashubian Lakeland. The club is open year-round daily from 8am to sunset. Non-members pay a greens fee (18 holes) of 230 zł ($92/£52) on weekdays and 280 zł ($112/£63) on weekends and public holidays. Taxis from Gdańsk cost about 120 zł ($48/£27).

Where to Stay

Sopot has a range of choice accommodation. Even if you're spending most of the day in Gdańsk, stay here if you want to be close to the beach and clubs. Gdynia, on the other hand, is short on well-located good lodgings. Some hotels ratchet up the prices during the Sopot Festival. The **Sheraton Hotel** (Powstańców Warszawy 10; ☎ **058/767-10-00;** www.sheraton.pl) has recently opened its doors in Sopot. Its location is superb, right by the pier and with the Grand Hotel as its neighbor.

Sopot

Grand Hotel Sopot by Sofitel ★★ Built in 1927, this stunning seafront hotel with a neo-Baroque façade is one of the most instantly recognizable landmarks in the country. Check into a sea-facing room for a definitive taste of Sopot high life and a taste of where the Polish rich and famous play. The building was spruced up in 2006, but it retains many of its original fixtures. Orchids adorn the sleek and modern rooms with fish-bone parquet floors. The black and yellow checkered tile in the bathroom exudes a 1960s look. The sea view doesn't leave your sight as you flex your muscles in the high-tech gym or splash in the indoor pool. In the French garden, the sea breeze caresses you while the vested staff is at your beck and call, ferrying you nibbles and cocktails.

Powstańców Warszawy 12/14. ☎ **058/520-60-00.** Fax 058/ 520-60-69. www.sofitel.pl. 127 units. June–Oct 630 zł–720 zł ($252–$288/£142–£162) single; 828 zł–918 zł ($331–$367/£186–£207) double; 1,260 zł–1,404 zł ($504–$562/£384–£316) suite w/park view; 1,800 zł ($720/£405) suite w/sea view. Jan–Mar and Nov–Dec 486 zł–576 zł ($194–$230/£109–£130) single and double; 900 zł–1,116 zł ($360–$446/£203–£251) suite w/park view; 1,296 zł ($518/£292) suite w/sea view. Breakfast 79 zł ($ 31.60/£17.80). AE, DC,

MC, V. Parking 60 zł ($24/£13.50). **Amenities:** Restaurant; 24-hour room service; concierge; conference room; dry cleaning; baby-sitting; gym; sauna (dry and steam); Jacuzzi; indoor pool w/water massage; massage; Wi-Fi; bicycle rental. *In room:* TV, dataport, minibar, kettle, hair dryer, iron, safe, umbrella.

Villa Sedan ★★★ This is one of the hotels locals like recommending to visitors, both for its beautiful rooms as well as for the excellent reputation of the competent staff. So if you can get a room here, take it. Commanding an enviable locale on a side of Monciak, the building is a typical example of early 20th-century villas in Sopot. The interior takes you back to Sopot's heyday. The cast-iron framed beds are topped with the most inviting bedspreads, while the wooden floorboards add to the coziness. The variety and abundance of fruits in the buffet will delight those jaded by routine hotel breakfasts. Regulars give double thumbs-up to the French cuisine at its restaurant. Savor the halibut laced with mushroom sauce or the pork sirloin while a musician tinkles away (on Friday and Saturday) on an exquisite antique upright piano.

Pułaskiego 18–20. ✆ **058/555-09-80.** Fax 058/551-06-17. www.sedan.pl. 21 units. June–Aug 300 zł ($120/£68) single; 380 zł ($152/£86) double; suite 480 zł ($192/£108); Sept–May 260 zł ($104/£59) single; 320 zł ($128/£72) double; suite 390 zł ($156/£88); weekends 10% discount. Rates include breakfast. Extra person 70 zł–80 zł ($28–$32/£16–£18). Children 5 and under stay free in parent's room. Children 6–12 40 zł ($16/£9). AE, DC, MC, V. Free parking. **Amenities:** Restaurant; bar; concierge; tour booking; laundry service; dry cleaning; gym and pool (2km/1 mile from hotel). *In room:* TV, complimentary Wi-Fi.

Willa Zacisze (Value) A new and excellent self-catering option in a restored town house located within a quick dash to the beach. The interior has refreshingly light-colored walls and mahogany-brown floors. You sleep on modern roll-out sofa beds. The cleanliness and staff friendliness are outstanding for accommodations in this price bracket. So, not surprisingly, rooms are booked out months ahead.

ul. Grunwaldzka 22A. ✆ **058/551-78-68.** Fax 058/551-78-68. zacisze.sopot@wp.pl. June 30–Sept 4 and Dec 30–Jan 1 240 zł ($96/£54) double. Sept 4–Sept 30 150 zł ($60/£34) single; 180 zł ($72/£41) double. Oct 1–Dec 29 and Jan 2–May 130 zł ($52/£29) single; 150 zł ($60/£34) double. Extra person 30 zł ($12/£6.80). MC, V. Free parking. *In room:* TV, kitchenette, kettle, plates, electric stove, pots, radio, CD and cassette player, complimentary Wi-Fi.

Where to Dine
Sopot

Bar Przystań ★★ FISH A veteran on the beachfront, this fish-fry is neither posh nor ramshackle. Join the queue at "Receiving Order" to place your order and choose from an array of freshly caught items ranging from eel to shark to tuna; there's also pickled and marinated fish galore. You will be issued a number—when your number is up, pay and collect some plastic utensils along with your catch served up on a cardboard plate. Besides beer, there are Italian and Chilean reds and whites. The wait can be agonizingly long on busy days.

Wojska Polskiego 11. ✆ **058/555-06-61.** www.barprzystan.pl. Fish 4 zł–8 zł ($1.60–$3.20/90p–£1.80) per 100g. AE, DC, MC, V. Daily 11am–11pm.

Cyrano et Roxane ★ (Finds) FRENCH Head west on Monciak from the pier; as you come up from the railway underpass, you'll suddenly slip into a less congested terrain and this lovely wine bar cum bistro. The short menu has mushroom quiche, liver and plum salad, and *moussur* (pork) slices marinated in a whole herb garden. The owners, a French husband and Polish wife team, are more than happy to talk *terroir*. They have 50 different labels from the South of France regions such as Bergerac and Bordeaux. Conversations are intermittently drowned out by the rumblings of trains chugging by.

Bohaterów Monte Cassino 11. ✆ **660/759-594**. Main courses 23 zł–33 zł ($9.20–$13.20/£5.20–£7.40), wine 7 zł–14 zł ($2.80–$5.60/£1.60–£3.15) per glass. MC, V. Daily noon–midnight.

Dobra Kuchnia ⓥ Value ⓕ Finds POLISH   It's a delightfully local experience in this students' hideout squirreled away around the corner from the tourist information office. Located on the first floor of a town house, it's unpretentious but arty. The hearty nourishment here is the kind of food Polish grannies used to make, such as *gołąbki* (meat-filled stuffed cabbage), roast chicken thighs, and beef roulade.

Jagiełły 6/1. ✆ **0696/451-969**. www.dobrakuchnia.prv.pl. Main courses 12 zł–21 zł ($4.80–$8.40/£2.70–£4.70). No credit cards. Daily 10am–8pm.

Rucola ★★ EUROPEAN   Stashed in the basement of the Museum of Sopot, Rucola is a charming place favored by locals for semi-formal meals. The interior resembles the den of a compulsive souvenir collector, plastered with tapestries, wood carvings, and bric-a-brac from India, Peru, Mexico, and elsewhere. The food is somewhat eclectic, too: anything from mussels to lentil soup. On a warm afternoon it's great to enjoy a coffee in the garden by the shadows of the lovely villa that houses the museum.

Poniatowskiego 8. ✆ **058/551-57-22**. Main courses 15 zł–48 zł ($6–$19.20). Daily 1–10pm.

After Dark in Sopot
Cafes & Pubs

Come Friday and Saturday nights, most of the cafes, pubs, and clubs on Bohaterów Monte Cassino Street keep their doors open till dawn. There's a velvet rope in some clubs, so be sure to gloss up and come with a clubbing attitude to get past the doormen.

Kawiarnia u Hrabiego ★ ⓕ Finds   A short march uphill on a side street of Monciak takes you to this petite and quaint 18th-century manor house of a countess, now converted into a dainty cafe and a site for ad hoc classical music recitals. The cloistered back garden is a great place to huddle for coffee, tea, mead, and sweets. Czyżewskiego 12. ✆ **058/550-19-91**.

Café Ferber ★   Considered a snobby spot by some, this is where flashy locals and visitors rub elbows. The interior has great blown-up black-and-white pictures of Sopot's heyday as a seaside resort, while the huge windows let you people-watch the passers-by on the street. Bohaterów Monte Cassino 48. ✆ **058/551-45-81**.

Galeria Kinsky   The house and birthplace of Klaus Kinski, a legendary German actor, is now a bar and restaurant. Posters and movies from the actor's career are on display. The place reflects the chaotic, mad, and wild spirit of Kinski's nature and works. Kościuszki 10. ✆ **058/802-56-38**.

Clubs

Kon-Tiki   A waterfront club north of the Grand Hotel. The crowd here is rated as the most "normal," in the complimentary sense of the word. Al. Mamuszki 21. ✆ **058/555-92-62**.

Mandarynka ★   It's still a much-talked-about name, though some claim it's a shadow of its former self. If you've been clubbing in Warsaw you'll find this place similar to the Cinnamon and the Platinum Club, but a few notches less haughty. Bema 6. ✆ **058/550-45-63**. www.madarynka.pl.

Showing This Summer

From June to the end of summer, **Copacabana Lounge & Summer SPA ★★**
((✆ **0514/161-316**) rigs up its giant marquis on the beach to the south of the
pier. The layout is slightly different every year, but you can expect a restaurant
and cafe, a bar and club with a VIP room, and a swimming pool. It's kind of a seasonal, makeshift beach resort that does everything from breakfast to dinner and
alcohol-laden, all-night dancing. Stargazers will enjoy sharing space with local
celebs and fashionistas.

PapryKA   Thoroughly enjoyable night out at a relatively laid-back bar and nightclub,
where nearly everything—from the leather sofas to the walls—is bathed in warm, red
hues. Great DJs and usually just quiet enough to converse under the music. Grunwaldzka
11. ✆ **058/551-74-76**. www.klubpapryka.pl.

Sefinir ★★   These plush tents are at the end of the pier, meaning it's the most seafront
premises you can find. It comes at a price: 25 zł ($10/£5.60) for a shot of Jack Daniels.
Głowica Sopockiego Molo. ✆ **0798/197-205**.

3 THE HEL PENINSULA

The Hel Peninsula, to the northeast of the Tri-City, is a pencil-thin strip of land that juts out
into the Baltic Sea. This picturesque stretch of windswept, sandy beaches and pine forests is
saturated with local holidaymakers in the summer months. Although the resort villages have
the usual trappings of kitschy amber shops and fish-fry shacks, the peninsula retains a
throwback-to-yesteryear charm. So much so, you can almost see a sepia glazing around you.

Aside from beachcombers, the area also reels in health-conscious vacationers who come
here for its microclimate of salubrious iodine-rich air. It is a place to wind down, but the
peninsula also has a reputation for high-speed pastimes. The Puck Bay is very shallow, making it a natural wading pool for beginner windsurfers; even 200m from the shore, the water
only comes up to your waist. However, daredevils take to these waters too. The winds pick
up enough gusto for old hands to get adrenaline kicks from kite surfing.

From end to end, the peninsula measures 34km (20 miles). At the northwestern tip,
where the strip of land joins (or, rather, leaves) the mainland, is the fishing port of
Władysławowo. And at land's end, so to speak, is Hel, another fishing port. In between
Władysławowo and Hel are the small villages of Kuźnica, Jastarnia, Chałupy, and Jurata.
All of them are tourist hubs. From the Tri-City, Hel is a popular destination for a day of
kicking about in the sand. In summer, if you plan to stay overnight or do any of the
watersports, book at least two months ahead. Off season, the special deals in the spa
hotels are the reason to come.

ESSENTIALS
Getting There
For day-trippers, the sea route to Hel is the most laid-back choice. If you're traveling by train
or bus, you can get off at Władysławowo or any of the resort villages en route to Hel.

BY BOAT **Water trams** *(tramwaj wodny)* (www.ztm.gda.pl/ferry.html) to Hel depart from Gdańsk (Motława Canal), Sopot (at the pier), and Gdynia (Nabrzeże Pomorskie; ☎ **0669/441-202;** www.zkmgdynia.pl). From late June to August, the water tram runs daily. Tickets are sold at the booths near the ferry landing. From Gdańsk it costs 18 zł ($7.20/£4.10), from Sopot it's 12 zł ($4.80/£2.70), and from Gdynia it's 10 zł ($4/£2.30).

BY TRAIN Regular trains to the peninsula leave from the Tri-City's train stations. The journey takes 1$^1/_2$ to 2 hours.

BY BUS There is minibus service from the northern side of Gdynia's bus station. The buses leave when they are filled up.

BY CAR From the Tri-City, take the E28 to Reda. Turn into Rd. 216 and head for Władysławowo. It should take 2 hours to reach Hel. It's an enjoyable drive passing by little towns, but keep in mind that the traffic can be a drag.

Tourist Information

You can find tourist information points along the villages on the peninsula. In Hel, the new **Tourist Information Point** (Wiejska 78; ☎ **058/675-10-10;** www.hel-miasto.pl) is near the ferry landing. From May to September, it operates daily from 10am to 6pm. The English-speaking staff assists with accommodation and updates you on public transportation schedules.

Getting Around

At Hel's train station, electric car operators mill around for customers. Prices are negotiable. Buses and trains run the length of the peninsula. In summer, there are 5 daily buses running from Hel to Władysławowo, costing 7 zł ($2.80/£1.60) one-way. *Note:* The main road can get quite congested around midday.

TOP ATTRACTIONS
Outdoor Activities

BEACHES Parts of the peninsula are so narrow, especially between Chałupy and Kuźnica, you could be caressed by the breeze from the Baltic Sea, then cut through pine woods and be facing Puck Bay on the other shore of the peninsula in just 5 minutes. In all of the villages, you will find signs and pathways leading to beaches.

DEEP-SEA FISHING In the villages, you'll find outfitters taking tourists out for cod fishing in the Baltic Sea. **Marian Wiśniewski** ★ (Kliprów 1, Chłapowo, Władysławowo; ☎ **0604/992-298;** www.neptun.intermedia.net.pl) is a merry, white-bearded sailor who runs such an operation year-round. He charges 150 zł ($60/£34) per person. If you're on your own, he'll slip you in with a group. The vessel leaves Port Władysławowo at 7am and returns 8 to 9 hours later. There's coffee and tea on board, but pack your own sandwiches. Marian doesn't speak English, but there's usually no communication problem once you're sailing away.

WINDSURFING, KITE SURFING & CATAMARAN SAILING Watersports lovers converge on Puck Bay from mid-June to the end of August. **BO Sport** ★★ (Chałupy; ☎ **058/674-37-42;** www.bosport.pl) has weeklong group and individual courses for all levels. For windsurfing and catamarans, course prices range from 590 zł to 940 zł ($236–$376/£133–£212), and include insurance and equipment. They can also rent wetsuits for the duration of the course. The kite-surfing courses come in three levels; individual lessons are 600 zł ($240/£135), and group courses are 400 zł ($160/£90). Although they claim to have English-speaking instructors, the command of the English language really varies from one instructor to another. BO Sport can arrange for accommodation in Arka Hotel in Jastrzebia Góra (10km/6 miles) away, but they don't arrange transportation between Arka and Chałupy. The rates from Sunday afternoon to Saturday evening are 462 zł ($185/£104) per person in a double room, and 360 zł ($144/£81) in a single room. They also rent out equipment if you do not want lessons. **Camp Solar** (Droga Helska, Chałupy; ✆ 058/677-89-67; www.obozy-windsurfingowe.pl) mainly caters to summer windsurfing camps for schoolkids. From May to October, they rent windsurfing gear and catamarans to tourists.

WHERE TO STAY & DINE

Most of the sleeping options here are in pensions and private rooms. These are usually rented out to vacationing families for weeks at a time, and they are unlikely to accept guests for one or two nights only. During the summer, advanced booking is advised. Camping sites also line the beaches. During peak season, some of them resemble congested refugee sites. As for food, there is a surfeit of fish and salad bars.

Chałupy 3 This friendly, beachside campsite, on the side of Puck Bay, is popular with surfers and has a friendly atmosphere. The BO Sport surfing school runs its courses here. You pitch your tent among families and young backpackers. The onsite **Surf Tawerna** eatery serves grilled meats and fish plus some Polish staples and is very popular with campers and day visitors. It has both indoor and alfresco seating. In the evenings, surfers, backpackers, and beachcombers congregate at the tavern to lap up beer and rowdy music.

Pole Namiotowe Nr. 3, Chałupy. ✆ 058/674-12-75. www.chalupy3.pl. 14 zł ($5.60/£3.20) adults; 12 zł ($4.80/£2.70) children 9 and under; 12 zł ($4.80/£2.70) 2-person tent; 13 zł ($5.20/£2.90) larger than 2-person tent. No credit cards. Parking 12 zł ($4.80/£2.70). **Amenities:** Restaurant; showers; toilets; food preparation area; grocery store; hairdresser; watersports equipment rental.

Jantar Hotel (Value) The mere mention of the hotel sends chills down the spine of some folks. This is a true example (as opposed to the mockups in Berlin) of a Communist-era hotel. Today, the complex is a holiday facility for the army, but in these capitalist times it is also open to the public. You'll get a very grassroots experience here. The clean and simple rooms are for double, triple, and quadruple occupancy. The service is, hmm, a cultural adventure. It is, however, a great value and is just steps away from the shore of Puck Bay.

Wojska Polskiego. ✆ 058/675-42-03. Fax 058-675-42-62. www.wzwjantar.pl. 196 units. June and Aug 31–Sept 13 and Dec 19–Jan 2 75 zł–95 zł ($30–$80/£16.90–£21.40) per person. July–Aug 95 zł–115 zł ($38–$46/£21.40–£25.90) per person. Jan 3–Apr 24 50 zł–65 zł ($20–$26/£11.30–£14.60) per person. Apr 25–May 65 zł–85 zł ($26–$34/£14.60–£19.10) per person. Half- and full-board packages available. MC, V. Parking 7 zł ($2.80/£1.60). **Amenities:** Restaurant; sauna; solarium; gym; billiards; tennis courts; parking; kayak rental; playground; BBQ pit; massage. In room: TV, minibar.

Hotel Bryza ★ With the Baltic Sea view and a sandy beach right at the doorstep, this hotel fills up quickly in the summer months. The rooms are adequate but not super modern. For a sea view, it'll cost more. Your alternative is to soak in the pool, which also faces the sea and is especially dreamy after sunset when it's lined with flickering candles. The spa has the whole gamut of body pampering options, from "caviar" facials to Balinese therapies; keep an eye out for off-season spa packages. The Polish cuisine and seafood at the restaurant are highly recommended.

Międzymorze 2, Jurata. ⒸⒷ 058/675-51-00. Fax 058/675-54-80. www.bryza.pl. 90 units. June 29–Aug 760 zł ($304/£171) double; 1,280 zł–2,460 zł ($512–$1,280/£288–£554) suite. May–June 28 and Sept–Oct 504 zł ($202/£113) double; 770 zł–1,470 zł ($308–$588/£173–£331) suite. Nov–Dec 21 and Sept–Mar 330 zł ($132/£74) double; 600 zł–1,470 zł ($240–$588/£135–£331) suite. In-season rates include breakfast and dinner. Off-season rates include breakfast only. Extra person 125 zł ($50/£28). Children under age 6 stay free in parent's room. Children 6–12 50% discount. Reduced rates from Thurs–Sun. AE, DC, MC, V. Free parking. **Amenities:** Restaurant; beach bar (in summer); cafe; billiards room; indoor pool; gym; spa center; tennis court. *In room:* A/C (in suites), TV, complimentary Wi-Fi.

4 ŁEBA & SŁOWIŃSKI NATIONAL PARK

Just two hours to the northwest of the Tri-City is a laid-back world of Polish-style seaside vacationing. Łeba (pronounced "where-ba"), a sleepy, quaint fishing village with miles of sandy beaches, is one of the much-loved Baltic shore sanctuaries valued for its clean air and clear waters. The village is also the entry point to Słowiński National Park, on the UNESCO's list of protected biospheres and famed for its "moving dunes."

Łeba and the sand dunes can be done as a day trip from the Tri-City. Or, like the Poles, you could stay for a night (or 14) for low-key repose by the Baltic Sea. If you only want to visit Słowiński National Park, the PTTK tourist information center in Gdańsk (see Gdańsk) organizes day trips to the park during the summer. The trips are infrequent and the schedule is subject to change depending on demand.

ESSENTIALS
Getting There
From the Tri-City, take the SKM to Lębork. From Lębork, buses run by **Boguś** (Ⓒ **059/862-93-00**) and **Tredetrans** (Ⓒ **059/863-19-09**) leave for Łeba every 15 minutes at 5.50 zł ($2.20/£1.20) per person. They drop you on pl. Dworcowy, just around the corner from the tourist information office. Total journey time is about 2 hours. If you are driving, follow the E28 highway in the direction of Słupsk, bearing right at Lębork. Journey time is about 1¹/₂ hours.

Getting Around
Getting around the village is manageable on foot. To get to Słowiński National Park, it's a 2km (1-mile) walk. There are bikes for rent outside the tourist information office. Bike rental company **Ciułałła** (on a yard opposite Sienkiewicza 4; Ⓒ **0696/042-119**) charges 4 zł ($1.60/90p) per hour. They also have bicycles with child-seats and children's bicycles. From May to September, **EKO-Tour Melex** (Ⓒ **0601/664-183** or 0663-682-608) runs trams to the park entrance, charging 5 zł ($2/£1.10) per person. They speak Polish only, so you might want to get the staff at the tourist information office to call them on your behalf.

Tourist Information
Stowarzyszenie Lokalna Organizacja Turystyczna Łeba (11 Listopada; Ⓒ **059/866-25-65**; www.lotleba.pl) is the local tourist office. In July and August it's open weekdays 8am to 8pm, Saturdays 8am to 6pm, and Sundays 10am to 4pm. Off season, it's open weekdays only from 8am to 4pm. You can get local maps, advice on rooms, and directions to the park here. Pick up the complimentary *Walking Through Łeba* for other attractions if you are spending more time here. Good Web resources for the area include **www.leba.pl** and **www.slowinskipn.pl.**

Getting Away

In summer, there are two to three buses leaving Łeba for Lębork every hour until 8pm. Get the current schedule from the tourist information office or at www.przewozy.info.pl. If you take an early train out of the Tri-City and spend 4 to 5 hours here you will still make the connection back to the Tri-City.

TOP ATTRACTION

Słowiński National Park ★ This remarkable landscape of wetlands and giant sand dunes, butted up against the Baltic Sea, is unique enough to be included on UNESCO's list of protected biospheres. The highlights here are the park's two lakes and the enormous, shifting sand dunes that rise to a height of some 40m (125 ft.).

The park has something for everyone. The protected wetlands make it a great spot for birders. The area is on the spring and autumn migratory paths of a vast number of bird species, making it a paradise for ornithologists keen to see sea eagles, eagle owls, mergansers, and auks. World War II history buffs will be interested to hear how the Nazis used the unique sandy landscape as a training ground for Rommel's Afrika Korps. The Germans also conducted early experiments in rocketry here. About 3.5km (2 miles) from the park entrance is the Rocket Launchpad Museum (Muzeum Wyrzutnia Rakiet), where you'll find an early and eerie-looking launchpad. And, of course, there's the amazing giant dunes themselves, stretching for a length of about 5km (3 miles). The dunes migrate up to 10m (30 ft.) every year. Plodding up the shifting sands with sea wind gusting is somewhat arduous, but you're rewarded with a mind-jolting "I can't be in Poland" vista.

All in all, there's a lot of walking involved, so have good shoes. If you're pressed for time, at the park's entrance there are bikes for rent (10 zł/$4/£2.25 per hour): pedaling will get you to the dunes in about 15 minutes. Those preferring to save foot power for scaling the sand dunes can take the electric-power trolley (15 zł/$6/£4) one-way). If you fast-track your visit you can be done in an hour, but most visitors stay for around 3 hours. It can get blustery even in summer, so bring a light jacket.

✆ **059/811-72-04.** www.slowinskipn.pl. Park admission 4 zł ($1.60/£1.10) adult, 2 zł ($0.80/55p) children and seniors. May–Sept 7am–9pm, Oct–Apr 8am–4pm. Parking 4 zł ($1.60/£1.10) per hour. Rocket Launchpad Museum Apr–Oct admission 14 zł ($5.60/£3.85) adult; 10 zł ($4/£2.75) children and seniors; 28 zł ($11.20/£7.70) family. The park entrance is 2km (1 mile) to the east of Łeba in the hamlet of Rąbka. Leave Łeba via ul. Turystyczna. On foot, it takes 20 minutes. Also see "Getting Around."

Outdoor Activities

DEEP-SEA FISHING Along the canal, numerous boats take visitors out to the Baltic Sea for cod fishing throughout the year. The boats depart at 5am and remain at sea for about 8 hours. **Marcel** (Lzbica 15A; ✆ **0502/481-907;** hotel_golabek@post.pl) has boats that hold 8 to 24 people, with a minimum group size as few as 2. The price per person is 120

Fun Facts Desert Shootings

Słowiński National Park has had its fair share of exposure to "lights, camera, action." Whenever a desert scene in Polish films was called for, the park often got the role. One of the most prominent movies shot in the park was *Pharaoh* (1966), a film set in Egypt and based on a novel by Polish writer Bolesław Prus. *Pharaoh* went on to garner an Oscar nomination for Best Foreign Film.

zł to 150 zł ($48–$60/£27–£34). Fishing equipment is provided. Your nourishment on board, naturally, is the catch of the day. Advanced booking is required. The English-speaking staff at Hotel Gołąbek (see "Where to Stay") can assist with the booking.

RIDING INTO THE SUNSET   If you've ever dreamed of horseback riding into the sunset on a Baltic Sea beach, here's your chance to live the fantasy. On the sandy shores of Łeba, the stables at **Gospodarstwo i Stadnina Koni Maciukiewicz** ★★ (Finds (Św Huberta 4, Nowęcin; © 059/866-18-74; www.nowecin.com.pl) organize rides that leave for the beach—about 4km (2.5 miles) away—each evening at 6 or 7pm. Once at the shore, you gallop away with cool wind in your hair and the sound of hooves thudding on the sand in your ears, feeling the steeds' glee as they chase the receding waves. Call a day in advance to book. The warm and friendly proprietors speak Polish, Russian, and German. The price for this dream is 44 zł ($17.60/£9.90) per hour. Time spent on the beach is usually 2 hours, but you can trot on longer. In season (late June to August), the minimum group size is 4; off season, it can be as few as 2. Wear comfortable riding pants and boots; the stable provides helmets. You should be at least proficient in trotting; they will give you a test ride at the stable to gauge your level of horsemanship. The stables are 3km (1.5 miles) to the south of Łeba. By car from Łeba, take Nowęcińska Street until you reach Hotel Soplica (Jeziorna 2, Nowęcin). The stables are behind the hotel. If you are traveling by public transportation, in season, there are taxis in Łeba or call **EKO-Tour Melex** (see "Getting Around"). Off season, with prior notice, the staff from the stables can pick you up from Łeba. If you're looking to stay overnight, they have four good value-priced standard rooms, at 50 zł ($20/£11.30) per person.

WHERE TO STAY & DINE

Łeba is a resort town, so there are plenty of guest rooms *(pokoje gościnne)* and camping sites. **Camping Leśny No. 51** (Brzozowa 16A; © 059/866-28-11; www.camping51.pti.pl) is open from mid-April to mid-October. It also has double and triple en suite rooms. **Pod Zegarem** (Kościuszki 92; © 059/866-24-49; www.podzegarem.pl) on the main street of Łeba has good basic rooms, with amenities such as restaurant, sauna, and solarium. A similar but slightly more expensive option is **Hotel** Gołąbek (Wybrzeże 10; © 059/866-21-75; www.hotel-golabek.leb.pl), located along the canal. *Note:* Most places will collect a "climate" tax of about 2 zł (80¢/45p) per person per day. For food, you'll find a multitude of fish and pizza eateries, delis, and bakeries on the canal embankment and along the main streets of Kościuszki and Nadmorska.

Hotel Neptun ★★   For some, this century-old villa on the shore of the Baltic Sea is a destination in itself. The building fell into disrepair after World War II; it's only in recent years that restoration work reinstated the *belle époque* ambience. Be sure to ask for a room with a sea view. Beyond the French windows, you'll see wind-twisted pine trees and seagulls gliding past. All rooms are in plush, modern classical style, each in a different color scheme. Rooms in the corner turrets are especially charming. It's worth splashing out on the suites for the additional space. The restaurant does Polish cuisine, and the house specialty is a traditional roast duck with apples and cranberry sauce. Attended by attentive but unobtrusive staff, you dine with an ocean view. In the morning, you'll wake up to the symphony of winds and waves. It's great for a romantic getaway or a restful break with the family.

Sosnowa 1. © 059/866-14-32. Fax 059/866-23-57. www.neptunhotel.pl. 32 units. June and Sept–Oct 395 zł ($158/£89) single; 470 zł ($188/£106) double; 650 zł–690 zł ($260–$276/£146–£155) suite. July-Aug 620 zł ($248/£140), 810 zł–850 zł ($324–$340/£182–£191) double; 1,080 zł–1,470 zł ($1,432–$588/£243–£331) suite. Jan–mid-Mar and Oct–Jan 2 355 zł ($142/£80) single; 395 zł ($158/£89) double;

570 zł ($228/£128) suite. April–May 365 zł ($146/£82) single; 420 zł ($168/£95) double; 615 zł–690 zł ($246–$276/£138–£155) suite. July–Aug rates include breakfast and dinner; other rates include breakfast only. Extra person 200 zł ($80/£45) July–Aug; 110 zł–150 zł ($44–$60/£25–£34) off season. Children 3 and under stay free in parent's room. AE, DC, MC, V. Free parking. From Kościuszki, after passing the canal turn right into Nad Ujściem followed by a left into Wojska Polskiego Street. The street turns right to Nadmorska Street. The first left on Nadmorska Street is Sosnowa Street. **Amenities:** Restaurant; bar; club; beauty salon; sauna; free bicycle rental; deck chairs; billiards; direct beach access; playground; outdoor pool; tennis court. *In room:* TV, minibar, hair dryer, safe, Wi-Fi.

5 MALBORK

Malbork's *piece de resistance* is the jaw-dropping Teutonic knights castle, the biggest brick-built castle in the world and a UNESCO World Heritage Site. The castle will effortlessly convert anyone into a devout fan of knights and Gothic grandeur. Malbork is only an hour's drive from Gdańsk, so it works perfectly as a day trip. Summer is the busiest period, but Malbork Castle makes an atmospheric sojourn into the medieval epoch at any time of the year.

ESSENTIAL INFORMATION
Getting There
Malbork is about 60km (36 miles) south of Gdańsk and 316km (190 miles) north of Warsaw.

BY TRAIN   Malbork lies on the main Gdańsk–Warsaw rail line. Departures from both cities are frequent. The trains arrive on Dworcowa Street, which is about a 15-minute walk from the castle. Taxis to the castle cost around 10 zł ($4/£2.30).

BY CAR   From Gdańsk, drive south along the E75 highway. Figure on about 45 minutes. From Warsaw, take the E77 and exit to Rd. 22 for Malbork. Journey time is about 4¹/₂ hours. There is paid parking on Piastowska Street, near the castle.

BY TAXI   From Gdańsk, a taxi ride costs about 250 zł ($100/£56) depending on traffic conditions. You can use **City Taxi Plus (*✆* 058/9686)**.

Tourist Information
The **Malbork Welcome Center** (Kościuszki 54; ✆ **055/647-47-47;** www.visitmalbork. pl) is open weekdays from 9am to 5pm and weekends from 11am to 3pm. If all you need is a map, any hotel will be able to give you one. In Gdańsk you can get the *Gdańsk, In Your Pocket* guide, which has a section on the minor attractions in Malbork.

TOP ATTRACTION
Malbork Castle ★★★   If you have time for only one medieval castle, then this is it. Following the knights' defeat in the early 15th century, the castle fell to the Polish kings, who used it as an occasional residence. After the Polish partition at the end of the 18th century, the Prussians took over Malbork and the castle, turning it into a military barracks. German control lasted until the end of World War II, when heavy fighting between Germans and Russians destroyed the town and left the castle in ruins. What you see today is the result of a long and steady restoration process that was completed only about a decade ago.

Moments Sundowner

Hop on the footbridge to get to the opposite riverbank from the castle to catch the day's end. The stunning vista of the sun setting over Malbork Castle coupled with the inkblot reflections on the River Nogat is an indelible memory.

Allow 2 hours or more to give the brick and masonry complex at least a cursory once-over. History aside, the architectural details—from trefoils to cinquefoils, friezes, gables, and arches—are all very arresting. It's breathtaking, also in the literal sense, to lose your-self in the corridors and spiral staircases. You enter the castle via a wooden drawbridge that takes you into the courtyard of the Middle Castle *(Zamek Średni)*. The building to your left houses an impressive amber collection and medieval weaponry. Another draw-bridge takes you to the High Castle *(Zamek Wysoki)*. Here you'll find the knights' dormi-tory, kitchen, and refectory. The castle's main square tower gives you a grand view of the complex. Do budget time for rambling along the river to view the castle from the exte-rior. The tickets come with a Polish guide, but you can wander off on your own. In July and August, there are three English-speaking tours a day (45 zł/$18/£10.10 per person). The museum is sometimes closed for special events, so call or check their website before heading out.

Starościńska 1. ✆ **055/647-09-78.** www.zamek.malbork.pl. Admission 30 zł ($12/£6.80) adults, 20 zł ($8/£4.50) children and seniors; family and group tickets available. Tower admission 6 zł ($2.40/£1.40) adults, 4 zł ($1.60/90p) children and seniors. Jul–Aug guided tour in English 11am, 1:30pm, 3:30pm; 195 zł ($78/£44) per group of 40. AE, DC, MC, V. Mid-Apr–mid-Sept Tues–Sun 9am–7pm; Apr 1–Apr 14 and Sept 16–Sept 30 daily 10am–5pm; Oct–Mar 31 Tues–Sun 10am–3pm.

Outside Malbork

If you're bitten by the Gothic bug, you won't want to miss out on the 14th-century castle and cathedral in **Kwidzyn**. The complex, featuring original interiors, now houses the **Kwidzyn Museum** ★ (Katedralna 1; ✆ **055/646-37-80;** www.zamek.malbork.pl). Kwidzyn can be an outing from Gdańsk or Malbork. Located 40km (24 miles) to the south of Malbork, it is served by regular buses and trains from Gdańsk and Malbork. Journey time is 45 minutes from Malbork and 2 hours from Gdańsk. If you're traveling by car, it's possible to squeeze Malbork and Kwidzyn into one day.

WHERE TO STAY & DINE

Along the river, there are plenty of eateries doling out in-season fish and Polish staples. **Kawiarnia Niucka** (Kościuszki 5; ✆ **055/273-48-36**) is a bakery stashed inside a shop-ping center. Locals endorse the sweet breads. It's open from 7:30am Monday to Saturday, so it's great for the morning caffeine fix. Another good source of sweet bread is on the steep Starościńska lane leading to the castle. Here you'll find a no-frills booth sporting a *Świeże Pączki* (fresh donuts) board. It opens early on Sunday, too.

Grot Hotel ★★ A spanking-new hotel built in 2007 and located just off Kościuszki Street, it's a 10-minute walk from the castle. The rooms have pinstriped champagne-colored wallpaper, fresh carpets, a minimalistic design, and spotless bathrooms. Choose a room facing the back street; the other side looks out to the busy Road no. 22. Kościuszki is a shopping street, so you'll have delis, restaurants, and ATMs close at hand.

Its city-modern restaurant has reasonably priced Continental fare such as mussels in saffron and white wine sauce.

Kościuszki 22D. ✆ **055/646-96-60.** Fax 055/646-96-70. www.grotohotel.pl. 18 units. Mid-May–mid-Sept 199 zł ($80/£45) single; 289 zł ($116/£65) double. Off season 179 zł ($72/£40) single; 259 zł ($104/£58) double. Rates include breakfast. Extra person 70 zł ($28/£15.80). Children 3 and under stay free in parent's room. Charge for smoking rooms 25 zł ($10/£5.60). AE, MC, V. Basement parking 20 zł ($8/£4.50). **Amenities:** Restaurant; bar; conference room; limited room service; laundry service; Internet terminal. *In room:* TV, hair dryer, complimentary Wi-Fi.

Hotel Zamek   Housed in a heritage building that was the Teutonic knights' former hospital, it's as near to the castle as you can get. It used to be the grandest shelter in town, but the old-fashioned brown sofas and heavy velvet curtains cast a somewhat ominous ambience (perfect, though, if you're after the brooding medieval mood). The rooms have small granary windows and either look out to the river or the car park. Beds are decked out with spotless sheets, and the marble-tiled bathroom is well scrubbed. In the hotel's **Restauracja Zamkowa** the Middle Ages theme reigns on. On chunky rectangular tables, you'll feast on good Polish soups and other usual suspects, while the formidable speakers blare out very un-medieval pop rock.

Starościńska 14. ✆ **055/272-33-67.** www.hotelprodus.pl. 42 units. May 16–Sept 16 259 zł ($104/£58) single; 310 zł ($124/£70) double. Apr–mid-May and Sept 16–Oct 216 zł ($86/£49) single; 259 zł ($104/£58) double. Nov–Mar 155 zł ($62/£35) single; 216 zł ($86/£49) double. Rates include breakfast. Extra person 72 zł–94 zł ($29–$38/£16–£21). AE, MC, V. Parking 15 zł ($6–£4). **Amenities:** Restaurant; bar; limited room service; laundry service. *In room:* TV, radio, dataport.

Gothic Café & Restaurant ★ INTERNATIONAL   Tucked below the amber exhibition hall of the castle is a breath of cosmopolitan cuisine not found elsewhere in Malbork. The compact menu, whipped up by an ebullient New York–trained chef, features a refreshing sea bass flavored with miso and black truffle and comes with *yuzu* sauce and fresh fruit (55 zł/$22/£15). If you feel like living it up, crunch on icy Russian Astrakhan

Knight Raiders

The Teutonic Order of the Hospital of St. Mary was founded in 1190 as a brotherhood to serve the sick. These warrior-monks took arms in the Crusades, fighting in the Holy Lands. However, upon sustaining a string of military defeats, they were forced to retreat to Europe. In 1226, Polish Duke Konrad of Mazovia enlisted the knights to subdue pagan Prussians in the West. Around 1276, the knights began construction of the Malbork Castle and named it Marienburg (the Fortress of Mary). The knights were ruthless and highly disciplined, and eventually came to rival the Polish kings for control over the vital Baltic Sea trade, including the amber trade. A century later, in 1410, Poles, along with Lithuanians and troops of other lands, joined forces to defeat the religious warriors at the epic Battle of Grünwald (also referred to as the "Battle of Tannenberg" in history books). This marked the beginning of the end of the knights' dominion in northwestern Poland. In 1457, King Kazimierz Jagiełło forced the knights to abandon the Malbork Castle and dispatched them to East Prussia. Today, the Teutonic Order still exists, but they are devoted to the wholly—and holy—peaceful endeavors of running schools and hospitals.

caviar (250 zł/$100/£70). Be sure to round out your meal with apple *racuchy* (fried yeast dough) or a hot apple pie with vanilla ice cream. Also bearing a U.S. accent are the soft chocolate-chip cookies. Those missing English-language press can pop in for the *Financial Times* or *Bon Appétit* magazine. In the mornings, they do good eggy items. To dine here without buying a ticket to the castle, call the restaurant and the staff will come to the entrance to let you through.

Starościńska 1. ✆ **055/783-464-828.** www.gothic.com.pl. Main courses 10 zł–55 zł ($10–$22/£2.30–£12.40). No credit cards. May–Nov daily 9am–8pm. Off-season daily 10am–5pm.

6 ELBLĄG

Elbląg is the starting (or finishing, depending on the direction of your travel) point of a one-of-its-kind canal in Europe: its only counterpart in the world is the Morris Canal in New Jersey. Boat trips on the Elbląg–Ostróda Canal can be described as a calm float coupled with a San Francisco cable-car ride through lush nature, most of which is conservation area. The canal, an engineering marvel, has been singled out by Poles as one of the nation's Seven Wonders, alongside Kraków's Wawel Castle.

Founded in 1246 by the Teutonic knights (see "Malbork"), Elbląg itself is a humble affair. Though the Old Town has been skillfully restored where the post-war houses blend harmoniously with the gables of burgher buildings, Elbląg is another example of Polish towns whose architectural gems were lost in World War II. Elbląg's proximity to Gdańsk makes it a good access point to the canal. In addition, the most interesting stretch is the first half of the canal, from Elbląg to Małdyty. Once you've had enough of pounding Gdańsk's cobblestone lanes, a leisure-boat ride on the canal is a welcome rest for weary feet.

ESSENTIALS
Getting There
BY CAR   From Gdańsk, take Road no. 77 followed by Road no. 22 into the Old Town. There's parking right by the Old Town on Rycerska Street. Within the Old Town, if you're early enough, there's parking around the church on Mostowa Street.

BY BUS OR TRAIN   The bus and train station are next to each other to the southwest of the Old Town. Regular PKS buses run from Gdańsk and take about 90 minutes. Similarly, there are regular trains from Gdańsk that take about 75 minutes. To get to the Old Town, tram nos. 1, 2, and 4 drop you off at the crossing of pl. Słowiński and 1 Maja, at the edge of the Old Town.

Visitor Information
There is a **tourist information point** (Brama Targowa; ✆ **055/611-08-20;** www.ielblag.pl) in the Market Gate in the north of the Old Town. From May to September, it's open daily from 10am to 6pm. Off season, it's open weekdays only from 10am to 4pm. If all you need is information about boat rides on the canal, the operator of the leisure boats, **Żegluga Ostródzko-Elbląska** (Wieżowa 14; ✆ **055/232-43-07;** www.zegluga.elblag.com.pl), is located in the Old Town.

TOP ATTRACTION
Elbląg-Ostróda Canal (Kanał Ostrodzko-Elblaski) ★   Have your binoculars ready as you sit back for a sedate boat ride through showpieces of nature and engineering.

Water-and-Railway

Built in 1884 under the commission of Prussian authorities, the Elbląg–Ostróda Canal was intended as a transportation channel for timber from the southern Ostróda region to the Baltic coast. As the terrain was too steep for traditional water locks, in 1836 Prussian engineer Georg Jakob Steenke came up with the design of incorporating slipways to negotiate the 100m difference in water level along the 82km (49-mile) canal. At the slipways, boats are mounted on steel trolleys and dragged up on rails to dry land, sometimes as steep as 45 degrees (this is where the San Francisco cable-car sensation comes in). The design was still deemed costly; Steenke had to lobby hard before the plan was accepted. It took more than 30 years to complete the project. The canal from Elbląg to Małdyty has all five slipways. Farther south, from Miłomłyn to Ostróda, two water locks were deployed. With the exception of short intervals, the canal has been in operation since 1860. It no longer serves the timber industry and is used solely for recreational purposes.

11

You'll journey through woods, swamps, and marshland where cormorants, grebes, gulls, graylag geese, and the occasional eagle wing by. You'll be stirred from your serene stupor when the boat reaches a slipway. A metal crate rises up from the water and scoops up the boat onto rail tracks on grassy slopes. Mind the weather forecast, since the best vantage points are from the deck seats. The booth seats below deck give you a "water-level" perspective. Bring your own snacks or buy from the nothing-to-write-home-about bistro on board. *Note:* This slow and easy journey is mainly about the peace and tranquillity of watching flora and fauna. While this appeals to adults, it could drive active kids 'round the bend—in other words, it's not really suitable for young children.

The boats, run by **Żegluga Ostródzko-Elbląska** (see "Visitor Information"), operate from May to September. At 8am, the boats depart from both Elbląg and Ostróda. The journey, from one end to the other, lasts 11 hours. If you're pressed for time, do the 5-hour Elbląg-Buczyniec ride, which covers the most interesting parts in terms of slipways. You must call at least a day in advance to book your tickets. At 7:30am on the day of the trip, pick up your tickets from a van on Bulwar Zygmunta. *Note:* Cash payment only. On busy days, as many as three boats, each with a capacity of 65 passengers, depart from Elbląg. When there are fewer than 20 passengers, the trip is cancelled. Although the canal is a major tourist attraction, the infrastructure for delivering passengers back to their starting points is spotty. If you are relying on public transportation, the best option is to take the trip to Małdyty. Boats arrive here at 2:30pm; a 2:54pm train gets you back to Elbląg in 30 minutes. The Małdyty's train station is near the boat landing, but it's an uphill pant to the station. The boat company organizes buses from Buczyniec to Elbląg on an ad hoc basis; call a day or two earlier to find out if this service is on. Yet another option is to take the Buczyniec-Elbląg return boat journey. The risk here is the seats may be fully taken up by passengers coming from Ostróda.

Boarding at Bulwar Zygmunta. May–Sept Elbląg–Buczyniec (8am–12:50pm) 70 zł ($28/£15.80) adult, 50 zł ($20/£11.30) children and seniors; Elbląg–Małdyty (8am–2:30pm) 75 zł ($30/£16.90) adult, 55 zł ($22/£12.40) children and seniors; Elbląg–Ostróda (8am–7pm) 85 zł ($34/£19.10) adult, 65 zł ($26/£14.60) children and seniors.

Hotel Pod Lwem (Kowalska 10; ℂ 055/641-31-00; hotelpodlwem.pl), a fine looking restored brick town house in the Old Town, is in the same price bracket as Elzam Gromada (see below), but the rooms are in contemporary style. The Old Town has plenty of informal eateries. **Restauracja pod Kogutem** ★ (Wigilijna 8/9; ℂ 055/641-28-82; www.podkogutem.elblag.pl) is a small country-style eatery with fairly priced and dependable Polish mainstays. More upmarket is **Kuchnia Wędrowca** (Wigilijna 12; ℂ 055/611-00-22; www.kuchniawedrowca.pl), but it has inexpensive lunchtime specials. Early birds can flock to **Piekarnia Raszczyk** (1 Maja 2), a bakery that also dispenses coffee and tea. It opens at 7am from Monday to Saturday, and 9am on Sunday.

Elzam Gromada   Conveniently located just outside the Old Town, the clean but plain rooms here have grey furniture and sparkling bathrooms. The hotel is a typical leftover of official hotels from the Communist era. What isn't typical is the updated at-your-service attitude from a staff that has a reasonably good command of English. The **Rattonowa** restaurant, so called after its rattan chairs, offers European cuisine in another "throwback to Communism" experience.

Pl. Słowiański 2. ℂ 055/230-61-91. Fax 055/232-40-83. www.gromada.elblag.pl. 112 units. May–Sept 250 zł ($100/£56) single; 300 zł ($120/£68) double. Off-season 210 zł ($84/£47) single; 260 zł ($104/£59) double. Rates include breakfast. Extra person 50 zł ($20/£11). AE, MC, V. Unguarded parking 25 zł ($10/£5.60). **Amenities:** 2 restaurants; bar; club; limited room service; gym; solarium; massage; sauna; 4 rooms for those w/limited mobility. *In room:* A/C, TV, radio.

Pensjonat Boss ★   This efficiently run pension is in the Old Town and around the corner from the boarding point for the canal boats, a major draw for the large number of German-speaking guests. The town house was renovated and adapted into a hotel in 1996. Expect rooms with light-colored walls, brown furniture, clean bathrooms, and a friendly English-speaking crew. **Pensjonat M.F.** (Św Ducha 26; ℂ 055/641-26-10; www.pensjonatmf.pl), a similar operation, is a few doors away.

Św Ducha 30. ℂ 055/239-37-29. Fax 055/239-37-28. www.pensjonatboss.pl. 13 units. May–Aug 160 zł ($64/£36) single; 230 zł ($92/£52) double; 300 zł ($120/£68) apt. Off season 150 zł ($60/£34) single; 210 zł ($84/£47) double; 300 zł ($120/£68) apt. Rates include breakfast. Extra person 50 zł ($20/£11). Children 3 and under stay free in parent's room. AE, DC, MC, V. **Amenities:** Bar; cafe. *In room:* TV, radio, kettle, complimentary Wi-Fi.

12

Northeast Poland

Retreating glaciers sculpted this "land of a thousand lakes," leaving behind lakes and islets, rivers, undulating meadows, woodlands, and rocky valleys in the Mazurian and Suwałki lake districts. This playground in nature is popular with vacationers looking to blend sailing, kayaking, and cycling with idyllic, rustic living. Nature buffs will love it here. The forests shelter a rich array of wildlife, from elks, wolves, beavers, and otters to birdlife such as cranes and owls. Turn a corner and you might lock eyes with a marsh harrier or catch a glimpse of a deer stealing a glance at you before vanishing. In spring and summer, you'll see the majestic fly-bys of storks. The top man-made attraction here is the Wolf's Lair, the site of an assassination attempt on Hitler in 1944. Moving east from the Mazury toward Poland's borders with Lithuania and Belarus, Prussian influence gives way to Russian Orthodox churches, eastern wooden architecture, and Belarusian music. To the south of the lakes is the Białowieża Forest, one of the last parcels of primeval forest in Europe

and an area where European bison still roam freely.

Even if rumble and tumble in mud and puddles isn't your thing, the scenic drives, selection of atmospheric shelters, and good, inexpensive regional food still make the Northeast an ideal place to unwind in nature.

In the major lakeside resort towns, room rates are higher due to their proximity to transportation terminals and other amenities. You'll find better value and more atmospheric rooms away from the main hubs. Some pensions and hotels, in addition to having their own fleets of kayaks and bicycles, throw in distractions such as mushroom picking, horseback riding, and day trips to local attractions or even guided tours to Poland's eastern neighbors. It's most convenient to navigate the terrain in a car, but with some planning you can get by with the network of trains and buses. Folks here seem to sense that you've gone out of your way to visit their backyard and are willing to go the extra mile to help you get what you need.

1 THE MAZURIAN LAKE DISTRICT

The Mazurian Lake District is a vast expanse of interconnected waterways that lie to the northeast of Warsaw. Lakes Śniardwy, Mamry, and Niegocin are famed for sailing, while Krutynia River has one of the most scenic lowland kayaking routes in Poland. Several organizers run multi-day sail, bicycle, and paddle (kayak) trips covering much of the region. For aqua adventurers, days can be spent out on lakes and rivers and nights on boats or in simple bunks along the way. Cycling routes are often designed to fit in pit stops at the Wolf's Lair (the site of a 1944 attempt on Hitler's life) and a monastery in Wojnowo. Dotted with resort towns and agro-tourist farms, you can basically set up camp anywhere, depending on your raison d'état.

Giżycko and **Mikołajki,** only 35km (21 miles) apart, are the common entry points to the Mazurian Lake District. The former was founded by Teutonic knights but severely damaged in World War II. In a strategic location on the northern shore of **Lake Niego-cin,** it's the largest sailing center in the Mazurian Lakes, where folks come to hire yachts and load up on supplies. Mikołajki, dubbed the Mazurian Venice, is in the middle of watersports traffic between **Lakes Mamry** and **Śniardwy,** the two biggest lakes in the region. It has a fair share of blinged-out holidaymakers. Both locations have scores of sailing, canoeing, and biking outfitters.

ESSENTIALS
Getting There
Giżycko and **Mikołajki** are about 320km (192 miles) from Warsaw and 280km (168 miles) from Gdańsk. The duo are served by trains (www.pkp.pl) and buses (www.pks.pl). From Warsaw, trains to Giżycko and Mikołajki take about 6 hours. Buses are better options and faster, taking about 5 hours. By car, you leave Warsaw on E77, switching to Road no. 61 in the direction of Ostrołeka, followed by Road no. 63 at Łomża. The journey takes about 4 hours. From Gdańsk, it's also 4 hours on the road. You leave the city on road E77, switching to Road no. 16. At Mrągowo, Road no. 59 goes to Giżycko, while Road no. 16 takes you to Mikołajki.

Visitor Information
Giżycko's tourist information center (Wyzwolenia 2; © 087/428-52-65; www.gizycko. turystyka.pl) is centrally located. July and August it's open weekdays 9am to 6pm and weekends 10am to 4pm. In September it's closed on Sunday. October to April it's open on weekdays only, 8am to 4pm, and in May and June it's also open weekdays 8am to 5pm. The helpful staff speaks English. Aside from maps, you can pick up listings of campsites and hotels, yacht and bicycle rentals, plus suggested cycling and kayaking routes. Guides cost about 150 zł ($60/£33.75) per day, and you need to book in advance. Filling a similar function, but only from May to September, is **Mikołajki's tourist information center** (Pl. Wolności 3, Mikołajki; © 087/421-68-50; www.mikolajki.pl). In July and August it's open daily 9am to 8pm. In May, June, and September it operates from Tuesday through Saturday 9am to 5pm.

The Mazurian Towns & Villages in Brief
Ruciane-Nida, the most southerly sizeable base, is the finishing point of the Krutynia River kayaking route. It is also a central point for cycling trips into the Mazurian Land-scape Park and Piska Forest *(Puszcza Piska).* The most northerly lakeside town is **Węgorzewo.** Most of the villages with historical interests, such as **Kętrzyn, Reszel, Ryn,**

Moments   **Stork Options**

A quarter of the world's white stork population roosts in Poland. Most of the 40,000 pairs have their base in Northeastern Poland. From May to September you'll see stork families in nests perched on lamp posts, chimneys, and pillars, and on the roofs of farm houses, pensions, or run-down heritage buildings. Storks winging by like ancient pterodactyls grace the skies. If you're lucky, you'll see one returning to its nest with a fish or a writhing snake to feed its brood. Come September, as the flock gets set to migrate to Africa, the juveniles take to the air for test flights.

and **Święta Lipka,** are to the west of Giżycko. **Krutyń,** a main village along the **Krutynia River** kayaking route, is 23km (14 miles) to the south of Mikołajki.

Getting Around

BY BUS & CAR Once you're in Giżycko or Mikołajki, you can get around in buses. The bus terminal in Giżycko is to the south of the center. In Mikołajki, the bus station is next to the Protestant church on the west side of the town center. A fairly extensive network of roads crisscrosses the area. Some of the roads can be a squeeze when a milk tanker or harvester gets in the way.

BY TAXI For short trips, taxis can be a solution. The average taxi rate is about 2 zł–2.50 zł (80¢–$1/45p–56p) per km. If you take a taxi out of town, you pay the fare for the empty taxi returning to its base. **Radio Taxi 9621** (© **0800/109-621;** www.radiotaxi-gizycko.com) operates from Giżycko.

BY FERRY From mid-April to October, ferries run by **Żegluga Mazurska** (Wojska Polskiego 8; © **087/428-53-32;** www.zeglugamazurska.com.pl) glide to Ruciane-Nida in the south and Węgorzewo in the north. These boats are a means of transportation as well as enjoyable cruises to nowhere-and-back. On some routes, the boats have canteens serving breakfast and warm meals. Get timetables at the tourist information offices, or read them off the boards at the departure jetties. A 3-hour round trip from Giżycko to Mikołajki on Lake Śniardwy costs 46 zł ($18.40/£10.35). In Giżycko, the departure point is on **Kolejowa 9** (✆ 087/428-25-78), which is right by the canal's embankment. In Mikołajki, it's on **3 Maja** (✆ 087/421-61-02), the embankment on the east side of the town.

EXPLORING THE AREA

Most visitors are here to enjoy nature and rural living while dabbling in sailing, fishing, kayaking, or cycling. There are cultural and historical attractions, but, truth be told, with the exception of the Wolf's Lair (see below) not many would travel some 300km (180 miles) just to see the minor Teutonic knights and Prussian castles or Baroque churches. Having said that, however, if you incorporate these minor attractions along with outdoor activities, or string them together as part of a drive in the countryside, they complement each other well as cultural interludes. If you are spending more time here, get a copy of *Across the Land of Great Masurian Lakes* by Stanisław Sieminski (30 zł/$12/£6.75; available in tourist information centers), which details the region's history, canals, forests, and wildlife.

Fans of church organs should keep an eye out for the May to September performances in Święta Lipka at the **Church of Our Lady** (Święta Lipka; ✆ 089/755-14-81; www. swlipka.pl). You can combine it with a visit to Reszel or the Wolf's Lair.

Reszel ★, 53km (31 miles) west of Giżycko, is a village much loved by Mazurian residents. It is likened to Kraków, but that's really stretching it. Nevertheless, there are charming 1850s buildings here that still sport their original-typeface signs and flank the cobblestone lanes. The key attraction is panting up the uneven steps of the tower of the 14th-century **Gothic castle (Zamek Reszel;** Podzamcze 3). For 500 years, the red brick castle was the seat of bishops. It now has a Polish restaurant where the dishes are reasonably priced, and a **hotel** (✆ 089/755-01-09; www.zamek-reszel.com) where rooms combine medieval ambience with contemporary creature comforts. Near the 14th-century Gothic **Church of St. Peter and St. Paul** is **Cukiernia Lodziarnia** (Wyspiańskiego 2; no phone), a third-generation family-run pastry shop that does a good job at flagging down locals and German cyclists with its cakes and ice cream.

The **Old Believers Monastery (Klasztor Starowierców;** Wojnowo 76, Ukta; ✆ 087/ 425-70-30; www.klasztor.com.pl) is listed in all the regional guides, but it's actually a very modest affair. It is mainly of interest to those tracing the roots of the Old Believers, a minority group that defied the reformations led by Patriarch Nikon for the Russian Orthodox Church in the mid-17th century. The last of the monastery's nuns passed away in 2006. The Orthodox chapel retains the golden religious icons. Down a path from the church on the bank of Lake Duś is a small cemetery with three-bar papal crosses. If you're not driving, the best way to get here is by bike along the Green Route. Kayakers on the Krutynia Trail to Ukta can access the monastery by detouring to Lake Duś. A quick browse of the compound will take no more than 15 minutes. For a longer stay, literally, you can check into the rough and ready rooms (35 zł/$14/£3.15 per person) above the chapel.

WOLF'S LAIR (WILCZY SZANIEC) ★★ A visit to the Wolf's Lair will leave you mulling over how different the course of history could have been if this attempted assassination on Hitler were successful. The Wolf's Lair was once Hitler's eastern command

Hit and Missed

The details of Hitler's attempted assassination at the Wolf's Lair read like a spy thriller (and indeed, *Valkyrie* (2008), the movie starring Tom Cruise based on these events, is just that). In 1944, the would-be assassin, Claus Schenk von Stauffenberg, an officer of aristocratic bearing, had come to see the war as unwinnable. He and other like-minded officers believed that if Germany had any hope of avoiding total annihilation, Hitler had to be stopped. On July 20, 1944, von Stauffenberg was dispatched to the Wolf Lair's to brief the Fuehrer and other top Nazi leaders on troop levels in the Eastern Front. He arrived at the meeting with a time bomb stashed in his briefcase. Just before the meeting started, he placed the briefcase near Hitler, activated the bomb, and left the room. The resulting explosion killed four people, but not the target. One of the generals had moved the briefcase just before it exploded, unwittingly saving the Fuehrer's life. Von Stauffenberg flew back to Berlin believing the assassination attempt had succeeded. Once Hitler recovered from his minor injuries, he ordered von Stauffenberg's arrest; the officer was executed by firing squad later that night. In the ensuing witch hunt, some 5,000 people were executed.

base and comprises a large camp of reinforced-concrete bunkers, some with walls as thick as 8m. The top Nazi leadership, including Hitler and Hermann Goering, maintained their own personal bunkers. Additionally, there were bunkers for communication and troop commands, a train station, an airstrip, and even a casino bunker. Hitler was a frequent visitor to the Wolf's Lair from its initial construction in 1941 until 1944, when it was abandoned just ahead of the Russian advance as the war drew to a close. In January 1945, the Germans dynamited the bunkers to prevent them from falling into enemy hands. The remains are what you see today. The moss-covered bunkers have been preserved in their original "destroyed" state. You are free to walk along the marked paths among the jarring, jagged, brick and concrete ruins sitting incongruously amid beautiful pine forests. With the exception of the multimedia film center, the more than 30 ruins are exposed to the elements.

Summer is the best time for unhurried explorations. It's worth hiring a guide to give context to the rubble. Guides mill around the entrance, charging about 50 zł to 60 zł ($20–$24/£4.50–£5.40) for 1¹/₂ hours of narration. A good guidebook with a map is *Wolf's Lair* by Stanisław Siemiński. It's available in souvenir booths in Gierłoż or more cheaply at the tourist information center in Giżycko.

Gierłoż (8km east of Kętrzyn). ℭ **089/752-44-29.** www.wolfsschanze.home.pl. From Giżycko, take the train or bus to Kętrzyn. Several daily buses run from Kętrzyn taking about 15 minutes. The Red Route cycling route takes you here. Admission 8 zł ($3.20/£1.80) adult; 5 zł ($2/£1.10) seniors, children, and students. Parking 10 zł ($4/£2.25). Tues–Sun 9am–sunset.

Outdoor Activities

SAILING The beauty of sailing in the Mazurian Lake District is that the interconnecting waterways allow you the freedom to waltz from one lake to another. In summer, however, it gets congested around Giżycko and Mikołajki. Spend a day sailing from Mikołajki to **Okartowo** (in the east) and you escape to relative isolation. Be sure to moor at **Lake Tuchlin** ★, a bird sanctuary. Similarly, you have nature to yourself (more or less) once you pass the lock at Ruciane-Nida into **Lake Nidzkie** ★. Serene, too, is the southeasterly **Lake Roś** ★. You get there by passing the lock in Karwik and slipping into the 6km (3.6-mile) Jegliński Canal. The lakes reward you with parades of grey herons, cormorants and ospreys, and stork galore. On the banks, elk skirt by belting out their mating tunes. You won't be bored by the bays and peninsulas of **Lake Dobskie** ★★ (northwest of Giżycko). Here, you find the peculiar **Cormorant Island** (W Kormoranów), where trees cannot grow, and Gilma Island, which reportedly was the site of an ancient pagan temple. **Lakes Dargin** and **Śniardwy** can be challenging for novices.

The sailing season lasts from May to late January. To avoid rubbing helms with other enthusiasts, May to mid-June and September and after are the best. But in July and August the weather is sunnier, and in the evenings you'll find merry beer-imbibing at all of the resort towns.

In the Mazury, yacht rentals abound. Some pop up and fold up just as quickly. The www.mazury.info.pl portal has an updated list of rentals. It is advisable to browse through local sailing magazines such as *Jachting* (www.jachting.pl) or *Żagle,* where you'll find many advertisements for outfitters. In July and August, advance reservations are a must. Locals sometimes book at two different locations and on the day of the trip check out the vessels before selecting one. *Caution:* When picking up a boat, look for any damages and report them before setting sail to avoid complications later.

One of the biggest marinas and outfitters is **Sailor** (Czartery Jachtów Sailor, Piękna Góra; ✆ **087/429-32-92;** www.sailor.com.pl) in Piękna Góra, situated just outside Giżycko. Another is **Tiga Yacht and Marina** (✆ **087/427-51-36;** www.tigayacht.pl) in the lovely marina of Sztynort (northwest of Giżycko), complete with a derelict heritage manor house, restaurants, hotel, and campsites. In Węgorzewo, **AHOJ Czarter** (Przemysłowa 10, Węgorzewo; ✆ **087/427-15-37** or **0602/398-208;** www.ahoj.pl) is another major player. mJacht (✆ **48-791-14-13-31;** www.mjacht.pl) has yachts scattered in marinas around the district. The friendly, English-speaking Daniel Zuchowski is ever ready to answer questions and make accommodation recommendations.

Note: If you don't have a sailor's license, the rental company will try to help you locate an English-speaking skipper. The going rate for skippers is about 200 zł–250 zł ($80–$100/£45–£56) per day plus meals. Depending on the size of the boat, expect to place a deposit of 500 zł–1,000 zł ($200–$400/£112–£225). The smallest boat for 4 could cost as little as 90 zł ($36/£20) per day. On the other end of the scale, a luxury yacht for 10, fitted with heat and showers, can command 800 zł ($320/£180) per day. Prices vary depending on the season. Before setting out, check with your rental agency to obtain local emergency numbers, water safety information, and local sailing customs.

CANOEING & KAYAKING The **Krutynia River** ★★ wins hands down as the loveliest lowland kayaking route in the country. The route starts in Sorkwity (35km/21 miles west of Mikołajki). The 102km (61 miles) will have you paddling from lake to lake via streams, moving east by zigzagging from north to south. Along the way, you pass the Mazurian Landscape Park. On the whole it is rated as an easy route, but from Zgon to Krutyń you paddle along Lake Mokre, a sizeable lake that requires care. If you're going solo or have kids in tow, a carefree and manageable route is from Krutyń to Ukta (about 4 hours). Most outfitters deliver both you and the equipment to the set-off point and then pick everyone up at any of the stopover or finishing points. The season begins in May and continues through October; mid-July to mid-August is the busiest.

For multi-day tours, there are various overnight options. Along the route, campsites run by **PTTK** (www.mazurypttk.pl) are located in Sorkwity, Bienki, Babięta, Krutyń, Zgon, and Kamień. The chalets cost about 25 zł ($10/£5.63) per person. To pitch your own tents, the fee is 15 zł ($6/£3.38) per person. Extra charges may apply for shower usage. If you don't want to rough it, ask your outfitter to deliver you back to your hotel. **Hotel Habenda** (Krutyń 42, Piecki; (*C* 089/742-12-18; www.habenda.com) does just that, packing you out for the day and ferrying you back to the hotel's comfort at day's end.

There are many outfitters in Krutyń, a one-main-street town. *Note:* There are no ATMs here—the nearest is in Piecki, 11km (6.6 miles) away—so make sure you have enough cash with you to cover rental, food, and accommodation expenses. As a guideline for rental costs, refer to **AS-Tours's** website ★★ (Krutyń 4, Piecki; (*C* 089/742-14-30 or 0601/650-669; www.masuria-canoeing.com), which has been in the business for about 20 years.

CYCLING   Nature-loving biking fiends could spend a week zigzagging the Lake District. Pick up the cycling routes from the tourist information office and a 1:50,000 map of *Wielkie Jeziora Mazurskie* by Tessa. For newcomers, a popular choice is the 60km (36-mile) Giżycko to Sztynort round-trip. You pedal northwest along Lake Dobskie to reach quaint Sztynort on the bank of Lake Dargin. Dismount here to see the 300-year-old oak trees in the park of the derelict 16th-century palace of the Lehndorf family. Pressing on, it's storks galore before you head south back to your starting point. The historical **Red Route** takes you westward from Giżycko to the Wolf's Lair. You can press on westerly to **Kętrzyn** to see a mid-14th-century Teutonic castle. Puff on another 13km (7.8 miles) on Road no. 594, and you'll come to the celebrated Baroque church in Święta Lipka. If you like panting on hilly inclines, then take the less crowded **Blue Trail** ★★ around Lake Gołdopiwo. For woody trails, head to the **Mazurian Landscape Park** to the south of Mikołajki.

Locals lug their bikes to these parts. Though most hotels have bike rentals for about 40 zł ($16/£9) per day that suffice for short rides, they may not have the well-maintained wheels and gears needed for longer trips. **Techmet TC** (Zwycięstwa 38, Piecki; (*C* 089/742-21-04 or 0607/132-314; www.rowery-mazury.com) has solid bikes you can rely on for 25 zł ($10/£5.60) per day, and they deliver them to your doorstep. There are no charges for delivery up to 20km (20 miles) from Piecki. Otherwise, it's 2 zł (80¢/45p) per km. When you're done, they'll pick them up from anywhere you have landed. Ask for Monika; she speaks English.

HUNTING   The wide expanse of woods and meadows is fertile ground for big- and small-game hunting. Most common are wild boar, deer, and birds. Hunting in Poland is strictly regulated. As such, it has the reputation as one of the top hunting grounds on the continent, attracting hunters from Scandinavian and other European countries. **Dzikie Mazury** (Wyszowate 44; (*C* 087/421-15-50; www.dzikiemazury.eu), 16km (9.6 miles) from Giżycko, is a licensed hunting office that organizes outings in the northeastern region. The autumn–winter season is from October to February, while the spring–summer season starts in May. Contact the office to sort out the paperwork for firearms and hunting permits prior to your arrival. Group size ranges from 2 to 20. A translator (360 zł/$144/£81 per day) accompanies each group. The company is affiliated with **Hotel Myśliwski** (Wyszowate k/Giżycka 44, Miłki; (*C* 087/421-15-50; www.hotelmysliwski.pl), which offers hunting and full-board lodging packages for 240 zł ($95/£54) per person.

ORGANIZED TOURS   A great way to explore the region is to combine cycling and canoeing. **Kampio** ★ (Maszynowa 9/2, Warsaw; (*C* 022/823-70-70; www.kampio.com.pl)

specializes in such trips, incorporating scenic stretches and historical attractions. The 7- to 8-day packages cost around 2,160 zł to 2,520 zł ($864–$1,008/£486–£567) and are popular with German tourists. They also have self-guided packages where they will arrange bikes and accommodations for you.

Where to Stay & Dine

Besides the places listed below, **Zamek Ryn** (Plac Wolności 2, Ryn; ℂ **087/429-70-00;** www.zamekryn.pl); **Kanu Klub** (Nowy Zyzdrój, Piecki; ℂ **089/742-00-14;** www.kanu club.pl), and—if you can tolerate kitsch—**Galindia** (Iznota k/Mikołajki, Ruciane Nida; ℂ **087/423-14-16;** www.galindia.com.pl), all have comfortable accommodations and restaurants that serve regional food. In Giżycko, moderately priced **Hotel Cesarski** (Pl. Grunwaldzki 8; ℂ **087/428-15-14**) is good for a day or two if you need a central location to sort out your bearings, but you won't want to dwell too long.

There is a surfeit of eateries doing fish, pizza, and grilled meat and sausages. And there's no shortage of grocery stores and delis for sailors to stock up supplies.

Around Giżycko

OLD MILL INN (KARCZMA STARY MŁYN) ★ This heritage mill dating from the turn of 20th century now operates as a small inn and restaurant. Although it fell into disrepair after World War II, the current owner, who took over in the '90s, has restored it lovingly. There are four small rooms in the attic; two look out to the tranquil lake and grazing cows on the rolling fields. Antique bed frames (two rooms have wrought-iron bedposts) stand on the pinewood floorboards. Throughout the petite, homey establishment, the emphasis is on bygone rustic life. The restaurant opens to the public late in the morning, which means if you spend the night you have the whole place to yourselves for an unhurried breakfast of pancakes and scrambled eggs. Visitors come for the regional fare such as *plińce*, a potato and pork patty drizzled with fresh mushroom sauce. It requires 40 minutes to prepare, so pacify your growling stomach with other country treats such as the sour milk with dill.

Upałty 2, Giżycko (10km/6 miles south of Giżycko). ℂ **087/429-27-18.** www.karczma-upalty.com. 4 units. July–Aug 170 zł ($68/£38.25) double; 260 zł ($104/£58.50) suite for 4. May, June, Sept 140 zł ($56/£31.50) double; 240 zł ($96/£54) suite for 4; Jan–Apr and Oct–Dec 120 zł ($48/£27) double; 200 zł ($80/£45) suite for 4. Rates include breakfast. Children 2 and under stay free in parent's room. Extra person 40 zł ($16/£9). 10% discount for stay above 1 week. AE, DC, MC, V. Head south from Giżycko on Road no. 63. About 8km (5 miles) from town, a left turn for Road no. 655 leads to the inn. **Amenities:** Restaurant w/fireplace and terrace; Internet terminal; BBQ pit; playground; bicycle and boat rental; day trip to Vilnius, Lithuania (Wed and Sat, 95 zł/$38/£21). *In room:* TV, no phone.

POD CZARNYM ŁABĘDZIEM ★★ Some say no trip to the Mazury is complete without a visit to this restaurant-inn-campsite-marina, situated on the southern bank of the picturesque Lake Niegocin. The 100-year-old stable with whitewashed walls reinforced by exposed dark wood beams has been converted into guest rooms and a restaurant. In the cottage-style rooms you'll find pinewood headboards and creamy bedcovers. Request the rooms at the lake's end (as opposed to the road). There's a common balcony for scenery appreciation. The barn-style restaurant buzzes with the hustle and bustle of vacationers while the resident dog weaves about lazily. The seasonal and regional menu is chalked up on a board. Waitresses in blue folk-style pinafores deliver *dzyndzałki* (regional *pierogi*), local lake fish such as *sieja* and *sielawa,* and excellent house-brewed beers.

Rydzewo k/Giżycka. ℂ **087/421-12-52.** www.gospoda.pl. 17 units. 150 zł ($60/£33.75) single; 220 zł ($88/£49.50) double; 320 zł ($128/£72) suite w/terrace. Weekend packages available. Rates include breakfast. AE, DC, MC, V. Parking 10 zł ($4/£2.25). **Amenities:** Restaurant; BBQ pit; bicycle rental; trips to Vilnius, Lithuania; fishing on Lake Niegocin; private pier w/access to lake; campsite w/showers. *In room:* TV, complimentary Wi-Fi.

Around Mikołajki

GAŁKOWO HUNTER'S MANSION (DWÓR ŁOWCZEGO) ★★ (Value) Belonging to the same Mazurian conservation group as **Oberża Pod Psem** (see below), this is rustic simplicity and genteel sophistication rolled up into one. The owner, Alexander Potocki (of Polish aristocratic lineage), led the restoration work of the heritage buildings. Rooms (some with shared bathrooms) are found in three wood and brick cottages, all which feature vintage farm and riding paraphernalia. Instead of TV you have vistas of wild meadows and forests. The **Knajpa u Targowiczan** restaurant is a busy operation all week from May to September. Off season, fans have to wait until the weekend. The seasonal compact menu has items that confound even those familiar with Polish cuisine. *Zsiadłe mleko z ziemniakami* (potatoes cooked in sour milk) is a peasant dish that's a rarity these days.

Gałkowo 46, Gałkowo (20km/12 miles south of Mikołajki). ℂ **087/425-70-73.** www.galkowo.pl. 20 units. May–Oct 100 zł ($40/£22.50) single; 135 zł ($54/£30) double; 220 zł ($88/£49.50) suite; 40 zł ($16/£9) extra person. Off-season 70 zł ($28/£15.75) single; 100 zł ($40/£22.50) double; 160 zł ($64/£36) suite; 30 zł ($12/£6.75) extra person. Children 4 and under stay free in parent's room. Children 12 and under 50% discount. AE, MC, V. Free parking. **Amenities:** Restaurant w/fireplace and kids' corner; vegetable and fruit garden; reading room; bicycle rental; access to horse riding.

OBERŻA POD PSEM ★★ (Value) You're assured of a taste of old Mazurian village life at this pension. The owners are ardent conservationists and champions of Mazurian folk culture. They salvaged the centenarian wooden buildings (some from other parts of the country) to set up a restaurant, an ethnographical museum, and rooms to let. The cottage, which sleeps 6, has functioning traditional heaters. The double rooms are less cluttered but in the same rural vein. Immaculate attention is put on details such as door handles, locks, and hinges. However, you can still access the Internet in the garden, which blooms with hollyhocks and wildflowers, while elk from the neighboring wildlife compound let out the occasional yelp. The informal homeyness extends to the restaurant, a magnet for foodies. *Wereszczaki* (pork braised in beetroot sauce) is a rare find anywhere in the country. The buckwheat and cottage cheese *pierogi*, wild boar *bigos* (hunter's stew), and the toffee pancake with poppyseeds are all must-eats. You can also take home locally made cheeses and wild boar pâté.

Kadzidłowo 1, Ukta. (12km/7.5 miles south of Mikołajki) ℂ **087/425-74-74** or **0601/094-641.** www. oberzapodpsem.com. 4 units. 120 zł ($48/£27) double; 250 zł ($100/£56.25) cottage for 6. Breakfast 15 zł ($6/£3). Extra person 20 zł ($8/£4.50). No credit cards. From Mikołajki, take Road no. 609. Turn right into a dirt road at the Kadzidłowo road sign. Free parking. **Amenities:** Restaurant; sauna w/traditional stone heating and a wooden barrel bathtub; campfire; ethnographic museum; cottage w/kitchen; rooms w/ common kitchenette; garden. *In room:* complimentary Wi-Fi.

---

2 THE SUWAŁKI LAKE DISTRICT

Arriving from the Mazury to the Suwałki *(Suwalszczyna)* Lake District, you can't help but notice how much wilder the terrain seems. You are not wrong. This most northeasterly part of Poland, whose borders touch Russia, Lithuania, and Belarus, has the lowest population density in the country. Even for Poles, this is uncharted territory.

The Suwałki region boasts the most talked about kayaking routes. The Rospuda, Czarna Hańcza, and Biebrza Rivers are linked by the Augustów Canal, resulting in over 100km (60 miles) of connected waterways. With the Schengen Zone agreement, you are free to wander into neighboring countries (except Russia) without a visa.

Augustów is a good stepping-off point into the region due to its strategic location amid lakes and parklands. Founded in 1550, the town lost most of its architectural beauty to battles ranging from the 17th century Tartar invasion to World War II, when 70% of the town was reduced to rubble. The regional capital is Suwałki, 30km (12 miles) to the north of Augustów. But the main roads and railway reach Augustów first before trundling northward to Suwałki and beyond. To the north of Augustów is the Wigry National Park, while Biebrzański National Park spans the southern rims. In the east is the Augustów Forest, one of Poland's largest continuous woodlands. Augustów is the finishing line for the Rospuda and Czarna Hańcza water routes. Via the Augustów Canal, you can access the Biebrza River.

The tourism infrastructure here is not as extensive as in the Mazury, but many outfitters are based in and around Augustów. Though it's mainly a summer destination, throughout the year the Suwałki region promises adventure bundled with serenity and a sense of time travel into the past.

ESSENTIALS

Getting There

By car from Warsaw, Road no. 61 leads you to Augustów. It's about 260km (156 miles) and 4 hours on fairly good and very scenic roads. From Giżycko, it's a 108km (65-mile) journey. Road no. 16 takes you here in about $1^1/_2$ hours. Daily trains (www.pkp.pl) and buses (www.pks.pl) leave from Warsaw and the towns in the Mazurian Lake District for Augustów. From Warsaw, the journey time for bus and rail is about $4^1/_2$ hours. The **railway station** (Dworcowa; ☎ **087/643-22-77**) is 3km (1.8 miles) from the center. The **bus station** (Rynek Zygmunta Augusta 18; ☎ **087/643-36-49**) is in the town square.

Visitor Information

The **tourist information center** (Rynek Zygmunta Augusta 44; ☎ **087/643-28-83;** www.augustow.pl) is in a modern building in the town square. In July and August, it operates Monday through Saturday from 9am to 5pm. The rest of the year, it's open weekdays only from 9am to 3pm. The earnest staff speaks passable English. Aside from maps and accommodation listings, they have bus schedules and current listings of bicycle, canoe, and kayak rentals, excursion organizers, and fishing information. For a city map, hop over to Korona (see "Where to Dine").

Getting Around

Most of the kayak and bike rentals and tour guides set up shop on Nadrzeczna on the south side of River Netta and on Portowa and Zarzecze on the northern bank. To get beyond Augustów you can arrange with your outfitter for transport; many are willing to collect you from Augustów. The **PKS** bus service (www.pks.suwalki.com.pl) serves the region.

Outdoor Activities

CANOEING & KAYAKING   The paddling season is from May to September, peaking in July and August. The best time to paddle on the Biebrza River is in late spring. In the summer, the reeds shoot up and water weeds clog the passage. To see the spring flooding on this river, you should aim for mid to late April. Outfitters cater to one- and multi-day outings, delivering paddlers and equipment to the drop-off points. When you're done paddling, call them and they'll come to ferry you back to your campsite or hotel. Since you pay for the transportation (about 2 zł/80¢/45p per km for up to 8 people), it makes economic sense to select an outfitter that is located closer to your chosen trail. In July and August, it's advisable to call at least a day ahead to book. Rental prices range from 25 zł to 40 zł ($10–$16/£5.60–£9) per day. For the Augustów Canal, have cash available for the locks, about 3 zł ($1.20/68p) per vessel. Get the schedule of the lock's operating hours at the tourist information office. In Augustów, the **Augustów Canoe Center ★★** (✆ **0501/274-244;** www.frontierpoland.com) not only will equip you but also will load you up with tips and advice. **Łukowy Kąt ★** (Stary Folwark 44; ✆ **087/563-77-89** or **0693/705-487;** www.wigry.info) has its base at the Lake Wigry starting point of the Czarna Hańcza route. Bogdan Łukowscy, the amicable owner, says he speaks "easy" English. He also runs a campsite and rents out rooms at 25 zł to 35 zł ($10–$14/£5.60–£7.90) per person. Another outfitter is **Hobbit ★** (Maćkowa Ruda 39; ✆ **087/567-88-97;** www.hobbit.suwalki.com.pl), which has several bases. One of them is on the idyllic Wigry peninsula.

CYCLING This is great cycling terrain because even in the peak of summer there aren't hordes of bicycles. There are plenty of well-marked routes, plus the Eurovelo (European cycle route) R11 crosses the region on its way from Athens to Oslo. The 1:85,000 laminated maps by ExpressMap are good resources. For quick tours around Augustów, the Blue Route takes you to the fringes of the majestic Lake Sajno and the Augustów Forest. Or pedal southerly along the Augustów Canal from Białobrzegi to the Borki water lock, and you'll see tree trunks where beavers have left their teeth marks. In general, the routes in Augustów Forest and Biebrza valley are flat tarmac, dirt, or sandy tracks. Farther afield in Wigry National Park and Suwałki Landscape Park, the undulating terrain means panting and puffing followed by exhilarating freewheeling. *Note:* You'll need a ticket (3 zł/$1.20/68p per day) for Wigry National Park (Krzywe 82, Suwałki; ✆ **087/563-25-40;** www.wigry.win.pl). It's open on weekdays from 7am to 3pm. In summer, it also operates on weekends from 9am to 4pm. Most kayak rentals and hotels have bikes for hire, too. In Augustów, **Jan Wojtuszko** (Nadrzeczna 62A; ✆ **087/644-75-40;** www.sprzetwodny.prv.pl) is a friendly, family-run water sports equipment rental. Their mountain bikes go for 25 zł ($10/£5.63) per day.

FISHING The Suwałki region is blessed with fish-rich clear waters. What makes it hassle-free for tourists is the consolidated information on where to fish and where to get your permits. The list of lakes for angling can be obtained at the tourist information office in Augustów or at the regional fishery office website (www.pzw.suwalki.com.pl). Permits, 12 zł to 20 zł ($4.80–$8/£2.70–£4.50) per day, can be bought at the **post office** (Rynek Zygmunta Augusta 3; ✆ **087/643-36-93**) or at some fishing equipment shops, such as **J. Kamiński** (Mostowo 24; ✆ **087/644-75-85**). The Wigry National Park's information center (see "Cycling") sells permits for lakes within its perimeters. If you need gear, you'll find no shortage of fishing equipment stores *(sklep wędkarstwo).*

ICE SAILING Winter in this region is much more severe than the rest of the country, giving rise to ice-sailing *(bojery)* opportunities. The sport resembles windsurfing on ice, an extreme sport practiced in very few places on earth. For it to happen, the surface of the frozen lake must be snow-free, a condition that is harder to come by in recent years. The best chance is in January and February. If you're tempted, get a Polish speaker to

Rivers (and Canals) Run Through It

The waterways are the perfect conduits for accessing the natural and man-made marvels of this area. The landscape varies from reed-filled marshlands to pine and coniferous hills. Connecting the 11 rivers and 7 lakes is the **Augustów Canal** *(Kanał Augustowski)*, a heritage canal dating from 1823, which is older than both the Suez and Panama Canals. From Augustów, it stretches east to the Niemen River in Belarus—never reaching the Baltic Sea in Latvia, for work was interrupted by the November Uprising (1830–31). The 101km-long (60.6-mile) waterway is a hydraulic engineering marvel with lovely water locks along the way. Part of the fun of kayaking on the canal is to be huddled into the narrow lock channels, bobbing up or down as the water level rises or drops.

The **Rospuda River,** the second longest in the Suwałki region, is rated as an intermediate kayaking route and also is one of the loveliest. It takes 5 days to negotiate the route if you start at the village of Supienie (68km/49 miles northwest of Augustów). The **Czarna Hańcza River** (to the northeast of Augustów) has a section for experts and another for novices. From Lake Hańcza (the deepest lake in the country) to Lake Wigry is a 47km (28.2-mile) route of adrenaline-pumping steep drops. Beginners can kick off from the picturesque Lake Wigry and meander from marshland into the woods of Augustów Forest. Along the riverside settlements, local peddlers tempt you with *pączki* (donuts) and cold beer. The woody stretch from Frącki to Mikaszówka is considered the prettiest.

contact Jarek Osa of **Nord** (Zarzecze 1; ✆ **0608/504-974**) at the *Schroniska Młodzieżowe* for equipment and user instructions.

WILDLIFE WATCHING   Ornithologists from around the world flock to this region. The early spring flooding of the Biebrza River more or less coincides with the return of migratory birds when, in Augustów, cranes, storks, and graylag geese fill the sky. On the canals, there are goldeneye duck, mergansers, and marsh harriers. May is when the birds do their courtship song and dance. September, as the nomads get set to bolt for winter, is another great time for bird-gazing. The ultimate bird safari is in the marshlands of Biebrza National Park to the south of Augustów. **Augustów Canoe Center ★★** (see "Canoeing & Kayaking") has customized tours. So does Katarzyna Ramotowska of **Biebrza Eco-Travel ★★** (Kościuszki, Goniądz; ✆ **085/738-07-85;** www.biebrza.com), who specializes in the **Biebrzański National Park** (www.biebrza.org.pl) area. Her itineraries, such as the "elk expedition" and "wolf tracking," are for hardcore and nascent naturalists alike. She also has special programs to get kids hooked on nature. In Sztabin (25km/15 miles south of Augustów), the bearded Adam Raczkowscy runs a farm-stay called **Dworek Na Końcu Świata** (Cottage at Land's End) (Koptytkowo 6, Sztabin; ✆ **0600/273-051;** www.rumcajsy. com). The quirky owner—who bears a resemblance to Rumcajs, a Central European cartoon character—rents rafts for day-long, sedate floats on the river for wildlife-spotting.

Beyond Poland

From Augustów, tour operators offer single and multi-day bus trips into neighboring countries such as Estonia, Latvia, Lithuania, and Russia. With the exception of Russia, the countries are within the Schengen Zone, so there's no visa hassles. You can look into the options offered by **Ela-Travel** (Rynek Zygmunta Augusta 15/2; ✆ **087/643-55-00;**

Where to Stay

In addition to their core business of supplying beds and meals, most properties are more than happy to get you kitted out for outdoor activities.

Augustów

DOM NAUCZYCIELA ★ (Value)   Right by the canal, this uninspiring, squat building hides remarkably comfortable rooms where the walls are a cheerful orange and the cotton bedsheets are whiter than white. The sparkling clean bathrooms have basic toiletries. The setup may remind you of Communist leftovers, but the service is helpful and warm. The restaurant is respectable, but you're a quick walk from other food sources.

29 Listopada 9. ℭ **087/643-20-21.** Fax 087/643-54-10. www.dn.augustow.pl. 48 units. 95 zł ($38/£21) single; 140 zł ($56/£31.50) double; 250 zł ($100/£56.25) suite. Breakfast 15 zł ($6/£3.30). Extra person 40 zł ($10/£9). Reduced rates for stays above 3 nights. AE, DC, MC, V. Parking 15 zł ($6/£3.40). **Amenities:** Restaurant; patio; gym; bicycle rental; tourist agency w/outings to Wigry and Biebrzański National Parks and kayaking on Augustów Canal and Czarna Hańcza. *In room:* TV, dataport.

SZUFLADA CAFÉ & BAR ★   Conveniently located on a side street of the main square, this new hotel has tastefully furnished, minimalistic modern rooms with squeaky clean bathrooms. Bedcovers, chairs, and carpets are coordinated in shades of brown. There are no elevators, but the friendly staff will help you with your luggage up the stairs. Tuck in to the pancakes (13 zł/$5.20/£2.90) at the cafe. They have 16 types in sweet and savory flavors, the best of which is the mushroom.

Ks Skorupki 2c. ℭ **087/644-63-15.** Fax 087/643-11-65. www.szuflada.augustow.pl. 7 units. May–Sept 140 zł ($56/£31.50) single; 170 zł ($68/£38.25) double; 300 zł ($120/£67.50) suite; extra person 60 zł ($24/£13.50). Oct–Apr 110 zł ($44/£24.75) single; 140 zł ($56/£31.50) double; 250 zł ($100/£56.25) suite; extra person 50 zł ($20/£11.25). Rates include breakfast. AE, MC, V. Parking 5 zł ($2/£1.10). **Amenities:** Cafe; bar; kayak and fishing trips. *In room:* A/C (some rooms), TV, dataport.

Outside Augustów

The Wigry National Park (see "Cycling") has seven forest lodges where the basic rooms with shared bathrooms are priced at 30 zł ($12/£6.75) per person. The oldest and most atmospheric lodge is the one in Gawrych Ruda. On the Wigry Peninsula, at the base of

Sounds of the Past

From the 1700s until World War II, the town of Sejny had a vibrant multicultural society of Jews, Poles, Lithuanians, Russians, and Germans. Although this diversity perished during the war, Sejny is one of the few places in Poland where the sound of Klezmer—a whirling, atmospheric Jewish dance music—is still alive. From July to mid-August, the **Borderland Foundation** (Fundacja Pogranicze; Piłsudskiego 37, Sejny; ℭ **087/516-27-65;** www.pogranicze.sejny.pl) hosts the Klezmer music festival in the **White Synagogue** (at the end of Piłsudskiego Street). Concerts are held on Tuesday, Friday, and Saturday from 8pm to 9:30pm, and tickets are 20 zł ($8/£4.50). During other times of the year, contact the foundation for the schedule. Sejny is 44km (26.4 miles) northeast of Augustów. There are hourly buses from Suwałki to Sejny taking about 45 minutes.

the Camaldolese monastery (Dom Pracy Twórczej) (see below), is **U Haliny** ★ (Wigry 12, Stary Folwark; © **087/563-70-42**). It's a farm-stay and campsite sharing the same magical location as Dom Pracy Twórczej.

DOM PRACY TWÓRCZEJ ★★ Constructed on a breathtaking and dreamy hilltop in the wilderness of the Wigry Peninsula, this complex is a former Camaldolese monastery dating from 1694. Even though it doesn't have 5-star trimmings, you'll still get more than monastic simplicity here with homey furnishings that are reminiscent of house-proud Polish grannies. The *erem* (hermitages used by monks for solitary contemplation) have private gardens, but also shared bathrooms that are on the lower level. A formal dining atmosphere permeates the **Dom Wigierski Restaurant.** The baked carp with berry sauce snatched the top place in a regional culinary showdown. On summer days, busloads of tourist come to visit the church, crypt, and the Papal Apartment, where Pope John Paul II resided in 1999. But at dusk, when a sublime serene peace pervades the compound and the peninsula, you'll have the place all to yourself. Your wake-up call is the twittering of birds and the chiming of church bells at 8:30am.

Stary Folwark. © **087/563-70-00.** www.wigry.org. 43 units. May–Aug 100 zł ($40/£22.50) single w/ shared bathroom; 150 zł ($60/£33.75) double w/shared bathroom; 170 zł ($68/£38.25) en suite double; 200 zł–300 zł ($80–$120/£45–£67.50) suite. Off season 80 zł ($32/£18) single w/shared bathroom; 120 zł ($48/£27) double w/shared bathroom; 140 zł ($56/£31.50) en suite double; 160 zł–240 zł ($64–$96/£36–£54) suite. Extra person 20 zł ($8/£4.50). Rates include breakfast. MC, V. Free parking. On Road no. 653 from Suwalki to Sejny; do not turn into Stary Folwark. Keep going and turn right at Ryżówka (about 3km/1.8 miles from Stary Folwark), then follow the signpost to the monastery. **Note:** Reception desk closes at 10pm. **Amenities:** Restaurant; cafe (July–Aug); complimentary Internet terminal. *In room:* TV, no phone.

GOŚCINIEC JACZNO (JACZNO LODGE) ★★★ (Value This cluster of stone and timber houses, on a peninsula in the Suwałki Landscape Park, is hemmed in by woods and the pristine, aquamarine water of Lake Jaczno. Since this lodge is far from Augustów, it's for those who want to stay put and enjoy their surroundings. The owners are architects who have designed every space—from the rooms, to the lounge and bar, to the rose bush and fruit-tree-strewn garden—to be picture perfect. People-shy guests have many cozy nooks and crannies to escape to both indoors and outdoors, including a secluded pier for admiring water lilies and storks. There are no restaurants in the vicinity, so unless you have a car you'll have to go full board. Neighboring farms supply the milk, cheese, and meat, and veggies and herbs come from the lodge's own patch. Swing in a hammock, try out the steep hiking and cycling routes nearby, or ask for the directions to farmsteads where you can milk cows or buy cheese. In winter, cross-country skiing gear can be obtained from the park office in Turtul.

Jaczno 3, Jeleniewo. © **087/568-35-90.** Fax 087/568-35-91. www.jaczno.pl. 15 units. Easter weekend, first weekend of May, July–Aug, Christmas and New Year week 230 zł ($92/£51.75) single; 290 zł ($116/£65.25) double; 380 zł–490 zł ($152–$196/£85.50–£110.25) suite. Off season 210 zł ($84/£47.25) single; 250 zł ($100/£56.25) double; 350 zł–440 zł ($140–$176/£78.75–£99) suite. Extra person 70 zł ($28/£15.75). Rates include breakfast. Lunch 35 zł ($14/£8). Dinner 25 zł ($10/£5.60). 50% meal discount for children. No credit cards. Free parking. On Rd. 655 heading north, go pass Jeleniewo toward Gulbieniszki. Turn left into Gulbieniszki and drive through the village of Udziejek (you'll pass Gościniec Drumlin on the way). The road becomes a dirt road. At a Y-crossing, you'll see the signpost to the right for Jaczno. From there on follow the Jaczno signposts, which are quite small and easy to miss. **Amenities:** Dining room; limited room service; dry cleaning; laundry service; 2 lounges w/fireplace; gym; sauna; *bania* (Russian sauna); billiard table; table tennis; boat; bicycles; pier; playground; campfire; BBQ pit; fishing rods; organized kayaking on Rospuda and Czarna Hańcza; sleigh rides; winter bonfire. *In room:* TV, minibar, complimentary Wi-Fi.

Good Food Center

The area has a number of specialties: The regional deli meat is *kindziuk,* chopped and seasoned sirloin cooked in a pig's stomach. *Kartacze* are chubby potato dumplings filled with lentils. The menus also feature *sielawa* and *sieja,* freshwater fish found in the lakes of northeastern Poland. For dessert, you'll see the pyramidal *sękacz* everywhere. The batter (whipped up from 40 eggs, 1kg flour, sugar, butter, lemon juice, and vanilla essence) is poured over a rotary spit and baked layer by layer, creating characteristic rings created while the dripping dough hardens into spiky stalactite.

Where to Dine
Augustów
Korona ★ REGIONAL   Although this basement restaurant does not score well for its modern pub decor, it makes up for it with genial service and good food. The trilingual (Polish, English, Lithuanian) menu features Polish classics including a well-rated steak tartare that will delight raw-food fans. If you're pining for non-Polish cuts, the Catalonian Serrano ham and chorizo platter (32 zł/$12.80/£7.20) will assuage your cravings. Bart, the merry English-speaking owner, recommends the pork chop in herb garlic sauce. Affiliated with Ela-Travel Agency, their complimentary map of the area is better than the one issued by the tourist information office.

Rynek Zygmunta Augusta 15/3. © **087/643-44-00.** www.korona.augustow.pl. Main courses 21 zł–40 zł ($8.40–$16/£4.70–£9). AE, DC, MC, V. Daily noon–midnight.

MASKA CONTINENTAL   Venetian, Balinese, and African masks stud the barrel-vaulted basement. Familiar food in tummy-padding quantities and friendly service are the strengths of this restaurant. The *golonka w piwna* (pork knuckles) takes 3 days to prepare, from marinating, braising, and roasting to braising again in beer. Vegetarian options include breaded mushrooms and risotto.

Rynek Zygmunta Augusta 9. © **087/644-72-13.** AE, MC, V. Main courses from 16 zł–30 zł ($6.40–$12/£3.60–£6.75). Daily 11am–11pm.

OGRÓDEK POD JABŁONIAMI ★★ (Finds REGIONAL   Yummy and fairly priced sustenance can be had in this informal alfresco eatery along River Netta. Run by an English-speaking young couple (Paweł and Sylwia), Paweł rustles up steaks (in garlic or pepper sauce) and pizzas and sautés the catch of the day, while Sylwia's mother upholds the traditional cuisine front with must-try chanterelle or pickled cabbage soups and *kartacze.* The serene garden has a kiddies' sandbox.

Rybacka 1. © **516/025-606.** Main courses 10 zł–40 zł ($4–$16/£2.25–£9). No credit cards. May–Sept daily noon–11pm (last order 10pm).

Outside Augustów
POD SIEJĄ ★ REGIONAL   This is popular as a fuel-stop for sports zealots and gastronomes alike. Scribbled on a placard are the seasonal and regional offerings: *kartacze, kiszka ziemniaczana* (a regional potato dish), roast suckling pig, *sielawa, świeżynka* (fried pork chunks and onions). A few notches more chic than the usual seasonal shacks in this

neck of the woods, this charming place has a wood-beam ceiling, brick fireplace, sun-dappled terrace, and free Wi-Fi thrown in.

Stary Folwark 48, Stary Folwark. ℂ **087/563-70-10.** www.sieja.suwalszczyzna.net. Main courses 5 zł–25 zł ($1.60–$10/£1.10–£5.60). DC, MC, V. May–Sept daily 10am–10pm.

3 BIAŁOWIEŻA

Białowieża, 2km (1 mile) from the Belarusian border, is synonymous with the European bison. Hunted to near-extinction by soldiers during World War II, the European bison has made a comeback in the sanctuary of the Białowieża National Park (BNP), one of Europe's last remaining parcels of primeval forest. The park covers some 1,000 sq. km (390 sq. miles), and since 1979 has been on the UNESCO list of World Natural Heritage Sites. In addition to bison, the park shelters populations of deer, lynx, black storks, beaver, and wolf, as well as hundreds of species of birds and a staggering variety of trees, fungi, mushroom, and insects. So, no surprise—it's inundated by scientists from around the world. However, the area has more to offer than just flora and fauna. History has left its marks on the landscape. The Białowieża Forest used to be the hunting grounds of Polish kings, Lithuanian princes, and Russian tsars. Aside from royal footprints, invasions and power shifts created an ethnic mosaic with influences from Russians, Lithuanians, Belarusians, Tartars, and Ukrainians, whose faiths range among Catholic, Orthodox, Islam, Protestant, and Adventism. Cycling in the woodlands is a great way to discover the onion-dome Orthodox churches *(cierkiew),* three-papal-cross cemeteries, 16th-century wooden architecture, and other historic monuments.

ESSENTIALS
Getting There
BY CAR   From Warsaw, take Rd. E77 in the direction of Białystok. At Zambrów, turn into Road no. 66; it leads you to Hajnówka. From there, Road no. 689 takes you into the village of Białowieża. The distance from Warsaw is 258km (155 miles), about 3^1/$_2$ hours, but could be longer due to road work.

BY TRAIN & BUS   There are daily trains from Warsaw's Warszawa Wschodnia Station (Lubelska 1; ℂ **022/473-72-97;** www.pkp.com.pl) to Hajnówka. Depending on service, the journey time is about 4^1/$_2$ hours. PKS buses, outside the train station, depart for Białowieża up to 8 times a day. There is also Oktobus (ℂ **0691/595-817;** www.oktobus. pl), a private bus company, with 5 daily services to Białowieża. The pickup point is also outside the railway station, near the church. The bus journey is about 30 minutes and tickets are 4 zł ($1.60/90p). Get off after Hotel Żubrówka, near the PTTK office. You can also take a taxi (ℂ **085/682-28-77**) from Hajnówka that costs about 70 zł ($28/£6.30).

Visitor Information
It would be ideal to make a pit stop at Hajnówka to swing by the **Białowieża Forest Regional Tourist Office** (3 Maja 45, Hajnówka; ℂ **085/682-43-81;** www.powiat. hajnowka.pl). They are open year-round Monday through Saturday from 9am to 5pm. The information stock here is extensive, covering attractions such as the orthodox churches in the area. Most importantly, they hand out good maps with cycling routes, which you don't get for free in Białowieża. From May to September in Białowieża, the

(Fun Facts   Number Crunching

The park area has about 440 European bison. An adult male can weigh up to 900kg; a female, 640kg. They may look like lumbering giants, but they are agile enough to clock 40km (24 miles) per hour when charging.

Tourist Information Point of Białowieża National Park (Park Pałacowy 5; ✆ 085/681-29-01; www.bpn.com.pl) is open daily from 9am to 5pm. The year-round facility is the **PTTK tourist agency** (Kolejowa 17; ✆ 085/681-22-95; www.pttk. bialowieza.pl). In July and August, it's open daily 8am to 6pm; from September to June, daily 8am to 4pm. They are a good source for hiring guides for the Strictly Protected Area (see below) and bikes and horse-drawn carts.

Getting Around

Cycling is a popular way of getting around during the warmer months. There are plenty of bike rentals at the rate of 5 zł ($2/£1.10) per hour or 25 zł ($10/£5.60) per day. The PTTK does day rentals only. At **Pensjonat Gawra** (Południowa 2; ✆ 085/681-28-04; www.gawra.bialowieza.com), they do multiday rentals. You'll also find that most accommodations have their own stash of bikes.

In season, bicycle rickshaws (✆ 0505/044-742) and "MELEX" electric cars (✆ 085/681-22-93) take visitors to the Bison Reserve and other points of interest. For the rickshaws, it's recommended that you book in advance. It's 25 zł ($10/£5.62) per hour for up to 3 passengers. The electric cars charge 15 zł ($6/£3.40) per person. The horse-drawn carts (see "Outdoor Activities") are meant as recreational rides rather than a means of transportation. But you can discuss with the drivers for reduced rates if you just need a drop-off somewhere. The private mini-bus service in the village is targeted at groups of 8 and more. Roman Buszko (✆ 0608/311-449) charges about 2 zł (80¢/45p) per km.

Top Attractions

Your first stop will probably be the **Palace Park (Park Pałacowy)** ★, built in 1890 for Russian royalty. The site was originally the hunting grounds of Polish kings. There is no admission charge and you can wander 'round the English-style lawns. The **Natural History Museum** (Park Pałacowy; ✆ 085/681-22-75), which has an interesting coverage of the ecosystem and the history of the area, is also located here. You'll immediately notice the "juvenile" 250-year-old oak trees in front the museum. To see older oaks, take the 3km (2-mile) yellow trail from the PTTK office to the **Royal Oaks (Dęby Królewskie)** ★. These magnificent specimens have clocked more than 400 years under their bark.

With exception of the **Strictly Protected Area** (SPA) (see below), the rest of Białowieża National Park can be accessed with or without a guide.

BISON RESERVE (REZERWAT POKAZOWY ZWIERZĄT) ★ (Kids) A ranch-style zoo showcasing a small but engaging selection of animals, namely the crowd-pulling European bison, from fully grown to young ones. Not to be missed are the *tarpans,* a species related to the extinct Eurasian wild horse that looks like something that has just stepped out of the Ice Age. Another attraction is *żubroń,* the result of crossing male bison with female domestic cattle. If you drag your feet, it will take an hour to see everything including the lynx, elk, wild boar, wolves, stags, and roe deer.

3km (1.8 miles) west of the Palace Park. ✆ **085/681-23-98.** Admission 6 zł ($2.40/£1.35) adult; 3 zł ($1.20/68p) seniors, students, and children. May–Sept daily 9am–5pm. Oct–Apr Tues–Sun 8am–4pm. Follow the green or yellow trails from the PTTK office. The Bison's Ribs (Żebra Żubra) trail passes by the reserve. Also see "Getting Around."

STRICTLY PROTECTED AREA (SPA; OBSZAR OCHRONY ŚCISŁEJ) ★★   The SPA is the oldest section of the park. A characteristic that distinguishes primeval parks from managed parks is that for the former no human intervention is permitted. So you'll find many dead trees left fallen (or standing) where they are. The name, along with the fact that you can access it only with a licensed guide, might lead you to think that this is a zone teeming with big game. The guides will tell you, "The problem with animals is, they move." You'll see birdlife, but mainly what you get is a fun stroll on muddy trails and wooden walkways among ancient foliage accompanied by an entertaining, fact-filled commentary on the park's origin and animal and plant life. They'll point out fungus like dead man's fingers (which you might have dismissed as "something black and moldy") and tree trunks pockmarked by eight species of woodpeckers.

The routine tour is 7km (4 miles) and 3 hours long. You spend about 30 minutes getting to the SPA entrance. There's an option to get there by horse-drawn cart (140 zł/$56/£31.50). The SPA is best in the morning when there is more animal activity. You can book a guide at any of the tourist offices or at the Natural History Museum, where you also purchase admission tickets to the SPA. If you book your guide at the museum, they can pool visitors together to split the guide's cost. No advanced booking is needed, but do call ahead to reserve a tour with Mateusz Szymura (✆ **0601/450-035;** bialowieza@ 02.pl), a particularly enjoyable guide at the BNP.

Park Pałacowy. ✆ **085/681-28-98.** Admission 6 zł ($2.40/£1.35). English-speaking guides 165 zł ($66/£37) per group of 20. Dawn to dusk. Closed during storms or flooding.

Outdoor Activities
In & Around Białowieża
EUROPEAN BISON SIGHTING   Although the image of the bison is slapped on every brochure, water, beer, and vodka bottle to promote the area, don't expect to encounter a bison lurking behind every tree. You are assured of seeing them in the Bison Reserve (see above). Sighting those living in the wild requires some luck and effort. ***Note:*** Bison are on the Red List of Endangered Species. As such, the BNP forbids activities that distress these animals, such as trailing them. Dogs are not allowed. Read the BNP's advisory on the dos and don'ts, and should you cross paths with a bison or a herd, keep your distance and do not startle them. You don't want tons of muscle charging at you.

To see the free-range bison, the BNP's recommendation is to go in winter, at dawn or dusk, to the feeding stations. A shortage of vegetation in the forest brings the bison out to these hay huts, which are accessible to the public. There are observation platforms by the three feeding posts to the north of Białowieża at Kosy Most, Czoło (near Stare Masiewo village), and Babia Góra. At any time of the year, the general advice from licensed guides is to go for a walk and try your luck. The yellow trail to Topiło, the red trail to Narewka, and the green trail (also called the Wolves' Trail) are tracks with reportedly higher probability of bison sighting. ***Note:*** Park regulations require you to stay on the marked trails. You shouldn't be overly discouraged about your chances. The locals are blasé about the bison, claiming that the animals often graze at the perimeters of their homesteads (between the villages of Narewka and Siemianówka).

CARRIAGE OR SLEIGH RIDE   Dashing through the woods (and villages) on a one-horse open sleigh or carriage is a popular pursuit targeted at visitors. Any tourist agency

Fun Facts **Would Bison Grass by Another Name Smell Just as Sweet?**

The "bison grass" in local favorite Żubrówka vodka is harvested from the Białowieża Forest. Despite the name, bison don't actually graze on it. You can buy the long, slim, fragrant blades from the souvenir booths outside the Bison Reserve. To make your own "bison grass" vodka, follow the instructions on the package.

and most of the lodgings can arrange this for you. The price for this alfresco repose is around 160 zł ($64/£36) for 3 hours in a carriage for four. The carriages also take visitors to the Bison Reserve and the Royal Oaks.

CYCLING   Cycling routes crisscross the villages around Białowieża and are great for getting acquainted with the rich ethnic character of the region. Pick up the English-language *Bicycle Routes in the Region of the Białowieża Forest* (available in Hajnówka's Tourist Information Office). The most interesting is the 16km (9.5-mile) **Land of Open Shutters** route, which takes you past orthodox churches, cemeteries with three-bar papal crosses, and 19th-century wooden cottages with ornate cravings. Cycling fiends can consider the 206km (123-mile) **Podlasie Stork Route,** which starts from Białowieża and ends in the Biebrza National Park.

WALKING   There are plenty of flat and relatively easy walking routes that you can pick up at the PTTK office. A popular track to get a feel of the primeval forest is the 4km (2.5-mile) **Bison's Rib (Żebra Żubra),** which is dotted with information boards about the plants. The green 11km (6.5-mile) **Wolves' Trail** takes you to the Hwoźna Protected Area, which has a similar feel to the SPA.

Where to Stay & Dine

The village has no shortage of guest rooms *(pokoje gościnne)*, especially along Waszkiewicza Street. In summer, even the most expensive rooms get snapped up.

Białowieża

BEST WESTERN HOTEL ŻUBRÓWKA   This four-star number delivers luxurious creature comforts in the form of tasteful reproduction of mahogany-colored period furniture, complete with striped wallpapers and shiny brocade bed covers. Its location next door to the PTTK office is ideal, but there is no view to speak of. The restaurant's decor is an overkill of deer antlers, pelts, and taxidermied animals. The menu is extensive-coverage plush regional exotica, such as wild boar carpaccio and Russian caviar with buckwheat *bliny*—and also the easier-on-the-pockets *kiszka ziemniaczana* (a regional potato dish).

Ul. Olgi Gabiec 6. ② **085/681-23-03.** Fax 085/681-25-70. www.hotel-zubrowka.pl. 74 units. 340 zł ($136/£76.50) single; 380 zł ($152/£85.50) double; 500 zł–900 zł ($200–$360/£112.50–£202.50) suite. Rates include breakfast. Extra person 75 zł ($30/£17). AE, DC, MC, V. Parking 29 zł ($11.60/£6.50). **Amenities:** ATM; restaurant; cafe; souvenir shop; bicycle rental; Internet terminal; nonsmoking room. *In room:* TV, fan, minibar, complimentary Wi-Fi, hair dryer, bathrobes (suites).

CEM GUEST HOUSE (CEM POKOJE GOŚCINNE) ★★ **Value Finds**   These guest rooms are stashed inside a modern stone, steel, and wood building that also houses the Palace Park's museum. That means, once the day visitors have tapered off, you have the park and all the grand oak trees to yourself. Almost. You share them with fellow guests, many who are researchers on field trips. The rooms are recently renovated to afford comforts similar to Hotel Białowieski's. The only hitch is breakfast. In print, the Park's restaurant opens at 10am, but off season, it's whenever they fancy. Get your breakfast supplies from the grocery stores along Waszkiewicza Street and borrow a kettle from the reception. Or skip over to Hotel Żubrówka, 10 minutes away, and blow 40 zł ($16/£9) on breakfast.

Park Pałacowy 11. ☎ **085/682-97-29.** hotel@bpn.com.pl. 15 units. 100 zł ($40/£22.50) double; 120 zł ($48/£27) triple. No credit cards. Free parking. Car entrance from Zastawa Street. **Amenities:** Bicycle rental; sauna; 1 room for those with limited mobility. *In room:* TV.

HOTEL BIAŁOWIESKI ★ (Value)   Situated at the far end of a street lined with *pokoje gościnne,* the rooms here are spacious, clean, and resemble cheerful showrooms of "Emilka" (a Polish brand specializing in veneered furniture). You pay more for rooms with balconies. The standard and deluxe rooms are fairly similar in levels of comfort, but the latter is slightly bigger. The hotel targets companies on team-building excursions, but it is also family friendly. If you dine here, go for the Króla Jagiełły *bigos,* which has more prunes and a drier consistency than the standard version, and the potato pancakes with chanterelle.

Waszkiewicza 218B. ☎ **085/681-20-22.** Fax 085/744-45-34. www.hotel.bialowieski.pl. 78 units. Mar 21–Oct 140 zł–210 zł ($56–$84/£31.50–£47.25) single; 150 zł–240 zł ($60–$96/£33.75–£54) double; 470 zł ($188/£105.75) suite. Jan 2–March 20 and Nov–Dec 23 140 zł–200 zł ($56–$84/£31.50–£45) single; 150 zł–220 zł ($60–$88/£33.75–£49.50) double; 440 zł ($176/£99) suite. Rates include breakfast. Children 4 and under stay free in parent's room. Extra person 40 zł ($16/£9). AE, MC, V. Parking 20 zł ($8/£4.5). **Amenities:** Restaurant; garden; playground; billiards; bike and canoe rental; bonfire; gym; sauna. *In room:* TV, Wi-Fi, hair dryer (in deluxe rooms).

HOTEL & RESTAURACJA CARSKA ★★ (Finds)   A must for fans of unique hotels, this property is housed in an old railway station constructed for Nicholas II, the last tsar of Russia. The station's waiting room has been converted into an upscale restaurant that is now a gourmand destination. The traditional regional dishes, like *solanka* (a Russian soup) and oatmeal cake (a regional Christmas Eve dessert), are plated with metropolitan flair. The tables on the platforms by the disused rail tracks are great for whiling away the afternoon. Once you hit your room, fit for a tsar and his entourage, you may not want to leave. Two duplex suites have been fitted into a water tower, with beds on one level and a spiral staircase up to the luxurious bathroom. There is a ground-floor room in a separate chalet. The adjacent *bania* (Russian sauna), complete with an outdoor wooden barrel tub, is easily the most refined in the area. End your day with Rasputin, a vodka and birch-sap tipple.

Stacja Towarowa 4. ☎ **085/681-21-19 or 0602-243-228.** www.restauracjacarska.pl. 3 units. 380 zł ($152/£85.50) guest room; 480 zł–580 zł ($192–$232/£108–£130.50) suite. Rates include breakfast. MC, V. Free parking. **Amenities:** Restaurant; *bania* (Russian sauna); bicycle rental. *In room:* TV, minibar.

Around Białowieża

PENSJONAT SIOŁO BUDY ★★ (Finds)   This homestead is for those who want a taste of rural living without forsaking clean toilets, hot showers, and espressos. Nestled in the middle of a cluster of four traditional chalets (with wood-shingle roofing) is a garden of apple trees, flowers, ferns, and fluttering butterflies. Rooms feature wooden or cast-iron bedposts, agrarian tools, and a smattering of Russian knick-knacks such as birch vodka bottles. The "settlement" captures the cultural heritage of the area as intended by the owners, who are folk history enthusiasts. **Karczma Osocznika,** a barn-style restaurant with long tables and benches for communal feasting, offers deliciously executed regional dishes such as Russian *solanka* soup, bison *bigos,* regional *hałuszki* (a baked potato dish), and *Marcinek* layered cream cakes. The prices? Similar to Warsaw's mid-level restaurants. But sipping *Obolon,* an unfiltered Ukrainian beer, by the campfire while an accordionist playing Belarusian music serenades under a star-speckled sky? Priceless.

Budy 41 (9km/5 miles west of Białowieża). ✆ **085/681-29-78.** www.siolobudy.pl. 11 units. 120 zł ($48/£27) single; 180 zł ($72/£40.50) double; 240 zł ($96/£54) triple. Rates include breakfast. Children under 6 stay free in parent's room. Children 6–17 50% discount. No credit cards. Free parking. From Białowieża's PTTK office, take the road toward Narewka. **Amenities:** Restaurant; museum; lounge w/ fireplace; kitchenette; bike and kayak rental; guides; bonfire w/Belarusian music; horse-drawn carriages; sleigh rides; horseback riding; *bania* (Russian sauna; 600 zł/$240/£135 including food and massage for up to 6 persons). *In room:* No phone, minibar.

Appendix A: Fast Facts, Toll-Free Numbers & Websites

1 FAST FACTS: POLAND

AMERICAN EXPRESS The American Express office in Warsaw's Marriott Hotel buys and sells traveler's checks and handles basic cardholder inquiries: **Warsaw Lim Center** (Al. Jerozolimskie 65/79; ✆ 022/630-69-52; Mon–Fri 9am–7pm, Sat 10am–6pm).

AREA CODES Poland's country code is 48 (011-48 from the U.S.). Area codes for cities include: Warsaw (022), Kraków (012), Gdańsk (058), Wrocław (071), Łódź (042), and Lublin (081).

ATMS/CASHPOINTS See "Money & Costs," p. 37.

AUTOMOBILE ORGANIZATIONS The Polish Motoring Association (Polski Związek Motorowy/PZM) (Kazimierzowska 66; ✆ 022/849-93-61; www.pzm.pl) is Poland's main automobile club. It promotes road safety, publishes maps, and conducts driving lessons. For visitors, the most useful service is its 24-hour nationwide emergency breakdown hotline: ✆ **9637.**

BUSINESS HOURS Stores and offices are generally open weekdays 9am–6pm. Banks are open weekdays 9am–4pm. Many stores have limited Saturday hours, usually 9am–noon. Large shopping centers and malls are open seven days a week from 10am until at least 8pm. Museums and other tourist attractions are often closed on Mondays.

CAR RENTALS See "Toll-Free Numbers & Websites," p. 285.

DRINKING LAWS The legal age for buying and consuming alcohol is 18, though ID checks are not common. Alcoholic beverages are widely available and can be bought just about anywhere, including convenience stores, tourist shops, grocery stores, and, naturally, in shops specializing in liquor. Though alcohol is easy to get, police take a dim view of public drunkenness, and fines for a night in the drunk tank are steep. The legal blood alcohol limit for driving is 0.02%—approximately one beer. Spot alcohol checks are frequent.

DRIVING RULES See "Getting There & Getting Around," p. 33.

ELECTRICITY Polish outlets follow the continental norm (220V, 50Hz) with two round plugs. Most appliances that run on 110V will require a transformer.

EMBASSIES & CONSULATES All foreign embassies are located in the capital Warsaw, though some countries maintain consulates in Kraków and other large cities.

The **United States Embassy** is located at Ujazdowskie 29/31 (✆ 022/504-20-00; http://poland.usembassy.gov). There's also a **U.S. consulate** in Kraków (Stolarska 9; ✆ 012/424-5100; http://kraków.usconsulate.gov).

The **embassy of Australia** is situated on the third floor of the Nautilus building (Nowogrodzka 11; ✆ **022/521-34-44;** www.australia.pl).

The embassy of Canada is at Matejki 1/5 (✆ **022/584–31–00;** http://geo. international.gc.ca/canada-europa/poland).

The **embassy of Ireland** is at Mysia 5 (✆ **022/849-66-33;** www.embassyof ireland.pl). Ireland also has an honorary **consular office** in Poznań (Kramarska 1; ✆ **061/853-18-94**).

The embassy of the United Kingdom is located at Al. Róż 1 (✆ **022/311-00-00;** ukinpoland.fco.gov.uk). The **British consular section,** which handles tourist services and emergencies, is located at the Warsaw Corporate Centre (2nd floor, Emilii Plater 28 (✆ **022/311-00-00;** ukinpoland.fco.gov.uk).

EMERGENCIES   In an emergency, dial the following numbers: **Police** ✆ **997, Fire** ✆ **998, Ambulance** ✆ **999, Road Assistance** ✆ **981** or ✆ **9637** (Polish motoring association/PZM). The general emergency number if using a cell phone is ✆ **112.**

GASOLINE (PETROL)   Unleaded gasoline, *benzyna*, is widely available; a green-marked tank with "95" is regular octane and "98" is high-test. Most stations are self-serve, but occasionally you'll still find a gas attendant. He'll fill up your tank and wash your windows, and expect a *złoty* or two as a tip. Gasoline is sold by the liter, with one U.S. gallon equal to about 3.8 liters. At press time, a liter of gas costs about 4.40 zł ($1.80/£1).

HOLIDAYS   Poland observes the following holidays: Jan 1 (New Year's Day); Easter Sunday and Monday; May 1 (State Holiday); May 3 (Constitution Day); Corpus Christi (ninth Thurs following Easter Sunday); Aug 15 (Assumption); Nov 1 (All Saints' Day); Nov 11 (Independence Day); and Dec 25 and 26 (Christmas). Offices, banks, museums, and many stores are closed on holidays, though some larger stores and restaurants remain open.

HOSPITALS   Medical standards in Poland are generally acceptable, and if something should happen during your trip, you can be confident that you will receive adequate care. In terms of private medical facilities, in Warsaw, the LIM Medical Center is centrally located in the Marriott complex and staffs a full range of English-speaking doctors and specialists (Al. Jerozolimskie 65/79; ✆ **022/458-70-00;** www.cmlim.pl/en). For dentists, the **Austrian Dental Center** (Zelazna 54; ✆ **022/654-21-16;** www.austriadent.pl) is highly recommended.

HOTLINES   The Polish national tourist organization and the police now operate a special tourist hotline in season from May through September (✆ **0800/200-300**) for visitors to check safety conditions and report dangerous situations. The hotline is available in English, German, and Russian.

INSURANCE   Medical Insurance   Foreign citizens are obliged to pay for any medical services they receive in Poland, so it's worth checking whether your home health insurance will cover you while you are abroad and, if not, how to supplement your insurance. Insurance providers offer a wide range of policies that are cost-effective and valuable for travelers.

Canadians should check with their provincial health plan offices or call **Health Canada** (✆ **866/225-0709;** www.hc-sc. gc.ca) to find out the extent of their coverage and what documentation and receipts they must take home in case they are treated abroad.

Travelers from the U.K. should carry their **European Health Insurance Card** (EHIC), which replaced the E111 form as proof of entitlement to free/reduced cost medical treatment abroad (✆ **0845/606-2030;** www.ehic.org.uk). Note, however, that the EHIC covers only "necessary medical treatment," and for repatriation costs, lost money, baggage, or trip cancellation, travel insurance from a reputable company should always be sought (www.travelinsuranceweb.com).

Travel Insurance The cost of travel insurance varies widely, depending on the destination, the cost and length of your trip, your age and health, and the type of trip you're taking, but expect to pay between 5% and 8% of the vacation itself. You can get estimates from various providers through InsureMyTrip.com. Enter your trip cost and dates, your age, and other information, for prices from more than a dozen companies.

U.K. citizens and their families who make more than one trip abroad per year may find an annual travel insurance policy works out cheaper. Check www.money supermarket.com, which compares prices across a wide range of providers for single- and multi-trip policies.

Most big travel agents offer their own insurance and will probably try to sell you their package when you book a holiday. Think before you sign. Britain's Consumers' Association recommends that you insist on seeing the policy and reading the fine print before buying travel insurance. The **Association of British Insurers** (✆ 020/7600-3333; www.abi.org.uk) gives advice by phone and publishes Holiday Insurance, a free guide to policy provisions and prices. You might also shop around for better deals: Try Columbus Direct (✆ 0870/033-9988; www.columbusdirect.net).

Trip Cancellation Insurance Trip-cancellation insurance will help retrieve your money if you have to back out of a trip or depart early, or if your travel supplier goes bankrupt. Trip cancellation traditionally covers such events as sickness, natural disasters, and State Department advisories. The latest news in trip-cancellation insurance is the availability of expanded hurricane coverage and the "any-reason" cancellation coverage—which costs more but covers cancellations made for any reason. You won't get back 100% of your prepaid trip cost, but you'll be refunded a substantial portion. **TravelSafe** (✆ 888/885-7233; www.travelsafe.com) offers both types of coverage. Expedia also offers any-reason cancellation coverage for its air–hotel packages. For details, contact one of the following recommended insurers: **Access America** (✆ 866/807-3982; www.accessamerica.com); **Travel Guard International** (✆ 800/826-4919; www.travelguard.com); **Travel Insured International** (✆ 800/243-3174; www.travelinsured.com); and **Travelex Insurance Services** (✆ 888/457-4602; www.travelex-insurance.com).

INTERNET ACCESS Internet cafes are ubiquitous throughout Warsaw, Kraków, and other large cities. Internet cafes generally charge around 6 zł ($2.40/£1.40) per hour of Internet use. Many hotels now set aside at least one public computer for guests to use. Nearly all hotels these days offer some type of in-room Internet access, either via LAN connection or wireless, and a growing number of cafes offer wireless Internet, though connections can be spotty.

LEGAL AID The police are authorized to collect fines on the spot for minor infractions, such as speeding. It's usually futile to try to argue your case and you're best advised simply to pay the fine and move on. For more serious crimes, there are few legal resources at your disposal. Contact your local embassy or consulate immediately.

LOST & FOUND Be sure to alert all of your credit card companies the minute you discover your wallet has been lost or stolen and file a report at the nearest police precinct. Your credit card company or insurer may require a police report number or record of the loss. Most credit card companies have an emergency toll-free number to call if your card is lost or stolen; they may be able to wire you a cash advance immediately or deliver an emergency credit card in a day or two. In Poland, to report a lost or stolen **Visa**, call

© **0800/111-15-69;** **MasterCard,** call © **0800/111-12-11.** To report a lost **Amex** card, call © **022/630-69-52** during business hours.

If you need emergency cash over the weekend when all banks and American Express offices are closed, you can have money wired to you via Western Union (www.westernunion.com), which maintains offices throughout Poland.

MAIL Postal rates vary by weight and it's always safest to have letters weighed at the post office in order to ensure the proper postage. The rate for mailing a postcard or light letter abroad will run about 3.20 zł ($1.30/70p). The postal service is generally reliable, but don't trust it for highly valuable packages or letters that simply must arrive. For that use FedEx, DHL, or another trackable delivery service.

MEASUREMENTS Poland uses the metric system. See the chart on the inside front cover of this book for details on converting metric measurements to non-metric equivalents.

MEDICAL CONDITIONS Be sure to bring along extra quantities of any prescription medications you will need on your trip. Poland's pharmacies are well stocked, but the pharmacist may not recognize your doctor's prescription. Also know the generic term for the drug (e.g. acetaminophen for Tylenol) since brand names can differ in different countries.

NEWSPAPERS & MAGAZINES You'll find newspapers and magazines widely available at kiosks in city centers and at train and bus stations, though most kiosks stock only Polish titles. English newspapers and magazines usually available include the *International Herald Tribune,* the *Wall Street Journal, The Economist, The Financial Times,* and *The Guardian.* In terms of local English publications, Warsaw has at least two good ones: the weekly *Warsaw Voice* and the monthly *Warsaw Insider.* Also look out for regular editions of the irreverent *Poland In Your Pocket* city guides for Warsaw, Kraków, Gdańsk, Łódź, Katowice, and Wrocław.

PASSPORTS The websites listed provide downloadable passport applications as well as the current fees for processing applications. For an up-to-date, country-by-country listing of passport requirements around the world, go to the "International Travel" tab of the U.S. State Department at http://travel.state.gov. Allow plenty of time before your trip to apply for a passport; processing normally takes 4–6 weeks (3 weeks for expedited service) but can take longer during busy periods (especially spring). And keep in mind that if you need a passport in a hurry, you'll pay a higher processing fee.

For Residents of Australia You can pick up an application from your local post office or any branch of Passports Australia, but you must schedule an interview at the passport office to present your application materials. Call the **Australian Passport Information Service** (© **131-232**), or visit the government website (www.passports. gov.au).

For Residents of Canada Passport applications are available at travel agencies throughout Canada or from the central Passport Office, Department of Foreign Affairs and International Trade, Alberta, ON K1A 0G3 (© **800/567-6868;** www. ppt.gc.ca). *Note:* Canadian children who travel must have their own passport. However, if you hold a valid Canadian passport issued before December 11, 2001, that bears the name of your child, the passport remains valid for you and your child until it expires.

For Residents of Ireland You can apply for a 10-year passport at the Passport Office, Setanta Centre, Molesworth Street, Dublin 2 (© **01/671-1633;** www.irlgov. ie/iveagh). Those under age 18 and over 65 must apply for a 3-year passport. You can also apply at 1A South Mall, Cork

(✆ **21/494-4700**) or at most main post offices.

For Residents of New Zealand You can pick up a passport application at any New Zealand Passports Office or download it from their website. Contact the **Passports Office in New Zealand** (✆ **0800/225-050** or **04/474-8100**), or log on to www.passports.govt.nz.

For Residents of the United Kingdom To pick up an application for a standard 10-year passport (5-yr. passport for children under 16), visit your nearest passport office, major post office, or travel agency or contact the **United Kingdom Passport Service** (✆ **0870/521-0410**) or search its website at www.ukpa.gov.uk.

POLICE The police emergency number is ✆ **997**. If calling from a mobile phone, dial ✆ **112**.

SMOKING Smoking rates tend to be higher in Poland than in the U.S., though increasingly cafes and restaurants are setting aside more tables for nonsmokers. Many hotels are now completely smoke free and almost all hotels offer nonsmoking rooms or rooms that are on totally nonsmoking floors. Be sure to request this in advance.

TAXES All taxes, including a 22% value added tax levied on most goods and excise duties on tobacco, alcohol, and gasoline, are already calculated in the purchase price. Buyers with permanent residency outside the European Union are entitled to reclaim VAT on purchases above 200 zł ($80/£45) provided the goods are permanently taken out of the EU within three months from the date of purchase. Look for shops with "Tax Free Shopping" in the window for details.

TELEPHONES Poland's country code is 48. To dial Poland from abroad, dial the international access code (for example, 011 in the U.S.), plus 48 and then the local Poland area code (minus the zero). The area code for Warsaw is 022. To call

long distance within Poland, dial the area code (retaining the zero) plus the number. To dial abroad from Poland, dial 00 and then the country code and area code to where you are calling. A call to the U.S. or Canada would begin 00-1.

TELEGRAPH, TELEX & FAX You'll find Western Union outlets throughout Poland for wiring money or to have it wired to you quickly, but this service can cost as much as 15 to 20 percent of the amount sent.

Most hotels have fax machines available for guest use (be sure to ask about the charge to use it). Many hotel rooms are wired for guests' fax machines.

TIME Poland is in the Central European Time zone (CET), 1 hour ahead of GMT and 6 hours ahead of the eastern United States. Daylight saving time is in effect from early spring until late autumn. Daylight saving time moves the clock 1 hour ahead of standard time.

TIPPING In restaurants, round up the bill by 10% to reward good service. Bellhops, taxi drivers, and tour guides will also expect a small amount in return for services rendered. Around 5 zł ($2/£1.10) is usually enough under any circumstance.

TOILETS Public toilets are a relative rarity, so you'll find yourself seeking out nearby restaurants or hotels and asking to use the facilities. This is usually not a problem. Some establishments will charge 1 zł (40¢/25p) for the privilege. Service stations and other places often have pay toilets for free or a nominal fee. Some public toilets still use the older symbols to designate men's and women's facilities: men are upside-down triangles; women are circles.

USEFUL PHONE NUMBERS U.S. Dept. of State Travel Advisory: ✆ **202/647-5225** (in the U.S.; manned 24 hrs.). **U.S. Passport Agency:** ✆ **202/647-0518** (in the U.S.). **Poland Traveler's Hotline:** ✆ **0800/200-300**.

VISAS Visitors from the U.S., Canada, the U.K., Australia, and New Zealand do not require visas for stays under 90 days. Nationals of other countries should consult the Polish Ministry of Foreign Affairs (general and visa information) (www.msz. gov.pl) or contact the Polish embassy in their home country.

WATER Tap water is generally safe to drink, but you may think twice about drinking from taps in older buildings with rusty pipes. If you have any concern, let the water run for a few seconds before drinking. Bottled water is cheap and widely available.

---

2 TOLL-FREE NUMBERS & WEBSITES

MAJOR U.S. AIRLINES
(*fly internationally as well)

American Airlines*
© 800/433-7300 (in U.S. or Canada)
© 020/7365-0777 (in U.K.)
www.aa.com

Continental Airlines*
© 800/523-3273 (in U.S. or Canada)
© 084/5607-6760 (in U.K.)
www.continental.com

Delta Air Lines*
© 800/221-1212 (in U.S. or Canada)
© 084/5600-0950 (in U.K.)
www.delta.com

Northwest Airlines
© 800/225-2525 (in U.S.)
© 870/0507-4074 (in U.K.)
www.flynaa.com

United Airlines*
© 800/864-8331 (in U.S. and Canada)
© 084/5844-4777 in U.K.
www.united.com

US Airways*
© 800/428-4322 (in U.S. and Canada)
© 084/5600-3300 (in U.K.)
www.usairways.com

MAJOR INTERNATIONAL AIRLINES

Air France
© 800/237-2747 (in U.S.)
© 800/375-8723 (U.S. and Canada)
© 087/0142-4343 (in U.K.)
www.airfrance.com

Alitalia
© 800/223-5730 (in U.S.)
© 800/361-8336 (in Canada)
© 087/0608-6003 (in U.K.)
www.alitalia.com

Austrian Airlines
www.aua.com
© 0801/40-4040 (in Poland only, not toll-free)
© 800/843-0002 (in the U.S. and Canada)
© 0870/1-24-26-25 (in the U.K.)

British Airways
© 800/247-9297 (in U.S. and Canada)
© 087/0850-9850 (in U.K.)
www.british-airways.com

CSA Czech Airlines
© 800/223-2365 (U.S.)
© 0871/663-3747 (in U.K.)
© 420/239-007-007 (Prague, not toll-free)
© 022/559-39-30 (Poland, not toll-free)
www.csa.cz

Finnair
© 800/950-5000 (in U.S. and Canada)
© 087/0241-4411 (in U.K.)
www.finnair.com

LOT
- ✆ 0801/703-703 (within Poland)
- ✆ 1 212 789 0970 (U.S.)
- ✆ 0845/601 09 49 (U.K.)
- www.lot.com

Lufthansa
- ✆ 800/399-5838 (in U.S.)
- ✆ 800/563-5954 (in Canada)
- ✆ 087/0837-7747 (in U.K.)
- www.lufthansa.com

BUDGET AIRLINES

Air Berlin
- ✆ 087/1500-0737 (in U.K.)
- ✆ 018/0573-7800 (in Germany)
- ✆ 180/573-7800 (all others)
- www.airberlin.com

BMI Baby
- ✆ 087/1224-0224 (in U.K.)
- ✆ 870/126-6726 (in U.S.)
- www.bmibaby.com

easyJet
- ✆ 870/600-0000 (in U.S.)
- ✆ 090/5560-7777 (in U.K.)
- www.easyjet.com

CAR RENTAL AGENCIES

Advantage
- ✆ 800/777-5500 (in U.S.)
- ✆ 021/0344-4712 (outside of U.S.)
- www.advantagerentacar.com

Alamo
- ✆ 800/GO-ALAMO (800/462-5266)
- www.alamo.com

Auto Europe
- ✆ 888/223-5555 (in U.S. and Canada)
- ✆ 0800/2235-5555 (in U.K.)
- www.autoeurope.com

Avis
- ✆ 800/331-1212 (in U.S. and Canada)
- ✆ 084/4581-8181 (in U.K.)
- www.avis.com

Budget
- ✆ 800/527-0700 (in U.S.)
- ✆ 087/0156-5656 (in U.K.)
- ✆ 800/268-8900 (in Canada)
- www.budget.com

Qantas Airways
- ✆ 800/227-4500 (in U.S.)
- ✆ 084/5774-7767 (in U.K. or Canada)
- ✆ 13 13 13 (in Australia)
- www.qantas.com

Swiss Air
- ✆ 877/359-7947 (in U.S. and Canada)
- ✆ 084/5601-0956 (in U.K.)
- www.swiss.com

Ryanair
- ✆ 1353/1-249-7700 (in U.S.)
- ✆ 081/830-3030 (in Ireland)
- ✆ 087/1246-0000 (in U.K.)
- www.ryanair.com

WizzAir
- ✆ 0904/475-9500 (U.K., not toll-free)
- ✆ 0703/503-010 (in Poland, not toll-free)
- www.wizzair.com

Dollar
- ✆ 800/800-4000 (in U.S.)
- ✆ 800/848-8268 (in Canada)
- ✆ 080/8234-7524 (in U.K.)
- www.dollar.com

Enterprise
- ✆ 800/261-7331 (in U.S.)
- ✆ 514/355-4028 (in Canada)
- ✆ 012/9360-9090 (in U.K.)
- www.enterprise.com

Hertz
- ✆ 800/645-3131
- ✆ 800/654-3001 (for international reservations)
- www.hertz.com

National
- ✆ 800/CAR-RENT (800/227-7368)
- www.nationalcar.com

Payless
✆ 800/PAYLESS (800/729-5377)
www.paylesscarrental.com

Thrifty
✆ 800/367-2277
✆ 918/669-2168 (international)
www.thrifty.com

MAJOR HOTEL CHAINS

Best Western International
✆ 800/780-7234 (in U.S. and Canada)
✆ 0800/393-130 (in U.K.)
www.bestwestern.com

Campanile (Campanile, Kyriad Prestige, Premiere Classe)
✆ 331/64-62-59-70 (France)
www.campanile.com.pl

Courtyard by Marriott
✆ 888/236-2427 (in U.S.)
✆ 0800/221-222 (in U.K.)
www.marriott.com/courtyard

Crowne Plaza Hotels
✆ 888/303-1746
www.ichotelsgroup.com/crowneplaza

Hilton Hotels
✆ 800/HILTONS (800/445-8667)
   (in U.S. and Canada)
✆ 087/0590-9090 (in U.K.)
www.hilton.com

Holiday Inn
✆ 800/315-2621 (in U.S. and Canada)
✆ 0800/405-060 (in U.K.)
www.holidayinn.com

Hyatt
✆ 888/591-1234 (in U.S. and Canada)
✆ 084/5888-1234 (in U.K.)
www.hyatt.com

InterContinental Hotels & Resorts
✆ 800/424-6835 (in U.S. and Canada)
✆ 0800/1800-1800 (in U.K.)
www.ichotelsgroup.com

Le Meridien
✆ 35321/493-0427 (regional number
   throughout Europe, toll)
www.starwoodhotels.com

Marriott
✆ 877/236-2427 (in U.S. and Canada)
✆ 0800/221-222 (in U.K.)
www.marriott.com

Orbis (Novotel, Mercure, IBIS, Etap)
✆ 0801/606-606 (in Poland)
www.orbis.pl

Qubus
✆ 071/782-87-65 (in Poland, not toll-free)
www.qubus.pl

Radisson Hotels & Resorts
✆ 888/201-1718 (in U.S. and Canada)
✆ 0800/374-411 (in U.K.)
www.radisson.com

Ramada Worldwide
✆ 888/2-RAMADA (888/272-6232)
   (in U.S. and Canada)
✆ 080/8100-0783 (in U.K.)
www.ramada.com

Residence Inn by Marriott
✆ 800/331-3131
✆ 800/221-222 (in U.K.)
www.marriott.com/residenceinn

Sheraton Hotels & Resorts
✆ 800/325-3535 (in U.S.)
✆ 800/543-4300 (in Canada)
✆ 0800/3253-5353 (in U.K.)
www.starwoodhotels.com/sheraton

Appendix B: Useful Terms & Phrases

1 BASIC VOCABULARY

There are a fair number of English speakers around, and nearly all hotels, tourist offices, and restaurants will be able to manage some English.

ENGLISH–POLISH PHRASES

English	Polish	Pronunciation
Hello/Good day	**Dzień dobry**	Djeen *doh*-bree
Yes	**Tak**	Tahk
No	**Nie**	Nee-yeh
Hi! or Bye! (informal)	**Cześć!**	Chesh-ch
Good evening	**Dobry wieczór**	*Doh*-bree *vyeh*-choor
Goodbye	**Do widzenia**	*Doh* vee-*djen*-ya
Good night	**Dobranoc**	Doh-*brah*-nohts
Thank you	**Dziękuję**	Djem-*koo*-yeh
Excuse me/Sorry	**Przepraszam**	Pshe-*pra*-sham
Please/you're welcome	**Proszę**	*Proh*-sheh
How are you? (informal)	**Jak się masz?**	*Yahk* sheh mahsh?
How are you? (formal)	**Jak się pan (to a man)/ pani (to a woman) ma?**	*Yahk* sheh pahn/pah-nee mah?
Fine	**Dobrze**	Dohb-zheh
Do you speak English?	**Czy pan/pani mówi po angielsku?**	Chee pahn/pah-nee *moo*-vee poh ahng-*yel*-skoo?
I don't understand	**Nie rozumiem**	Ne-yeh roh-*zoom*-yem
How much is it?	**Ile kosztuje?**	Eel-eh kosh-*too*-yeh?
Menu	**Menu**	Men-yoo
The bill, please	**Poproszę o rachunek**	*Proh*-sheh oh *rahk*-oo-nek
Cheers!	**Na zdrowie**	Nah-*zdroh*-vyeh
Bon appétit!	**Smacznego**	Smahch-*neh*-go

English	Polish	Pronunciation
Where is . . . ?	**Gdzie jest . . . ?**	Gjye yest. .?
the station	**dworzec**	*Dvoh*-zhets
a hotel	**hotel**	*Hoe*-tel
a restaurant	**restauracja**	Res-to-*ra*-tia
the toilet	**toaleta**	Toy-*le*-ta
Do you have . . . ?	**Czy jest. .?**	Chee yest . . . ?
When?	**Kiedy?**	*Kye*-day
What?	**Co?**	Tso
Today	**Dziś/Dzisiaj**	Jeesh/*jee*-shay
Tomorrow	**Jutro**	*Yoo*-tro
Yesterday	**Wczoraj**	*Fcho*-ray
Good	**Dobry**	*Doh*-bree
Bad	**Niedobry**	Nee-yeh *dob*-bree
More	**Więcej**	*vyen*-tsay
Less	**Mniej**	*Mer*-nyey

DAYS & MONTHS

Poniedziałek (po-nye-*jya*-wek) Monday
Wtorek (*fto*-rek) Tuesday
Środa (*shro*-da) Wednesday
Czwartek (*chfar*-tek) Thursday
Piątek (*pyon*-tek) Friday
Sobota (So-*bo*-ta) Saturday
Niedziela (nye-*jye*-la) Sunday
Styczeń (*sti*-chen) January
Luty (*loo*-ti) February
Marzec (*ma*-zhets) March
Kwiecień (*kfye*-chen) April
Maj (mai) May

Czerwiec (*cher*-vyets) June
Lipiec (*lee*-pyets) July
Sierpień (*sher*-pyen) August
Wrzesień (*vzhe*-shen) September
Październik (pazh-*jyer*-neek) October
Listopad (lees-*to*-pat) November
Grudzień (*groo*-jyen) December
Rano (*ra*-no) In the morning
Po południu (po po-*wood*-nyoo) In the afternoon
Wieczorem (vye-*cho*-rem) In the evening

GENERAL

Apteka Gate
Brama Gate
Cmentarz Cemetery
Cukiernia Cake shop
Dolina Valley
Dom House

Droga Road
Dwór Country manor
Dworzec Station
Główny Main, as in *Dworzec Główny* (Main Station)
Góra/Góry Mountain/mountains

Granica Border
Jaskinia Cave
Jezioro Lake
Kantor Currency exchange office
Katedra Cathedral
Kawiarnia Cafe
Kemping Camping
Kino Cinema
Klasztor Monastery
Kościół Church
Księgarnia Bookshops
Miasto Town
Most Bridge
Ogród Garden
Piekarnia Bakery
Plaża Beach
Poczta Post Office

Pogotowie Emergency
Pokój Room
Policja Police
Prom Ferry
Przystanek Bus stop
Ratusz Town hall
Restauracja Restaurant
Rynek Market/town square
Skansen Open-air museum
Stary Old, as in *Stary Miasto* (Old Town)
Teatr Theater
Ulica Street. Abbreviated to ul.
Wieża Tower
Zajazd Inn
Zamek Castle
Zdrój Spa

NUMBERS

1 **Jeden** (*ye*-den)
2 **Dwa** (dvah)
3 **Trzy** (tshi)
4 **Cztery** (*chte*-ri)
5 **Pięć** (pyench)
6 **Sześć** (sheshch)
7 **Siedem** (*she*-dem)
8 **Osiem** (*oh*-shem)
9 **Dziewięć** (*jye*-vyench)

10 **Dziesięć** (*jye*-shench)
11 **Jedenaście** (ye-den-*nash*-che)
12 **Dwanaście** (dva-*nash*-che)
15 **Piętnaście** (pyent-*nash*-che)
20 **Dwadzieścia** (dva-*jyesh*-cha)
30 **Trzydzieści** (tshi-*jyesh*-chee)
50 **Pięćdziesiąt** (pyen-*jye*-shont)
100 **Sto** (sto)
1,000 **Tysiąc** (*tee*-shonts)

SIGNS

Ciągnąć/Pchać Push/Pull
Dla panów/Męski Men
Dla pań/Damski Women
Kasa Ticket office, cashier
Nieczynny Closed, out of order
Nie dotykać Do not touch
Nie palić No smoking

Otwarty/Zamknięty Open/Closed
Toalety Toilets
Uwaga Caution
Wejście/Wyjścia Entrance/Exit
Wolny Vacant
Występ wzbroniony No entrance
Zajęty Occupied

2 MENU TERMS

GENERAL TERMS

Filiżanka Cup
Gotowany Boiled
Grill/z rusztu Grilled
Łyżka Spoon
Marynowany Pickled
Mielone Minced
Nadziewany Stuffed/Filled
Nóż Knife

Pieczeń Roast
Słodki Sweet
Słony Salty
Surowy Raw
Świeży Fresh
Talerz Plate
Wędzony Smoked
Widelec Fork

BASIC FOODS

Bułka Rolls
Chleb Bread
Cukier Sugar
Drób Poultry
Frytki French fries/Chips
Grzyby Mushroom
Jajko Eggs
Jarzyny/warzywa Vegetables
Kanapka Sandwich
Kiełbasa Sausage
Makaron Noodles, pasta
Masło Butter
Ocet Vinegar

Olej Oil
Orzechy Nuts
Owoce Fruits
Pieprz Pepper
Ryby Fish
Ryż Rice
Ser Cheese
Śmietana Cream
Sól Salt
Surówka Salad
Szaszłyk Shish kebab
Twaróg Cottage cheese
Zupa Soup

BEVERAGES

Gorąca czekolada Hot chocolate
Herbata Tea
Kawa Coffee
Biała White
Czarna Black
Miód pitny Mead
Mleko Milk
Piwo Beer
Sok Juice
Sok jabłkowy Apple juice
Sok pomarańczowy Orange juice

Wino Wine
Białe White
Czerwone Red
Słodkie Sweet
Wytrane Dry
Woda Water
Gazowana Sparkling
Niegazowana Still
Mineralna Mineral
Wódka Vodka

CAKES & DESSERTS

Budyń Milk pudding
Ciastko Cake/slice of cake
Ciasto drożdżowe Sweet yeast bread
Czekolada Chocolate
Lody Ice cream

Makowiec Poppyseed cake
Pączki Donuts
Sernik Cheesecake
Szarlotka Polish-style apple pie
Tort Layered cream cake

Baranina Mutton
Bażant Pheasant
Boczek Bacon
Cielęcina Veal
Dorada Sea bass
Dorsz Cod
Dziczyzna Game
Dzik Wild boar
Gęś Geese
Golonka Leg of pork
Indyk Turkey
Jagnięcina Lamb
Kaczka Duck
Karp Carp
Kotlet schabowy Breaded pork cutlet

Kurczak Chicken
Łosoś Salmon
Makrela Mackerel
Pasztet Pâté
Polędwica Tenderloin
Pstrąg Trout
Sarnina Venison
Śledź Herring
Szynka Ham
Wątróbka Liver
Węgorz Eel
Wieprzowina Pork
Wołowina Beef
Zając Hare
Żeberka Ribs

FRUITS, GRAINS, NUTS & VEGETABLES

Buraczki Beetroot
Cebula Onion
Cytryna Lemon
Czarne porzeczki Blackcurrant
Czereśnie Wild cherries
Czosnek Garlic
Fasola Beans
Groch Lentils
Gruszka Pears
Grzyby Mushrooms
Jabłko Apple
Kalafior Cauliflower
Kapusta Cabbage
Kapusta kiszona Sauerkraut
Kasza Gryczana Buckwheat

Kurki Chanterelle
Maliny Raspberries
Migdały Almonds
Morele Apricots
Ogórek Cucumber
Orzechy włoskie Walnuts
Pieczarki Button mushroom
Pomarańcze Orange
Pomidor Tomato
Śliwka Plum
Szparagi Asparagus
Truskawki Strawberries
Winogrona Grapes
Wiśnia Cherries
Ziemniaki Potatoes

MEALS

Śniadanie Breakfast
Obiad Lunch
Kolacja Dinner

Na miejscu Eating on premises (as opposed to take away)
Na wynos Take away

3 MENU GLOSSARY

Barszcz or **barszcz czerwony** A clear broth made from beetroot, sometimes comes with pasta pieces.
Barszcz ukraiński White borscht.
Bigos Hunter's stew made from pickled cabbage, sausage, and sometimes game meat.
Bryndza A soft cheese made from sheep's milk.
Chłodnik A summer cold soup; pink, creamy, and made from young beets.

Ćwikła z chrzanem   A slightly sharp condiment made from beetroot and horseradish **293**
served with meats and cold cuts.

Gołąbki   Cabbage leaves stuffed with a mixture of rice, minced meat, and sometimes
mushroom. A Polish version of the Greek *dolma.*

Grochówka   Bean soup, sometimes served with sausage.

Jajecznica   Scrambled eggs.

Kajmak   A thick and sweet light brown mixture made from milk and sugar. It is
often added to cakes, tarts, and *mazurek.*

Kapuśniak   A very sour pickled cabbage soup.

Kartoflanka   Potato soup.

Kawa po turecku   Poland's rendition of Turkish-style coffee where coffee grounds are
added to a glass and hot water is poured directly on top.

Kisiel   A jelly-like dessert made from milk and corn or potato starch.

Knedle   A steamed bread bun. The sweet version is stuffed with prunes (*z sliwkami).*

Kompot   A syrupy drink made from boiled fruit.

Kopytka   A kind of potato dumpling that is similar to gnocchi.

Kotlet Schabowy   A breaded pork cutlet that is a national staple.

Krupnik   A clear soup made from barley, it often comes with boiled vegetables and
chunks of meat.

Leniwe pierogi   Similar to *kopytka* but made with cottage cheese, usually a dessert.

Makowiec   A sweet poppy seed roll, usually a Christmas and Easter treat but available year-round.

Mazurek   A dessert for Easter, but available year-round. The shortcrust pastry is
topped with *kajmak* or chocolate and decorated with dried fruit.

Mizeria   A salad of thinly sliced cucumbers dressed with cream and dill.

Naleśniki z serem   Pancakes filled with cottage cheese.

Nalewka   Vodka infused with fruits, nuts, spices, or herbs.

Oscypek   Smoked cheese from the Tatry region, usually made from a combination of
sheep's and cow's milk.

Pierogi   Dumplings, usually filled with minced meat, cabbage, and mushroom.
Sweet versions are stuffed with seasonal fruit such as strawberries (*z truskawkami*) and
blueberries (*z jadodami*).

Pierogi "Ruskie"   A savory *pierogi* stuffed with potato and cottage cheese and served
with fried onions.

Pyzy   Steamed bread bun.

Racuchy   Fruit fritters; the most traditional is made from apples.

Rosół   A clear chicken broth.

Sztuka mięsa   Literally, it means a piece of meat. It's normally boiled pork or beef,
served plain with sauce.

Zrazy zawijane   Beef roulade, normally filled with a mixture of vegetables, bacon,
and mushrooms.

Żurek   A sourish soup made from fermented rye. Often comes with potatoes and
sausage.

INDEX

See also Accommodations and Restaurant indexes, below.

RESTAURANTS

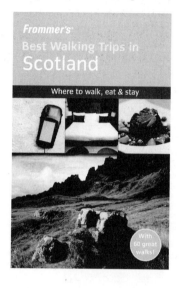

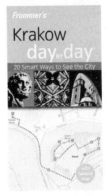